Historical Aspects of Ross
Volume II

by

**Philip Anderson, Joyce M. Briffett,
Joan Fleming-Yates, Heather Hurley, Margot Miller,
C.A. Virginia Morgan, John Powell & Ian Standing**

Ross & District Civic Society

in association with

Logaston Press

ROSS-ON-WYE & DISTRICT CIVIC SOCIETY
secretary@rosscivic.org.uk

LOGASTON PRESS
Little Logaston, Woonton, Almeley,
Herefordshire HR3 6QH
logastonpress.co.uk

First published by Ross-on-Wye & District Civic Society
in association with Logaston Press 2010
Copyright © Author of each chapter 2010

ISBN 978 1 906663 48 3

Set in Times by Logaston Press
and printed in Great Britain by
CPI Antony Rowe

*This book is dedicated
to the late Graham Hurst,
former Chairman and President
of the Ross-on-Wye & District Civic Society*

Acknowledgements

Acknowledgements and thanks are due to David Clark, David Campion, Bob & Lyn Channon, the late Mr Jack Coombes, Dr Frank Crompton, Rhys Griffith, Mrs Mary Hopson, Sue Hubbard, Dr Timothy Mowl, Peter Pember, Richard Powell, Mr Bill Price, Dr Colin Price, Carol Probert, Dr Keith Ray, N.B. Redman, Mrs V.J. Robbins, Elizabeth Semper-O'Keefe, Mr Colin Michael Southall, Brian Thomas, Tim Ward, E. & I. Williams, Sheila Williams, Scott Wilson, Daphne & Jane Wyatt, Sarah and John Zaluckyj and the various churchwardens, parish councillors and local residents who have helped or provided information in one way or another.

The authors are also grateful for the assistance given by the staff of Herefordshire Record Office, Hereford City Reference Library, Ross-on-Wye Library, Ross Market House Heritage Centre, *Ross Gazette*, Hereford Cathedral Library, Gwent Record Office and Monmouth Museum together with Hentland with Hoarwithy PCC, the Society of Friends in Ross-on-Wye and Andy and Karen Johnson of Logaston Press.

Unless otherwise stated the illustrations are from the individual author's collections.

Heather Hurley, Co-ordinator and Chair of the Publications Committee.

Contents

List of Subscribers in alphabetical order

Annetta Anderson

Elizabeth Bailey

Mrs J. Bottomley

Simon Clarke

Simon Clarke

Simon Clarke

Simon Clarke

David Collin

Richard and Jenny Cook

Janet Cooper

Peter and Madge Crocker

David and Leila Dawson

Keith and Brenda Glover

John Goodrich

Philip Gray

Herefordshire Libraries

Herefordshire Libraries

Herefordshire Libraries

Herefordshire Libraries

Herefordshire Libraries

Herefordshire Libraries

Herefordshire Libraries

Herefordshire Libraries

Herefordshire Libraries

Eithne Holcom

R. Houghton

Heather Hurley

Jon Hurley

Aileen Hurst

Andrew and Heather Jackson

Andrew and Heather Jackson

Mervyn James

P.B. Lee

Didi Lodge

Carol and Chris Lowndes

Richard Mayo

Margaret and Owen Morgan

Virginia Morgan

Melody Morgan-Busher

Miss F.E. Okell

Alan Parslow

Mary Sinclair Powell

Shirley Preece

Shirley Preece

Shirley Preece

Shirley Preece

Dr C.D. Price

Nancy Rees

Nancy Rees

Miss D.F. Roberson

R.R. Roberts

Ross Market House Heritage Centre

Ross Old Books

Marc Russell

John Saul

Mrs R.E. Skelton

Fenny Smith

Prebendary Andrew Talbot-Ponsonby

Brian Thomas

David Whitehead

Graham Williams

Sheila Williams

Foreword

The late Graham Hurst was the prime mover in establishing the Ross-on-Wye and District Civic Society's series of Pink Publications as a contribution to the recorded historical knowledge of Ross and its environs. They form part of the literary scene in this part of Herefordshire, nationally and internationally. Graham's aim was to capture the local history which might have become lost because of omission rather than intentional neglect. The first Pink Publication was produced in 1993 and has its origins in a sixth-form project at John Kyrle High School.

The first ten Pink Publications were published in 2000, as the Ross Civic Society's Millennium project, in *Historical Aspects of Ross*, a single volume in hardback.

This second volume is also wide ranging in covering topics from the 1st to the 20th century. The authors, all expert in their particular area of local history are from many backgrounds and their enthusiasm is infectious. The subjects covered include a Celtic Saint, the Quakers, Domesday entries, Ross Workhouse, Stained Glass, Hoarwithy Church, Recusants, a Scholar, Corn Milling and Brewing.

It has been my privilege and pleasure to have been involved in the production of the individual papers in this volume by preparing the manuscripts for publication.

Dr Colin Price
Secretary, Ross-on-Wye & District Civic Society Publications Sub Committee
1993-2009

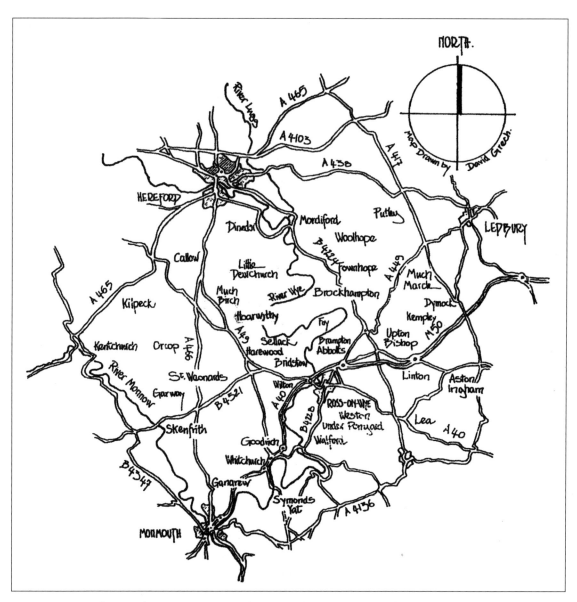

General Location Map showing the area around Ross-on-Wye

CHAPTER 1

The Ross Union Workhouse 1836-1914

Introduction

A new Community Hospital stands at Dean Hill, Alton Street, Ross on what was the site of the Ross Union Workhouse. This chapter tells part of the story of those who lived and worked in the Workhouse between 1836 and 1914.

Until 1834 and the new Poor Law Amendment Act, the poor were the responsibility of their respective parish. Justices of the Peace decided on the local Poor Rate and this was levied on occupiers of land and property. Parish officials — paid Overseers — were appointed to obtain the funds and, together with the Churchwardens, distribute 'relief' to the needy poor. Stringent settlement regulations, outdoor relief and, in many parishes, a Poor House or House of Industry, were the basic features of the support of the parish poor. However, in many impoverished rural areas, householders were exempted from paying rates and their rents were often subsidised by the parish. Initiative and mobility of labour were discouraged by the Settlement Laws, with labourers surplus in one region unable to seek work in another.

By 1830 the Poor Rate accounted for one fifth of the national expenditure. Resentment at the injustice of its administration, and poverty causing riots and machine burning in many rural areas, resulted in the setting up of a Commission to conduct a nationwide survey. Questionnaires were circulated to every town and country area. The Poor Law Report of 1834 includes the following questions and the answers from Ross:

> Q — 'What are the classes of manufacturers, workmen or labourers in your Parish whom you believe to be most subject to distress?'
> A — 'We have no manufactories. I consider that the number of mechanics and labourers are about equal who feel distress.' (Mr John Hardwick, Asst Overseer for Ross Town answered)

A further question elicited the information that a journeyman mechanic would average £40pa and a labourer in 'average employment' for 10 months £18 5s. 6d.pa, 'But in many instances the labourer has a good garden to his cottage, which enables him to keep a pig, that would be worth when slaughtered, £5 or £6'. After ascertaining that a married man's wife could earn 9d. per day, and his four children from 6d. to 3d. per day, the family's annual income could be as much as £30 4s.

> Q — 'Could the Family subsist on these earnings, and if so, on
>   what food?'
> A — 'That must depend on the price of food.'
> Q — 'Could it lay by anything? And how much?'
> A — 'No.'

Key : Ross Union Boundary ——————
Union District Boundaries — · — · — · — · -
Parish Boundaries . . . .

Ross Poor Law Union in Herefordshire, 1836
Ross Union also included Lea (Gloucestershire) and Ruardean (Gloucestershire),
and Aston Ingham and Linton were added in 1894

Even before the answers were properly analysed, legislation was rushed through in 1834 and the huge bureaucracy of the Poor Law Commission was born.

Parishes within a 10-mile radius of a market town were to combine in supporting a centralised Union Workhouse. The officials manning the house and those dispensing relief in the parishes were to be paid out of Union funds, funds that came from all the parishes in the Union.

The workhouse was primarily a haven for those who could not work or maintain themselves because of youth, age, infirmity or incapacity. The poor who would not work and were able-bodied were not encouraged to apply for workhouse entry — indeed the disincentives of hard and repetitive work, a dull (but adequate) diet, restrictive rules and minimum comfort all combined to make the workhouse a last resort. At the same time the New Poor Law sought to discontinue outdoor relief — the able-bodied no longer received it just because they were in need, but if they insisted they could not find work, they were offered a place in the workhouse — the dreaded 'Workhouse Test'. On entry, married couples were separated, the sexes segregated and children over 7 removed from their mothers. The inmates were not prisoners. If they gave the Master three hours notice they could leave as long as they changed back into the clothes they had come in with. However the children (often abandoned as illegitimate or unwanted), the aged, the infirm and the mentally handicapped inmates did remain for long periods in these institutions.

The architecture was designed to indicate order, efficiency and confidence in the new social order. The high walls, the forbidding design and the impressive size of the new workhouses proclaimed a regime of deterrence and authority.

'Out-relief', despite the central body's ruling, did continue and from the Minutes it appears that the Ross Union Guardians were generally kindly towards those in need.

Administration
The rules for Union administration were clearly laid down by the Poor Law Authority. Boards of Guardians were elected annually, on a restricted property-based franchise. Women and manual workers could not become Guardians until this property qualification was abolished in 1894.

A Master and a Matron were in charge of the running of the workhouse reporting to the Board at their fortnightly meeting. Usually the workhouse was served by a Medical Officer, a Porter, a Schoolmaster, a Nurse and a Curate. The paid Clerk was the linch-pin of the Union and he normally had legal training. Out of the workhouse, district based Relieving Officers were responsible for identifying and maintaining the paupers who were not eligible to enter the workhouse but were eligible for 'out-relief' — this was in the form of bread, money, clothes and shoes.

The Guardians and the Union Treasurer were Honorary Administrators. Their main aim was to restrict expenditure on poor relief in their areas. The meetings carefully recorded in the 27 Minute Books detail their decisions. They approved tenders and checked trades-peoples' estimates and invoices. They scrutinised the Master's and Relieving Officers' Day Books and Accounts. They appointed and dismissed staff and debated the claims for relief sent in by paupers. However, the Poor Law Commission had to sanction most of the Guardians' decisions and this often caused tension. While the Guardians wanted to keep the ratepayers' costs down, locally, the Commission wanted to defend itself from criticisms of the new, more ruthless system, nationally.

Within the workhouse the Master ruled. He ensured that every inmate obeyed the rules — these were usually displayed on the walls of the wards. He saw that the dietary prescribed by the Central Authority was rigorously rationed out to each resident. He conducted prayers; with his wife he supervised the sick and attended the dying. He maintained careful records

Statement of Expenditure by Parish in 1866

4

of all income and expenditure and was present at the regular Board meetings. Any pauper issued with an order for entry into the workhouse had to be admitted, the Master or Matron supervising the pauper's reception, with a compulsory bath and a change into workhouse clothes. The newcomer was then sent to his or her ward or dormitory.

Finance

The initial purchase of the site and the cost of the building, completed in 1838, were met by an Exchequer loan and the repayment costs debited to the 30 contributing parishes. The ongoing maintenance and administration costs of the workhouse and the inmates were considerable. Initially these were met by half-yearly 'calls' on the parish rates based on the average of their respective expenditure over the previous three years. As the regional system consolidated, each parish had its call assessed on the relief, indoor and outdoor, given to its particular poor over the previous half-year. Thus in hard times and bad weather the rate would be higher, with the paralleled difficulty for the ratepayers in meeting the demand. In 1861 the contribution system changed, with property rather than poverty the basis for parish payments towards the common expenses of the Union. In 1865 a common rate was levied on all the parishes in each Union so that the poorer ones were subsidised by the wealthier ones.

Tradesmens' Accounts for the Ross Union in October, 1862

The responses to these 'calls' were often delayed. Sometimes the Overseers responsible were fined in the Magistrates' Courts for late or non-payment of parish dues. Assets such as parish-owned property were sold and the proceeds sent to the Union Treasurer for investment, subsequent dividends helping to defray parish expenditure. Any personal pension, legacy or savings belonging to a pauper was taken over by the Union Treasurer and used to defray the beneficiary's maintenance costs, while he or she received relief of any sort. Some revenue was raised from work done by the workhouse inmates. Stone broken by the able-bodied men was sold for road building, and the oakum shredded by the women was sold. Pigs were regularly bought and fattened and sold at a small profit. In later years some cost saving was made by vegetable growing on land rented for the purpose.

The salary of the schoolteacher was subsidised by the Treasury from 1848, but the rate depended on the competence of the teacher. One schoolmaster refused to be examined! From 1888, as a consequence of the Local Government Act, the Union Officers' salaries were paid from the County rather than the Poor Rates.

All these systems had to be initiated, supervised and audited. Occasional discrepancies are noted and rectified. The few recorded embezzlements, by Overseers and Collectors to the Guardians, resulted in punishment for the perpetrators. Unfortunately the ledgers and day books are not in the local Record Office. All the regular calls on the parishes are noted in the Minute books, as are the Masters' and Relieving Officers' accounts. Details of the building and repair costs are recorded and the payments and expenses are cross-referenced with the relevant account numbers. The clerical and book-keeping systems must have been very onerous to maintain. The Clerk was responsible for their efficiency and accuracy.

Even without access to the ledgers and account books most of the financial negotiations of the Union can be derived from the Minute books.

Buildings

There had been a smaller workhouse just for Ross Parish on the site at Dean Hill, with access to Corpse Cross Street, as it was then called. The land had been bequeathed by Jane Furney in May 1728 for the use of the Parish of Ross, 'for ever'. A barn stood on the ground, but by 1819 a record of the Benefactions of the Parish Church and the Poor of the House notes 'the now Workhouse and garden'. In December 1809 James Powles acquired a 99 year lease of a plot of garden ground, part of these premises. The next reference found is in the replies to the 1834 Poor Law Commission queries. One answer records that there were then 18 adults and 5 children living in the Ross Parish Workhouse; the cost per person including clothing, was 3s. 3d. per week and another 9d. each per week covered the costs of the establishment.

After the introduction of the New Poor Law, a meeting was convened to secure the agreement of the Ross ratepayers to sell the workhouse and its land to the new Union for £500 plus interest at 5% pa.

The Guardians of the Union commissioned Mr Plowman of Oxford as the architect and a tender to build a new workhouse was accepted from Thomas Tristram of Ross; his figure was £2,200 but with alterations and fees the final cost of the building was £3,650. The existing inmates were duly moved to the smaller workhouses at Weston-under-Penyard and Upton Bishop, from which it is presumed that the earlier building was completely demolished whilst the new one was built.

Delays and problems are listed in the Minutes, but on 2nd January 1838 the newly appointed Master and Mistress, Benjamin and Mary Ann Jeffreys, received 53 pauper residents in the new building designed to accommodate 160. But problems remained; for example the 'warming apparatus' did not function properly. In turn the contractor suggested springs should be fitted on the doors as the inmates habitually left them open, so allowing the heat to escape! In 1838 the House contained 80 residents and was reported as full. This was queried by the Guardians as reported in the Minute Book on 5th November 1838 but was explained (at a meeting held on 12th November) that changes made to the rooms had led to 'deficient accommodation'. Alterations were made both in accommodation and, in 1839, to allow baking on the premises. This bread was supplied to both those in the workhouse and to the outdoor poor as their relief.

A well was sunk to such a depth as would ensure 'a supply of water at all seasons', but this supply was to prove insufficient. Mr John Phipps sent in his estimate for a new pump (see below).

Drains were a recurring nuisance; in 1840 leave was sought from the Reverend Ogilvie to 'drain the fever wards through the adjoining Glebe Garden'.

In 1858 a new Dead House was built and the previous one converted as a bathroom for the boys. (Deceased paupers were always taken back to their own parish for burial).

By 1862 the workhouse was proving too cramped, and under pressure from the Poor Law Board the Guardians decided to look for a site for a new and larger building. However, it was subsequently decided to enlarge the existing building and, after much negotiation, in 1868 Glebe land was purchased for £700. Plans were invited for an entirely new workhouse and five designs were submitted under false names — the Guardians had added the incentive of an award of £40 for the chosen plan. At a special meeting the Board conducted a 'minute examination to discover the special merits of each plan'. The set of designs under the motto 'IDONEUM' was selected and it transpired that it came from Messrs Haddon of Hereford and Great Malvern. In September 1872 tenders were invited for the construction of the buildings, but significantly these were described as alterations and not a new workhouse. There was reference to Messrs Haddon's plans in the 18th May 1872 edition of *The Builder*: they were completed at a cost of 'less than £34 per head of inmates and preferably 6 shillings per cubic foot of the entire building'.

The lowest tender in the sum of £7,849 was chosen from John Everal of Great Malvern as follows:

Extract from the Minute Book
(HRO K42/407, p.256)

		£
1.	Principal Building	3,670
2.	Infirmary	1,535
3.	Fever Building	645
4.	Receiving Buildings etc	850
5.	Vagrants' Wards	897
6.	Boundary walls and roads etc	252
		£7,849

Priority was given to the construction of the vagrants' wards, on the north-east of the site. These itinerants were always a cause for concern in the neighbourhood, particularly when casual work was scarce. The new buildings increased the size of the workhouse substantially. As there is no mention of the inmates having to move it is possible that some of the 1836 buildings remained.

In 1874 there is reference to the need to 'arch over' the well in the old Workhouse 'leaving a hole for a pump to be put up if hereafter necessary such hole to be covered with a flagstone'. The architects' reports describe the two entrances, one from Alton Street and the other next to Dean Hill. Also the cost of a new wall between the workhouse property and the property bordering Corpse Cross Street was estimated at about £65, whilst the one bounding the cottage property 'which abuts on Dean Hill would be about £30'. By February 1874, Mr Everal had completed the work. An interesting order by the Master is his request for 31 pokers and 31 shovels which were required for the different fireplaces in the new buildings. Also 13 galvanised pans for earth closets for the Infirmary and other buildings were ordered from Messrs Perkins & Bellamy of Ross, at 3s. each.

*The workhouse
shown on the 1889 Ordnance Survey*

But the workhouse was still too small. Plans were therefore requested from Mr Pearson of Ross for an extension but these needed amendment by the Local Government Board (May 1875). Despite pressure, the Guardians would not agree to further expense and baulked at Mr Pearson's insistence on payment for his plans — he wanted '£36 for them but would reduce this to £25'. Heated exchanges in the board room led to Captain Power's 'desire to resign as Chairman of the Board'. One Guardian used strong terms of condemnation of the Board's proceedings — 'Dishonest, Disgraceful and Dishonourable' — in defence of Mr Pearson's position. Eventually apologies were tendered, the plans approved and Mr Pearson instructed to take out the 'quantities'. He estimated that, if old materials were re-used, the extensions would cost £3,000. But all the tenders were rejected as too costly.

A year later the School Inspector issued a critical report. The schoolteacher was over-streched and no progress had been made with the completion of the workhouse since his last visit. In reply to the Guardians' query as to the possibility of modifications to his plans, Mr Pearson reported that 'the only buildings that can be erected without interfering with the old part of the [work]House are the wings for the accommodation of the men and women adjoining the principal buildings'. In May 1881 it was resolved that a house and buildings in Alton Street adjoining the Stone Yard should be bought, and one of the Guardians, Mr Brunsdon, was to offer £150 on behalf of the Board. In 1882 Mr Kemp tendered £45 10s. to pull down and rebuild the north-eastern boundary wall.

The workhouse was becoming increasingly over-crowded and in 1889 it was decided that Mr Pearson's plans should be implemented, and under his son's directions (Arthur Pearson) tenders were again sought. These included for a new kitchen and dining room, but unfortunately the plans have not been found. The architect of the new Community Hospital

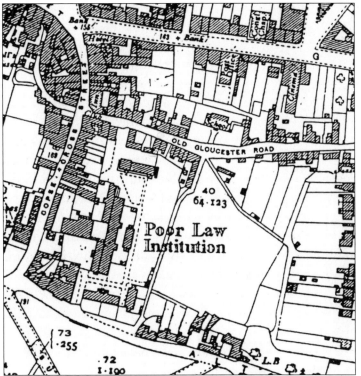

This revision c.1927 of the Ordnance Survey Map shows a significant extension of the workhouse compared with the map opposite

has deduced that the principal spine building was extended to the south-west. This time a tender for £4,350 was accepted from Messrs Henry Millward of Leominster and the works completed in 1890. Accommodation was now available for 200 inmates.

In 1904 the board room was enlarged and improved. It was also rented out to local organisations including for an Art and Craft Exhibition in 1909. An office for the Sanitary Inspector was rented and a telephone installed in the building. The bake-house was demolished and instead the bread was supplied by a local baker. The new laundry and kitchen was also used by schools for laundry and cooking lessons. These further building projects cost £4,900.

New vagrants' wards were completed in December 1911, built by William Bevan for £175; this avoided the need to send 'casuals' to lodgings. By 1913 the demand for accommodation had fallen and it would have been possible to allow classification of the inmates according to the principle, but not the practice, of the 1834 Act. An article in the *Ross Gazette* of 14th May 1914, reports a Poor Law Conference in West Malvern where the difficulties of implementing classification were discussed.

A summary from a Survey by the Royal Commission on the Historical Monuments of England (1994) gives the following details of the site:

Parishes	Guardians elected	Names of Guardians qualified to act in the Parishes where no Guardians have been elected
Ballingham		Clement Cade
Brampton Abbotts	Daniel Dew	
Bridstow	William Wylie	
Brockhampton		William Stallard
Foy		William Jones
Goodrich	Thomas Powell	
Harewood	Charles Andrews	
Hentland	Thomas Meats	
Hope Mansell	Cornelius Morfell	
How Caple	John A Hollings	
King's Caple		James Price
Llandinabo	Richard Howells	
Llangarren	Geo Woodall Lloyd / Frederick Price	
Llanwarne	George T Taylor	
Lea Bailey	Cornelius Morfell	
Lea Gloucester	John Lodge	
Lea Hereford		
Marston		Thomas Barnett
Pencoyd	Revd M Coke	
Peterstow	William Dew	
Ross	Wm Cary Cocks / Joseph Pearce / Thomas Morfell / William Bonnor	
Ruardean	John Vaughan	
St Weonards	W V Foxwell	
Sellack	Thomas Dew	
Sollershope	Joseph Jill	
Tretire	Frederick Price	
Upton Bishop	Henry Chellingworth / Thomas S Bradstock	
Walford	Isaac Theyer	
Weston	William Bennett	
Yatton	William Gibson Ward	

Ross Union Guardians by Parish in 1861

Ross-on-Wye Workhouse buildings in 1951 (Michael Raven)

The site is small and irregular and the buildings were erected close together. To the west of the main entrance on Alton Street were the administrative offices and receiving wards: to the east were the infirmary and fever wards. The main building, in the centre of the site, followed the corridor plan which was favoured for workhouses throughout the country between the 1840s and the 1870s. To its west was the dining hall, kitchen and laundry, to its east was a schoolroom and to the north a casual ward block.

The land comprising the workhouse premises was assessed for valuation purposes in April 1914:

Acreage – 2 acres 29 perches	Original gross value	£14,746
	less Tithe	£3
		£14,743
	Original assessable site value	£ 1,035
	Therefore Assessable Site Value	£13,708

The only building remaining after the demolition of the workhouse/Dean Hill Hospital in October, 1995

With all the rebuilding, alterations and extensions, it is estimated that over £16,000 of Union funds was expended on the workhouse buildings. This was in addition to at least £1,800 on land purchases.

Between 1913 and 1992 the workhouse changed its name and function. From 1913 it was called the Poor Law Institution renamed the Pubic Assistance Institution in 1929 until 1943 when it became the Ross Social Welfare Institution. In 1948 it was called the Alton Street Hospital, and more recently the Dean Hill Hospital. Local people used to call it the 'Spike'. This is a colloquial name for a casual ward; to sleep in the workhouse was to go 'on the Spike'.

In 1976 there was a total of 113 beds. A maternity ward with 4 beds was situated above the Receiving Ward. Lilac Ward accommodated the long stay Age Care residents, and Holly and Oak Wards the female and male adults with learning difficulties. A physiotherapy unit and administrative offices occupied the building where the Guardians met so regularly. Only this building remains, as illustrated in the photograph above, taken the day before the construction of the new Community Hospital began.

Medical Relief
The licensed 'Medical Gentlemen' contracted by the Board of Guardians were required to attend all the sick paupers in the Union, usually by referrals from the Relieving Officers. The Union supplied basic medicines but unusual items had to be bought in. From 1865 to 1868 a dispensary was opened at the workhouse with a qualified dispenser, Mr John Cotton, and the Medical Officers' salaries were reduced by '10£ per cent' and, in a later entry, 'the Board would supply bandages, leeches and syringes where ordered by the Medical Officer' (MO). In 1875 Mr Kemp was engaged to convert the Register Office to a dispensary but later there were many complaints as the Dispenser was frequently absent and, in one case,

a women had walked from Llangarren for her medicine. The local chemist benefited — in April 1878 the Guardians chided the Dispenser to 'keep up his stock of drugs so far as is consistent with proper freshness so as to render it unnecessary to make purchases in the Town'. Mr W.S. Rootes and Mr C.E. Thomson were the first Medical Officers, with the Union divided into two districts. When the Union workhouse opened in January 1838, Mr Thomson took on its care at a salary of £15. Until 1842 the MOs were paid on a contract basis and their charges in 1839 were:

> For every single case within 2 miles of Ross the charge would be
>   5s. and beyond that distance 7s. 6d.
> For all Family cases within 2 miles of Ross 7s. 6d. and beyond
>   that distance 8s. 6d.
> For all midwifery cases 8s. 6d.
> For all fractures and dislocations and for amputations and
>   operations for hernia £1 1s.

From 1839 Edmund Jones was appointed MO in charge of the workhouse and his kindly service ended in 1863 with the Guardians' tribute to his 'assiduity and attention to his duties'. He was also the Public Vaccinator, earning 1s. 6d. for every successful case, but since many people did not return for checking on the seventh day he often worked for nothing.

Smallpox is first mentioned as prevalent in August 1838, and the Master was told to have all the children vaccinated. In 1840 Mr Jones undertook to visit all the out-paupers on specified days at Old Gore, Hope Mansell, Llangarren, Hoarwithy and Ross. He had to keep 'two books one of which would note the residence of every person successfully vaccinated' and give them a certificate. The Poor Law Board issued frequent directives, and later on proceedings were taken against parents who did not allow their children to be vaccinated. Through their relative isolation the inmates of the workhouse were protected, but in May 1859 John James of Goodrich was admitted 'suffering from smallpox'. The Overseer responsible was criticised as the Guardians said the case was 'not one of sudden and urgent necessity'.

Other infectious diseases are reported, outside, and the use of a fever ward was recommended to cope with any sudden influx of sick paupers. In the early years Mr Jones's concern about the severe diarrhoea prevalent in the workhouse led to his report to the Board that 'although this complaint has and usually does prevail in the Autumn in all places, yet in the workhouse it had been much aggravated and increased by the unwholesome nature of the atmosphere created by the present method of warming three of the wards which, while the temperature consistently varies, tends neither to ventilate nor purify the air as a common fireplace does which in my opinion would prevent the present close and disagreeable smell

The Isolation Ward, east of the Infirmary

and great deposit of water upon the doors and walls.'

After the considerable extension of the workhouse in 1874 the MO, Dr Thomas Jones, told the Board that 'the newly erected infirmary and infectious wards are ready for occupation' and 'the Master was directed to avail himself of the extra accommodation at his disposal'. But the fever ward was only used once, until 1909, when nine children and the Matron were taken ill with scarlet fever. In 1912 six children were isolated there, suffering with scabies. In 1884 water closets were substituted for the earth closets in the Fever Ward.

The 'itch' was a problem: in 1856 Mr A. Willmott, the House MO, had to report on the number of such cases. He said it was on the decline and 'expressed the hope that it would soon be good rid of entirely'. One 4-year-old child contracted the itch whilst in the workhouse but the Board decided to discharge his mother so that she could go into service and 'to keep the child in the Workhouse until he could be cured of the disease without compelling his mother to remain with him in the House'.

The Board paid a subscription to the hospitals they used, and an application for one was received from the newly established Eye and Ear Hospital, Hereford, in November 1883. Much care and cost was given to the disabled, the blind and the deaf and dumb paupers. One boy, Samuel Hodges of Ross, was sent to the Deaf and Dumb Asylum, Old Kent Road, London for board and instruction, and in March 1861 he became an apprentice to Mr Joseph Evans of Ross, Basket Maker, with the Board arranging the indenture payment and also 'to supply his fit out'.

Many single expectant pauper mothers came in to the workhouse to have their babies and had to occupy the same room as the mothers who were lying in. It appears that mothers could look after their infants, but there were sad cases of desertions.

A nurse was employed for most of the period but there was a remarkable 'turn over' in the job, with at least 18 in the post between 1838 and 1914. Sometimes there were no answers to the advertisements and the Matron had additional work, but 'thus the salary and rations of a nurse were saved'. An inmate applied for the post once, but as she could not 'read writing' she could only act as assistant to the Matron at a salary of £10pa, subject, as were all decisions, to the sanction of the Poor Law Authority. Another nurse was summarily dismissed for 'insubordination' and the porter resigned at the same time. In 1898 it was resolved that dying and bedridden patients were to be removed from the sick ward and a hospital trained nurse was appointed.

The Guardians were consistent in their efforts to save ratepayers' money. An example is this Minute in January 1850: 'Dr Jones applied for the payment of a fee of one guinea to Dr Barratt for assisting him to amputate the thigh of a pauper in the workhouse. The Board, considering that all such expenses were paid by Dr Jones's salary, felt necessitated to reject the application.' At this time Dr Jones's salary as MO for the Workhouse was £25 per annum, and he earned a further £60 as MO of one of the Districts. There were generous Guardians. Mr Hall at his request was permitted 'to erect at his own expense a pole etc in the yard for the boys in the Workhouse to exercise themselves in gymnastics'.

After the Public Health Act of 1872 a Medical Officer of Health should have been appointed for the whole Union 'including that portion of the parish of Ross under the supervision of the Ross Town Commissioners'. The salary was to be £70 per annum, and an Inspector of Nuisances was also to be appointed at an annual salary of £60. But the Guardians hesitated; they wanted to see what other Unions were doing!

Initially the water supply was from the well, later it was obtained from the River Wye. Fortunately for the health of the inmates an 'unlimited and always consistent supply' of spring water was laid on from Mr Turnock's property, Merrivale, in 1879.

It was ironic that the Urban Sanitary Authority had to report a nuisance at the workhouse arising from a cess-pool. The proposed solution wondered whether 'an outlet be obtained into the town sewer running down Corpse Cross Street?'

Minute Book entry for 1st June 1840, showing the diet (HRO K42/407, p.323)

Food and Diet

The 'less eligibility' test for workhouse entry required that the diet for those receiving 'inside' relief should not be better than that available to the lowest paid employee outside. The Central Authority drew up different

Dietary Tables and the one chosen by the Guardians had to be strictly followed and copies printed 'in large type and hung up in the most public places in the Workhouse'. 'Dietary No. 1' was initially selected for the adults, but was replaced by one recommended by Mr Cary Cocks. This applied only to the able-bodied adults. The diet for the aged and the sick was unchanged.

The children under 9 had a different diet:

5 – 9 Years		1 – 5 Years		Under 1 Year	
Bread	8 oz	Bread	7 oz	Bread	6 oz
Meat	4 oz	Meat	3 oz	Milk	? pints
Cheese	1 oz	Cheese	1 oz		

However in 1857 the Medical Officer for the workhouse altered their diet 'with a view to remove the scorbutic disease which exists among them'.

The aged and infirm had extras like tea, sugar and butter. In 1858 the Master told the Board that all the able-bodied paupers and children over 9 years of age should have a pint of milk and water at suppertime. But the vagrants did not fare so well.

Parsnips were ordered by the hundredweight (cwt), onions by the peck or bushel. Oatmeal came from Scotland in 5cwt supplies (average price £1 per cwt). Land at Ashfield was leased for vegetable cultivation, and in 1895 the Royal Cross Estate, opposite the workhouse, was bought on the understanding that it should never be built on: until the 1960s it was cultivated productively. Tenders for potatoes occur frequently in the records, but in 1846 and 1883 crop failures led to difficulties: 'it appearing that there was great difficulty in obtaining potatoes, it was resolved that rice and other vegetables should be use alternatively with potatoes as a temporary expedient.' Meat was supplied mainly by one contractor: he was very indignant when, in 1872, Australian beef and mutton, at 6d. per lb, was ordered from Mr J. Hill, a grocer. Earlier there was official criticism of the diet for the feeble minded: 'the meat is always boiled'.

The Local Government Board, in an attempt to improve health standards, suggested that fish be tried: 'the inmates to have 8oz of cooked fish each, on Saturdays'. It was not a success. The Master reported that 'in many cases the inmates would not touch it and that on the second occasion he had cut up a cheese and given it in lieu of fish.' It was resolved that fish dinners be discontinued.

Bread was the most important item in both inside and outside relief. From May 1839 until March 1890 it was baked on the workhouse premises, and the succession of bakers, (sometimes assisted by the lads in the house) earned £1 per week, later augmented by 1s. 6d. per week for every sack (280lb) of flour over 12 sacks, baked per week. The bread

Minute Book entry for 10th March 1879
(HRO K42/407, p.883)

was taken to the 'outstations' by the contractor in his bread cart; in September 1883 the list of outgoings includes: 'H. Digwood paid for conveyance of bread 17s. 0d. per wk. Conveyance of dead 3s. 6d. per journey'. Years earlier the Guardians, always parsimonious, thought the bread delivery costs too high and invited tenders 'for the construction of a light sprung wagon with covered top capable of holding about 320 loaves of bread'. However the project was too expensive and the bread deliveries contracts continued. The 4lb loaves cost between 4d. and 10d. each, for the purpose of parochial reimbursement, and they were marked with an indented 'R.U.' Regrettably the Relieving Officer for the vagrants was suspected of cutting this mark off the bread and selling the loaves, and was dismissed. Quality control was practised by the Board, from samples produced from each tender. In one case the workhouse baker blamed his poor product on the flour. The contractor, Mr J.B. Whittard (of Whitchurch), indignantly responded by arranging for his employee to bake in the workhouse with his flour and the usual barm (used instead of yeast). An 'excellent loaf was produced therefrom' and the workhouse baker was 'censured and cautioned'.

Restriction of food was used as a punishment, but never with children, nursing mothers or the aged. Wine and brandy were frequently ordered from Mr Purchas of Ross. In 1872, the auditor criticised the Master for the quantity of brandy used. He had an unusual explanation: it had been ordered by the Medical Officer to be given to the nurse as there had been an 'inmate of one of the wards with frost-bitten feet and the toes gradually decayed and fell off, the effluvia from the sores being so offensive that the Nurse could not discharge her duties without stimulants and the brandy referred to above was given to her.' A résumé of indoor costs compiled in 1914 notes that in 1904, 32½ gallons of whisky and spirits were purchased, whereas for the year ending 31st March 1914 the quantity amounted to only 2½ gallons.

As the years went by the diet became more varied, and more generous. Tea was available to the inmates generally but it was weak! — 'ordered that 1oz of tea be used with 8 pints of water instead of with 10 pints of water as hitherto'. The diet for the officers was more liberal than that of their charges. In March 1838, Sir E.W. Head, the Assistant Poor Law Commissioner, recommended that rations 'as for seven should be allowed for the

17

Master, Matron, Nurse and School mistress'! All the officers had a beer allowance, or were given 'three halfpence a day in lieu'.

But there were good times. Following the tradition of a good Christmas dinner being provided by public subscription in Ross Parish, one of the founder Guardians, Nathaniel Morgan, proposed that this should continue in the workhouse. A dinner of roast beef and plum pudding was therefore given to all the inmates every year on Christmas Day.

Christmas celebrations at the hospital, c.1930s.
(Photo courtesy of Mrs. V.J. Robbins)

An entry for December 1879 reads: 'the usual dinner to be provided to the Inmates of the House on Christmas Day with exception of bad characters who may come in immediately.' On Christmas Day 1909, the whole day's fare is noted:

> Breakfast: Bread 8oz. Butter ½oz. Tea 1 pint and milk and
> arrowroot per sick dietary.
> Dinner: Cooked meat, vegetables and Christmas Pudding with
> one pint of Ale or mineral water.
> Supper: Bread 6oz. Butter ½oz. Tea 1 pint and 4oz. Sultana Cake.
> Extras: Male Inmates – 1oz. tobacco each
> Female   – 2 oranges
> Children   – oranges and sweets.

Other special occasions were celebrated with 'good dinners': the Central Board sent a circular to all the Unions sanctioning a change in the dietary on Her Majesty's Coronation, her Marriage and her Jubilee. At the Coronation of King Edward VII the diet was:

> Cold Meat, pickles, salad, fruit tarts
> Beer and ginger beer for men, also tobacco
> Tea and sugar for women

Towards the end of this period, with growing awareness of nutritional requirements in a balanced diet, those in the workhouse were probably better fed than their friends and relatives outside.

Children

The children in the workhouse came in with their destitute parents, or were brought in on their own to relieve the financial pressures on their families. Many children were born in the workhouse and sometimes they were abandoned there. The rules in 1847 dictated: 'so long as any mother is suckling her child she ought to have access to it at all times except when she is at work, and the child ought not, even then, to be completely beyond the mother's reach.' Children under 7 could sleep in the female wards. After the age of 7, according to the classification system, the boys and girls were separated, sleeping in male and female dormitories.

Outside the workhouse there were complex rules for the different pauper children's needs. In the early days widows, and deserted or separated wives, could have relief for their children under 7, and the authorities could not remove those children. After 7, if her case was justified, a mother could send the child into the workhouse without accompanying it.

In 1838, nationally, in the workhouses of 478 Unions sending returns, there were 42,767 children under 16 representing 44% of the total workhouse population. In 1840 this number had risen to 64,570 of whom 56,835 were aged between 2 and 16.

Relief was allowed to illegitimate children under 16, and this was deemed relief to the mother as long as she remained unmarried or a widow. But discrimination against such children is recorded. In 1866 an illegitimate little girl was being nursed by a Mrs Griffiths. She had complained already to the Board that when the child had a fever the District Medical Officer had refused to call. He had rationalised this, when summoned before the Board, saying he believed the child 'was suffering merely from a cold and that he did not feel justified in attending illegitimate children without a special order'. The case worsened. Mrs Griffiths applied for out-relief for her charge, but, following the rules, 'the Board refused — but, as the mother had deserted it, consented to take the child into the Workhouse.' The putative father, who worked at the Royal Hotel stables, was ordered to pay 1s. 6d. weekly towards the child's maintenance.

As late as 1905, when 'boarding-out' of workhouse children was regarded as a better upbringing than that within an institution, illegitimate children of able-bodied women in the workhouse were not included in those to be selected.

There are many references to the Clerk's attempts to coerce fathers into supporting their offspring. On one occasion he was directed 'to see the women now in the Workhouse and ascertain whether there was sufficient evidence to enable the Guardians to obtain

Bastardy Orders upon the alleged children of their Putative Fathers.' The next meeting reported developments. In one case the Clerk reported that the child had died, and that 'thus there was an end to the case'; with a second woman 'there was no corroborative evidence on which to obtain a summons against the alleged putative father of the child'; in a third case 'the mother was to be removed to the Parish of her settlement'.

A particularly poignant example of the distress of poverty is the offer of a reward of £1 'to any person giving such information as shall lead to the apprehension of the person who left a child about 5 weeks old at the door of the house in Smallbrook — whereby it became and is now chargeable to the Union.'

The children in the workhouse were better educated than many of their fellows outside. As early as 1839 the Master was told to provide the schoolroom with six slates and pencils for the use of the children under the schoolmistress's care and the chaplain (Mr Brasier) was to be requested to order 'what books may be wanted for the children's use'. Mr Thomas Blake was the schoolmaster from 1848 to 1853, and his list of articles required included a desk. The Guardians dispensed with the desk request, but said he could 'procure books etc from the British and Foreign School Depot' at a cost of £5. Later, maps of England and Palestine, and a tuning fork were purchased. A grate was fitted in the schoolroom, a clock was supplied and in 1874 the Clerk was asked to thank Mr F. Cooper, who had written on behalf of subscribers presenting a harmonium 'to be used in the Workhouse School'. School inspections were generally satisfactory, but in 1876 it was reported that there were 58 children in the school, of whom 30 were boys, too many for the schoolmistress to manage.

Industrial training was introduced. This was part of the central policy and the aim was to teach practical skills. The girls were instructed in cooking and household tasks, the boys in manual and horticultural work. At one stage the baker was enlisted as the Industrial Trainer and lads in the bakery were useful assistants. For a short period some children over 7 were sent to Hereford Industrial School at a cost of 3s. per week each. With the introduction of compulsory education from 1874, the children outside the workhouse had to attend school. Indeed the Guardians had to pay their school fees (usually 3d. per week) and later, children of non-paupers were entitled to have their school fees paid by the Union. But there was some discrimination: the Local Government Board told the Guardians they had no authority to pay the Ferry Toll for non-pauper children going to school!

From 1846 grants had been available to pay the salaries of qualified schoolmasters and mistresses, but two years later these were graduated according to the teacher's proficiency in the classroom. Some Guardians in other Unions objected: 'to teach writing and arithmetic to pauper children was to give them advantages superior to those of the children of the independent labourer.'

The first schoolmistress, in 1838, was the ex-matron of Ross Workhouse, Mrs Mary Griffiths. She was directed to 'walk out with the children when the weather is sufficiently fine' for set times and 'to put the children always to bed'. After she resigned in 1839, there was a succession of 17 single teachers. The annual salary was £25 with full board, lodging and washing. Some elected to have 'three halfpence a day in lieu of beer'. In January one year the mistress was blamed because, it was alleged, she had 'not properly attended the children and had allowed their feet to become very sore from chillblains'. At the next meeting her resignation was reported. Subsequently, her successor 'sent two letters of an objectionable nature to the Nurse and Matron so she is expected to resign'. When the schoolmistress left in 1892 it was resolved not to fill the vacancy, and the children attended the Board School. The Industrial Trainer was to look after them out of school hours and the Cook was appointed to the post. By 1905 there were only six children to be so instructed, so the post was abolished. Boarding-out of children aged over 3 was recommended and in 1911, 16 children were sent out to foster-homes.

The Central Authority always had the goal of giving the children of the poor a good start in life. With this aim they often had to persuade the Guardians to spend Union funds. Ross Union seems to have been generous and caring in its responsibilities to the young. Physically handicapped children were sent to specialist homes, orphans were sent to the Orphans' Home at Leominster and Müller's orphanage in Bristol. When young mothers left the house with their children, their requests for clothes or shoes were usually granted. In February 1862 one eloquent entry reads: 'Clerk to ask for sanction of Poor Law Board about the proposed allowance of a suit of clothes to the value of £1 5s. 10d. to George Meek an able-bodied Pauper chargeable to Weston-under-Penyard on his leaving the Workhouse for the purpose of procuring his own living. He has been in the Workhouse nearly all his life and consequently has no clothes of his own.' At the next meeting the letter of sanction was read.

When the boys reached the age of 12 they were employed or apprenticed. Despite the Central Authority's reservations about apprenticing children, except for physically disabled youngsters, Ross Union both arranged and supervised many such commitments. One boy, aged 14, was apprenticed to a plasterer in Ross, another to a tailor, another to a basket maker in Linton. In these and many other cases, the term, the premium and the wage to be paid (or invested in a Savings Bank) is detailed. In 'binding' Henry Bell King, a deaf and dumb boy, the Guardians required the Relieving Officer to attend before paying the second moiety of the premium. They 'expressed their satisfaction at the progress of the lad' and authorised the payment. Domestic service was the usual employment for girls. A certificate as to their fitness was obtained from the Medical Officer and agreements were prepared and signed. The boys and girls were usually given an outfit before leaving the workhouse. In one case the girl was to be paid £3 per annum; in another 1s. per week. When one of the schoolmistresses retired she applied to take a girl orphan inmate for 12 months as a domestic servant. One girl returned to the house after only 6 months service with a family.

She complained that she had been ill-used, the mistress having thrown a bucket of pigs' wash over her. The employer did not deny this and said that she had thrown three bowls of whey over the girl who was very 'saucy'. The Guardians did not pursue the matter but demanded the 6s. 8d. due as wages to the girl, which was put to the credit of the Union.

A few treats are described. In June 1851 all the children in the workhouse were taken to a Railway Fete held on Ross Cricket ground. There was a proviso: '8 tin dishes be lent for the purpose of the Fete. Mr Minett [the Clerk] undertaking they will be safely returned.' In 1865 the Poor Law Board refused to allow payment of travelling expenses of 5s. each for three unsuccessful applicants for the post of schoolmistress. The Guardians made a collection between them and 'as there remained 9s. the Clerk was directed to hand this over to the Master to provide a treat for the children in the Workhouse.'

As with the aged, the policy with regard to children in the workhouses became more lenient. A circular in 1891 sanctioning newspaper and book purchases for the older people stated that toys could be bought for the children. From 1901 birth certificates recorded the address as 3 Alton Street rather than the Workhouse (or the Public Assistance Institution). Where children were boarded out regular checks on their health and happiness were made by members of the Special Ladies Committee as well as the Medical Officer. Only children under 3 remained in the workhouse nursery, with the exception of 'ins and outs', the term for temporary inmates. The rates increased with this more liberal attitude, from 3s. 10½d. in the £ in 1904 to 4s. 6½d. in the £ in 1914. The outlay in boarding-out was blamed, as foster-parents received 5s. each per child, much more than pauper parents received for out-relief for each of their children.

Traders who supplied the Ross Union in 1914

With hindsight the benefit to the children can be imagined. They had escaped the numbing boredom of an institutionalised life, where there was no challenge, no room for initiative and no future. The workhouse had been a refuge, but they had to live in the real world.

The Able-bodied
This classification differed between those living outside and those inside the workhouse. Outside it defined those able to be, or in, employment. Able-bodied males were aged between 13 and 60, able-bodied women between 16 and 60, none of whom were mentally or physically incapacitated.

Outside relief was not to be offered to the able-bodied: if they were out of work and destitute, their only relief was to be in the workhouse. The Poor Law Central Authority believed that this would incite all able-bodied people to find work and subsistence without burdening the Poor Rates.

In Ross Union, many exceptions to this rigid rule are recorded in the Minute Books. Examples include a machineman earning 2s. per day, when he could work, with five children, none of whom were able to work, who was granted 'a pair of trowsers value 8s. 6d.' A widower with eight children, the youngest only 14 days old, earning 8s. per week asked if the baby could come into the workhouse as he was sick. As his illness was considered to be only temporary this was granted. In the severe weather of February 1888 an able-bodied man in Goodrich was granted relief, for two weeks, of 3s. and 12lbs of bread, valued at 1s. per week. A non-settled pauper, living in Westbury Union had been receiving 4s. per week, paid by them but debited to the Ross Union. On the death of the pauper's wife the Ross Clerk wrote to the Westbury Clerk suggesting that the 'pay' should be reduced to 2s. 6d. per week, which was agreed. As mentioned, able-bodied women had to come into the workhouse if their husbands were ordered in. Single women, widows with children, deserted mothers and mothers of illegitimate children were, if they were able-bodied, given out-relief according to their needs. There were some restrictions on the period of time that this could continue.

The value of the relief was in the ratio of one-third bread (or in kind) and two-thirds money (or pay). Medical relief, if prescribed by the Medical Officer, could consist of meat, milk or wine. A query was directed to Dr T.J. Jones, MO for St Weonards District as to the large quantities of wines and spirits ordered in May 1888. In cases of desertion, rewards were offered for the apprehension of the errant parents and their names and description were published in the *Poor Law Gazette*. In 1851 the Master was asked to prepare a list of all the children in the workhouse deserted by their parents, or without parents. The refrain that follows the details of each case is 'and leaving them chargeable to the Parish of — .'

Sometimes the fathers enlisted, but they were traced. One such deserted boy, left in the workhouse, posed a problem with regard to his settlement. After extensive enquiries 'the Master was directed to take the lad to Cardiff and the Clerk to allow the cost of his journey.' On another occasion a reward of 10s. was offered to apprehend a delinquent husband: he was caught and sent to Hereford Gaol for three months. A year later the reward was £2 for information about a man who had deserted his wife and children, with out-relief ordered for the children as 'they are within the age of nurture'. In bastardy cases, too, putative fathers were relentlessly pursued where there was sufficient evidence to convict them.

In all the circumstances, after the first distress of destitution had been overcome, the able-bodied men and women in the workhouse must have been very restless and the authorities provided hard and repetitive work as a means of avoiding disturbances.

The tasks would have included for the men, care of the pigs (whose profitable sales are frequently recorded), vegetable growing on the allotments rented from Messrs Collins (1862) and later on the land opposite the workhouse. Also wood chopping, stone breaking, water carrying (this in 1855, perhaps due to the frost), and on one occasion, 'painting the woodwork in the House and Mr Turnock [a Guardian] to get the paint'. The 1914 Minute Book records several cases of 'house labour' employed in decoration and minor repair work. The able-bodied women, when free from care of their young children, would have to do all the chores of the large establishment. The clothes mending may have been unsatisfactory because an entry in 1882 reads: 'Resolved to appoint a tailoress to repair inmates' clothes — to be paid wages with rations'.

On entry to the workhouse the paupers were taken into the separate receiving wards, bathed and given workhouse clothes (their own were kept to be returned on discharge). They were examined by the House Medical Officer, classified and shown to their stark quarters. In the evenings it was dim in the wards because although Mr Harris, the proprietor of the Ross Gas Works supplied metered gas to the 'new' workhouse in 1873, the Guardians 'struck out fifteen of the proposed lights'!

As the Minute Books only record routine administrative and management procedures, they are enlivened when accounts of misbehaviour and the consequences are described. In all these predicaments the Guardians were anxious to conform with the rules and regulations of the Central Authority.

There are several reports of boys and women absconding — but the censure is greater when the escapees are in workhouse clothes as this was theft. Other reports note that a woman had a bottle of brandy hidden in her clothes when admitted. Some of the younger women's names recur, either for refusing to work or being insolent. The usual punishment was up to 12 hours isolation in the refractory ward and an alteration in the diet! However when a young mother was one of the troublemakers, she was exempted from punishment as she was breast-feeding her baby.

The rules stated that any inmate with a complaint should forward it to the Board of Guardians and represent the case themselves at the fortnightly meetings. An 11-year-old boy of a violent disposition was defended by his mother in an unusual manner — she addressed a letter to the Board Chairman and threw it out of the window. She complained that the Master had beaten her son, but on examination it transpired that the boy had been expelled from the workhouse school for using very indecent language to the girls and since then he had been breaking stone during the usual hours. The Master admitted that he had 'administered corporal punishment to him on two or three occasions but only to a proper and moderate extent; and the boy was of so violent a disposition that he had once attempted to strike the Master with a besom.' The Board dismissed her complaint. As she repeated her aggressive behaviour later they were probably justified. An imbecile woman charged with deserting her illegitimate children was remanded temporarily in Ross Lock-up in November 1849 and a few months later she is reported as complaining that the Master had punished her unfairly. One malicious inmate accused the Master of giving food to one of the younger women secretly. The Guardians dismissed this, saying his character was unimpeached. He, Mr Smith, reported to one meeting that 'the male inmates of the workhouse had been in the habit of getting out of their yard over the wall into the women's yard.' It was resolved that 'Mr Joseph Drew be employed to do what is necessary in preventing any communication between the two yards — and also to do what repairs are necessary to the oven.'

But the Master's troubles were not over. One of the Guardians 'had been informed that some of the female paupers had on several occasions, dressed themselves in men's clothes and got into the men's ward.' The informant repeated her story to the visiting committee; on investigation it was verified that this had occurred, 'but it appeared that it had been done as a frolic and not with any criminal intent. The men's clothes had been removed from where they were necessarily kept after they are taken off until they are washed.' The report continued: 'The Committee place little or no reliance on the testimony of the witnesses, as to the disgusting acts of immorality which they allege to have taken place but supposing their statements to be true inasmuch as all parties kept the facts from the Master and Mistress no blame is attributable to them and it only proves the very depraved character of the female inmates themselves.'

In the years 1838 and 1840, and after the 1870s, Guardians were pressurised by the Central Authority to reduce their grants of out-relief. When this was combined with severe weather, or agricultural depression and loss of employment, the workhouse held more able-bodied, turbulent people. The discipline of the school and the apathy of the infirm ward would have offered a welcome contrast for the overworked Master and Matron.

The Aged, Infirm and Sick Poor

These three classifications of the poor were treated kindly under the 1834 Poor Law Act. Out-relief was always available to them as a means of avoiding destitution and the workhouse alternative was only offered to them when their living conditions, or state of health, necessitated this. However the out-relief so generously offered was accompanied by vigilant examination of the financial circumstances of their children or relatives, with a view to reimbursing the Poor Rates of their respective parishes: so much so that many poor people tried to avoid asking for relief for the aged in their families. Medical relief was available to them through personal application to their District Relieving Officer.

The aged and infirm poor, initially described as the 'impotent poor', were those aged over 60; infirm meant those permanently incapable of obtaining paid employment.

The sick poor were not only able to apply for medical relief but could be brought into the workhouse for treatment and nursing. In 1861 a non-resident pauper, Sarah Gardner who was 'bedridden and very ill', was authorised by the Clerk of Westbury-on-Severn Union, where she resided, to be brought to the Ross Workhouse in a fly. Ross Board agreed to bear the expense, and as she came from Walford, that parish was debited in due course.

When the elderly came in they were able to enjoy some privileges. After an 1847 ruling, aged married couples could stay together, if they wished, whereas all other age groups were strictly segregated as regards sex. The aims of the Act had been that inmates of different age groups should also be kept separate, but in most mixed general work-houses, as in Ross, this did not happen. Also the classification was negated by house-hold chores and general tasks, and by the statutory prayers: also, probably, communal meals.

However peace and quiet in the twilight of their lives was not to be enjoyed by the aged in this workhouse! In August 1839 the elderly women complained of the noisy behaviour of the younger women. The committee appointed by the Guardians to investigate the problem presented a most illuminating report: they met 'to investigate the complaint made to the Board as to the want of proper classification of some of the inmates of the House & of disorderly conduct arising therefrom. These irregularities are wholly confined to the female apartments.' The report details the accommodation arrangements and continues: 'it appears that last week there were 20 sleeping in room No 57, viz 14 girls from 9 to 16, 3 women between the ages of 70 and 80 and 3 able bodied women with children (two illegitimate) — and there were at the same time 17 sleeping in No 58 viz 7 women with children, 6 of them illegitimate, 2 women whose husbands are in prison (one with an infant child), 1 women deserted by her Husband & 7 other able bodied women one of them (who has since left the House) very much diseased with syphilis. These two rooms are opposite each other with only a narrow landing place between them and the doors being unlocked at night while the inmates were there it follows that between 7 & 8 in the evening and 6 in the morning there is no restraint upon the inmates of these rooms of whatever character or age as they are thus indiscriminately mixed together.' The Chaplain, the Rev Mr Brasier, reported that the two elderly women, 'on being called upon with others on Sunday to receive the Sacrament, declined assigning as a reason that they had been so much disturbed by bad language and general confusion in the room that they had been unable to prepare themselves for it.' The practical solution offered was to close up the doorway of one room, and reopen it at the far end with access to a separate staircase. Also plans to build over the Fever Ward or the board room were put forward by the committee.

Some deference was paid to the needs of the aged and infirm — their dietary needs were met in a slightly more indulgent way. A historian of the period reports that the policy of uniformity affected even these few luxuries — 'it had been found that the old men and women who were allowed weekly allowances of tea and butter would not take their teas simultaneously or consume their little pats of butter evenly.' This distressing deviation from the dietetic uniformity led the Central Authority to suggest the withdrawal of the privilege, in favour of simultaneous service of a certain quantity of liquid tea and of portions of 'bread and butter'. It is to be hoped that the Master, Mr Henry Smith, did not take up this suggestion.

The aged and infirm were set light tasks, such as wood chopping or bundling, hoeing or weeding and sewing, mending and household work for the women. However as cards and all board games were banned, the evenings must have been long. The whole routine was regimented with rigid times for meals, rising and going to bed.

From 1895, the policy on eligibility for relief was changed. Also there was a new ruling as regards Guardians' eligibility for election. Until then they had had to be wealthy landowners: from 1895 the more modest landowners could be elected to represent their respective parishes. (Ross Parish had four elected Guardians, Walford and Llangarron two and the others one elected Guardian each). Also the number of women Guardians increased significantly.

Newspapers came into the workhouse and acknowledgements to the *Ross Gazette* and *Man of Ross* are recorded. The Ross Cottage Hospital donated periodicals and in 1901 a library was set up. From 1883 the men over 60 were permitted one day in every two months out of the workhouse, and those over 70 one day in every month without application. Under the strict Poor Law rules the women inmates were only allowed out accompanied. However in 1908 the men's privilege was restricted — only deserving cases enjoyed this temporary freedom.

Most of the rural areas suffered a more stringent ruling under the Outdoor Relief Prohibitory Order (1844-1911) as it was those areas that had, in the opinion of the Poor

Law Central Authority, misused relief. Also the able-bodied in urban areas could not avoid periods of unemployment as trade and industrial development fluctuated. The strictures of this order in rural areas included the insistence that the wives of able-bodied men, even if ill, had to accompany their husbands into the workhouse if relief was required.

The sick poor received the best treatment available; cleanliness and discipline were the aim, but some of the nurses employed were erratic in their behaviour, judging from accounts of flirtations with the porters, insubordination with the Master and, on one occasion, theft from a patient. The sick were, in later years, isolated in the Infirmary — this was separated from the main building in line with central policy. From 1867 the 'outside' sick poor also had greater consideration and care and persons receiving relief on account of temporary sickness were visited fortnightly by the Relieving Officer. National awareness of hygiene and dietary health requirements influenced the regulations affecting workhouses and the infirm and sick were the beneficiaries. Here the extensions in Ross of 1890, together with brighter rooms, better ventilation, segregation from the younger inmates (in 1908 the old men were removed from the boy's dormitories to their own rooms) and more varied diets, were all improvements.

In 1908 with the introduction of Old Age Pensions — 5s. per week to all aged over 70 whose annual income was less than £21 (and a Graduated Pension where the total income was between £21 and £31) — the elderly were able to escape the stigma of pauperism. Children could afford to maintain their aged parents and, in theory, their numbers in the workhouses should have decreased. In Ross this appears to have been the case:

Aged admitted to Ross Workhouse (over 70 years)
1909 — 32   1911 — 24   1912 — 16

The sick poor also benefited; in 1898 a professional nurse was recruited at a salary of £30pa with beer allowance, board, lodging, washing and an indoor uniform provided. By a previous Nursing Order, no pauper ward attendants were permitted.

One of the essential skills in nursing was midwifery. In 1909 a night nurse was needed, as the Infirmary was full. Women in the community began to play a more prominent part. They had always been involved in private charity work and from 1897 joined visiting committees to inspect the home conditions. Later women Assistant Relieving Officers were able to help ameliorate conditions out in the parishes — a forerunner of the later District Nurse service.

A simple clerical innovation — the Case Paper System — came in generally around 1911. This provided a continuous record of each pauper family's history and needs.

Relaxation of the rules, concessions in diet and general improvement in comfort must have made the lives of the aged, infirm and sick more tolerable. Tobacco and snuff were allowed for both sexes and 'dry tea' allowed to the older women. Later, cocoa and coffee were added as treats for both sexes in the older age group. Fixed mealtimes were abandoned and cubicles built in the dormitories. Mixed day rooms were introduced and a report in 1914 thanks the proprietors of the Ross Picture Palace for 'allowing the inmates to attend every Saturday during the year'. One Union was granted the right to provide a harmonium, chargeable to the Poor Rates, for the use of the inmates in the workhouse. Here in Ross, the gift of an organ was much appreciated. Mr Rex Roff, the last Master, used to play it in the chapel to accompany the hymn singing.

Lunacy

In contrast to the harsh attitude towards the able-bodied paupers and the vagrants, the New Poor Law Administration dealt kindly with lunatics and the 'feeble minded'. At least 12 Acts regulating their care were enacted between 1774 and 1890. In 1885 Commissions of Lunacy were set up. The vigilant Commissioners caused the Ross Guardians much irritation as they made regular, rigorous inspections of the workhouse.

One of the reports, in April 1873, outlines the conditions:

> At my visit to this Workhouse today, I saw all those classed here of unsound mind; they are five women, one of whom only was in bed, and but for slight indisposition.
> This house is still overcrowded and the means at the disposal of the Master and Matron for securing the personal cleanliness of the inmates inadequate. For 120 inmates of whom 60 are children, there is one portable bath; the only other bath is that in the receiving ward. This necessitates I am told 10 persons being washed weekly in the same water — a most objectionable practice. The house diet, giving only 3oz of solid meat in 3 days of the week, is too low for persons classed as insane and extra diet should be given to all of them. I learnt that there was no closet for either of the female sick wards. The dress supplied is sufficient — I trust that when the additions to this Workhouse, too long delayed, but now in progress, shall be completed, the imbecile class may be accommodated in the infirmary, as far as possible, that there they may have fixed baths with hot and cold water supply pipes. The bedding which I inspected was clean but under blankets are required. The ground for exercise is, it seems, limited temporarily by the building operations; the imbeciles capable of walking abroad should I think, be frequently taken beyond the premises.

Long before the New Poor Law (1834), each parish had been responsible for its own feeble minded or imbecile parishioners and from 1832 licensed private houses and, later, County Asylums for the lunatics, were approved by the Justices and inspected regularly by a physician. Mr Millard's, at Portland House, Whitchurch, was the nearest licensed asylum to Ross and in 1847 he wrote to the Guardians detailing an increase from 10s. to 12s. with details of his charge of 12s. per week for each pauper lunatic which included for board, lodging, washing, medicine, medical attendance, attendance of a servant and clothing. Dr Gilliland had a similar establishment in Hereford, but after 1851 the patients were removed, with the Relieving Officer, to the newly opened Joint Counties Asylum at Abergavenny. The lunatics are listed, together with their removal and maintenance expenses. Occasional cures and discharges are noted and also the deaths.

The cost of maintaining pauper lunatics was repaid by their respective parishes and, where possible, some of this was recouped from their relatives. Monies found on a 'wandering lunatic' — £35 15s. — had to go in a separate account, so that all the expenses incurred could be deducted and the balance transferred to common charges to meet his maintenance costs. Two years later the Relieving Officer 'put into the hands of the Clerk part of a watch, a chain, a ring and a brooch' which had belonged to the man: he had since died in the asylum and had no known relative.

There is very little indication of the lives of the feeble minded living in the workhouse, but it is known that when they were harmless and physically fit, they did simple household chores and in many cases looked after younger children. They mixed with other inmates despite official pressure to segregate the classes. As late as 1908 two babies were in the care of two imbecile women. The Guardians were not in favour of sending the mentally retarded to asylums unless their conduct endangered the other inmates, mainly because their maintenance costs at the asylums were higher than in the workhouse and it was time-consuming and often impossible to recover these costs, with the inevitable rise in the charge on the Poor Rates.

In the workhouse, assessments were made 'as to who were supposed to be fit subjects for a lunatic asylum'. However, at a later date two Guardians considered that at least ten of the lunatics confined in the various asylums 'were suitable for treatment in this Workhouse if suitable accommodation could be provided for them'. The early policy was that all the sick poor, which included the mentally defective, should be maintained in their own home areas but if any 'persons of unsound mind' found their way to a workhouse they were to be detained. By legislation a dangerous lunatic could not be detained in a Union work-house for more than 14 days and during that time they had to be examined, segregated and restrained if necessary, before assessment and removal to an asylum. After the establish-ment of the Lunacy Commission in 1855, many lunatics were moved out of workhouses into asylums, but as the Webbs' put it — 'this was more than made up by the increasing tendency to seclude the village idiot so that the Workhouse population of unsound mind actually increased.'

Recorded cases in the Ross workhouse include a man whose noisy behaviour had caused much trouble. A report signed by the Master, Matron, MO and three inmates (two with a cross — 'his mark') declared that the man's 'mental derangement' was such that finally he had to be strapped to a bed. He was certified by the MO for the workhouse, Mr Edmund Jones, as being of unsound mind 'and the accompanying order signed by Wm Bridgeman Esq for his conveyance to the Asylum'. But he was sent back on the following morning by Mr Millard who had refused to receive him. The Board requested Mr Millard's attendance and explanation at their next meeting, but he sent a letter instead, which read: 'I hereby certify that the patient's mental faculties are more or less enfeebled from paralysis yet he cannot be deemed insane.' A female lunatic who had been very disruptive in the workhouse was sent to the same place and Mr Millard was consulted before she was 'enlarged' (discharged). However she was fortunate — 'if she prove not to be a dangerous lunatic, the vestry of Walford had reported, through the Chairman, that a meeting of the Ratepayers had been lately held on the subject and that she could be taken care of, if enlarged, at a charge of 5s. per week.'

In the latter years of the 19th century the number of pauper lunatics increased alarmingly and some were boarded out with relatives or friends, the Hereford County Asylum at Burghill reporting that it could not accommodate any more female patients. Later that year, 1895, it was suggested that a mild case in the asylum belonging to Ross Union could be exchanged for a bad case in the workhouse. Two upper rooms in the Receiving Ward buildings were prepared with a communicating door to an attendant's room. The nurse was offered 15s. per week (with board and lodging) and the Master was authorised to buy a 'straight-jacket'.

At this time in Burghill Asylum, there were 407 inmates (186 males and 221 females) and of these 53 belonged to Ross Union (24 men and 29 females). The weekly maintenance charge per patient was between 8s. 9d. and 9s. 0½d. per week.

The 1901 Commissioners' Report stated that there were 4 men and 9 women imbeciles in the workhouse, and that looped pipes in the WCs had to be cased in to prevent them being used to commit suicide.

Children over 5 years old presented a problem if they were mentally retarded. In 1907 an advertisement in the *Ross Gazette* invited applications for a foster home for a little imbecile girl, Daisy, with an allowance of 5s. weekly plus 10s. a quarter for her clothing. Sadly, after a month Daisy was sent back to the workhouse. In 1904 a Royal Commission recommended that all mentally defective persons should be taken out of the Poor Law administration and placed under the direction of the Lunacy Authority Councils. The Act of 1913 placed this duty upon County Councils. Separate institutions for the different categories was the aim, but the First World War intervened and only the urgent cases were removed. An authority on the subject estimates the national numbers in 1914 as 1% of the whole population, 'between 400,000 and 500,000 of either sex, of all ages, the great majority of them being at some period in their lives, either in receipt of poor relief or nearly destitute — and it is estimated that the feeble-minded still constitute at least one fourth of the total inmates of the workhouses.'

Vagrancy

The newly built Union workhouses provided convenient 'bed and breakfast' stops for the casual poor or vagrants. No out-relief was to be given to this class of pauper but they had to be admitted to the workhouse if they were in real need. The Central Authority policy was strict with vagrants all through this period, although greater concern developed for the health and comfort of the other classes of pauper as time went on. Deterrence was the aim: they were to be accommodated in basic lodging houses, or in separate wards in the work-house. A bath on entry was compulsory; there were no fires in their wards; smoking and card playing was forbidden and their bedding was to be 'inferior' to that of the inmates — 'coarse straw or cocoa fibre in a loose tick'. Their diet was restricted. Above all they had to complete a task before being released. The tasks varied with age, sex and health of the vagrant, but they were alike in being tedious. Oakum picking was one: oakum was tarred old rope, delivered unbeaten or beaten, ('junk' in the Minutes). The picked product was sold for caulking ships' decks and boards. Chopping wood, pumping water and gardening were other tasks. However stone breaking was the major work, and the tramp cells had sieves through which the occupant had to push his broken stones before he could leave.

The first record of a vagrant arriving is described in Minute Book 2, on 23rd November 1840:

> Daniel Burke states that on Thursday the 5th Inst. he went into a Shed in the Parish of Goodrich — there he remained till 4 o'clock the next evening (Friday) when some Woman came to him and gave him some refreshment, he then remained in the same Shed till 4 o'clock the next evening (Saturday) when some Gentleman came to him & gave him in charge of the Constable who took him to a Magistrate, from thence to a Beer house, gave him some Beer, then took him home, afterwards turned him out of his house, he that night slept in a Shed near the Constables with two Pigs. The Constable took him into his house the next morning (Sunday) where he remained till Tuesday evening when he was brought to the Workhouse in a Wheelbarrow covered with a Cider hair — it rained all the way to Ross.

The Constable's action was justified by the fact that the vagrant was paralysed and he judged that 'the Pauper would be less shaken in a Barrow than in a cart or a small wagon'.

Mr Henry Smith, the Master, had the duty of relieving the Wayfaring Poor 'in and at' the workhouse door. In October 1848 a 'wayfaring woman whose name was unknown' was given refuge as she was very ill. On recovery she wanted to leave but was 'kept to obtain the opinion of the Board', although the Medical Officer judged that she was not a 'proper subject for a lunatic asylum'. The Minute continues: 'on her appearance before them the Guardians

Inside of Vagrant's Cell at Dore Workhouse (by kind permission of Ewyas Harold WEA Study Group)

ascertained that she was a Welch woman and not able to speak but little English — and having expressed her great distress at being kept in the House the Board told the Master there were no reasons to detain her in the House against her will.'

Possibly through overcrowding in the workhouse, John Halford, Relieving Officer for Ross, was directed to select a 'barn or some convenient and suitable place near Ross to place vagrants & wayfarers applying for lodgings — and to provide straw to be placed therein and employ a person to cleanse the same from time to time.' Two houses in Brampton Street were rented from Mr Richard Jackson, for 2s. per week. In 1856 a letter is recorded complaining about the use of Black Lion Court for the use of vagrants. The following year the owner, Mrs Brewer, gave the Board notice to quit and the Clerk was asked to enquire whether premises at the top of Corpse Cross Street could be 'letted'.

In 1862 the Board considered that 'a considerably greater number of vagrants were relieved in this Union than in any neighbouring Unions' and recruited the Superintendent Constable, Charles Hopton, stationed in Ross, as Assistant Relieving Officer for vagrants at a salary of £5 per annum. After examination, if the vagrant was considered eligible for relief, he would be given a ticket which entitled 'the applicant to a night's lodging in the vagrant ward and 1lb of bread from the Union Workhouse on the following morning' — 3 months later the Board reduced the bread allowance to ½lb. A system of passes, or tickets, issued by neighbouring Unions was tried, with the incentive that vagrants producing such a pass could have 8oz bread, those that did not just 4oz. But the system failed — the Tramp

Master's Book 'showed that less than 5% of vagrants relieved in the Ross Union had come with "Way Tickets".' (February 1869).

The new workhouse extension of 1872/3 included male and female vagrant wards, with six hammocks for 'one half of the male wards and the female wards to be supplied with bedsteads'. In March 1874 the wards were ready for occupation and, in line with the local Government Board's rule, placards were printed and placed in each ward 'stating the task of work required to be performed also the Diet to be allowed to the different classes of tramps'. The Ross 'visitors' were ingenious. A Minute in 1874 requests tenders from local ironmongers 'for the alteration of the stone screens, the spaces at present being so wide that an arm may be put through and fastenings tampered with and also that the tramps are enabled to push large stones through the openings instead of breaking them.' Messrs Perkins and Bellamy's tender, at 3s. 9d. per screen was accepted. At this time able-bodied vagrants were required to break 5cwt of stone each for one night's stay. In April 1883 an edict went out that the task of work for a vagrant detained during the day was to be increased to 8cwt of gravel. A Minute, a few months later, reported the Clerk's return showing a considerable reduction in 'vagrants' admission and nights lodgings'.

There are records of stone being delivered to the workhouse by local suppliers and in 1879 the Guardians had a large surplus of broken stone, which they sold to the Highway Board at 4s. per cubic yard. The Highways Board was also 'asked to provide, deliver and stack at the workhouse all the stone required for breaking by the Paupers and Tramps and to pay the Guardians 1s. 6d. per yard for breaking such stone.'

Female tramps and children were normally accommodated in the lodging houses, and the women given tasks of oakum picking. This unpleasant work had been prohibited for female convicts in prisons in 1896, but a Poor Law Conference Report of 1900 noted that 'many country Masters expect female tramps to pick 2lb of unbeaten oakum and keep them prisoner until it is done.'

The rise in vagrancy between 1847 and 1848 was repeated in 1895 and 1910. Responsibility for all Poor Law administration was taken over by other Departments by 1907, except for the continuing deterrent regime for vagrants exercised by the Boards of Guardians. The anomaly was they were solely concerned with their own Union's needs and the tramps, wayfarers or men looking for employment were itinerants. Only by discouraging their stay in the workhouse could savings be made on the rates. Thus local and national statistics must be doubtful as they do not record the many people sleeping rough, but without 'tasks'!

In 1911 new Tramp Wards were built on workhouse land: the porter's salary was increased by £2 10s. per annum and he was given a uniform, which the Guardians Committee considered would give him more authority. The police were no longer required to assist and the Master was, in recognition of his added work, also given an allowance of £10 per annum.

An analysis of the average number of inmates in the house in 1913 and 1914 shows little change, i.e. 91 in 1913 and 89 in 1914, but the average number of casuals relieved in Ross per fortnight changed dramatically in the last four months of 1914:

	Jan–Aug	Sep–Dec
1913	227	180
1914	160	87

The Clerk noted, on 26th November 1914, that 'No casual applied for admission on Tuesday last. A most unusual occurrence.'

There was a general reduction in poverty helped by the Welfare Reforms from 1910. During the First World War vagrancy almost disappeared as Army Service and vacancies in unskilled jobs provided opportunities for work. These Ross statistics reflect this national trend. Sadly vagrancy and poverty returned.

Reflections

It is difficult to summarise the many aspects of the New Poor Law and its effects in the Ross Union.

The policy of the Central Authority was, initially, aimed at discouraging the poor of all classes from seeking relief. Thus the workhouse functioned as a deterrent for the helpless paupers as much as for the underpaid and unemployed poor.

Fortunately the Ross Guardians, along with many other Boards of Guardians, appeared to have been more lenient towards the poor for whom they were responsible. Over time, nationally, the system became less rigid. Contemporary criticism and up-to-date analysis are reflected in the following quotations:

> I consider the Workhouse as now organised is a reproach and disgrace peculiar to England: nothing corresponding to it is to be found throughout Europe. (Robert Pashley [1805-1859] Barrister and QC, *Pauperism and Poor Laws*, Longman, Brown Green, & Longman, [1852])

> There was to be one institution in each union for all classes of pauper. It was to be a place which, whilst it provided the full requirements of physical welfare, starved both the will and intelligence, and forced the pauper into a condition of blank mindedness. (Sidney and Beatrice Webb, *English Poor Law Policy*, p.82, first published 1910)

The New Poor Law Administration was a combination of Victorian free market economics, with a vast bureaucratic machine of government; with all this, however, all this Victorian corporatism, the edifice was baffled by its own paupers. (Summary from a talk given at a course on Poverty and Poor Law, School of Continuing Studies University of Birmingham September 1994)

Alton Street Hospital Staff in 1938 outside the dining hall with master and matron, Mr and Mrs Roff, seated. (Photo courtesy of Mrs V.J. Robbins)

CHAPTER 2

The Catholic Martyrs of the Monnow Valley

Introduction

Recusancy was the term used to describe the failure or refusal to attend church in accordance with the Act of Uniformity. These people were mainly Roman Catholics. How did this split in the religious life of this country come about and what is its relevance in the Monnow Valley? The geographical situation of the Monnow Valley with the River Monnow not only being the border between England and Wales but also the boundary between the diocese of Hereford and Llandaff, together with its remoteness and difficult terrain, fostered a spirit of independence and conservatism amongst the inhabitants. The traditions of the old Marcher lordships with their feudalism still lingered on and made it easy to ignore the statutes which distant London tried to impose on them. The countryside was very hilly and thickly wooded and it was easy to hide and find refuge.

The political reformation under Henry VIII when he broke irrevocably away from the jurisdiction of Rome changed the Church in England and Wales forever. This continued during his son Edward's short reign. His daughter, Mary Tudor, returned to the Catholic Church of Rome and for the five years of her reign there were extreme penalties against both Protestants and Puritans.

When Elizabeth I came to the throne in 1558 you can imagine how confused most people were. Would she carry on as her sister Mary had done or would she return to the religion of her father Henry VIII? The population of the country was divided on this subject. On one side there were those who supported Mary and these included all the bishops who had been appointed by her. The remainder of the bishops had either been burned at the stake or had fled overseas. Then there was the bulk of the people in the country who wanted a Catholic Church of England without the servility to Rome and which was reformed from the abuses which had gathered round it during the Middle Ages. During

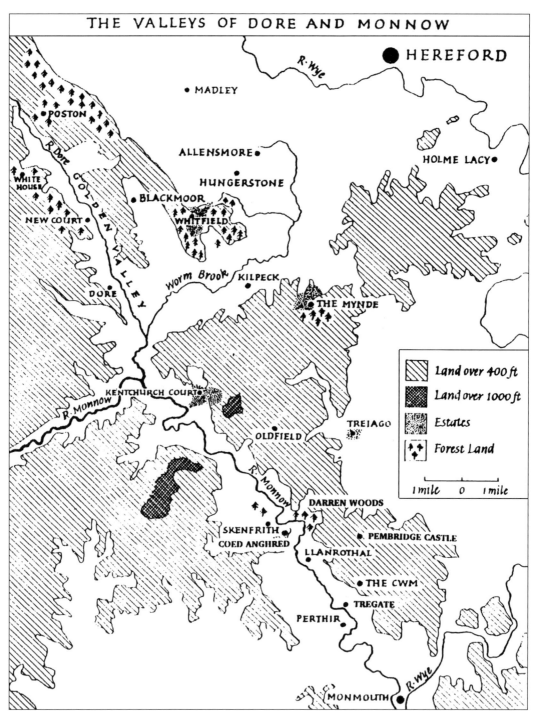

THE VALLEYS OF DORE AND MONNOW

● HEREFORD

R. Wye

● MADLEY

● POSTON

● ALLENSMORE

HOLME LACY ●

WHITE HOUSE

● HUNGERSTONE

R. Dore

● BLACKMOOR

GOLDEN VALLEY

NEW COURT ●

WHITFIELD

● DORE

Worm Brook

● KILPECK

● THE MYNDE

Legend:
- Land over 400 ft
- Land over 1000 ft
- Estates
- Forest Land

1 mile   0   1 mile

KENTCHURCH COURT

R. Monnow

TREIAGO

● OLDFIELD

R. Monnow

DARREN WOODS

SKENFRITH

● PEMBRIDGE CASTLE

COED ANGHRED

LLANROTHAL

● THE CWM

● TREGATE

PERTHIR

R. Wye

MONMOUTH ●

Map showing the places mentioned in the text (courtesy of Roland Mathias)

the first years of her reign Elizabeth re-established the Church of England and the Acts of Uniformity and Supremacy were passed. These Acts established Elizabeth as head of the Church and required a uniform service for all churches. There were stiff penalties for anyone who refused to conform to this one establishment. The queen's subjects were bound to attend church every Sunday unless they had a lawful excuse to absent themselves. A fine of 12d. was levied by the churchwardens on each occasion of absence and the money was used for the benefit of the poor of the parish.

At first, Elizabeth was quite tolerant of those who refused to accept the new regime. It was sufficient if Papists, as the recusants were called, stood in the porch of the Protestant church during the sermon and many Roman Catholics conformed to this extent. This was accepted as a denial of their religion. The stauncher Catholics called this practice schismatic. However, the determination of the Pope to humiliate Elizabeth caused the atmosphere between the Government and the recusants to deteriorate.

In 1570 there was a formal trial of Queen Elizabeth in Rome, witnesses being found from among the recusants who had fled from England. Elizabeth was found guilty, excommunicated and deposed and all her subjects were dispensed from their oath of allegiance to her. The verdict was smuggled to England and nailed to thc door of the Bishop of London's Palace by a man called John Felton. This was a disaster for the recusants. With the passage of time, Elizabeth's anti-Catholic legislation became increasingly severe. The threat to the security of the throne and the physical safety of the queen was blamed on the Jesuit Mission, Spanish interference and the intrigues of Mary Queen of Scots. Roman Catholic men were leaving England for the continent where they were training at Catholic and Jesuit Colleges as priests and missionaries and returning secretly to England and Wales to preach and convert.

In 1571 an Act was passed against bringing in and putting into execution Bulls and other instruments from the see of Rome, along with importing any crosses, religious items such as pictures and beads or other suchlike vain and superstitious items. Anyone singing Mass was fined £113 and imprisoned for a year. £10 per month was paid by anyone keeping a recusant schoolmaster. In 1581 another Act was passed which imposed a penalty of £20 per month for anyone over the age of 16 who refused to attend church.

In 1585 there was an Act against Jesuits and Priests. Anyone who helped them was condemned to death. A further Act against recusants was passed in 1587 stating that anyone in default of paying the £20 per month fine resulted in the seizing of two-thirds of their land and property. This Act set the pattern for the next hundred years. In 1593 another Act forbade recusants to stray more than 5 miles from their homes without a licence. The fines from recusants became an important contribution to the national exchequer.

Following the death of Elizabeth and the accession of James I in 1603, hopes were high that the Catholics would be treated with more tolerance as James had no desire to persecute them. He genuinely hoped that a reconciliation with Rome might be possible. This greatly encouraged the recusants, and priests poured into the country hoping for a mass movement towards Rome. Their hopes were all rudely shattered by the Gunpowder Plot of 1605.

Following this event, the severity of the legislation increased. All recusants had to receive the sacrament of the Lord's Supper. The penalties for failing to do so were £20 per month for the first year, £40 for the second year and £60 per month in each subsequent year. The crown could also refuse the £20 monthly fine and instead seize two-thirds of the land of a rich recusant.

After the Gunpowder Plot, James I imposed an Oath of Allegiance which denied that the Pope had any power to depose the king. Some English Catholics took the Oath on the grounds that the Act was political rather than religious. By the Acts of 1610 and 1611 recusants who refused to take the Oath of Allegiance were imprisoned, while recusant wives were forced to pay £10 per month, forfeit one-third of their husband's lands or go to prison. It was forbidden to send children to be educated overseas or support foreign colleges.

After the Civil War during the Commonwealth period some tolerance was given to Catholics. The Cavalier Parliament, however, in 1661 pressed for a law against dissenters which became the first of four Acts that became known as the Clarendon Code: all magistrates had to take the Oath of Allegiance (1661); the Church of England was the only form of worship tolerated (1662); all dissenting ministers were forbidden to come within 5 miles of any corporate town neither were they allowed to teach (1665); and not more than five persons unless of the same household or the established church, were allowed to assemble for worship in houses (1670).

The Test Acts stipulated that anyone holding a position of trust under the Crown must take the Oath of Allegiance and receive the sacrament of the Church of England. Anyone who refused was fined £500 and became ineligible for other offices. They were also debarred from prosecuting suits in Law and Equity and from becoming guardians or executors.

James II, who was a Catholic, became king in 1685. Churchmen were worried how a Catholic head of the established church would use his power. James insisted that Catholics should be free to serve him both in the army and state regardless of the Test Act and demanded that the Declaration of Indulgence be read in all churches. Both Church and State were convinced that the foundations of political life were in jeopardy and in 1688 James's daughter Mary and her husband, William of Orange, were invited to take the throne.

This opened up a new period in the history of Catholicism in this country. E. Watkins in his book *Roman Catholicism in England* (Oxford 1957), called it 'the most dispiriting period of their history, of persecution without heroism, of martyrdom, of exclusion from government, a period of defections and diminishing numbers.'

In 1696 an Act forbade Catholics to become members of the legal profession or to inherit or purchase land. Another Act of 1715 required every Baptist to register his name and real estate with the Clerk of the Peace for his county.

Eventually the Catholic Relief Act of 1791 enabled Catholics to worship freely in their own churches and in 1817 commissions of every rank in the army and navy were open to Catholics. Finally, in 1829, the Catholic Emancipation Act was passed.

It is against this background that the events which took place over a period of 300 years must be viewed.

With so much oppressive legislation, maintaining faith in the Roman Catholic church was not easy. How well or conscientiously the Acts were carried out varied throughout the country. There were many land-owning Catholic families with wealth and influence and not all bishops regarded recusancy with any urgency. It was easy to support the persecution of 'Papists' in general but not so easy when it came to prosecuting neighbours, friends or members of the family. All large groups of recusants included at least one member of the gentry whose houses formed the base of operations for itinerant priests.

Many recusant families lived in south Herefordshire and Monmouthshire. Catholics crossed and recrossed the River Monnow which flowed through well wooded country. Priests from Herefordshire moved into Monmouthshire in times of danger. It was easy for squire, tenant and priest to conspire together against the government in distant London. The area was remote, hilly and dense woodland made it easy to hide. Recusancy in Wales was almost exclusively confined to the counties formed out of the Marches of Wales.

During the reign of Elizabeth and James I about 2% of the population aged 16 and over were convicted recusants. Monmouthshire had the most convicted recusants in the country with 117 recusant households per thousand, Lancashire second with 112, Durham third with 31 and Herefordshire fourth with 25. Seventeen English countries scored less than 10.

The Riot

Before the financial inducement and possible fines imposed on churchwardens, I suspect that most villages turned a blind eye to the recusants in their midst. Everyone was a Roman Catholic anyway until the reign of Henry VIII and most people just gradually absorbed the new religion. In an area like the Monnow Valley with few outside influences, recusants seemed to be in the majority. Throughout the 17th century there are long lists for every parish in the valley. From the beginning of the 17th century the churchwardens had to report to the Ecclesiastical Court all misdemeanours in their parish. These were written in the Acts of Office Book which is now in the Hereford Record Office.

There follow some examples between the years 1673 and 1681 for the parish of Garway which was in the Archenfield Deanery:

> Jacob Pritchard for burying his child in the churchyard without acquainting the minister.

> Thomas Maddox for ill language, giving abusive words to the minister and such like and for not frequenting the church. Fined 2s. 2d.

> William Baskerville, George Loop, William Williams, Thomas Williams, Thomas Pritchard. For being Papists and absence from Church.

> Luke Preece and Jane Davies. For failing to prove their marriage held in a private house in Llanrothal by an unknown priest.

However, there were problems attached to non attendance at church. There were three times in life when the church was essential. First, at birth when not to have been baptised meant eternal damnation, although this baptism could be done illegally by an itinerant priest. A marriage could also be performed by a priest even though once again, illegal. But death was different — there was a body to be disposed of. It was an illegal burial which started all the trouble.

Whilst we are all familiar with the Gunpowder Plot of November 1605, few people realise that here in Herefordshire there was plot and uprising of Catholics earlier the same year. For a period of six weeks from the Tuesday of Whitsun week until the month of July a state of lawlessness persisted.

It all started in the village of Allensmore, 5 miles south-west of Hereford. Alice Wellington, the recusant wife of Thomas Wellington, a yeoman, died excommunicate and was refused burial by the Vicar of Allensmore, Richard Heyns. The Catholic community in the area were furious and very early on the morning of Tuesday 21st May 1605, buried Alice in the churchyard by torchlight with all the Catholic ceremonial including candles and bells. Richard Heyns immediately went to the Bishop's Palace in Hereford and gave the names of those in the burial party whom he had recognised. A list of 25 names was subsequently received by Bishop Robert Bennett and included those of James Coles from Hungerstone, a weaver, his wife and daughter. He was known to act as massing clerk to Roger Cadwallader, a priest. Also listed was Phillip Giles, who 'bare the crosse'.

Three days later the High Constable of Hereford visited the district with a warrant issued by the bishop to arrest three men who had participated in the burial. They first went to the hamlet of Hungerstone to arrest James Coles and William Chadnor, both weavers who worked in adjoining rooms. A struggle ensued and Chadnor was chased for some distance but managed to escape, whilst Coles grabbed a knife and wounded two of the constables. Then the third man named in the warrant, Leonard Marsh, joined in the struggle. Coles managed to escape and the constable headed back towards Hereford with only Leonard Marsh as a prisoner.

Then William Marsh, brother of the prisoner, appeared. He shouted to the constable to wait until William Morgan of Treville Park had a word with him. This was refused. William shouted to his brother to resist. Suddenly the constable's party was surrounded by 40 or 50 men armed with bows and arrows, staves, bills and swords. They demanded that the constable tell them where he was taking the prisoner. Outnumbered and outweaponed the constable, after giving grave warnings of the consequences of the tumult and rebellion released the prisoner. The constable went straight to the bishop who at once dispatched the news of the riot to the Privy Council in London.

The Privy Council's first reaction was to counter the violence with stern repression. The king, in a speech made on June 9th to the Judges at the Court of Greenwich, made it plain that there was no longer any need to spare the blood of recusants and that Herefordshire men should serve as an example. However, the council was loath to use force in the king's name for fear of provoking a general uprising. They thought it best to get several of the rebel leaders into their hands and that the magistrates of Herefordshire should try to trap the leaders themselves.

By the beginning of June, Bishop Bennett had decided to arrest William Morgan of Whitfield in Treville Park. Today, Whitfield is an early 18th-century house up a 2-mile drive from the Hereford/Abergavenny road. In the early 17th century it was probably not

Whitfield

much more than a rather grand farmhouse. Mass was said there by Roger Cadwallader, a seminary priest who was martyred at Leominster in 1610.

A little after midnight on 5th June the bishop, accompanied by Sir James Scudamore of Holme Lacy, MP for Herefordshire, and Sir Roger Bodenham of Rotherwas whose wife was Lady Bridget, daughter of Sir Humphrey Baskerville of Eardisley, set off for Whitfield. Sir Roger had been described by the Bishop as 'countenancing all priests and recusants'. Sir James was a Papist but behaved with discretion.

However the bishop's party was expected. At least 60 men, maybe as many as 100, armed with bows, pikes, bills, swords and javelins were lying in wait, some 20 or 30 of whom were positioned in a dell called the Cockett. It was not planned that there should be a direct attack on the bishop's party but only if there was an arrest and then Morgan was to be rescued. Among the waiting men were James Coles, William Chadnor and Leonard Marsh, and reinforcements were expected from the recusants in the Monnow Valley. Their leader was a man called Thomas Pritchard. Then something unexplained happened. Perhaps William Morgan felt he had enough influential friends to speak for him, whilst it is known that Sir Roger Bodenham had some sympathy with the recusants as well as having some influence over Thomas Pritchard. In any event the ambush was called off, the magistrates searched the house and took away a number of incriminating letters written by Morgan, whilst Morgan himself was arrested and sent to London.

Most of the ambush party went into hiding. It is presumed that, as Allensmore and Treville Park lie close to the River Monnow and Monmouthshire, a county 'almost wholly corrupted' according to the bishop, Monmouthshire is where they headed. Monmouthshire was also out of the bishop's jurisdiction being in the Diocese of Llandaff.

On the Sunday following the fiasco at Treville Park, 300 people with weapons in their hands, assembled for Mass at the Darren chapel on the Herefordshire bank of the River Monnow in the Parish of Garway. Expecting trouble, many of them lingered on over the Monday and Tuesday. Among them were William Hugh of Monmouthshire and servants of William Vaughan of Llanrothal equipped with bows and arrows, together with James his shepherd carrying a forest bill and a long hanger (a sword). One of the bishop's men who ventured too close was roughly handled but no one else put in an appearance. The bishop had a problem. As he put it, 'if we go out with a few we shall be beaten home; if we levy any strength we are descried and they are all fled into the woods and there they will lurk until the assizes be past.'

On Wednesday 19th June the Justices made their biggest effort yet. Sir James Scudamore, William Rushall, Rowland Vaughan and Thomas Kyrle of Walford with a strong force searched the Darren and villages adjoining, house by house, all that night and the day following, making a 30 mile sweep along the borders of Monmouthshire. They found altars, images, books of superstition, relics of idolatry, but hardly a living soul apart from the occasional child or old woman. The villages were desolate. The entire population had fled westwards and southwards into an even more unpredictable Wales.

According to the bishop only one man was caught. There is a strong local tradition in this area that this man was an outlawed priest called Ainsworth whom the Justices surprised in the Darren woods and beheaded on the spot. According to the legend this took place by a spring of water and that the rocks around this spring were stained with his blood. It is said that the stones around this well are still strongly marked and are especially bright after being soaked in water for a few minutes. There is no proof that this violent act happened in 1605 but there is strong evidence that it could have happened in 1679 at the time of Titus Oates's allegations.

The Justices returned to Hereford with no result from their intensive search. A report reached the king on Sunday 23rd June that the Bishop of Hereford had not only been resisted but had fled for his life. A thousand Catholics were reported to be in arms at one spot alone and a full scale rebellion was feared. Dr Bennett sent his own report of the situation but many believed he was only trying to make excuses for his own incompetence.

Raglan Castle (Cadw reconstruction drawing by Alan Sorrell)

The Privy Council were very undecided how to deal with the insurrection in the Monnow Valley. They tried putting the blame on the magistrates who 'failed to carry out their orders with that dexterity which was contemplated by the King and Council'. Some, including the king, were all for sending an armed posse against the Catholics, but others feared that force would fail in so recusant a county with the result that the revolt would spread.

It was decided that the Earl of Worcester, by reputation a stiff papist, would be sent to calm the situation. He was a personal favourite of the king and as his seat was Raglan Castle he was the natural overlord of the area. He was to talk to the recusant leaders and quell the revolt. Hopefully, as a Catholic himself, they would trust him and defer to his authority.

He arrived in Raglan on Saturday 29th June and this was the beginning of the end of the rebellion. The earl decided that the affair should be played down. The first six days after his arrival he spent contacting the recusants. The priests and others who might suffer serious punishment got away and were out of reach, no doubt deliberately warned. The earl had 'a few fellows of the baser sort' put into prison, more to show that he had done something than because they deserved punishment. The tumult in the Monnow Valley was at an end.

However, the strong presence of the Catholics persisted. Several rich and influential families lived in the valley including families from other parts of the country who had moved there because of its remoteness.

In a house called The Cwm at Llanrothal in 1605 lived William Griffiths and his wife, William's sister Jane together with her son John and his wife Sara of London amongst others. All were rich and staunch Roman Catholics. William had travelled widely and was in touch with the English Jesuit Mission. It is thought that Robert Winter and Humphrey Lyttleton, who were being sought in connection with the Gunpowder Plot, were hidden at the Cwm. Other dangerous recusants were listed as residing at Tregate and Penhir.

The Cwm

The Cwm, sometimes known as Coombe, means wooded valley, shelter or hollow. The present house was rebuilt in 1830 on the foundations of an old house which was pulled down. Originally the old house was known as Lower Cwm.

The Cwm is the parish of Llanrothal about 3 miles north of Monmouth. A line of hills rises above the River Monnow and The Cwm rests in a slight hollow about a mile and a half along a quiet lane which branches off the main Hereford to Monmouth road at Welsh Newton.

During the 17th century the area was densely wooded and the lane was a stony track which led past The Cwm to Llanrothal Church. A branch off this lane leads to the

Manor house of Tregate and on over the Monnow to St Maughans. About two miles further upstream are the Darren woods and Skenfrith. Pembridge Castle is half a mile uphill from The Cwm.

The Society of Jesus, or the Jesuits, were associated with The Cwm for more than 100 years. The Jesuits were a company of ordained priests who, in 1540, took vows of obedience calling themselves

The Cwm, Llanrothal c.1960

the Company of Jesus. The Jesuit organisation was military and trained as an elite corps to carry out the wishes of the Pope. They were privileged, paying no taxes and were exempt from other Papal orders. Their aim was to educate, to preach and hear confession. Wherever there was educational work to be done the Jesuit Colleges were important instruments for Catholic influence and propaganda. The two men associated with the foundation of the Society of Jesus were Ignatius Loyola and Francis Xavier.

At the time of the disturbances in 1605, The Cwm was occupied by William Griffiths and his wife. William was an important Glamorgan landowner and despite the fact that he had forfeited two-thirds of his estate he was still able to settle his family at The Cwm. He was a prominent Catholic layman. He had travelled many times to the continent and was in touch with the Prefect of the English Jesuit Mission. He was the eldest of six brothers and close by in Llanrothal lived his sister, Jane Griffiths, who had resumed her maiden name after the death of her husband John Watson. Her son John and his wife Sara were also staunch Catholics. It is also probable that one of his brothers, John or James, a doctor of medicine, was residing at The Cwm with his wife Mary.

The exact date of the earliest Jesuit connection can only be guessed at but it is probable that there was a Jesuit Training College established as early as 1595. During 1605 Father Jones, known as 'the Fyerbrande of all', who had said Mass at the Darren was a frequent visitor. When he became Superior of the Jesuits in 1609 he made his headquarters at The Cwm where he remained, dying in office in 1615. Father Salisbury, who was chaplain to Lady Frances Somerset at Raglan Castle, succeeded Father Jones in charge of the Mission of North and South Wales in 1615. He took a lease of The Cwm and surrounding land as a Jesuit headquarters. The property was owned by the Earl of Worcester who was obviously aware of the Catholic activity there.

In 1622 the English Mission had been created a vice province by Rome and The Cwm was created the College of St Xavier, the other Colleges being St Ignatius in London and St Aloysius in Lancashire. For administrative purposes the Jesuits divided England and Wales into districts which they called Colleges or Missions. The Mission of St Francis Xavier covered South Wales, North Wales, Monmouthshire, Herefordshire, Gloucester and Somerset. Later, in 1676, a separate North Wales Mission was formed.

After the Earl of Worcester's death in 1628 The Cwm was let by his son to Father William Morton on a 99 year lease. Management and profits from both Cwms was entrusted to a local Catholic named Peter Pullen.

In the Monmouthshire and Herefordshire area Catholics made little attempt to hide their religious practices. Large congregations gathered in Abergavenny to say Mass. Several times a year pilgrimages were taken to the Holy Mountain, the Skirrid Fawr, and Mass was said at the chapel of St Michael at the summit. A local magistrate claimed to have seen a great crowd 'with beads in their hands' (*Journal of the House of Commons* 14 p.467). The presence of a College at The Cwm must have been known locally as their cart was sent regularly to Monmouth for provisions.

This state of affairs lasted for over 50 years. During this time many priests served at the College of whom the longest serving was Father Thomas or John Harris. He became a Missioner at The Cwm in 1639 and was still there 37 years later in 1676 but is believed to have died before the raid on the College.

There does not seem to be any record of the Civil War (1642-46) affecting the Jesuit College at The Cwm although Pembridge Castle not far away was besieged. The Kembles garrisoned the castle for the king in 1644. In 1646 the Roundhead Colonel Birch ordered that the castle should be slighted. According to contemporary documents, a peace conference was held in 1646 at Tregate Castle, the home of William Barry, between Sir William Fleming, representing the king, and high ranking officers or the Scottish army which was then near Ross. It proved abortive and the Scottish army, commanded by Lord Leven, moved on to Hereford.

The Plot

Charles I was executed in 1649 and his sons Charles and James were brought up as exiles in France. In 1660 Charles was invited to return as Charles II to help restore unity and stability to the nation.

The Parliament of 1661 was strongly Anglican and Royalist. The Acts known as the Clarendon Code which were passed during the next few years were mainly aimed at Puritans but the Catholics could also be prosecuted under them. In 1673 Parliament passed the Test Act prohibiting non-Anglicans from holding any civic or military office. Gradually, a tide of anti-Catholic panic began to rise. The fire of London in 1666 was rumoured to have been started by Catholics and in 1681 an inscription to this effect was engraved on the Monument in London. The anti-Catholic feelings rose to panic in 1678 with allegations by Titus Oates, subsequently described as the 'greatest liar in history'. Oates, who was an Anglican clergyman who had been thrown out of the Navy for immorality, and his accomplice Israel Tonge, revealed a Jesuit plot against the king and his subjects. The murder of the king was to be followed by a massacre of Protestants and the handing of the crown to James, Duke of York. Panic spread throughout the country and many innocent Catholics were put on trial or died as fugitives.

A co-conspirator was William Bedloe, a Monmouthshire man born in Chepstow. He had been imprisoned for fraud and theft and had recently been released from Newgate prison. He gave Parliament detailed accounts of conspiracies which involved leading Monmouthshire and Herefordshire Catholics. According to Bedloe, uprisings were planned and a great army was to assemble in Radnor and march to Milford Haven where there was to be a Spanish invasion.

Evidence of the strength of Roman Catholicism in the Monmouth/Hereford area was also collected by John Arnold of Llanfihangel Court near Abergavenny and John Scudamore of Kentchurch Court near Pontrilas (Plate 3). John Arnold was the grandson of Sir Nicholas Arnold, who as a reward for supporting Thomas Cromwell at the Reformation was given Llanthony Abbey in the Black Mountains. His second son John established himself at Llanfihangel in 1626. This John's eldest son, also John, was born in 1634 and succeeded to the estate in 1665. Arnold was a rabid Protestant and Whig politician who had a long-standing feud with the Catholic Earl of Worcester. The Scudamores of Kentchurch Court were the senior branch of the family who had lived in the area since the Norman conquest. John Scudamore was a lapsed Catholic.

Llanfihangel Court (A. Copping)

The magistrates of the counties of Monmouthshire and Herefordshire were split between those who supported the Earl of Worcester and were Popishly inclined, for example, Henry Milbourne of Llanrothal Court, and those who opposed the earl such as John Arnold. A proclamation that ordered the magistrates to arrest and bring to trial all priests and Jesuits, was bound to cause local problems.

In March 1678 a Commons Committee had considered 'the danger the nation is in by the growth of Popery' and before this committee appeared Mr Greenhaugh, Vicar of Abergavenny, John Arnold and John Scudamore. Both Arnold and Scudamore told the committee that The Cwm was a Jesuit residence. The Commons had been informed in 1670 and 1674 about the existence of the college but the support of local justices of the peace had insured that nothing was done. However, in the climate of the Titus Oates plot the support of the local gentry gradually faded. Action was taken by the House of Lords and a letter was sent to the Bishop of Hereford:

> Upon information given to this House of a place in Herefordshire called Combe that the said house and three hundred pounds (P.A.) belongeth to the Church of Rome and that five or six Jesuits commonly reside there and that in the Chapel there Mass is said there constantly and that the place is commonly called and known by the name of the Jesuits College by the Papists. Upon consideration that thereof it is ordered by the Lords Spiritual and Temporal in Parliament assembled that it be, and is hereby recommended to the Lord Bishop of Hereford, calling to his assistance such Justices of the Peace of the said County as his Lordship shall think fit, to enquire into the information aforesaid, and think necessary for finding out the truth of the matter of fact concerning the said place called Combe and to give this House a full account thereof so soon as His Lordship conveniently can.
>
> Jo. Browne, Cleric Parliamentor

Dr Herbert Croft, Lord Bishop of Hereford, was one of the nine children of the Catholic Sir Herbert Croft of Croft Castle, Herefordshire. Sir Herbert sent his third son, Herbert, to St Omers, a Jesuit college 24 miles from Calais, and in 1622 Herbert was admitted to the English College at Rome. Back in England, Herbert Croft was persuaded by the Bishop of Durham to return to the Church of England. Eventually he was made Dean of Hereford and then in 1662, Bishop of Hereford, and he carried out a vigorous campaign against Romanism.

On 7th December 1678 Bishop Croft and his agent Captain Scudamore searched The Cwm. This raid was not altogether successful as no Jesuits were found at the college. The Superior of The Cwm, Father Lewis, and the six resident priests (Fathers Humphries, Draicott, Philip Evans, Charles Pritchard, Ignatius Price and John Archer) had departed.

The bishop composed *A Short Narrative of a Discovery of a College of Jesuits at a place called the Combe* (published in London in 1679), to which he added 'a true relation of the knavery of Father Lewis, the Pretended Bishop of Llandaff, now a prisoner in Monmouth Gaol'.

In this narrative the bishop describes the Upper Cwm as a 'fair and gentile house wherein there are six lodging chambers, each one a convenient study to it, with a standish (inkstand) left in them. The other house is also a good country house, with several chambers and studies, but the furniture is removed, we cannot find whither. There are one and twenty chimnies in both houses and a great many doors to go in and out, and likewise many private passages from one room to the other.'

The bishop's party also discovered vestments, bottles of oil, a box of white wafers, Popish pictures, some relics, a little saint's bell and an incense pot. Two cart-loads of books were found in a pig-cot. Some of these were written by 'principal learned Jesuits and include catechisms, ordinances from Rome, Welsh Popish books and many others'. All these books were taken to Hereford Cathedral Library where many of them remain to this day.

The Martyrs

The madness engendered by the Titus Oates plot resulted in the arrest of over 2,000 Roman Catholic priests. Two of these were from the Monnow Valley.

John Kemble was born at Ryd-y-Car Farm, St Weonards in 1599 the son of George Kemble. His mother was a Morgan of Skenfrith. He was 6 years old when the Whitsun Riot took place. About 1620 John entered the English College in Douai and was ordained a priest in 1625. Three months later he returned home and became an itinerant priest tramping about the well known tracks in the Monnow Valley saying Mass and administering sacraments in Catholic houses.

In June 1630 his brother George leased Pembridge Castle in the Parish of Welsh Newton (Plates 4 and 5). After the damage done in the Civil War, George Kemble repaired the castle and the family continued to live there. Father Kemble spent most of his time there and in his old age probably lived there permanently. In a corner of the castle there is still a chapel where John Kemble said mass.

Father Kemble was well known to John Arnold and John Scudamore and believed them to be his friends. At this point Father Kemble could have escaped capture. He was warned by friends of the danger he was in but he replied that as he had not many years to live it would be an advantage to him to die for Christ rather than in his bed.

So on a cold January day in 1679 an old man of almost 80 was arrested by John Scudamore and taken the 6 miles to Kentchurch Court where he was charged and detained overnight. John Scudamore's wife and children were Catholics and very fond of Father Kemble whom they had known all their lives. Next day he was taken to Hereford Gaol to await trial.

He was tried at the Spring Assizes on 31st March 1679 and he was indicted simply as a seminary priest charged with having offended against Statute 27 Elizabeth I, which equated being a priest ordained overseas with treason. He was found guilty and condemned to be hanged and drawn.

On 23rd April the House of Lords ordered that John Kemble, David Lewis and two other priests who had been convicted on similar charges should be brought to London for questioning. The journey for John Kemble must have been very difficult as his age and probable arthritis made riding almost impossible. It is said that he was strapped like a pack onto his horse. Nothing came of this examination as they all denied any knowledge of the Plot and the priests were sent back to their respective counties. On the return journey John Kemble was allowed to walk most of the 135 miles back to Hereford. He was back in Hereford Gaol early in June.

Friends in Hereford tried to secure a reprieve and while in Gaol he had many visitors including John Scudamore's wife and children.

John Kemble's grave
in Welsh Newton churchyard

On the day of execution, 22nd August, Father Kemble was taken to Widemarsh Common, a place of public recreation just outside the City of Hereford. Before leaving prison he was asked if he had any last requests. He said he wished to be able to finish his prayers and to smoke a pipe for the last time. Mr Digges, the Under Sheriff sat down with him and together they smoked their pipes. The priest was then bound to a hurdle on which he was dragged, feet first, to his execution, which is believed to have taken place at the north-west corner of the common between where the Leominster road branches off and the front of the Bulls Head Inn.

John Kemble mounted the cart and addressed the large crowd assembled on the common.

It will be expected that I should say something but as I am an old man it cannot be much, not having any concern in the plot neither indeed believing there is any. Oates and Bedloe not being able to charge me with anything when I was brought up in London, though they were with me makes it evident that I die only professing the Old Roman Catholic Religion, which was the religion that first made this kingdom Christian ... I beg of all whom I have offended to forgive me for I do heartily forgive all those who have been instrumental or desirous of my death.

After he was hanged his body was cut down and beheaded but not quartered. His nephew Richard Kemble was allowed to have the body which he put into a coffin which was buried at the foot of the Cross in Welsh Newton churchyard. The grave is marked by a flat tombstone. Father Kemble's left hand, enclosed in a reliquary, is venerated at St Francis Xavier's church in Hereford and in the Roman Catholic church in Monmouth are kept the altar, vestments and missal used by him at Pembridge Castle. Every August there is a pilgrimage to his grave on the Sunday nearest to the anniversary of his death. On Sunday 25th October 1970, Father Kemble the Martyr was canonised.

Father David Lewis, a Jesuit, was born in Abergavenny in 1616 and was one of nine children. His father was Principal of the Royal Grammar School in the town, which had a reputation for producing men of scholarship. He was either a Protestant or a church Papist, i.e. one who conformed outwardly to the Established Church. His mother was a strong Catholic.

After his parents died, possibly of the plague, David decided to enter the English College at Rome having been received into the Church of Rome during a visit to Paris. He was aged 21 and during the next seven years studied philosophy and theology. He was ordained in 1642.

David Lewis returned to his native Monmouthshire in 1648 and, making his headquarters at Llantarnam Abbey near Newport, he visited Catholic houses over a wide area. He was very generous to the poor which earned him the title Tad y Tlodion — Father of the Poor. A man of learning and considerable eloquence, Father Lewis frequently preached in both Welsh and English.

Twice during the 30 years that he spent in the area David Lewis was Superior at The Cwm, between 1667-1672 and 1674-1679, and held that position when he was arrested.

As soon as Father Lewis realised how serious the danger from the Bishop of Hereford was, he evacuated The Cwm immediately. However, four of the six priests living at The Cwm were to die as a result of the Plot, and Father Lewis himself had already been arrested by the time the raid was made on The Cwm.

A Short
NARRATIVE
Of the Discovery of a
College of Jesuits,
At a Place called the
COME,
In the County of *HEREFORD*:

Which was sent up unto the Right Honorable,
The Lords Assembled in PARLIAMENT,
at the End of the last Sessions, by the Right
Reverend Father in God *HERBERT*, Lord Bishop of
Hereford, according to an Order sent unto him by the said Lords,
to make diligent Search, and return an Account thereof.

To which is added
A true Relation of the Knavery of
Father LEWIS,
The Pretended Bishop of *Landaffe*;
Now a Prisoner in *Monmouth* Gaol.

London, Printed by *T. N.* for *Charles Harper*, at the *Flower-de-luce* against *St: Dunston's Church in Fleetstreet.* 1679.

---

(2)

See the Examinations of Mr. Boothby, Lord of the Mannor. them, having Lands belonging to them worth about Threescore pounds *per Annum*; (they pay Taxes at Eight and fifty pounds *per Annum*.)

This Estate did formerly belong to *Edward* Lord Marquis of *Worcester*, who by his Lease dated *Novemb.* 10. in the Twelfth year of King *Charles* the I. did Lett it for Fourscore and nineteen years to one *William Morton*, who dying, left it to one *Robert Hutton* living in *St. Giles's in the Fields*, London, stiled Merchant; which *Hutton* hath by his Lease dated the second day of *February* 1677: and sealed and delivered in the presence of *William Ireland*, *John Fenwick*, *J. Groves*, set the *Lower Come* to one *William Williams*, for One and twenty years, at Forty pounds *per Annum*: And he hath likewise made a Letter of Attorney to one *Peter Pullen* a Servant, intrusting him with the management of the Profits of both the *Comes*, which is dated the 27th day of *April* 1678. and the Witnesses to it are *W. Ireland*, *Jo. Fenwick*, and *William Cornelius*.

One

(3)

One of these Houses is a fair gentile House, wherein there are six lodging Chambers; each one a convenient Study to it, with a Standish left in them, besides several other lodging Rooms.

The other House is also a good Countrey House, with several Chambers, and Studies to some of them, all in very good repair: But the Furniture now removed, we cannot yet find whither.

The remaining Dwellers in the House, who were but Under-Servants, will not confess: They are apparently Perjured; For they flatly denied, upon Oath, several things, which were made out by others, and then they confessed them.

There are One and twenty Chimnies in both Houses, and a great many Doors to go in and out at; and likewise many private Passages from one Room to the other.

These Houses are seated at the bottom of a thick woody and rocky Hill, with several hollow places in the Rocks, wherein Men may conceal themselves; and there is a very private

54

Father David Lewis,
one-time Rector of the Cwm

John Arnold had promised an additional reward to that offered by the government for the capture of David Lewis. This proved too much of a temptation to William James, a servant of David Lewis, who led six armed men to arrest him. Lewis was taken to the Golden Lion Hotel in Frogmore Street, Abergavenny where he was examined by William Jones, Recorder of Monmouth who charged him with having remained in England after having taken orders in the Roman Church contrary to the law of Elizabeth's reign. William James swore he had seen the priest at mass at least 20 times.

After being committed on a charge of treason, Lewis was given the alternative of spending the night in a guardroom at the Golden Lion or spending the night as Arnold's guest at Llanfihangel Court. As he and Arnold were well known to each other he accepted the invitation. The next morning he was taken to Monmouth Gaol where he spent two months. He was given a good lower room for which a friend paid 14s. a week inclusive of fire, candle and linen.

Many highly coloured rumours circulated about Father Lewis and some were published. A pamphlet entitled *A true Relation of the Knavery of Father Lewis* was attached to the account of Bishop Croft's raid on the Cwm. Father Lewis was supposed to have cheated a woman out of her savings by promising to free her father's soul from purgatory. First of all he said this could be done for £100 but when she said she had only £30 he said he would take that.

During May 1679 Lewis was taken to London with Father Kemble and was interviewed by Oates and Bedloe and once again denied any knowledge of the Plot. On 23rd May he was returned to Usk Prison.

The execution took place at Usk on 27th August 1679, according to tradition at a spot just outside the town where the present Catholic Church now stands. His execution was not a popular measure. He was so well known locally that a large crowd gathered to say farewell. His last speech took the text from St Peter's First Epistle: 'Let none of you suffer as a murderer or as a thief; but if as a Christian, let him not be ashamed'. He declared he was dying for religion alone and felt no shame.

The gallows were a makeshift affair, so low that a trench had to be dug. In the trench beneath the gallows was placed a stool. After the rope was placed round Father Lewis's neck the stool was removed. The body was disembowelled but not quartered. Some of those present dipped pieces of cloth into the dead man's blood to be treasured as relics. The body was given an honourable burial in Usk Parish Churchyard, the crowd who had attended the execution joining the funeral procession. The grave is to the left of the entrance to the church and is covered with a large flat stone cracked through the centre. No inscription can now be read. In recent years a replica has been placed alongside this original stone bearing an inscription describing Father Lewis' martyrdom and his canonization.

Father Lewis's replica gravestone in Usk Parish Churchyard

On Sunday 25th October 1970 in the Basilica of Saint Peter, Rome, there was a Solemn Canonisation of the 40 Blessed Martyrs of England and Wales by Pope Paul VI. During the Mass of Canonization, the Westminster Cathedral Choir sang music by William Byrd (1543-1623), himself a staunch Catholic and a persistent recusant. The choir were especially honoured, on this occasion, to be permitted to substitute for the Sistine Choir. And so John Kemble and David Lewis who were killed for their religious beliefs became numbered among the Saints.

Coed Anghred

Although the bishop's raid on The Cwm was the virtual end of the Jesuit College it survived another 100 years as a Mission. In 1684 there were four priests at The Cwm, in 1712 seven missioners, in 1750 still seven missioners and in 1771 ten missioners.

Apart from missionary work, the priests were engaged in writing and translating theological and devotional treatises in Latin, Welsh and English. A few works were printed abroad and a small number of Welsh works are still extant. For a time during the 18th century, the centre of influence moved to Perthir about 2 miles north of Monmouth in the parish of Rockfield. The Catholic Powell family had lived at Perthir for generations and the male line ended in 1715 in three unmarried sisters. The estate was inherited by their cousin Michael Lorymer.

The English and Welsh Catholic Church from 1688 till 1840 was divided into four districts, the London, Midland, Northern and Western districts. Each was headed by a Vicar-Apostolic. The first Vicar-Apostolic of the Western District was Matthew Pritchard.

Perthir provided the headquarters of the Western District and a home for Bishop Matthew Pritchard until his death in 1750. Mass was said regularly in the house and the family names occur in the recusant lists of the 18th century. The house is now demolished and the stone gateway that adorned the garden was removed to Clytha Park, Abergavenny where it is known as the Perthir Gate. In 1840 Monmouth and Hereford were taken out of the Western District to form the Welsh District.

The Catholic religion survived in the border country. There were still 440 named recusants in the County of Monmouth in 1771 compared with 541 in 1676. The area was backward, undeveloped and poor agriculturally with very bad communications. There were no large urban centres with their influences. Welsh was the most common language spoken. Many, if not most of the landed aristocracy were Catholic and their servants and tenants tended to follow their lead. In the first part of the 18th century the two greatest landowners, the Earl of Worcester and Lord Abergavenny, were both recusants and local families like the Vaughans of Courtfield, the Milbournes of Wonastow and Llanrothal and the Joneses of Llanarth were resident locally and although not wealthy, had enormous

The Perthir Gate at Clytha Park, Abergavenny in 1998

The Catholic Church at Coed Anghred

influence. It is in the homes of these families that the centres of Catholic worship survived.

And so in the Monnow Valley the old Catholic faith was never really lost. Not being able to erect chapels, worship had to be in private houses, for example in an upstairs room in the Robin Hood Inn in Monnow Street, Monmouth.

The first Catholic Relief Act of 1778 exempted Catholics from most of the penalties to which they were still liable, provided they took the Oath of Allegiance. By 1793 a new chapel had been built in Monmouth. In 1829 the Catholic Emancipation Act was passed giving Catholics the same privileges as those attending Protestant churches. Within 15 years of this Act a Catholic church was being built in the Monnow Valley. The site chosen was remote on a steep hill between Skenfrith and Cross Ways.

The *Catholic Directory* for 1845 under the County heading for Monmouthshire reads:

Coedangrol, Skenfrith. A chapel is being built here, and a mission is being contemplated for the sake of three former congregations in this part of Monmouthshire.

The foundation stone of what turned out to be an example of typical English parish church, was blessed and laid on 1st August 1844 by the Vicar General of the Welsh

District, the Very Reverend Dr Thomas F. Rooker. The builder was Mr C. Lawrence of Monmouth. The church was registered with the Quarter Sessions at Usk on 13th March 1846, 'as a place of congregation or assembly for religious worship'. The name of the church was 'the Church of the Immaculate Conception of the Blessed Virgin Mary'.

On 5th September 1846 there was a notice in the *Monmouthshire Merlin* advertising the opening of the church:

<blockquote>
The solemn dedication
of the
New Catholic church at Coed Anghred
Near Skenfrith, Monmouthshire

is fixed for the 22nd of September. All Clergymen attending the procession, are requested to bring with them a cassock and a surplice.

Morning Service. High Mass, Coram Pontifice, will commence at Eleven a.m., Sermon after the Gospel, by the Right Rev. Bishop Brown V.A.W.

Afternoon service. Vespers and Benediction, at Three p.m. Sermon by the Very Rev. Dr Rooker, V.G.

Cards of Admission, 5s., 2s. 6d. and 2s. may be had of Mr T. Dubberley, Silversmith, Agincourt Square, Monmouth; or at the church on the morning of the dedication.

There are three Inns, Good stabling, in the village of Skenfrith, near the church.

Refreshments will be provided in the Schoolroom adjoining by Mr Evans, White Swan, Monmouth.
</blockquote>

The opening was extensively reported in the *Monmouthshire Beacon* and the *Catholic Directory* for 1847 described St Mary's as a 'Beautiful church, with a good Mission house and School House adjoining', but it also added that the means to support the incumbent was as yet wanting.

Coed Anghred narrowly missed becoming a place of great importance. In 1852 John Brown the Catholic Bishop of Apollonia and Vicar General of the newly formed Welsh District was looking for somewhere to build the Cathedral Chapter of Newport. Sites were offered at Chepstow, Usk, Pool Hall and at Courtfield. Among these offers was one to build at Coed Anghred. The land at Belmont, Hereford given by Mr Wegg-Prosser was the place finally chosen and Belmont Abbey was built.

St Joseph's Foreign Missionary Society of the Sacred Heart, Mill Hill in London was started in 1869 by the Mill Hill Fathers founded by Father Herbert Vaughan of Courtfield, and for a brief while they ran a small school at Coed Anghred. The following report was sent to Mrs Mary Hopson of Tregate from Mill Hill and is marked 'From an unknown newspaper August 1880':

This school was opened at Coedangred, near Monmouth, on the Feast of Our Lady's Assumption (August 15th). The object of this school is to prepare, for the higher studies at Mill Hill any youth who has a strong desire to study for the Foreign Missions, and

OPENING OF THE CHURCH OF THE IMMACULATE CONCEPTION OF THE B. V. M. OF COEDANGRA, NEAR SKENFRITH, MONMOUTHSHIRE.

This beautiful church, situated on an eminence above the village of Skenfrith, was solemnly dedicated on Tuesday, the 22nd inst., by the Right Rev. Dr. Brown, Bishop of Apolonia, V. A. of the Welsh district, assisted by a number of the clergy. Hitherto, the Catholics scattered over this tract of the country, the remnants of congregations, that at no very distant period had their own pastors and chapels, have been deprived, in great measure, of the consolations of religion, by their great distance from any place of worship, and it is lamentable to see how many have in consequence fallen away. It may easily be imagined, therefore, with what satisfaction those who still retained feelings of religion, watched the progress of the new building, and with what eagerness they crowded to the ceremony of the dedication. So great was the number that attended from the neighbouring congregations to witness a scene so pleasing in the eyes of faith, that scarcely half of them could gain admittance, though the church was completely crowded, amongst the company present were Lord Southwell, Wm. Jones, Esq., of Clytha, Miss Jones, Messrs. Philip, Edward, and Wyburn, Jones, of Lanarth, Mr. and Mrs. Plowden, from Rotherwas, Mr. and Mrs. Monington, from Sarsefield, Mrs Witham, Miss Salvin; the choice of the music was most select, and the choir under the skilful management of Mr. Henry Field, of Batt, was most effective. Miss Whitnall, of Liverpool, whose first ideas on the true character of church music every one must acknowledge by her powerful tones and pure enunciation of religious feelings, told forcibly upon a people bent down in the solemn act of worship, and the effect was what alone should be aimed at, admiration lost in devotion.

Before 11 o'clock the bell sent forth its tones from the castellated tower, and every place was occupied; the procession advanced from the sacristy, outside the church, to the west entrance chanting the *Quam delecta Tabernacula*, psalm 83; and passing through the midst of the assembled multitudes, formed around the altar, and the service began. High mass was sung by the Rev. Thomas Shattock, of Prior Park, assisted by the Rev. J. Dawson of Cortfield, and Rev. Wm. Woollett, of Pontypool, as Deacon, and Sub-deacon. The Rev. J. Bonomi acting as master of the ceremonies. After the gospel, his lordship, in cope and mitre, advanced to the centre of the altar, and preached a most impressive sermon from 2 Cor. c. 6, v. 16, "For you are the temple of the living God." After illustrating the zeal of the faithful of all ages in decorating material temples dedicated to divine worship, he took occasion of the spiritual temples of the holy ghost in the souls of men, which it was of infinitely more consequence to decorate by the practice of every christian virtue, for order to fit them for heaven.

After the high mass there was an elegant cold collation laid out in the new school room by Mr. Evans, of the White Swan, Monmouth. The poor members of Christ were not forgotten on this occasion; a liberal charity being distributed to about one hundred and twenty of the most needy, "lest they should faint by the way, some having come from afar." The evening service was chanted alternately by the choir and officiating clergy at the altar with very pleasing effect. The very reverend Dr. Rooker, V.G., of Wales, preached an eloquent sermon from Luke 10, v. 23, "Blessed are the eyes that see the things which you see;" shewing that the blessing of our Saviour's coming was not confined to those whom he was then addressing, but intended for all future generations to the end of the world; and that his present hearers had great reason to rejoice at the additional opportunity of having the ancient faith of this country, which was the same which Christ and his apostles taught, preached amongst them, and the holy sacraments left by Christ to his church, administered to them. The whole was concluded with the solemn benediction of the blessed sacrament, and the people separated delighted with what they had heard and seen.

The edifice was erected by Mr. C. Lawrence, builder, of this town, and evinced great taste and ability. It is of the early English order of architecture, and was much admired by the congregation.

Monmouthshire Beacon, 3rd October 1846

who is at least sixteen and not more than twenty years of age. The school is placed under the guardianship of Father Marianus, the worthy pastor of Coedangred, who laboured for seventeen years in the Foreign Missions. The school commences in the presbytery with four students and a teacher; all of them from Lancashire. To the great delight of the fervent little congregation of Coedangred the inauguration of the school was the occasion of a somewhat, to them unusual solemnity. The altar of this beautiful church was decked in its best ...

There were five students, three entered in August and September and the other two in May 1881. There were two teachers, James Hanifan and Richard Joseph O'Halloran was appointed Master of Discipline in October 1880. Unfortunately the school's stay at Coed Anghred was short-lived. A document from Mill Hill states:

The school has been transferred from Coedangred to Kelvedon in Essex. The little secluded mission of Coedangred, among the hills of Monmouthshire, was well adapted for an Apostolic School. Moreover His Lordship the Bishop of Newport and Menevia and his Chapter were quite agreeable to let us have the full use of the premises and the land attached to them. But it would have necessitated a considerable outlay of money for the purpose of enlarging the presbytery. This has been providentially avoided by the offer of Kelvedon.

From that time on there was a slow decline in the attendance at St Mary's. One of the main problems always had been the 'means adequate to support an incumbent'. The Catholic population in the district was declining and there were seven incumbents between 1880 and 1900. A statement dated 10th June 1907 was sent from the Diocese of Newport to the Prior of Belmont Abbey:

The Church of St Mary, Coedangred, Skenfrith, was opened in the year 1848. It was built, not by the subscriptions of the faithful, or by public collections, but with money given to Rev Thomas Abbot by a single benefactor. Coedangred is six miles from Monmouth, and is situated in a scantily populated and inaccessible district, about a mile from the small country village of Skenfrith. There is no railway station nearer than Monmouth. The reason why the church and presbytery were built in this solitary place was at that time there were, as I am told, some five or six Catholic farmers round about, the neighbourhood, being then owned, as it is yet by a Catholic proprietor. The late Lord Southwell, who then owned the estate, endowed it to the extent of £1,000. Other small investments by Fr Abbott and the rent of a few acres of glebe, bring the endowment up to about £90 or £100 a year.

A Catholic cemetery adjoining the church was established about 1847, and there are a good many interments ...

It was very soon perceived that there would never be any congregation. The Catholic farmers gradually disappeared. There is now one such family, living about two miles away. This is nearly the whole congregation. The average attendance at Mass on Sundays is seven. The loneliness of the presbytery makes it difficult for the priest to keep a housekeeper, or to supply himself with coals etc. The Bishop has been obliged to accept the services of any priest who would consent to live there; with the result too often of the most unsatisfactory nature.

What the Bishop now proposes, is to sell the land and buildings (the latter, including the Church, would probably be pulled down) and apply the proceeds, together with the endowment, to the founding of a new mission in the neighbourhood. The cemetery, of course, would be reserved, the enclosure wall made secure and the cemetery itself, although closed for interments, reverently looked after.

Finally, in 1910, St Mary's Church Coed Anghred was closed. The last recorded marriage in May 1910 was of, rather appropriately, Margaret Bennett of the Darren, the place where all those years ago in 1605, the bishop had tried to stop the Catholics gathering for mass. The last burial and a baptism were in July 1910.

The church was not demolished until after the First World War and part of the presbytery remained standing until the 1950s. The only building now remaining is part of the coach house. Some of the stone taken from the church was used to secure the churchyard walls and some was taken to the nearby mansion of Hilston. It is understood that stone was taken to Pembridge Castle which had been bought in 1912 by Dr Hedley Bartlett and was being extensively restored.

It was some years before another Roman Catholic Chapel was built in this district. I have been told that for a time mass was held in a room at the Broad Oak Inn and before that at a bungalow on the site of the now demolished Priory Motel at Skenfrith. By the 1930s the Roman Catholic Chapel, a rather plain wooden building, was built at Broad Oak and is still in use today.

It is not easy to find what is now left of St Mary's Church, Coed Anghred. About half a mile up a steep lane known as Lint Hill which runs from Skenfrith to Crossway, there is a track off to the left. Here is a footpath sign with a chained swan showing that this is part of the Monnow Valley Walk. To the right of this track are some rusted railings and the remains of some broken steps where the entrance drive to the church commenced. When I visited the site about 1997 the churchyard was completely overgrown and it was impossible to see any sign of the tombstones which had been painstakingly recorded by Mary Hopson in 1984. All evidence of the church had been obliterated. It was therefore a very pleasant surprise to find, on a more recent visit, that the owners of the churchyard had erected new fences and cleared away all the brambles and nettles. Most of the tombstones are too weathered to read and many are fallen down or leaning over, but it was possible to see the last remaining evidence of a Catholic edifice in the Monnow Valley.

Not everyone was happy about the Catholic Emancipation Act of 1829 as is shown by this contribution to the *Monmouthshire Beacon* of 10th February 1838:

'Our church and no surrender'

'Tis now the hour when Popish power
For desperate conflict rallies,
And flings her brand throughout the land,
And pours her poisoned chalice.
Now, Britons! now, with dauntless brow,
Back, bold defiance send her;
And swell the cry though earth and sky,
'Our church - and no surrender.'

Remembering all the bloodstained thrall
Of Popish persecution,
O! may ye feel the martyr's zeal
Inspire your resolution!
Your native land now calls your hand
From slavery to defend her -
Let earth and sky ring back the cry,
'Our church - and no surrender.'

Shall Priests regain their iron reign,
Our holy Churchmen dooming
To rope and rack, to sword and stake ,
And molten fires consuming?
To Jesuit knaves shall we be slaves,
Or trust their mercies tender?
No! whilst on high is heard the cry,
'Our church - and no surrender.'

Her altars pure shall long endure,
By bigotry unshrouded;
And sacred shine, in light divine,
The shrines of faith unclouded.
As nought on earth can raise her worth
Nor greater glories lend her,
So loud be heard our rallying word,
'Our church - and no surrender.'

Through traitors base her fame disgrace,
O'erawed by mob-debaters,
And dastard flee, or bend the knee
To rebel agitators;
Our maiden Queen enthroned is seen
Our glorious faiths defender,
And raises high the patriot cry,
'Our church - and no surrender.'

CHAPTER 3

The Beautification of Hoarwithy Church

Introduction

St Catherine's Church in Hoarwithy (Plate 6) is recognised by the architectural historians and writers of guide books as a remarkable Victorian building. 'A masterpiece, the brilliant work of a bold and confident architect' and 'without a doubt this is the most exciting Victorian church in Herefordshire', are just two examples of the praise that has been lavished upon it.

Writers have been particularly struck by the way that the building and its setting evokes memories of Italy. 'On a summer day the loggia of Hoarwithy hangs over the valley of the Wye as an Umbrian church might over the Tiber' writes one, whilst another puts it more succinctly: 'The stones of Venice come to the banks of the Wye'.

Its hilltop site, its east end apse, its campanile and its cloister round two sides have generally led to the church being called 'Italian', 'Italianate' or 'Italian Romanesque', but in truth there is a more complex mix of influences. Indeed the official listing covers most possibilities by declaring it 'eclectic *Rundbogenstil* [i.e. round arched style] with Byzantine, French, Venetian, Lombardic, Tuscan and Sicilian Romanesque influences', and to this list one could surely add the influence of Herefordshire's own Norman churches and their sculpture.

Visitors to the church who explore the passage behind the altar find, beneath the central of the five apse windows, a rather battered brass plaque with faded red and black lettering inscribed:

To the Church of God and in memory of
William Poole MA
Prebendary of Hereford Cathedral
and Vicar of Hentland with Hoarwithy for forty six years
the above windows are dedicated by his personal friends
in token of their affection and esteem.

He restored and beautified this Church at his sole cost
and devoted his energies and talents to promote the
best and highest interests of those living in the parish
October 1903

To examine how this 'beautification' resulted in the splendidly unique blend of styles seen today, one needs to delve into the life and career of William Poole and his architect, John Pollard Seddon. But first, consideration must be given to the church Poole found when he came to Hoarwithy.

The Original Church

In the 19th century Hoarwithy was, as it still is today, within the parish of Hentland. Although there is some documentary evidence of there having been a 13th-century chapel in Tresseck, a hamlet close by, there does not appear to have been any mediaeval chapel in Hoarwithy itself.

By the 19th century the old village of Hentland, adjacent to the parish church, had shrunk, whilst the size of Hoarwithy, nearly two miles away, had grown because of the increase in river traffic and the turnpiking of the road to Ross in 1749. It must have been these circumstances that led to Her Majesty's Commissioners for Building New Churches erecting a church in Hoarwithy in 1843.

The Church Building Commission had been set up in 1818, because it was apparent that there was insufficient church room for the country's rapidly expanding population. A deficiency of 2½ million church places had been estimated. The authorities were worried that without the pastoral care of the Established Church the poor would fall an easy prey to revolutionary agitation, especially when inflamed by the impassioned oratory of the ministers of the Nonconformist churches.

Between 1818 and 1856 the Commissioners, with the aid of government grants, were responsible for building more than 600 new churches. The great majority of these were in the expanding industrial towns, and it is rare for such a rural location as Hoarwithy to be accommodated, but presumably the local diocese made a case on the basis of population shift within Hentland parish, which the Commissioners accepted. A book on this subject, *Six Hundred New Churches* by M.H. Port (1961), contains lists of the Commissioners churches derived from the Commission's Annual Report and its returns to Parliament, but curiously these omit Hoarwithy. However there seems no doubt that the Commission was responsible, because the Hereford Record Office holds a Deed of Conveyance, dated 26th June 1843, of glebe land from the Dean and Chapter of Hereford and their lessee to Her Majesty's Commissioners for Building New Churches, under the 'Act for building and promoting the building of additional churches in populous parishes' of 1818.

The Commissioners almost invariably acquired good sites for their churches and they certainly achieved this aim here. The church was built where its successor is today, perched above the river on a small hill, which Prebendary Hawkshaw, a Curate of Hentland from 1842-1845, said had been 'as bare as the palm of my hand' when he first knew it. The church had no dedication and was known only as the Chapel of Ease. Its present dedication to St Catherine dates only to the early 20th century, after William Poole's death.

The Commissioners had a statutory duty to build as cheaply as possible, and therefore their churches tend to be plain and unornamented. According to Prebendary Hawkshaw 'a sort of oblong box for a mission church' was put up, and this is confirmed by a photograph dated 1866 in a Hopton family album held in the Record Office, which shows a simple, gabled building, with no tower or external decoration. Permission to consecrate was granted on the 28th August 1843, suggesting that only a short construction period was required. The dimensions of the new chapel were 57' 10" east to west and 31' 8" north to south, so that the building was rather broad for its length compared to a normal church profile. This was presumably to make best use of the confined site, which slopes down steeply on three sides and is cut into the hillside on the north side. These dimensions subsequently provided the proportions of Poole's church whose main body is of almost the same measurements.

Walling from the old church remaining at the north-west corner of the present church

Some accounts suggest that the 1843 church was a brick building with round-headed windows, and that the latter caused Poole to adopt a similar style in his 'beautified' church. Indeed *Lascelle's Directory* of 1851 calls it 'a neat modern brick building'. However, the above mentioned Hopton album photograph of 1866 clearly shows that the building is of local sandstone and has Gothic lancet windows with pointed heads. This is confirmed by the *History of the Deanery of Archenfield* published in 1903 after Poole's death, but based on his notes, where it is stated that traces of the old church, 'a very ugly and plain building, devoid of any architectural beauty' can still be seen in a small portion of the north-west wall. This wall can still be seen today and is of stone.

Moreover on the exterior of the south wall of the nave there is a clear change in the stonework at a level of about three feet above the cloister floor, the stones below this point being more roughly carved and requiring thicker mortar joints than those above. This presumably indicates Seddon's work being built upon the earlier stone base.

It seems unlikely that the church would have been built in brick and then encased in stone and had its fenestration changed, before Poole and Seddon's transformation. In any case Gothic was the approved style for Commissioners' churches in a rural setting, rather than brick, for which there is little vernacular tradition in the region. So the references to a brick building remain something of a mystery.

However that may be, Hoarwithy now had a chapel of ease which in 1870, just before the Poole/Seddon changes, is listed in the Diocesan Church Calendar as providing 240 sittings, whilst the parish church of Hentland accommodated 180.

The Benefactor — William Poole

Family Background
Chronologically at least, William Poole was a true Victorian. He was born in 1819, the same year as Queen Victoria, and died just over a year after his sovereign on 6th March 1902. He was the youngest of the five children surviving into adulthood of Edward and Katherine Poole of the Homend in Stretton Grandison parish. The Pooles were a long established gentry family, who owned land in several parishes in the county and in Radnorshire. They had also acquired, via an 18th-century marriage, holdings on the borders of Yorkshire and Durham. Down the generations they had intermarried with their neighbours, the Hoptons, whose house, Canon Frome Court, was only a mile from the Homend. (Both houses survive but are now in multiple occupancy.) In William's generation both his eldest brother and eldest sister married Hoptons.

At the time of William's birth, work was in progress to provide the old half-timbered family home with a smart new classical entrance front. For this his father had engaged the services of Sir Robert Smirke, architect of the British Museum, whose work in Herefordshire also includes Eastnor Castle and the Shire Hall. In 1825 Edward Poole also commissioned a picturesque lodge for the Homend estate from the office of the famous John Nash. So his young son was growing up with the work of two fashionable London architects around him.

Education
William Poole was educated at Rugby School and Oriel College Oxford. He thus came into contact during his formative years with important men who influenced not only him but Victorian society as a whole.

First, during his time at Rugby his headmaster was the famous Dr Thomas Arnold, who did most to create the ethos of the Victorian public school. His stated priorities were 'first religious principles, secondly gentlemanly conduct, thirdly intellectual ability'. His brand of muscular Christianity with its emphasis on character and moral fibre certainly seems to have had an impact on Poole, 'who always spoke with the greatest affection [of Dr Arnold] as having done much to model his former life', as his obituarist was later to write.

He then went up to Oriel at a time when it was the hotbed of the Oxford Movement, whose chief protagonists John Newman, John Keble and Edward Pusey were all fellows there. These theologians emphasised the continuity of the Anglican Church with its pre-Reformation Catholic past. They stressed the importance of the sacraments and adherence to the Book of Common Prayer. They wanted a Church that was concerned with spirituality and its expression through ritual. The activities of this group were a key element in the Victorian Anglican revival.

In some cases adoption of these principles led men to a 'High Church' position, where ritualism was greatly stressed, or even, as in the case of Newman, to conversion to Catholicism. Poole and the majority of his fellow clergy did not go down this route, but the notions of evangelism and morality that stemmed from the Oxford Movement certainly remained influential. Poole was able to absorb these influences at first hand and his obituarist notes that he formed life-long friendships with men who were at college with him.

He graduated as a Bachelor of Arts in 1841 with a degree in *Litterae Humaniores*. The fact that it was a fourth class degree perhaps suggests that he was not especially gifted academically.

Career

Poole was ordained deacon in 1845. He served as curate at St Weonard's and Lugwardine before being made perpetual curate, and shortly afterwards Vicar of Hentland with Hoarwithy in 1854.

The question arises of why he came to Hentland. It was not unusual for the younger sons of gentry to take a church living, but this was usually in their home parish or another parish where the living was in the family's gift. Hentland was a poor parish with no connections to any of the important gentry families.

Was there any indiscretion or unhappiness in his youth? Is there any significance in the enigmatic message on one of the wreaths at his funeral from Miss Trafford (presumably from the landed family of Hill Court and Michaelchurch Court): 'In loving memory of first days'? A more prosaic, but more likely explanation is that he was driven by a genuine sense of mission.

Missionary work was accorded great importance by the Oxford Movement, and, whilst this was mostly carried out in foreign lands or amongst the urban poor, Poole may well have felt the need to evangelise in his native county. Later on, when he was campaigning for increased financial support for poor rural benefices, he was to write 'Without the bribe of wealth, of the charm of society, or the excitement of numbers, she [the Church] carries the sweet music of the Gospel to these lonely and distant parishes. These ill-provided places of the Church are the unfinished angles, the open chinks, through which danger can find its way.' Hentland, a parish so under-provided with the Gospel that a new chapel had to be built, may therefore have seemed a suitable place for him to follow his vocation.

He remained vicar of Hentland until 1901 and during this 47-year span wrought enormous improvements in the parish through his energy and generosity. As well as beautifying Hoarwithy Church, he funded the building of a new vicarage, a school, and next door to the church a reading room combined with a Sunday School and a residence. He had the parish church at Hentland restored and a vestry added. He set up a new grocery store and when old cottages became free he had them reconditioned for re-let. His building schemes helped prevent local unemployment and allowed local men to be trained in the building trades.

He was in control of nearly everything that happened in the parish. He set up a clothing club, a coal club, a penny bank and a free library. He organised sports and personally supervised the children's education, devising syllabuses, composing hymns for them to sing and writing poetry and stories for them to read. He was a magistrate for 57 years, the chairman of the Highways Board and a trustee of the Hoarwithy Bridge Company.

He also took a large share of diocesan work. He was quickly appointed Rural Dean of Archenfield in 1856 and Prebend of Wellington Major in 1857. He was later offered, but declined, a Canonry. He often took a prominent part in discussions at the annual diocesan conference and two organisations owe their origins to him — the Church Union (for the improvement of church choirs) and the Society for Augmentation of Poor Benefices.

The latter was one of his major campaigns. He read a particularly well prepared paper to the 1880 diocesan conference in which all the benefices of the diocese

The former vicarage

were itemised. He recommends that £200pa should be the minimum benefice income and notes that 90 benefices fall short of this figure. He goes on to make some very practical suggestions for supplementing these benefices through investing diocesan capital, requesting aid from the Ecclesiastical Commissioners, approaching the patron of the living etc. He backs up his arguments with examples of successful schemes in other dioceses. He even managed to preach a sermon on this subject at a Three Choirs Festival. The charity being supported at this Festival was for assistance to the widows and orphans of the clergy, but Poole took the opportunity to broaden his appeal and delivered his sermon on 'The defaults of society towards poor clergy'.

But perhaps Poole's biggest contribution outside the confines of his own parish was in the field of education. He became a governor of Hereford County College and secretary of the Diocesan Board of Education. His reasons for wishing to improve educational standards are set out in a letter of 1858 (subsequently published) to the agriculturalists resident in the Ross Union. This followed Poole's discovery that the candidates of a prize that had been set up to encourage farm servants to keep up their learning were very few. In the letter he sets out the benefits of ongoing education, emphasising that it is better for master/servant relationships for the labourers' mental and physical condition to be improved. He writes, 'my own experience fully confirms what has been so often stated, that the most ignorant are also the most prejudicial and insubordinate, the most ready to believe all ill of those richer than themselves, the most hard to disabuse of suspicions however unfounded.' So Poole's support for education was perhaps a means of preserving the status quo, rather than (as modern day liberalism would have it) for the empowerment of the masses. One of his obituarists was to confirm that he was 'in politics a staunch conservative'.

However, he was also a campaigner against social evils of the day, as evidenced by his paper on Mop Fairs — 'Old Mops Mended, not Thrown Away'. Labourers came to these fairs to be hired, 'to be picked out in the street like a bullock or a sheep, to be chosen by length of arm, or breadth of chest, or power of sinew, to be put to paces like a cart colt, to have points examined like a calf or a filly, to be taken by a master of which they know nothing, who knows nothing of them, to a place of which they have never heard, without character asked, or any particulars given.' The fairs had a reputation for drunkenness and vice, so that 'little by little the proprieties of everyday life drop out of sight and many a young person has to look back on some long anticipated Mop as the cause of good principles weakened, of modest habits undermined, and, it may be, of a fair character stained for ever.'

Typically his solutions comprised practical ideas, e.g. putting hiring on a more respectable footing via a registrar sitting in a hall, mixed with severity — putting in force with a special strictness laws against drunkenness, etc — and the provision of healthy alternative activities, such as a well organised plan of games and sports.

Interests

Whilst Poole's chief preoccupation was undoubtedly his work, he also found time to pursue his interests, of which one was foreign travel. As a young man in 1842/43 he went on a kind of Grand Tour, writing letters to his mother from Vienna, Greece, Corfu, Rome, Naples, Florence and Milan. He made other trips to Italy and his travel journal of 1862 survives, recording a journey of over 2,500 miles around France.

He was also a keen student of the history and topography of his native Herefordshire. He was a member of the Woolhope Club for 39 years, although he never seems to have held office or presented a paper. However in the Hopton Collection in the Hereford reference library there are 15 volumes of his manuscript notes on various aspects of the county. He was especially interest in 'pedigrees', drawing detailed family trees of local gentry with their seats, heraldry etc. He also wrote of 'Herefordshire Worthies', such as Nell Gwynne, and made extracts from wills, taxation documents and parish registers. He was a great compiler of lists — parishes with their area and population, county clergymen, writings on the county (a *Bibliotheca Herefordiensis*) and so forth.

The church as depicted in the History of Archenfield, *1903*

The book a *History of Archenfield with a Description of the Churches in the old Rural Deanery* was published after Poole's death in 1903, compiled by his successor as Rural Dean, Prebendary Seaton. But the preface makes clear that Poole had done much of the preparatory work and had commissioned a well known illustrator, T. Raffles Davison, to make sketches of all the churches in the deanery and had then had these engraved at his own cost.

In both his foreign travels and local studies, Poole's writings evince an interest in architecture. In his 1862 journal he describes churches he had visited, including many in the Byzantine style in the south of France. He also notes, 'nothing in France, perhaps, more striking than the view of the Cité of Carcassone'. (This was a famous restoration by the eminent French architect Viollet-le-Duc.) 'The castle was, like all government buildings in France, under repair and, as Carcassone furnished M. Viollet with the main ground for his theory as to the wooden galleries being suspended from walls, it is likely, since he is the appointed restorer, that his theory will not suffer from want of a good specimen of antiquity.'

His local history manuscripts include pencil drawings of buildings, their features and floor plans. Even a book of sermons includes doodles of arcades and lancet windows, and (intriguingly in view of the style of Hoarwithy Church) notes on 'old basilicas converted into churches', with four churches in Rome cited as examples.

Personality

The only likeness we have of William Poole is the copy of his portrait, painted when he was 73, which hung in the reading room at Hoarwithy. Beneath the beard and side whiskers we see a stern, rather ascetic face. It is an authoritarian figure, but perhaps with a hint of a retiring nature also.

William Poole from his portrait in the church

What we can glean of his personality to add to this image comes chiefly from three sources: his own writings, his obituaries and the researches of Barbara Fleming. In 1950, Mrs Fleming took up residence in what had been Poole's vicarage, and she had the advantage of being able to talk to people with memories of the vicar in his later years. In 1960 she gave a talk about him on the BBC Home Service, the script for which survives.

His reputation is that he was something of a tyrant. This is epitomised by Barbara Fleming's story of a later vicar visiting a dying man in the village in the 1930s. The vicar tried to comfort the old man about his fear of dying, at which the latter exclaimed 'Oh! It's not God I am afraid of meeting — it's William Poole.'

There are certainly stories to suggest that Poole was a difficult man in his later years. On encountering a child with a hole in her pinafore, he would poke his finger in the hole and rip it further open, and then send her back to school to learn how to mend it. When a woman wore beads he disapproved of, he ripped them off her. And to a postman who was moving to a new round, he said brusquely 'Well, we shan't miss you, for you never came to church.'

Poole's brand of Anglicanism was stern, conservative and muscular. A flavour of his no nonsense approach can been seen in these notes in his common place book: 'When you go out on a cold day you shudder at the sharpness of the wind, but when you have taken hard exercise, that same cold wind comes but as a pleasant refreshment — apply to affliction — discipline — trials of all sorts.'

His views on morality are unequivocal. He gave a sermon in Hoarwithy Church in 1858 which he thought important enough to have printed under the title 'God's judgement on a common sin'. In it he says 'a simple life of modest decency: marriage undefiled and pure: these are the two roads for Christians to choose between. Anything else is fornications ... idleness is the mother of opportunity, and opportunity is the doorway of sin ... Let [your daughters] never learn to be idle, and wander about from house to house, and not only to be idle but to be tattlers and busybodies.' And so on in similar vein.

In his common place book he notes: '"Toleration" allows unbelief a free hand — in society — in books — in magazines. Gods laws weakened'. He is also scathing about the play *Quo Vadis*, later a Hollywood blockbuster, then playing at the Adelphi Theatre: 'Crude sensationalism and quasi religious sentiment. Conversions, brought about under the influence of sexual passion. Sacred texts employed as mere ingredients in a sexual hodgepodge. Received by several hundreds of people with unbounded enthusiasm.'

Part of Poole's inscription: 'Keep thy foot when thou goest to the House of God'

His theme of total obedience to God's laws is enshrined outside the west door of Hoarwithy Church, where, in the mosaic pavement, he had inscribed the words 'Keep thy foot when thou goest to the House of God'. This is a quotation from the *Book of Ecclesiastes* which continues 'and draw nigh to hear. For much better is obedience than the victims of fools, who know not what evil they do'. A modern translation (*New English Bible*) is 'Go carefully when you visit the house of God. Better draw near in obedience than offer the sacrifice of fools, who sin without a thought'. Did Poole intend his 'Keep thy foot' to also mean a prosaic 'Mind the step' as a sort of humorous double meaning? It is possible, but one tends to think not.

But with all this fierceness there is another side to William Poole. He wrote 'when you rise in the morning form a resolution to make the day a happy one to a fellow creature', and he seems to have followed this precept. His acts of generosity in supplying Hoarwithy with a new building and new facilities have already been noted. He also looked after the sick, sending a rabbit and a bottle of wine to pensioners who were ill, and let some of the old people live rent free in the cottages he owned. His devotion to the spiritual and temporal welfare of his flock is apparent.

He never married and according to his niece, Madeline Hopton, this was 'because he thought it not right to hand on an inheritance of insanity which had appeared in members of his family.' Whilst one could not justifiably say that an inheritance of insanity was apparent in his behaviour, there is nevertheless a certain lack of balance in his character. His list making and other writings have a meticulous, almost obsessive, quality. He seems determined to be in charge of everything that happened in the parish, and there are stories of him whipping the cloths off the top of baskets to see what their owners were carrying. In modern parlance we would probably call him a control freak. An obituarist noted that he was naturally of a retiring disposition, and this perhaps contributed to the unsympathetic way he asserted his authority.

He was extremely persistent and compromise was not in his vocabulary. As his obituarist puts it in appropriately polite language, 'Having a high ideal of duty, he never shrank from expressing his views, and although he might not at once attain his object he never swerved from supporting his views until if possible his ideal was attained.' He goes on to recall some 'remarkable words' from a speech by the then owner of Pengethley Court who said 'I thought him to be self opinionated, but now I feel convinced that he was right, and that I was wrong; and that he had at heart the one object of what he deemed best for the welfare of his parishioners.' No doubt the feelings about Poole's persistence from those who encountered it varied according to whether or not they agreed with the view he was championing.

The final summary of this complex man can best be left to the wife of one of his curates who said of him 'So good, so grand, so autocratic and so often — so difficult'.

Death

Poole finally retired in 1901. Given the energy with which he fulfilled his duties, and a physique that was not particularly strong, it was a triumph of the will over the flesh that he remained in post into his 82nd year.

He returned to his family home at Homend, which had lately been empty and, notwithstanding his increasing frailty, took a keen interest in the building extensions he put in hand there.

However on the 6th March 1902 he died peacefully siting in his chair at Homend, the cause of death being certified as 'failure of the heart's action'. All his siblings and their spouses were already dead, and he was survived only by two nieces, daughters of his sister Frances, who had married James Hopton. He made provision for his nieces in his will, but most of his estates were left to more distant male Hopton relatives.

His funeral at Stretton Grandison was a grand affair. The Bishop of Hereford officiated at the committal of the body to the vault, attended by the dean and clergy from all over the diocese. Many of Herefordshire's landed families were represented. When his remains were buried in the family vault, he having no other immediate relatives, it was closed 'for ever'. He had for some time been spoken of as 'the last of the Pooles'.

He is commemorated by a brass plaque in Stretton Grandison Church, and a stained glass window depicting St Dubricius at Hentland (Plate 8). In Hoarwithy Church there are the stained glass windows already mentioned, although it would not have been unjustified for any inscription to his memory there to have used the words from Sir Christopher Wren's tomb in St Paul's Cathedral: 'If you seek my monument look around you'.

The Architect — John Pollard Seddon

Career

John Pollard Seddon was Poole's junior by eight years, being born in 1827, and died four years after his client in 1906. His father, Thomas, was a furniture manufacturer who was at the very top of his profession. He had the largest furniture making business in London and, in partnership with the upholsterer Nicholas Morel, had supplied furnishings for Windsor Castle as part of George IV's large scale revamping of the building.

John Pollard did not follow into his father's business, but became a student of T.L. Donaldson, who was a minor architect but was later important as one of the main instigators of the Royal Institute of British Architects. In 1851 Seddon established his own architectural practice in London, and in the following year, when on a job in south Wales, he met a fellow architect, John Pritchard. Pritchard had been brought up in the cathedral close at Llandaff and was an expert in ecclesiastical architecture.

Seddon's University College of Wales, Aberystwyth

Pritchard and Seddon were in partnership for the next 11 years during which they were Diocesan architects of the Llandaff Diocese and built or restored many churches in south Wales. Seddon also found work over the border in Herefordshire, including his early works for William Poole.

When the partnership broke up in 1863, Seddon returned to London but kept his contacts in Wales and Herefordshire. In fact probably his greatest building — along with Hoarwithy Church — was built in Wales in 1864-66. This was the enormous building on the sea front at Aberystwyth that was first conceived as the Castle House Hotel, but, when the client ran into financial difficulties, soon became the University College of Wales, part of which it remains today. The bold bow fronted section on the sea front and the double tower on the entrance side to the rear have been described by a leading architectural authority as 'among the grandest and most boldly plastic fragments produced in the period. Neither Oxford or Cambridge has anything of comparable quality.'

After this time Seddon tended to leave most architectural work to a succession of partners and collaborators, whilst he concentrated on restorations and a variety of design work including furniture, metalwork, ceramics, tiles, textiles and stained glass. He also wrote and lectured extensively on architecture and was recognised as one of the leaders of his profession. He remained in practice until shortly before his death, one of his last designs being for the stained glass windows at Hoarwithy dedicated to his late client.

Influences

A big influence on Seddon seems to have been his involvement with the Pre-Raphaelite painters and, through them, with William Morris and his circle. The contact was via his younger brother Thomas who was an artist in the Pre-Raphaelites' circle. When he died young in 1856, his best painting *The Valley of Jehoshaphat* was presented by subscription to the National Gallery and thus became the first Pre-Raphaelite painting to enter a public collection.

John Pollard continued to join in social gatherings with his late brother's friends and commissioned work from them, including a reredos painted by Rossetti for Llandaff Cathedral. He also designed a cabinet, shown in the mediaeval court of the International Exhibition of 1862, on which various Pre-Raphaelite painters painted panels depicting the marriage celebrations of King René of Anjou. He even designed Rossetti's retirement bungalow in Birchington-on-Sea, where (rather incongruously) this larger than life figure died.

From these influences Seddon derived a passionate belief in the unity of the arts. Architecture, painting, design and the decorative arts should, he felt, combine to create a total work of art. He also pre-figured Morris' founding of the Society for the Protection of Ancient Buildings in his respect for old materials and his advocacy of sympathetic restorations. In an 1866 lecture he called on architects to 'to preserve un-mutilated the precious structures which have descended to them as heirlooms from the past — not to be wantonly altered to serve a passing purpose, but tenderly and reverentially cared for to hand down in no worse condition to generations yet to come.'

These influences make Seddon a more rounded, and less dogmatic, architect than many of his contemporaries. As a young man he made tours of the continent and was prepared to combine details derived from a variety of sources in an eclectic way. His partner towards the end of his career, John Coates Carter, wrote that 'he was far the most original of the Gothic revivalists; for though among the strongest in his love for and belief in the revival, he was always a modern rather than a mediaevalist ... and in his work almost alone among the early revivalists was it impossible to trace the origin of the detail to any particular mediaeval style or building.'

Other Buildings

There are a number of churches close to Herefordshire built during the time of Seddon's partnership with Pritchard, for instance at Llandogo, Wyesham and Redbrook. These tend to be constrained by budget, and probably by the need to conform to diocesan requirements, and thus are fairly unadventurous in the approved Gothic idiom. But there are still some interesting and unusual touches. To take an example, the prominent belfry at Llandogo is an open stone structure which has been described as 'a sort of pulpit in the sky', which is exactly what it looks like.

It is of some local interest that one of Pritchard and Seddon's pupils was F.R. Kempson, the leading Herefordshire-based Victorian architect. His most famous buildings are the Hereford Library in Broad Street, and what is now the Royal National College for the Blind in College Road. Both these buildings show inventiveness in their detailing, which one feels Kempson may have picked up from his time with Pritchard and Seddon.

After leaving Pritchard, Seddon was able to introduce more variety into his churches. At about the same time as designing Hoarwithy he was also working on Adforton,

Herefordshire; Ullenhall, Warwickshire; and Ayot St Peters, Hertfordshire. Curiously all these churches are apsidal, rather than square ended, at their east end, but are otherwise very different. Seddon does not seem to have minded what brand of churchmanship his churches were required for, and the church at Ullenhall, for example, has a very Low Church arrangement.

Adforton near Wigmore, completed in 1875 is particularly delightful. A very simple design, costing under £1,000 to build, it nevertheless contains well-crafted furniture and achieves a notably calm and harmonious atmosphere. Its one touch of exuberance is the font designed by Seddon, whose bowl is sculpted on the outside with fishes caught in a net.

Two fine examples of Seddon's restoration work can be seen by going into Monmouthshire. He restored and partially rebuilt the church at

The font at Adforton

Grosmont, but the mediaeval feel of the building has been successfully retained, and at Llangwm Uchaf there is a magnificent mediaeval wooden rood screen, whose discreet restoration by Seddon can hardly be discerned.

The School of Science and Art in Stroud

Finally, a late building is to be found not far from Herefordshire, the School of Science and Art in Stroud, Gloucestershire, built between 1890-99. This is a splendid stone Gothic building, capped by a French looking tower where it turns a street corner. The side of the building is decorated by sculpture appropriately depicting leading scientists and artists, and on the corner a bust of Queen Victoria is flanked by a galleon on one side and a locomotive on the other.

Involvement with William Poole

Seddon and Poole knew each other over a long period of time. Seddon's first job at Hentland church dates from 1853, just before Poole became vicar. Seddon carried out restoration work and was probably responsible for the new north porch.

In 1857/58 the new vicarage where Poole was to live for the rest of his career was built to Seddon's designs, and in 1859-60 Seddon's new Hentland School was erected. Both buildings date from the time of the Pritchard and Seddon Partnership and are in a fairly conventional Gothic style. Both received mainly favourable notice from the *Ecclesiologist*, a publication that was the upholder of the 'correct' style of Gothic architecture.

Former Reading Room and Sunday School (to the left)

In 1866, although Seddon was now in London, Poole went back to him to design the vestry for Hentland Church. He also made designs for the lych gate. Then in 1868 Poole commissioned plans to alter an old house below Hoarwithy Church into a reading room, Sunday School and residence.

All these buildings survive today. The Hentland parsonage is now an old peoples' home and the school is a private residence, and both these show some alterations from when they were first built. The Hoarwithy building is very little altered and although in a Gothic style composes well with the Italianate church above when viewed from across the River Wye. The reading room continued to be used as a parish room into the new century, until 2009 when the whole building was refurbished. The main Seddon/Poole collaboration, Hoarwithy Church itself, of course, followed on and will be looked at in detail below.

The two men seemed to have retained their friendship. In the Hopton papers, and thus presumably from Poole's collection, is a copy of Seddon's paper read to the RIBA in 1873 on his work on shoring up Grosmont Church tower. Perhaps Seddon gave it to him. The copy of Poole's portrait which hung in the reading room carries a label stating that the original was by 'Miss Seddon'. This presumably is the Miss M. Seddon who exhibited two portraits at the Royal Academy in the 1890s and is also the Miss Maud Seddon who did figure studies for a stained glass window whose insertion Seddon supervised at St Margaret's Westminster in 1893.

It seems from this that Poole maintained contact with the Seddon family into old age and of course it was the elderly John Pollard Seddon who after Poole's death designed his memorial windows at Hoarwithy.

The Project — the Beautification of Hoarwithy Church

Chronology

The chronology of the project is somewhat uncertain. Poole's mother died in 1870, his father having died back in 1848. He would then have more income from the family estates at his disposal and it seems likely that this triggered the work at Hoarwithy. There are a few designs by Seddon for some details of the church which date from 1874. It may, however, be that some work started earlier because in the 1872 church calendar the number of sittings in the church are shown as 180, having been 240 earlier.

In the 1874 church calendar there is a list of churches in the diocese built or extensively restored since 1860, in which Hoarwithy does not appear. Neither, however, does it appear in similar lists published through the 1870s and 1880s, nor indeed does Hentland feature in the lists showing the value of benefices. One assumes that Poole was just not cooperative in supplying information of this sort to the compilers of the calendar.

It seems that there was certainly major work going on around 1878 and 1879. There is a copy of extracts from a letter in Poole's handwriting with prices (either estimates or actual costs) for elements of the building work. This includes a reference to the mosaic in the nave — i.e. the floor of the central aisle — in 1878 (£410 10s.). Other items to which the date 1879 is appended include such basic elements as the 'Tower to 1st' (level?) costing £1,650, the block floor, the cloister roof, arch stones, chancel stops and two windows. There is also reference to mosaic work in the ceiling and chancel, but as this amounts to only £152 it can hardly be for the great Byzantine mosaic scheme over the chancel that is seen today. 1879 is also the date in the Morris & Co. Catalogue of Designs for the stained glass window designed by Burne-Jones which occupies the topmost window at the west end.

Kelly's Directory of 1879 still refers merely to 'a chapel of ease' as it had done in former years. However, in an article in *Building News* in 1883 the building is referred to as 'built some years ago from the designs of Mr J.P. Seddon', and by 1885 *Kelly's* describes it as 'in Byzantine style'. It seems therefore that the major building work must have finished around 1880.

It is interesting that according to the plaque in memory of Poole, 'he restored and beautified this church' rather than 'rebuilt' it, and this must have been how the work was viewed. By keeping the proportions of the old church and leaving old walls where possible, Poole probably tried to keep the church available for worship during building works as much as he could, although there must have been times when this was impossible, such as when the nave walls were breached and rebuilt with new windows.

The choir stalls were installed in 1883 and the prayer desk in 1884, but in 1885 the building is described as 'far from complete', although this presumably referred to unfinished interior features and perhaps some exterior embellishments. The continuing work of 'beautification' does seem to have slowed down after this and this may have been due to the agricultural depression of the 1880s. Poole's income would have been mainly from agricultural rents, as even the family's northern estates were distant from industrial areas.

Indeed there is evidence of unfinished work at the church to this day. Apart from the bare walls and plain glass windows of the nave, which Poole must have hoped to decorate, there are a number of patently unfinished details. For instance, two rough blocks of stone protruding from the lower stages of the campanile tower face visitors as they ascend the path from the road, and these must have been intended for sculpture. Likewise the interior opening of the belfry giving on to the chancel has carvings over only half of this perimeter, and the truncated roof beams nearest the chancel arch remain unpainted. There is also the figure of an angel prettily drawn on the stonework above one of the carved capitals which looks as if it is a marker for more carving not carried out.

It is said that Poole was increasingly in dispute with the church authorities about his project and also had some undignified arguments with his workmen about their pay. One also wonders whether Poole's creation was valued by his contemporaries. The description in *Jakeman and Carver's Directory* of 1902 seems rather unenthusiastic: 'A conspicuous and unusual object in the English countryside'. Perhaps as Poole grew older and more cantankerous, and with his income reduced, he began to grow weary of the whole thing. Certainly he did not, as might have been expected, leave any money in his will towards the further improvement or maintenance of the church.

Architectural Style

The most remarkable thing abut the Italian Romanesque architecture of Hoarwithy is that it was built at a time when hardly any other new church in the country adopted this style.

There had been something of a revival of the Romanesque in England in the 19th century, either in a continental style or in the English Romanesque, i.e. Norman style. This had started with Picturesque neo-Norman castles, such as Eastnor, and in the 1840s a few Romanesque churches were built. Examples are Wilton in Wiltshire, an Italianate church richly endowed by the Herberts, Earls of Pembroke, of Wilton House, and at St Peters, Cheltenham in an English Norman style. But then English church architecture entered a period when only an historically accurate English Gothic Style was acceptable, and indeed only Gothic of the 'Middle Pointed' period, around 1300. This was deemed the high point of the style, coming after the more basic earlier forms but preceding the 'debased' version of the Perpendicular period.

Even when broader thinking came in around 1860 and different versions of English and continental Gothic were built, there was hardly any return to the Romanesque, and it was not until the 1890s that this again became more common, led by the Catholic Church, in particular with the neo-Byzantine Westminster Cathedral.

The only immediate precedent for Hoarwithy seems to be St Barnabas, Oxford, built between 1869 and 1872. This has an apse, round-headed windows and an Italianate campanile, not unlike Hoarwithy's, and, standing on low-lying ground near the Oxford canal has a definite feeling of Venice about it. The benefactor here was Thomas Combe, head of the Oxford University Press (and, incidentally a major patron of the Pre-Raphaelites, whom Seddon must have known). He was a zealous high churchman who wanted a church for Anglo-Catholic ritual and saw its early Christian style of architecture as a way of empha-sising the continuity of the church of his day with the early pre-Reformation Church.

This however would not seem to be William Poole's motivation at Hoarwithy. As we have seen his churchmanship was of a more rugged and down to earth kind. Hoarwithy has the liturgical arrangements recommended by the Oxford Movement and widely adopted by the 19th century Anglican Church, such as an altar raised by a series of steps and stalls for a surpliced choir, but, for all its Italian and Byzantine features, it is not designed to accommodate a High Church ritual. Nor is there anything at Hentland to suggest such a thing. Poole's views on Catholic ritual can be seen in an extract from his travel journal about watching a mass, 'with its endless signs and genuflections and the obsequious attend-ance of the red robed urchins who rang the bell with great vehemence, making it a point of honour to make as much noise as possible, and winking his success even at the most solemn moment to his fellow cherub, for the costume suggested this rather than a thing of flesh and blood, made to play and run and brace itself up for a real and active manhood.'

No, it was not churchmanship but aesthetics that led William Poole to build as he did. He dearly admired what he had seen in Italy and southern France, and no doubt carried images of this architecture either in drawings or in his head. He certainly did not despise English architecture of the Gothic period, writing of English cathedrals as 'these vener-able buildings, which taken as a whole are probably unmatched in any nation, in any creed upon the Earth.' However, he did not care for 'that painful type of modern Gothic of which England has to bear the odium.'

Another contributing factor may have been the constraints of the site. Prebendary Hawkshaw observed that Poole 'did not like to pull it down [the 1843 church], and he could not turn it into anything Gothic, so he built round the mission church the present Byzantine church which he is understood to have copied from one in the south of France.' Could this perhaps mean that, because of the steep slopes, there was just no room to add to the mission church the long chancel and transepts that would be *de rigueur* for a Victorian Gothic church?

Many of the earlier neo-Romanesque churches of the 19th century have a stark quality about them, caused by their angular profile and plain round windows, unrelieved by the mouldings and other decorative detail of a Gothic church. This also made them cheaper to build, which was often an attraction.

However, at Hoarwithy, Poole's money and Seddon's ingenuity have avoided this, largely by building in a red sandstone appropriate to the area, by wrapping the elegant cloister or loggia around the lower half of the south and west elevations (Plate 7), and by achieving a striking composition at the east end. This consists of the apse flanked by two lower half-apses, and, resting against the southern half-apse, the campanile tower with the opening to the cloister punched through it. What a dramatic spectacle this provides as one ascends the steps from the roadway!

Hoarwithy's Romanesque east front

Other, more subtle, details enliven the architecture (see also Plate 6). These include the use of Roman tiles on the roof, the round arched 'Lombardic' frieze just under the roofline at the east and on the campanile, and the way the shallow pitch of the cloister roof contrasts with the steeper pitch of the main nave roof. Notice also the way the roofline of the western range of the cloister, which becomes the narthex or porch for the west door, is higher than the southern range, and how the large opening as its south-west corner itself is not completely regular, being divided into three groups of four bays each, nor are the south windows of the nave above,

Hoarwithy Church from the south

which are in a 1:2:2:1 rhythm. The western elevation is perhaps the least satisfactory, the broad gable, inherited from the dimensions of the earlier church, being punctuated by three rows of windows, which seem small in proportion, one at the top, three in the middle and seven below.

There is a wealth of carving on the exterior. The capitals of the columns in the cloister have different animals and interlaced foliage, reminiscent of, although not directly copied from, the 12th-century Herefordshire School of Romanesque sculpture. In the tympanum over the west door is the figure of a seated Christ raising his hand in benediction surrounded by symbols of the Evangelists. This follows the 12th-century

Interlace carving on the cloister arcade

The clenched fist

Herefordshire School even more closely and one can see the influence of Poole's local history interests here.

Less obvious to the eye are the panels of sculpture with animals and interlace which run up the edges of the gable at the west end, whilst there is something even more strange round the corner, where an opening at the end of the western porch gives on to the north side of the building. A moulding over the arch of the opening terminates on one side in a carving of a snail and on the other a clenched fist. Whilst these could be just the whim of a carver, one supposes, knowing Poole's personality, that he must at least have sanctioned them and they probably meant something to him.

Interior Decorations and Furnishings

Amongst the writings transcribed by Poole into his commonplace book are extracts from William Morris's lectures, including his famous dictum, 'have nothing in your houses that you do not know to be useful or believe to be beautiful'. The interior of Hoarwithy Church shows that Poole set out to apply these words to the House of God. The results suggest that Poole, in his usual uncompromising way, went for the best of everything, and, if he could not achieve this, would rather have nothing at all, so that the nave, for example, remains largely bare.

It was reported in 1885 that the 'complete scheme of decoration' was in the hands of George Fox, an upmarket interior designer of country houses, who had worked at Longleat House, Wilton House, Warwick Castle and in the 1860s and 1870s at Eastnor Castle, which is where Poole may have come across him. It is debateable how much Fox actually contributed. Certainly some of the details were designed by Seddon, and it is difficult not to think that much was designed, or at least highly influenced, by Poole himself.

Starting at the west end, 10 of the 11 stained glass windows were designed by Seddon. They depict saints, patriarchs and angels in stiff poses, typical of early stained glass and chiming in well with the Byzantine east end of the church. They are in very pale colours and it is interesting that Poole in his travel journal notes that at Bordeaux Cathedral he saw 'some good modern glass ... the best I have ever seen — very pale in it colouring and subdued ... it did not offend — but rather produced actual pleasure — a good thing to say of modern glass.'

However, the single window at the apex of the west gable is quite different, being a splendid example of a William Morris window, made to a Burne-Jones design, and depicting a trumpeting angel in more definite colours that in the windows below. In the Morris catalogue it is dated September 1879, so must have been made for the original building campaign. Why this glass of such a different style from its companion windows was selected is a mystery. Seddon's connections with the Morris circle may have had something to do with it, although by this time Seddon was falling out with Morris over details of church restorations and what he felt to be a lack of transparency in Morris glass.

In the nave roof the stencilled design on the king posts and struts appears to be by Fox, being akin to some of his country house work. The fairly plain Gothic font is the sole survivor from the earlier chapel. The only stained glass in the nave is in one of the pairs of windows on the north side and depicts Judah (Plate 8) and Levi. These wonderfully lively figures were designed in about 1885 by Hugh Arthur Kennedy, a designer whom Seddon praised (and presumably recommended). The pulpit of white marble with maroon porphyry panels and ramped sides is based on examples in Italian churches. The mosaic pavement along the centre aisle is probably by Seddon, being similar to some of his tile designs. The brass lectern was the gift of Poole's parishioners on his resigning the living. There is a story that this is a back-handed tribute, because he was known not to care for furnishings in brass.

The glory of Hoarwithy is the richly designed chancel. The four columns in grey marble veined in red, their richly carved white marble capitals including figures of the four evangelists, the purple, white and green marbles of the chancel floor, and the altar in marble with

The chancel drawn by T. Raffles Davison in the History of Archenfield

A carved capital with evangelist's head in the chancel

lapis lazuli panels all contribute to this effect and evoke the great churches of Italy and southern France. In the words of the 1903 *History of the Deanery of Archenfield*, 'the whole chancel is a triumph of colouring, rich yet sober, and is a monument of exquisite taste throughout.'

The high point literally and figuratively of the chancel decoration is the gold mosaic of Christ as ruler of the world in the half dome above the altar (Plate 10). By the last quarter of the 19th century pictorial mosaics were not uncommon in Anglican churches — there is for instance a splendid Herefordshire example on the chancel walls of Moreton-on-Lugg by Salviati of Venice. But what is unusual in an Anglican church is to depict a figure of Christ in a dome in the style of a Byzantine Pantocrator. The best known example of this is in the mosaics installed at St Paul's Cathedral in the 1890s, but there a rather aesthetic Christ is depicted, sitting on a rainbow amongst clouds and surrounded by Pre-Raphaelite angels.

At Hoarwithy on the other hand, a stern authoritarian Christ holding the orb of the world in his hand, gazes out in a way more in keeping with the Byzantine churches that Poole would have seen and with his own religious attitudes. The mosaic was designed by Ada Currey who worked for the firm of James Powell & Son. At St Paul's the mosaic caused an outcry because of this 'Popish and Byzantine' work being included in a Renaissance Protestant Cathedral, and one can imagine that there were similar reactions in Herefordshire about the Hoarwithy version.

Seeming rather to intrude into the Byzantine scene are the rather bucolic choir stalls and prayer desk dating from 1883 and 1884 respectively. The stalls are made of oak from the Poole estates. They have semi-domed canopies in a Renaissance style, but above these are Gothic gables, on and between which are carved figures of 12 saints local to Wales and the border. Prebendary Hawkshaw said that Poole intended to have six male saints and six female saints, but in the event could only find three women.

The prayer desk has a front panel showing the miraculous birth of St Dubricius and the saint as Archbishop of Llandaff, whilst the sides depict lively scenes of St Dubricius miraculously producing cider from a previously empty cask, and him casting out a devil in the form of a bat. Hawkshaw said that the cider production was deliberately hidden on the side furthest from the congregation lest it should offend the weaker brethren, and that the bat was originally a real devil. Poole, however, did not like the idea of a devil between him and the congregation and got it changed, later receiving a bill for 'changing his satanic majesty into a bat'.

Poole was no doubt keen to install these depictions of local history and his parish's patron saint, but *The Builder* was not impressed. Their reviewer writes: 'whether it is worth while, or even in any sense suitable, to decorate a modern church with these rather foolish legends, to which, it will be observed, no moral whatever attaches, is a question we do not discuss, and which we should, perhaps, be told was out of our province. We give the desk merely as a good piece of work in design and execution, rather inclining to wish that both architect and carver may on another occasion light upon an historical subject better worth treating.' The architect of both the choir stalls and prayer desk was in fact Seddon, and the carver was Harry Hems of Exeter. Hems was a prolific carver of church fittings, who had a taste for publicity. He collected over 26,000 cuttings relating to his career and employed two clerks to keep them in albums. This trait can be detected at Hoarwithy because, of the fine things there, only the choir stalls and prayer desk found their way into the building trade press and because, most unusually Hems has inscribed his name on St Dubricius's miraculous cask.

Another feature of the chancel to be mentioned is the hanging lamps copied from those in St Mark's, Venice. They each depict the lion of St Mark, who once held a book inscribed *'Fiat Lux',* but these were all cut off when the lamps were stolen (although fortunately later recovered). Elsewhere in the metalwork is a head which seems to be a green man with foliage issuing from its mouth. The organ on the north side is a later inclusion, replacing a harmonium which accompanied Poole's choir. An 1895 report of a District Festival of Parish Choirs held at Hoarwithy says that the singing was 'aided by the excellent acoustic properties of the church'. The later organ stands in what was once the vestry and covers a mosaic of a peacock, said to be used by Poole to warn his choirboys against the sin of pride.

Finally there are the five stained glass Poole memorial windows in the apse, depicting Christ as the Light of the World in the centre flanked by the four Evangelists. These windows had previously contained plain glass so as to light the ceiling mosaic. They were designed by the elderly Seddon as a final tribute to his long-standing friend and patron. Architect and patron had combined over a period of some 30 years to leave us this remarkable building to admire and use today.

CHAPTER 4

Domesday Book entries for the district around Ross-on-Wye

Introduction

This chapter is written in two parts. The first part explains how the Domesday Book was compiled and the detail of the format. The second part lists the entries including that part of the English/ Welsh border country called 'Irchenfield' now known as Archenfield.

A.G. Bradley in his book *Herefordshire* published in 1915, says of 'Irchenfield': 'Domesday book tells us about these people [of Archenfield] and their particular territory, which like the county has more or less the shape of a diamond. Its two western sides are formed by the Worm Brook and the Monnow, its eastern sides by the twisting Wye. Its northern point almost touches Hereford, while its lower extremity actually touches Monmouth. This was the district of Archenfield.

'Now when the Mercians drove the Welsh over Offa's Dyke, the Silurian Welsh of Archenfield were permitted to remain unmolested, with the privilege of retaining their laws, their customs, and their language. They had probably encouraged this treatment in some way, and thoroughly justified it by a staunch loyalty to their Saxon ruler, earl or king, and a most determined hostility towards their Welsh brethren beyond the Dyke. They remained as it were a little state within a state, under their own Welsh laws, but sending six of their number as representatives to the Shire Mote at Hereford. The most curious privilege of those cherished by them is thus expressed, "When the Army marches against the Enemy (the Welsh) they form by custom the vanguard in the advance and the rearguard in the return." The Welsh of the 40 odd parishes of Archenfield, then, were never disturbed, nor were those of the adjoining district of Ewyas, afterwards attached, which came into the county under much the same curious conditions.'

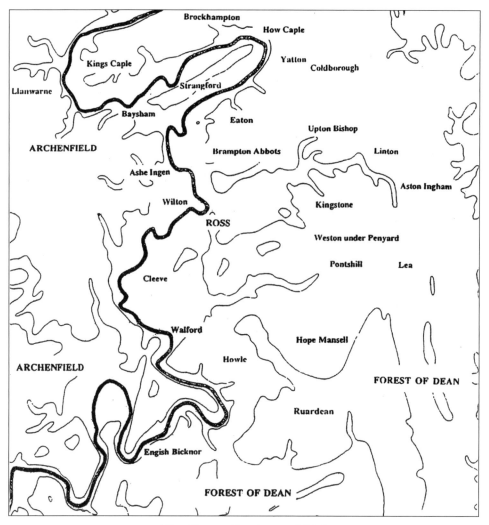

The Ross district at 1086

The map shows the landholdings that are listed in the Domesday Book. The exact location of villages and hamlets in 1086 is uncertain because the settlements sometimes occupied different sites than they do today. Nor does Domesday Book much about earlier landscapes. There is no clue that the Roman town of *Ariconium* once stood at Weston-under-Penyard and that an Iron Age fort and probable settlement were built on Chase Hill.

In 1086 the southern border of Herefordshire did not end at Bishopswood and Hope Mansell as it does today. Most of the Ross district east of the River Wye lay in Bromsash Hundred which also took in much of the Forest of Dean. West of the river was Archenfield. This was a borderland district rather than an English hundred. It reached west to Pontrilas and Garway, and, in 1066, north to Kilpeck. Although east of the Wye, Howle and Kings Caple also lay in Archenfield. Beyond the extent of the map were the probable Domesday landholdings of Ballingham and Harewood. The relative lack of information about settlements within Archenfield suggests an emptiness which is certainly false.

The contour lines are at approximately 100 and 600 feet above OD.

What is the Domesday Book?

The Domesday Book is a hand-written document, in two volumes, that was compiled during the year 1086AD, on the orders of King William. It is a survey of the people and places in England at that time. It is our earliest major public record and it provides information about some 13,000 places in the kingdom. For many localities the Domesday Book contains the oldest surviving written record.

Volumes 1 and 2 survive as original manuscripts in Latin. They are sometimes called Great and Little Domesday; occasionally they are referred to as Exchequer Domesday. Herefordshire is covered in Domesday Book Volume 1 and the information has been massively condensed from the data that was originally gathered by the king's commissioners. Volume 2 covers, with more detail, the counties of Essex, Norfolk and Suffolk, counties that are missing from Volume 1. The theory is that Volume 2 is a circuit return that reached Winchester too late for inclusion. Both volumes are held at the Public Record Office.

There is another other important and related manuscript, the Exon Domesday, which is held at Exeter Cathedral. This is an early but incomplete draft of the circuit return for the south-western counties and contains greater detail than appears in Volume 1.

From eastern England there also survive two 12th-century texts that were probably copies of drafts of the local returns, or information gathered for it. They are respectively the Inquisito Comitatus Cantabrigiensis and the Inquisito Eliensis. It is possible that these were copies made by landowners for their own use.

Other items of interest include an account written in 1086 by Robert Bishop of Hereford, of two inquests carried out in that year, one being Domesday and the other a geld inquest. Lastly, there are some later copies of Domesday information made by the royal court and by monasteries, nowadays termed Domesday Satellites. One of these, known as the Herefordshire Domesday, was made *c.*1160-70. It has some contemporary updating in the margins that has helped to identify some of the Herefordshire 'manors' mentioned in Volume 1. It is

William the Conqueror and his half brothers (from the Bayeux Tapestry)

preserved at Balliol College and a facsimile was published by the Pipe Roll Society in 1950. Copies are held by Hereford City Library.

The name of Domesday is early but not original. A document of *c.*1176 relates that the survey was, by then, '… called by the native English, Domesday, i.e. the Day of Judgement … [because] when this book is appealed to … its sentence cannot be quashed or set aside with impunity.'

Why was it compiled?

No written record has survived to tell us the exact reasons for the making of the Domesday Book. The Anglo-Saxon Chronicle states that the king was at Gloucester with his counsellors at midwinter 1085-86, and that he held 'very deep speech with his wise men about the land, how it was held, and with what men …'.

We can only speculate as to why King William caused this survey, or inquest, to be compiled. However, the resulting 'book' had many uses. It recorded who held land from the king and the king's own royal manors; hence the survey could be used as a land register. It also recorded the size of each holding and the tax assessment. Thus the king could check that he was not being cheated by those paying the taxes, or by the collectors.

Some of the land carried a duty for the holder to render military services; thus the king had a record of where soldiers might be raised in time of need. The survey would also assist the king and his officials to have a better knowledge of the geography of the kingdom in an age when maps did not exist.

The Victorian scholars, J.H. Round (1895) and F.W. Maitland (1897) saw the purpose of the survey or inquest as a 'geld book' or taxation document. Later minds, in particular J.E.A. Jolliffe (1937) and V.H. Galbraith (1961), viewed it as a register of fiefs and titles that underpinned the feudal ideas that arrived in England with the coming of the Normans.

In Anglo-Saxon England quite a lot of land was owned by individuals. When William won the English crown he decreed that the kingdom and all its land belonged to him. He granted lands to his followers not as gifts or freeholds, but as leases to tenants. Each holder had to swear an oath requiring fealty to William, and thereafter pay services and taxes to him. William's new system of landholding laid the foundations of the feudal system which later developed more fully in England than in any other part of Europe.

How was it compiled?

The king sent reliable officials and scribes to all parts of his kingdom. They gathered the required information by asking a standard set of questions. This type of exercise was called an Inquest. The Anglo-Saxon Chronicle records:

January: Ploughing

… the King had muckle thought and deep speech with his wise-
men about this land, how it was set, and with what men. Then he
sent his men over all England into each shire and let them find out
how many hundred hides were in that shire, and what the king had
himself of land or cattle in those lands, or what rights he ought to
have in the twelve month from the shire. Also he let them write
about how much land his archbishops had, and his bishops, and his
abbots, and his earls and, though I tell it longer, what or how much
each man had, that was landsitting in England, in land or cattle,
and how much it was worth. So very narrowly did he let them sheir
it out that there was not a hide nor a yardland nor – it is shameful
to tell, though he thought it no shame to do – so much as an ox or
a cow or a swine was left, that was not set down in his writ: and all
these writs were brought to him afterwards.

Today, England is administered through its civil parishes, districts, counties (shires),
and regions. In 1086, the administrative units used were the 'manor', the hundred and the
shire. This was the Anglo-Saxon system rather than a Norman one. The Norman administrators organised the survey data into a standardised format which they presented in
Domesday Book county by county. For each county there was a numbered list of landholders starting with the king and then descending through archbishops, bishops, abbots,
and other church holders, followed by earls, barons and on down to the smallest holders.
Then followed the holdings and associated information for each, arranged under hundreds.
To see the result, readers should refer to a facsimile such as the 20th-century edition by
Phillimore, or to the coloured county facsimiles reproduced by the Ordnance Survey during

the 1860s. In this account the entries for the Ross district are arranged alphabetically and thus the original Domesday layout is not followed. The terms used in the local Domesday entries are explained in the glossary at the end of this chapter.

In each shire the king's officials met with the county sheriff and the officials of the hundreds. Local juries were also sworn in to validate the information. At each place the king's officials posed the same questions:

> What is the name of the manor?
> Who held it in King Edward the Confessor's time?
> Who holds it now?
> How many hides are there?
> How many plough teams are held by the lord and the tenants?
> How many villagers, smallholders, slaves?
> How many freemen and sokemen?
> How much woodland is there?
> How much meadow and pasture?
> How many mills and fisheries?
> How much land has been added or lost?
> What was the manor worth in 1066 and now?
> How much land was held by freemen at the time of King Edward,
>   when King William granted it, and now?

The answers to these questions were recorded by the scribes and conveyed to some central place, probably Winchester, where the information was copied and re-arranged under the name of the person who held each manor. The works of V.H. Galbraith, *The making of Domesday Book* (1961) and, especially, *Domesday Book – Its place in administrative history* (1974), contain fascinating, deductive accounts of how this was done.

Scholars have been publishing accounts of their research on Domesday Book since the 1700s. Galbraith (1974) contains a useful review of work carried out from 1833 to 1918, whilst Roffe (2002) covers relevant work published up to 2002.

What do the Domesday entries tell us?

Each entry is recorded in Latin in a condensed and abbreviated format. Even the precise, modern translations are so short of words that they do not seem to make much sense on first reading.

The key to understanding the information is to remember that each entry consists of the answers, in the order of the standard questions that were asked. Where there was no answer, the entry simply passes on to the next question.

The other obstacle to understanding lies in the jargon. Words such as lordship, hides, virgates, sesters etc. conceal meaning and implications that are not obvious. The glossary and the notes supplied under each entry should help to explain them.

The entries tell us something about the settlement and landscape of the locality at that time. They record the existing estates, or 'manors', and what they were called in 1086. However, we are not told where the villages and hamlets lay and we should not assume that the settlements stood exactly where they do today. Some of the Domesday 'manors' did not thrive in later centuries; a few shrank to hamlets or even single farms, and some seem to have disappeared completely.

These Domesday 'manors' were not the Saxon vills nor the later manors, although the latter developed from them. The 'manor' of Domesday was a land unit or holding, an estate or a territory, which someone controlled. This person or institution was termed the lord. The sense is that of a landlord rather than a noble.

The entries tell us who the landlords were and they give an idea of the amount of land in the 'manor'. We learn from the number of ploughs how much was arable and from other questions how much was pasture, meadow and waste.

Some of the entries describe fairly simple estates or 'manors' such as Brampton and Ross. Others like Cleeve with Wilton were more complicated and they had 'sub manors' within them. These facts hint as to how the estates were organised in Anglo-Saxon, and earlier, times.

Each entry shows how completely the Normans had taken control of England since the Conquest. Almost without exception the original Anglo-Saxon landholders had been replaced by Normans and others, many of whom had assisted William as soldiers in the invasion. But William did not grant the entire land of the kingdom to others. He kept the lands that had belonged to King Edward (and after to King Harold, although Domesday Book rarely refers to Harold as a king). Such land was termed 'Terra Regis' i.e. land of the king (royal demesne). Much of this land was leased in the normal way but some estates operated as royal manors. Linton and Cleeve are good examples in the Ross district. William also acquired the lands of any landholders who rebelled.

A ship of the fleet of Duke William transporting troops for the invasion of England (from the Bayeux Tapestry)

Computation of the entries in Domesday Book indicate that over 15% of the cultivated land was in possession of the king in 1086 and to this must be added some 25 or so royal forests including locally the Forest of Dean and other woods near Ross. The Church was also a major landholder. In 1066, 24.6% of the land of Herefordshire belonged to the abbeys and churches and this grew to 29.6% by 1086. In Gloucestershire the figures were 31.5% and 31.8%. In Worcestershire the Anglo-Saxon church in 1066 held a staggering 65.5%, but this figure had reduced to 52.9% by 1086 (Ballard, 1906). Individual entries also show that gifts and grants to French abbeys of local lands and churches were underway by 1086. The information in the Domesday entries is a valuable historical tool. It gives us a glimpse of England under the last Anglo-Saxon administration and it provides detail about the local area in the Norman Period, just 20 years after the Battle of Hastings. This is a very useful point from which to study the growth and development of localities and settlements. This subject is further considered in the section on boundaries.

The local landscape, 1066-86

Much statistical work has been carried out on the information contained in the Domesday Book, especially by H.C. Darby and I.B. Terrett in *The Domesday Geography of Midland England* (1954), and by J.N. Jackson in the Woolhope Naturalists' Field Club centenary volume *Herefordshire* (also published in 1954).

Darby and Terrett systematically present data on such matters as settlements, prosperity, population, hides, ploughlands, plough teams, values, Welsh custom, woodland, forests, enclosures, meadowland, fisheries, wastes, salt, mills, churches, urban life, iron and sheep. However, although the work contains much useful detail, it is dominated by statistics. Rowley (1983 and 1986) has published more readable accounts of the landscape in the early, and later, Norman period.

From their work and from the entries themselves, we can begin to envisage the area around Ross as a landscape of woodland and royal forest interspersed with agricultural settlements. One suspects that in 1086, the area that stretches

Harold and Stigant (from the Bayeux Tapestry)

from Lea, through Hope Mansell, to Bishops Wood was not much different from what is there today, apart from the more recent buildings, agriculture and tarmacadam. However, to the north and west of Ross-on-Wye, there were probably rather more trees and woods than now. Ross was still an agricultural settlement and a century would pass before it began to develop into a town. Although the Domesday entries tell of the settlements and the size of their agricultural lands, we do not know much more about them. It is known that some late Anglo-Saxon settlements appear to have had open field systems and, if they existed in south Herefordshire, these were most likely to be found to the north and west of Ross. Seebohm (1883) and Hart (2000) provide details of the royal estate of Tidenham, Glos., just before the Conquest. It is possible that the 'manors' of Ross and Cleeve were organised in a similar way.

Darby and Terrett calculated the number of heads of households in the county to be 4,453 whilst Sir Henry Ellis's study calculated a figure of 5,368 including tenants-in-chief, under-tenants and urban dwellers (Ellis, 1883). To arrive at a total population for the county it is necessary to multiply these totals by an estimated number per household. J.N. Jackson used a multiplier of 3.5 to produce a total county population range of 16,000 to 20,000. Such figures are highly tentative and it should be remembered that the average life span was short. Recent work on historic populations suggests that previous figures may be too low. Dyer (1993 and 1994) provides some useful discussion and references.

Darby and Terrett indicate that the number of people per square mile in the Ross area was around six, slightly less than the eight of central Herefordshire. There is no data for Archenfield, part of which lay in the Ross district. Most of the settlements were small and they lay in the borderland between England and Wales. There was no precise national boundary.

County, hundred and manorial boundaries

The Mercian shire counties were created in late Anglo-Saxon times, probably before 1016, to facilitate the collection of men and ship money for defence. Herefordshire's boundaries were influenced to some extent by the Diocesan boundary that had existed since the late 7th century (Hillaby 1976; Thorn and Thorn 1983), but the western boundary with Wales was uncertain. Thus the county once included part of what is now south Shropshire, and much of the Forest of Dean, now within Gloucestershire. The 'manors' of Alvington, Ruardean, Redbrook, Staunton and Whippington, now in Gloucestershire, were recorded in the Herefordshire folio and the parishes of some of them remained in the Hereford diocese until 1542. Moore (1987), discusses some of the previously unidentified Herefordshire entries in this part of Gloucestershire.

Hundreds were the administrative subdivisions of the shires, each with its hundred court to oversee the collection of taxes and other matters. This is why the lands of each tenant-in-chief are arranged under hundreds in Domesday Book. In 1086, Herefordshire contained 19 hundreds, plus the district of Archenfield. The boundaries of several are not known. Only five of their names survive among the 11 hundreds of the present day. The extent and existence of individual hundreds varied over the centuries. In 1086, Ross lay within the Hundred of Bromsash. This was a large hundred that was bounded to the east by Gloucestershire and to the west by Archenfield. Today, Ross-on-Wye lies in the Hundred of Greytree.

Individual hundreds consisted of a number of 'manors' or estates. These would have possessed defined boundaries that must have originated long before 1066. These boundaries would be well known to their lords and residents, and also to the officials of the hundreds.

During the 12th century, manorial lords often founded churches in their manors. In time this led to another set of boundaries — those that defined the exact extent of parishes. Just as manorial boundaries were important for legal and tax reasons, parish boundaries defined the area from which churches gained their congregations, their tithes and other income. Manorial and parish boundaries were often coterminous. They have importance for local historians.

The first editions of the Ordnance Survey large scale plans depict parish and other boundaries before much change and rationalisation was made to them. They thus provide valuable clues to past landscapes. Some parts of them stretch back to Domesday and before. Angus Winchester (2000) has produced an excellent account of parish and township boundaries.

Classes of people listed in the Domesday Book

Domesday Book was not a social history book but a register of landholders and taxation. It uses terms to denote various classes of people. These terms doubtless had a clear meaning at the time but no definitions were handed down to us. The definitions below are what we have come to understand as the meanings:

The Lord of a Domesday 'manor' was the person or institution holding land direct from the king. In the entries below we find this was sometimes a person and at others a church or a monastery. The king kept some 'manors' for himself and in these he was the lord.

Freemen were non-noble holders of land.

Smallholders (Bordarius) were low in rank and they held substantially less land than the villagers. The normal holding was about 5 acres but many had only a garden with their home. They were agricultural labourers. Like the villagers they were tied to the lord. The Anglo-Saxon equivalent was the kotsetla or cottager.

Slaves belonged directly to the lord. They had no land and they were bought and sold. Their children were automatically slaves. Sometimes they were freed to relieve the lord of the burden of feeding them when they became less able to work. Freed slaves were sometimes called boors. The church frequently owned slaves.

Thegns were Anglo-Saxon landholders or lords of middle rank, often a soldier who held his land in return for military service. Post 1066, the term thane meant a person holding land from the king by special grant.

Villagers (villanus) were the highest ranking tenants of the manor. The normal amount of land held by a villager was a virgate, also known as a yardland, of 30 acres, but some had less. Although not slaves, the villagers were tied to the lord through their land. They were not free to leave the lord or the manor. To the lord the villagers paid rent and customary services such as a number of days ploughing the lordship land, harvesting, fencing and so forth. The Anglo-Saxon equivalent was the gebur.

Welshmen are mentioned in some entries. The reason for this is not clear but it may be to note that they paid the Welsh customary dues of honey and sheep rather than money. In the entry for Archenfield the Welshmen had specific duties to perform for the lord.

The entries for the Ross District

The entries are arranged alphabetically by their modern names. The name of the Domesday hundred appears next, followed by the 1086 landholder. The translated entry follows. The 1086 name of the holding is italicised in upper case. Interpretative comment follows each entry.

Archenfield

> In *ARCENFELDE* the King has 100 men, less 4, who have 73 ploughs, with their men. In customary dues they give 41 sesters of honey, 20s. in place of the sheep that they used to give; 10s. for hearth tax. They do not pay tax or other customary dues, except that they march in the King's army if ordered. When a freeman

dies there, the King has his horse and arms. The King has one ox when a villager dies. This land was laid waste by King Gruffydd and Bleddyn before 1066; therefore what it was like at that time is not known.

This district adjacent to Ross-on-Wye and lying between the Rivers Wye and Monnow, was known as Archenfield. It was won from the Welsh King Gruffyd by Harold *c*.1063. It existed as a distinct district, rather than as a hundred and it formed a border area between England and Wales. Archenfield had special customs and some of them are listed in Domesday Book, in addition to the entry above. They included aspects of law dealing with killing, thefts and concealment. They also note that the king had three churches in Archenfield and that the priests carried the king's despatches into Wales. Before 1066 it was the custom of the men of Archenfield to form the vanguard for an army advancing into Wales and to form the rearguard on its return.

The actual Domesday entry for Archenfield is unusual in that it encompasses a district rather than the individual landholdings it contained, some of which appear under their respective landholders. These were: Ashe Ingen, Baysham, Birch, Garway before 1066, Howle Hill, Kilpeck, Kings Caple, Llanwarne Much Birch, Penebedoc, Pontrilas and, possibly, Strangford. Both Howle Hill and Kings Caple lay east of the Wye whilst Wilton, part of Cleeve, lay west of the Wye but not in Archenfield. That Archenfield was formerly

a Welsh district is shown by the Welsh customary dues of sheep and honey.

The place-name *Arcenfelde* may derive from urchin or hedgehog thus giving 'felde or land of the hedgehog'. This animal appears in heraldic arms of the Abrahalls of Foy, and was later used by John Kyrle of Ross for his crest and other applications.

Ashe Ingen (part of Cleeve, near Ross-on-Wye)
In Archenfield
Land of the King. Held by Alfred of Marlborough.

> Before 1066 there were in this manor [Cleeve] 2 hides less a virgate which are in *ASHE* [Ingen]. Alfred of Marlborough now holds them. [Earl] Harold held them at the time of his death. The Shire states that they belong to the Manor of Cleeve. [Elsewhere is stated] Alfred also holds *ASCIS*. It was waste before 1066. I man with 1½ ploughs. He pays 10s in revenue.

This was a small manor north of Bridstow. It is now not much more than a single farm. At Domesday it was part of the larger manor of Cleeve. A virgate was 30 acres.

Aston Ingham
In Bromsash Hundred
Held by Ansfrid of Cormeilles.

> Godfrey holds *ESTUNE* from him [Ansfrid]. King Edward held it. 2 hides which pay tax. 1 plough in lordship. 4 villagers and 9 smallholders with 8 ploughs. 8 other men who pay nothing; 2 ploughmen. A mill which pays nothing. Value before 1066 was 50s. Now 100s.

This was a small simple manor with plenty of arable. Formerly it was a royal manor. It had prospered under new lords and doubled in value over the 20 years from 1066. It may have included what is now Aston Crews.

Ballingham?
In Archenfield
Land of the king.

> Gilbert son of Thorold holds a manor there. 4 free men there with 4 ploughs. They pay 4 sesters of honey and 16 pence in customary dues.

This entry, folio 1.51, follows Garway folio 1.50 which in turn follows the entry for Archenfield. No specific place is recorded and thus the 'there' of the entry is ill defined. Thorn and Thorn place the entry to Ballingham. 1.52 is also nameless, but Thorn and Thorn consider it is Harewood.

Baysham
In Archenfield
Land of the king.

> *BAISSAN*. Walter holds it from him. In the time of King Edward Merwin held it. 2 ploughs in lordship; 14 men with 7 ploughs. They pay 5 shillings in customary dues. Value 30s.

Baysham lies in the neck of the Sellack peninsula, west of the Wye, probably represented by modern Baysham Court and surroundings. There was considerable arable farming.

Bridstow

There was no entry. The area was part of Cleeve Manor (see below).

Brampton Abbotts

In Bromsash Hundred
Held by St Peter's Abbey, Gloucester and St Guthlac's Church, Hereford.

> St Peter's Church of Gloucester holds *BRVNTVNE*. 2 hides; 1 pays tax; the other is free from tax and from every customary due. In this free hide 3 ploughs in lordship; 5 villagers and 5 smallholders with 5 ploughs. 16 slaves. Value £4.
> In the other hide 1 villager and 1 smallholder with one plough. A mill at 8s. Value 10s.
>
> St Guthlac's Church holds *BRVNTVNE*. 1 hide which pays tax. Land for 2 ploughs. It was and is waste. However it pays 5s.

The holding of 3 hides has been subdivided, probably well before 1066; the 1 hide portion may have been a thane's holding before passing to St Guthlac's. It was out of cultivation and had been so at least since 1066. In contrast, the portion held by St Peter's is tenanted and farmed. Notice how the abbey's own farm is in the free hide and thus exempt from taxes and dues. Note also the number of slaves (probably working the Abbey's farm) compared with the numbers of villagers and smallholders.

Brockhampton

In Greytree Hundred
Held by the Canons of the Church of Hereford.

The Wye Valley at Capler by S.P.B. Mais, c.1937

In *CAPELFORE* there are 5 English hides which pay tax, and 3 Welsh hides which pay 6s. a year to the canons. In the 5 hides is 1 plough in lordship. 8 villagers with 7 ploughs. Meadow 3 acres. In the time of King Edward 70s., later, and now as much.

This was a sizeable landholding belonging to the church canons. The home or lordship farm's arable was small with just one plough, but it may also have used those of the villagers by customary service.

Cleeve

In Bromsash Hundred

Land of the king.

> The King holds *CLIVE*. Earl Harold held it. 14½ hides, with a detached part called *WILTONE*.
>
> In lordship 4 ploughs; 20 villagers, a reeve, and 11 smallholders with 16 ploughs. 9 male and 5 female slaves and 1 ploughman. 2 mills at 6s. and a fishery which pays nothing. To this manor belong as many Welshmen as have 8 ploughs; they pay 10½ sesters of honey and 6/5d. St Mary's of Cormeilles holds the church of this manor, a priest and the tithe, with 1 villager.
>
> In King William's Forest there is as much land of this manor as paid 6 sesters of honey and 6 sheep with lambs before 1066.
>
> Of this manor William Baderon holds 1 hide and 3 virgates; Godfrey holds 1 virgate.
>
> Roger of Lacy holds half a fishery which belonged to this manor before 1066; 25 measures of salt from Droitwich then belonged there also.
>
> At that time there were in this manor 2 hides, less 1 virgate, which are in *ASHE* [Ashe Ingen]. Alfred of Marlborough holds them now. Harold was holding them when he died. The Shire states that they are this manor's. This manor pays £9 10s. of blanched pence.

This was a large manor won by Harold from the Welsh not long before he became King of England. At the Conquest all Harold's lands passed directly to William. It lay south of Ross and north of Walford presumably including what is now Hom Green and Hill Court. Wilton was a detached portion west of the Wye. There was a large arable demesne farm and numerous tenant villagers and smallholders also engaged in arable cultivation. It appears that the Welshmen, perhaps those in Wilton, owed or rendered the services of 8 further ploughs.

The church with priest, tithes and tenant had been granted to an abbey in France. The holdings of William Baderon and Alfred of Marlborough were probably sub-manors based on an earlier thane's holdings. Cleeve, like Linton, was a complex estate. Both warrant further research. The words relating to salt are unclear in their meaning. They may suggest that some of the renders made to the king of salt from Droitwich were destined here; possibly for the salting of fish caught from the River Wye.

The mention of some of the manor's land lying within the king's forest suggests that the boundary of the Forest of Dean ran as far north as this in 1086. Alternatively, local woodland belonged to the king and was thus termed forest.

Coldborough
In Bromsash Hundred
Held by Durand of Gloucester.

> Durand also hold *CALCHEBERGE* and Bernard from him. Gunnar held it. I hide which pays tax. 1 plough in lordship and one slave. The value is and was 64d.

This was a small manor, very similar to Weston and Pontshill which Durand also held. The area today is Coldborough Park. It would be interesting to research the park's present day, and older, boundaries to see if it is based on the Domesday Coldborough 'manor'. See also Yatton.

Eaton, The Hill of
In Bromsash Hundred
Held by Alfred of Marlborough.

> *EDTUNE*. Earl Harold held it. 2½ hides which pay tax. 1 plough in lordship. 9 villagers, and 6 smallholders with 7 ploughs. Value before 1066 was 50s.; later and now 40s.

Eaton is north of Ross-on-Wye, half a mile north of Brampton Abbots. Today it is known as the Hill of Eaton. At Domesday it was a medium sized manor with plenty of arable farming, but it had declined in value since the Conquest. Today it comprises a few scattered dwellings situated on ancient roads that run down to the Wye.

Fownhope
In Greytree Hundred
Held by Hugh Donkey.

> Hugh also holds *HOPE*. Thorkell White held it. 15 hides, ten pay tax. In lordship are 3 ploughs. 14 villagers and 10 smallholders. 2 priests with a church which has ½ hide of land. A reeve, a smith and

a carpenter. They have 25 ploughs. 18 male and 3 female slaves; a mill at 5s. 3 fisheries which pay 300 eels. The lord has 12s. 4d. from the waste land. Hugh gave one member of this manor to a man-at-arms of his, with one plough.
Value before 1066 £12; later £15, now £16.

Fownhope was a large landholding. Much arable land is indicated by the many people and the 25 ploughs. Note the mention of a church with 2 priests.

Foy
No entry. Possibly within the manor of Strangford, on the Sellack peninsula.

Garway
In Archenfield before 1066.
Land of the king.

> *LAGADEMAR* was in Archenfield in the time of King Edward. There were 4 carucates of land. Herman holds this land. 3 small-holders with 3 oxen.

Garway lay on the western edge of Archenfield. For carucate, see the glossary.

Gorsley
No entry. Some of what later became Gorsley probably lay in Linton but much of the area was probably waste and woodland e.g. modern Queen's Wood.

Harewood
See note under Ballingham.

Hoarwithy
No entry. Possibly lay within the manor of Kings Caple.

Garway Church as illustrated by H.T. Timmins

Holme Lacy

Dinedor Hundred
Held by the canons of Hereford.

> In *HAMME* there are 6 hides that pay tax. 2 ploughs in lordship. 16 villagers, a priest, a reeve, a Frenchman and 4 boors. Between them they have 20½ ploughs. 1 male and 2 female slaves; meadow 10 acres; woodland ½ league long and wide.
>
> A church called *LADGVERN* is in this manor... [see Llanwarne below.]

A medium sized manor with a great number of ploughs. The 'boors' were slaves who had been freed. There was ample meadowland for hay with which to feed plough oxen during the winter. Although far from Ross, Holme Lacy is included because of the connection with Llanwarne in Archenfield.

Hope Mansell

Hundred of Bromsash
Held by William son of Baderon.

> William son of Baderon holds *HOPE*. Leofric and Edwulf held it as two manors. 4 hides which pay tax. Solomon holds it from William. In lordship 2 ploughs; 1 villager and 1 smallholder with 1½ ploughs. Value before 1066, 40s.; now the same.
> A third part of this manor lay in the lands of St Peter's Church of Gloucester, in the time of King Edward, according to the testimony of the County.

Mowing in August (from the Bayeux Tapestry)

This was clearly two landholdings, possibly of 2 hides each, held by the Anglo-Saxons Leofric and Edwulf. The two holdings have been combined and are now held by the Norman William who appears to have leased the holding out to Solomon. The holding seems to comprise the lord's farm and two other tenant farms.

How Caple
In Greytree
Held by the canons of the church of Hereford.

> In *CAPEL* are 5 hides which pay tax. In lordship 3 ploughs. 9 villagers and 1 smallholder with 8 ploughs. 1 male and 2 female slaves. A mill at 3s. meadow 8 acres. Value in 1066, 70s.; later and now 60s.

Another sizeable estate with plenty of arable cultivation.

Howle Hill
In Archenfield
Land of the king.

> Godric Mapson holds *HVLLA*. Taldus held it in King Edward's time. In lordship 2 ploughs; 4 ploughmen; 1 female slave. 12 villagers and 12 smallholders with 11 ploughs; they pay 18 sesters of honey. 1 smith. 1 fishery. Value 40s.

Howle Hill today is not a village; at Domesday it may have been a dispersed settlement with extensive arable cultivation, on the upland plateau on the English side of the River Wye, yet in Archenfield. Payments of honey were a Welsh custom, used in Archenfield. At Domesday Howle Hill also included part of the River Wye, possibly at modern Bishopswood, where the fishery may have been. Note the reference to iron-working implied by the presence of a smith.

Kilpeck
In Archenfield
Land of the king.

> William son of Norman holds *CHIPEETE*. Cadiand held it in the time of King Edward. In lordship 3 ploughs; 2 slaves. 4 ploughmen and 57 men with 19 ploughs; they pay 15 sesters of honey and 10s. they pay no other tax or service except in the army.

Kilpeck was the most northerly settlement with a specific entry in Archenfield. There was extensive arable farming. Payments followed Welsh custom. The army services are described under Archenfield.

Kings Caple
In Archenfield
Land of the king.

> William [of Baderon] also holds *CAPE*, and Walter from him. King Edward held it in lordship. 5 Welshmen with 5 ploughs; they pay 5 sesters of honey, five sheep with lambs and 10d. Value 30s. I Frenchman with one plough.

A small royal manor with some Welsh customary payments. Let out.

Kingstone (near Weston-under-Penyard)
In Bromsash Hundred
Held by St Mary's Church of Cormeilles.

> St Mary's Church of Cormeilles holds 2 hides in *CHINGESTUNE*. They pay tax and do service in Gloucestershire, but the men who live there plea in this Hundred to give and receive right.

This small manor illustrates the problems of being close to a boundary. Today, Kingstone is a small hamlet between Weston and Rudhall.

Lea
In Bromsash Hundred
Held by St Peter's Abbey, Gloucester.

> The Church itself holds *LECCE* by gift of Walter of Lacy. Ansgot held it in the time of King Edward. 1 hide which pays tax. He could go where he would. In lordship 1 plough; 2 slaves; 1 smallholder. The value was and is 10s. 1 more plough possible.

This was a small landholding. The Anglo-Saxon Ansgot was not tied to this estate. That 'He could go where he would' indicates that he was not tied to a more powerful lord. His Norman successor, Walter, subsequently gave Lea to the church, presumably to ensure prayer for the fate of his soul. '1 more plough possible' shows that the manor was thought to be capable of more cultivation. A further part of Lea appears under Linton, see below.

Linton

In Bromsash Hundred

Held by the king. One small portion, formerly in Lea, was held by William son of Baderon.

> King William holds *LINTVNE*. King Edward held it. There were 5 hides. It paid a fourth part of one night's revenue. Now it is extremely reduced. In lordship 3 ploughs; 10 villagers and 5 small-holders with 12 ploughs. 6 slaves; a mill at 8d.
>
> 1 Frenchman who holds half a hide which paid 4s. in the time of King Edward. This manor, as it is now, pays £10 of white pence.
>
> Of this manor St Mary's of Cormeilles holds the church, a priest with his land, and the entire tithe, and 1 villager with 1 virgate of land.
>
> Ansfrid of Cormeilles holds 2 hides of this manor; two villagers and 9 ploughs.
>
> William of Baderon holds 1 virgate of land which lay there in King Edward's time.
>
> Ilbert the Sheriff has in his revenue of Archenfield all the customary dues of honey and sheep which belonged to this manor before 1066.
>
> William son of Norman has from it 6 sesters of honey, 6 sheep with lambs and 12d.
>
> William son of Baderon holds one virgate of land at *LECCE*, the King's manor. Leofstan held it; he could not withdraw from this manor. 1 plough; nothing more. The value was and is 3s.

Unlike Lea, Linton was a large and complicated holding. It was a royal manor in King Edward's time and it contributed a quarter of the cost of board and lodging for the king and his court for one night. There were plenty of ploughs and people. They were served by a church with a priest although the church and its tithes had been gifted previously to an abbey in France. There were various sub-holdings in the manor. The existence of dues to Archenfield, despite Linton being in the English Hundred of Bromsash, suggests a loss from Wales in late Anglo-Saxon times.

Llangarron

No entry, presumably covered under Archenfield.

Llanwarne

In Archenfield but a dependency of Holme Lacy in Dinedor Hundred
Held by the canons of Hereford.

> A church called *LADGVERN* belongs to this manor [the entry
> appears under Holme Lacy].
> 3 ploughs there, but this land of the church does not pay tax. A
> priest pays 2s. from it. Roger of Lacy holds this land under the
> Bishop. Earl Harold held this manor wrongfully because it is for
> the canon's supplies. King William restored it to Bishop Walter.
> Value before 1066 £9; now £8.

This was part of Archenfield and mis-appropriated from the Bishop of Hereford by Earl
Harold shortly before he became king.

Much Birch

In Archenfield
Land of the king. Held by Roger of Lacy.

Sentinels of the Marches, c.1937 (S.P. Mais)

> Roger of Lacy holds *MAINAVR*. Costelin held it before 1066. Now his son holds from Roger. There are 4 ploughs. He pays 6 sesters of honey and 10s. Roger has a Welshman who pays 5s. and 1 sester of honey.

The size is not stated but is sufficient for 4 ploughs. Note the sub-letting from king to Roger of Lacy to Costelin's son; also the Welsh customary payment of honey.

Penebedoc
In Archenfield
Land of the king.

> Roger [of Lacy] also holds *PENEBEDOC* and Novi holds it from him. He also held it in the time of King Edward. 4 ploughs. The land pays 6 sesters of honey and 10s.

It is not known where this 'manor' lay in Archenfield.

Peterstow
No entry. The area may have been within Wilton and thus part of the manor of Cleeve.

Pontshill
In Bromsash Hundred
Held by Durand of Gloucester.

> Durand holds *PANCHILLE*, and Bernard [holds it] from him. Gunnar held it; he could go where he would. 1 hide which pays tax. 6 smallholders have three ploughs. The value was and is 6s.

Pontshill today is a small hamlet set between Lea and Weston-under-Penyard. At Domesday it was a small manor with its own 'free' lord, and a handful of tenant smallholders.

Pontrilas
In Archenfield
Land of the king.

> Alfred of Marlborough holds *ELWISTONE*. Earl Harold held it. 1½ ploughs in lordship. A priest, 3 villagers, 4 smallholders and 4 slaves with 5 ploughs. They give 3 sheep. Value 30s.

Pontrilas was the most westerly settlement of Archenfield. Beyond, lay the upper reaches of the River Monnow draining the Black Mountains.

Ross

In Bromsash Hundred

Held by the church of Hereford and mentioned as belonging to the canons.

> In *ROSSE* 7 hides that pay tax. In lordship 1 plough; another would be possible. 18 villagers, 6 smallholders, and a priest with 23 ploughs. 3 slaves; a mill at 6s. 8d.; meadow 16 acres. The woodland is in the King's protection. The villagers pay 18s. in dues.

See also the last line of the entry for Upton Bishop.

The lands of Rosse were large and under considerable arable cultivation. The canons' home farm was small, so presumably they derived income from the many tenant farms. The mill may have been at Brookend. The 16 acres of meadow would be the best grasslands for hay needed to feed the plough oxen during winter. Although not mentioned as such, the presence of a church is indicated by the priest.

The woodland was probably on Chase and Penyard Hills and possibly part of the royal Forest of Dean. Hart (1947, p.168), reports the entry to mean 'the wood of Ross was included in the Forest, as was also some woodland pertaining the manor of Cleeve …', whilst Thorn and Thorn 1983, use the words 'The wood is in the King's Enclosure'. But the Domesday scribe wrote the words '*Silua. e[st] in defensu regis*' which suggests 'The wood is in the King's protection'. There are no surviving written bounds of local royal forests in 1086, and none before the Forest of Dean was expanded between 1150 and 1216.

In 1282, the year of the oldest surviving perambulation, Chase and Penyard Hills were within the bounds of the Forest of Dean, although the bishop's chase at modern Bishops Wood was outside the bounds, having been disafforested in 1260 (Hart, 1947). Chases were private hunting grounds regulated under common law. Royal forests were regulated by forest law and the right of hunting in them belonged exclusively to the king.

Ruardean

In Bromsash Hundred

Held by William son of Baderon.

> William son of Baderon also holds *RUUIRDIN*. Soloman holds from him. Hadwic held it. 4 hides pay tax. 3 ploughs would be possible in lordship. 1 smallholder, 2 villagers and one Welshman with 3 ploughs. The value was and is 30s.

Sellack Church as illustrated by H.T. Timmins

This upland manor in the royal Forest of Dean was under-developed, especially the lord's home farm. It may be that stock farming was preferred to arable cultivation. Today Ruardean is in Gloucestershire.

St Weonards

No entry, probably part of Archenfield and one of the three churches may have been there.

Sellack

No entry. A small Domesday manor called *EDTUNE*, was the only manor within the Hundred of Sellack. This may have been at Strangford, between later Foy and Sellack. However, the Archenfield 'manors' of Baysham and Ashe Ingen occupied the eastern end of the Sellack peninsula. See Strangford.

Sollers Hope

In Greytree Hundred
Held by Ansfrid of Cormeilles.

> *HOPE*; Hagen held it; he could go where he would. 5 hides which pay tax. Richard holds it from Ansfrid. 2 ploughs in lordship and 11 slaves. A man at arms holds 1½ hides. He has 1 plough and 1 smallholder. A mill at 5s. 3 more ploughs would be possible. Value before 1066 £4; later £3, now £4.

This is an interesting manor leased out to Richard by Ansfrid. However, the manor was not tied to its lord; in Hagen's time 'he could go where he would'. A significant part of the manor is held by a man at arms — a soldier, who probably undertook military services, when needed, in return for his land.

Strangford

In Sellack Hundred
Land of Hugo Donkey. Held by Elric.

> *ETONE* Elric held it from Thorkell White. Half a hide. 2 men with 2 ploughs. They pay 2 sesters of honey. The land does not pay tax.

The identification of the location of Etune with Strangford is based on evidence from the Herefordshire DB. Thorn and Thorn (1983) include a lengthy note about this and the hundred of Sellack.

This was a tiny 'manor', perhaps no more than 60 acres and no apparent home farm.

Upton Bishop

In Bromsash Hundred

Held by the church of Hereford and mentioned as belonging to the canons.

> In *VPTVNE* 7 hides which pay tax. 2 ploughs in lordship; 18 villagers, 11 smallholders, 2 boors and a priest; between them they have 28½ ploughs. 5 slaves; meadow 4 acres; 1 hedged enclosure; woodland which pays nothing. The villagers pay 20s. in customary dues.
>
> These three manors, Walford, Ross and Upton are assessed at £14.

The lands of Upton Bishop were as large as those of Ross. There were more ploughs, but much less meadow. Half of a plough means 4 oxen — half the size of the usual team of 8. The two 'boors' were slaves who had been freed. The 'hedged enclosure' is translated from 'haia' or modern 'Haie' — a term generally associated with deer parking within woodland or forest. See also Walford.

Walford

In Bromsash Hundred

Held by the church of Hereford and noted as belonging to the canons.

> In *WALECFORD* seven hides which pay tax. In lordship 1 plough; two more would be possible. 6 villagers and 4 smallholders with 5 ploughs. Meadow 14 acres; 3 hedged enclosures. The villagers pay 10s. for the waste land.

See also the last line of the entry for Upton Bishop.

Although the size was similar to Ross and Upton Bishop there were far fewer ploughs and thus much less arable cultivation. There was plenty of meadow so some stock farming was possible. The mention of 3 hedged enclosures is curious (see also the comment under Upton Bishop); they may have been what we would call fields made within woodland, perhaps with some specialised purpose such as deer parks.

Reaping in June (from the Bayeux Tapestry)

Weston-under-Penyard

In Bromsash Hundred
Held by Durand of Gloucester.

> Durand also holds *WESTVNE*, and Bernard from him [see also Pontshill]. Gunnar held it [in the time of King Edward]. 2 hides which pay tax. 2 smallholders have 1 plough; a further 3 ploughs are possible. The value is and was 4s.

Weston was small and under-utilised for arable. Note also the lack of mention of woodland This suggests that the wooded Penyard Hill was not part of the manor.

Wilton

A dependency of Cleeve in Bromsash Hundred. See Cleeve.

Yatton

In Bromsash Hundred
Held by the king.

> In *GETUNE* Hwaetmen held 1 hide which paid tax. He could go where he would. Hugh held it from Humphrey the Chamberlain [i.e. the king's]. He paid and still pays 30s. Before 1066 this land was thaneland, but afterwards it was changed to reeveland. Therefore the King's officials state that this land and its dues are being taken away from the King.

This interesting entry shows that in King Edward's time the land was held by a free thane, probably in return for military service to the king. Since the Conquest this state of affairs had changed with loss of money and service to the king.

Edward the Confessor (from the Bayeux Tapestry)

Glossary

Blanched pence, white pence. see: Money.

Carucate. A measure of land that is thought to be equal to a hide and, possibly, also to a ploughland. If correct, '3 carucates' would mean land for three ploughs. It may well also have a taxation use.

Customary dues. A form of words describing routine payments in cash, kind or services.

Fishery. Fisheries in the area around Ross-on-Wye would comprise the exclusive right to take fish from the rivers and streams by means of wooden fish traps, and by other means such as nets, set in favourable locations. The fish would include salmon, trout, coarse fish and eels.

Forest. An area of un enclosed territory with defined metes and bounds, consisting of heaths, wastes and woods and sometimes even farmlands and settlements, in which the right of hunting was reserved to the king. These royal forests were administered under forest law by central as well as local officials. The Forest of Dean was such a forest. It included, at one time, Chase and Penyard Hills (see also the discussion below the entry for Ross). Another entry (1.53) hints at Archenfield being a forest although no other reference occurs in Domesday or elsewhere.

Hide. Hide had two meanings. It was sometimes a measure of area amounting to 120 acres; see also: virgate. Mostly, the hide was a unit of tax liability. When an entry states '1 hide' it generally meant that the 'manor' had a liability to pay a sum of tax equal to x, whilst a 7 hide 'manor' would pay tax of 7x. In the entries the hidage gives us an idea of the worth of the 'manor'. Thus a small but productive manor might be assessed at more hides than a larger manor with few people and little farming. To gain an idea of the area of a 'manor' the numbers of ploughs and people should also be taken into account.

Hundred. Anglo-Saxon in origin. A group of 'manors' that was collectively responsible for providing ship money and arms for defence. Hundreds also operated courts and had their own officials. Groups of hundreds formed the shires or counties.

Lordship. That part of the 'manor' which the lord used and farmed for himself is described as 'in lordship'. Historians often use the term demesne, or home farm for the same thing.

'Manor'. Domesday scholars frequently used the word 'manor' when referring to the units of landholding detailed in Domesday Book. The word derives from the Domesday Latin word *manerium*. No simple definition is possible because the 'manors' differed greatly in their size and complexity. Some were no more than single farms, but others had multiple, detached dependencies or berewicks. Sometimes these were even in different hundreds. In the Ross district, the 'manors' of Cleeve and Linton demonstrate complexity. The manor of the Middle Ages developed from the Domesday units.

Money. Accountants at the time of Domesday used pounds, shillings and pence, but the only money in circulation was the silver penny. This was sometimes broken in half to make halfpennies. There were 12 pennies to the shilling and 20 shillings to the pound. The value of the cash depended on the weight of silver it contained. This guarded against penny coins that were smaller than they should be. Another problem was debasing; i.e. the reduction of the quantity of silver by the addition of less valuable metals. Some entries mention blanched or white pennies; they refer to the need for assay to ensure the face value of the coins.

Plough. Many entries state the number of ploughs in lordship, and those belonging to the tenants. A standard plough team was drawn by 8 oxen. Mentions of half ploughs should not be read literally; they mean half a team which is four oxen. It is thought that a team was capable of ploughing one hide. Thus the number of ploughs should provide some idea about the amount of land under arable cultivation. There are some pitfalls to interpretation; the tenants' ploughs would be used for the lord's land as well as their own, so that the lord's arable was often larger than is suggested by the teams in lordship. Some authorities believe that the ploughs represent another, perhaps older, basis for taxation. If this is so, calculations of the extent of arable from the ploughs is fraught. Perhaps the best solution is to use the numbers of ploughs as a relative guide to size and activity.

Sesters. A measure of volume, but the exact amount is not known. A sester of honey is thought to have been about 32 oz.

Smallholders. See p.100.

Slaves. See p.101.

Villagers. See p.101.

Virgate. There were 4 virgates to the hide. Thus a virgate was 30 acres.

Waste. Land that was other than woodland, pasture, meadow or arable; unused or uncultivated land.

Plate 1 Ross (LOWV)

Plate 2 Dean Hill Hospital

Plate 3 Kentchurch Court

Plate 4   Pembridge Castle (Logaston Press)

Plate 5 Pembridge Castle Chapel

Plate 6 Hoarwithy Church

Plate 7 Hoarwithy Church cloisters

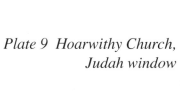

Plate 8 Hentland Church, Poole window

Plate 9 Hoarwithy Church, Judah window

Plate 10 Hoarwithy Church: mosaic above the chancel

*Plate 11 Aston Ingham,
daffodils and rabbits*

*Plate 12 Hope Mansell,
St Francis*

*Plate 13 Weston-under-
Penyard, St Francis*

Plate 14 Ross, Dragon

*Plate 16 St Weonards,
Flemish panel*

*Plate 15 How Caple, First World War
memorial window detail*

*Plate 17
Llanwarne, Justice*

Plate 18 Goodrich Castle Chapel, Millenium window

CHAPTER 5

Stained Glass in the Ross-on-Wye area

Introduction

The objective of this chapter is to guide readers to some of the more interesting stained glass windows in the Ross area, and to set these windows into the context of the development of stained glass in this country as a whole.

It covers the area within a radius of about 7 miles of Ross, to St Weonards to the west, Little Dewchurch to the north, Much Marcle to the east and the county boundary to the south. Even in this limited area there are over 40 churches, most of which have stained glass of some kind, and to attempt coverage of every window, or even every church, would make tedious reading. A selection has therefore been made based on artistic or historic interest. I apologise in advance if a favourite window has been omitted.

It must be emphasized at the outset that the story of stained glass in this area is largely one of the Victorian era and later. The survival rate of mediaeval glass is not high anywhere in the country and this area, in contrast to some other parts of Herefordshire, is particularly impoverished in this respect. There is a little 16th-century Flemish glass imported in later centuries and a couple of interesting 17th-century windows, but the rest is of the 19th and 20th centuries.

Although the last 20 years has seen a revival of interest in Victorian art and architecture, stained glass of this period remains largely disregarded. Sometimes it is just ignored like some sort of ecclesiastical wallpaper, for instance many church guide books say no more than 'the glass is modern', although this could well mean over 150 years old. Sometimes it is actively disliked and criticized. It is certainly true that there is much mundane Victorian glass and some that is downright atrocious, but it is hoped that this chapter will be able to show that there is also plenty of glass of considerable merit and interest from this period and the years that followed.

An outline history of Stained Glass in Britain

Very early in the history of glassmaking it was discovered that, by adding different metal oxides to the glass mix in its molten state, different colours could be obtained. By this process the glass is coloured all the way through and is known as 'pot-metal' glass. Pieces of glass of different colours, and clear glass, can be cut into shapes and then pieced together, held by strips of grooved lead known as 'cames'. At some stage — it is not known exactly when — it was found that details of features, drapery, foliage etc. could be painted in monochrome on to the pot-metal glass, resulting in the 'stained glass' (which should more properly be called 'painted glass') familiar to us today.

Stained glass was of early importance to the Church because, along with wall-paintings, it was the 'bible of the poor' by which narrative scenes could be shown to an illiterate congregation. But glass also had symbolic properties, representing Christ as the Light of the World shining into the church. The glass itself, being hand blown, had imperfections which gave an extra sparkle and radiance, and it was sometimes seen as a magical substance.

The earliest surviving stained glass of any size in this country is that from the late 12th century at Canterbury Cathedral. At this period small narrative panels appear within geometric shapes and borders of stylized foliage. The individual pieces of glass are small and the images are defined almost as much by the way they are leaded together as by the painting. The dense patterning and deep colours, especially red and blue, give a rich, jewel-like effect.

Into the 13th century windows grew bigger and lighter interiors were demanded, so narrative painted glass was set within areas of clear or 'grisaille' (greyish-tinted) glass. Foliage became naturalistic and figures were commonly put under architectural canopies of increasing elaboration.

In the early 14th century there was a breakthrough when yellow stain (also known as silver stain) was invented. It was found that silver nitrate painted onto clear glass turned yellow on firing, the heavier the application the denser the colour, (the first true 'stained-glass'). This meant that for the first time a single piece of glass could carry different shades of colour, and the technique was commonly used for depicting hair, crowns, trimmings on clothes and the like. Also at this time stained glass makers turned more to a colour palette of earthy red-browns, yellows and greens, and the style of drawing became softer and more naturalistic. Eaton Bishop, near Hereford, is an excellent place to see glass from this period at close quarters.

After a hiatus in the years following the Black Death, the 15th century turned back to red and blue pot-metal glass, but used with plenty of white glass and stain. Later in the century, and into the 16th, Flemish glaziers had a great influence introducing richer colours and more exotic imagery. Robust and vigorous depictions spread right across windows, without respecting the architectural divisions. At about this time came the invention of enamel stains of different colours that could be applied to white glass, so that pot-metal glass need no longer be used to obtain colour.

And then in the 1530s came the Reformation. Suddenly imagery and colour in churches was frowned upon. It is likely that the number of stained glass windows purposely destroyed was relatively small, but their maintenance was ignored, they became damaged and were eventually removed without replacement. Stained glass manufacture continued in parts of northern Europe, with increasing use of enamel paints, but in this country installation of new windows virtually ceased for nearly 200 years, except for a brief revival under Charles I and Archbishop Laud around 1630.

In the 18th century there was a growing antiquarian interest in mediaeval glass amongst collectors such as Horace Walpole and a few makers made new windows, but using enamel paints in a romantic and decorative style, rather than with mediaeval techniques. The church at Great Witley, Worcestershire has some marvellous examples. By the 1820s and 1830s some makers returned to using pot-metal glass and making more use of leading in the composition of their windows. There was a growing realization that glass was by its nature a two-dimensional medium and was not so suitable for the pictorialism and perspectives of easel painting.

But it was the regeneration of the Anglican Church towards the end of the 1830s that really revived stained glass. Gothic architecture in a correct mediaeval style and mediaeval colour and imagery returned in a big way. Augustus Welby Pugin was the architect and designer who led this movement and under his influence Victorian glass at first took on the characteristics of the earlier mediaeval periods with simplified and stylized figures and scenes. However, different stained glass artists soon wanted to form their own personal, recognizable manner and incorporated later mediaeval features with more complex, more pictorial scenes, and built in some non-mediaeval originality in colour and design.

Stained glass soon became enormously popular as a memorial to individuals connected with a church, while the demand for memorial sculpture fell rapidly away. This was a period when large numbers of new churches, requiring new stained glass, were built. It is estimated that there are about 80,000 Victorian stained glass windows in England and Wales. Later in the century stained glass also became popular in domestic houses and secular public buildings. To meet the demand some large firms, such as Hardmans and Clayton and Bell, grew up employing many artists and glass makers in production line techniques. Inevitably quality sometimes suffered, but at their best all the big studios were capable of turning out excellent windows.

A change of direction occurred thanks to William Morris and his followers. Their early windows were still in the Gothic idiom, with subdued colours, but around 1870, particularly with the designs of Edward Burne-Jones, their windows took on the more sculptural qualities of Michaelangelo and the Italian Renaissance and the colours became much lighter. This change matched the general shift at that time towards more liberal, more secular and less pietistic attitudes.

Alongside this movement the older-style Gothic Revival styles carried on, often becoming stereotyped and lacking in vitality. An important maker who moved away from the stereotype was Charles Kempe, whose windows reflected a 15th-century style, with subdued colours, intricate detail and much use of white or silver glass. His work appealed to the Aesthetes of the 1880s.

Towards the end of the century the influence of the Arts and Crafts movement was felt in stained glass. The ethos of this movement was that the designer of the glass should carry out, or at least supervise, all subsequent stages of producing the window, in contrast to the factory methods of the large firms. There was an emphasis on naturalism in design, stemming from pre-Raphaelite paintings. 'Early English', or slab, glass was often used. This was thick, uneven glass which gave a pleasing texture to the window. One of the problems of mediocre Victorian glass was that it was produced mechanically in thin rolled sheets, giving a flat finish, lacking in sparkle.

The first half of the 20th century saw a continuation of the styles of the 19th century. Several firms followed in the Arts and Crafts idiom, with the Bromsgrove Guild being the leading practitioners in the West Midlands. At the same time windows in the older style of Victorian trade glass continued to be made. Right up to 1939 windows that could have been made 70 or 80 years earlier were still being produced, and indeed some were from designs dating from that period. The tragedy of the First World War was a great generator of new windows, some as memorials to individuals who were killed in action and some to the fallen generally.

In the second half of the century stained glass became more experimental. Artists like John Piper and Marc Chagall produced fresh, more impressionistic, designs. Some designers adopted the sharp, angular style of the Cubist movement. Others designed purely abstract windows, relying on subtlety of pattern and colour to make an impact. At the same time a cosier, more representational tradition continued, but increasingly depicting more secular subjects, such as local topography, flora and fauna instead of overtly religious ones. By now nearly all the big glass firms had closed and typically stained glass work became an industry of small businesses, sometimes consisting of just one person with a studio and kiln at the end of the garden. Finally the Millenium gave a fillip to glass makers, as churches and secular organizations commissioned windows to mark the occasion.

A Chronological Description of Local Stained Glass Windows

Mediaeval

The Ross area possesses only one window where the majority of the glass is mediaeval, and even this was brought from elsewhere. This is the east window of the **Parish Church of St Mary in Ross-on-Wye**.

The glass was originally commissioned by Thomas Spofford, Bishop of Hereford from 1421 to 1448 for the Chapel of St Thomas in the Bishop's Palace at Stretton Sugwas. This was one of the many palaces owned by the bishops and was not used by them after 1503. The building gradually fell into disrepair and was eventually demolished in 1792.

It was soon after this that the glass came to Ross, probably presented by the bishop of the day. The first definite mention of its existence in the church is in a guidebook of 1818. A photograph taken before the 1873 restoration of the church shows that elements of the stained glass were incorporated in a large east window without any stone tracery and with the glass held by iron bars forming a rectangular pattern.

However, as part of the restoration, the present east window was installed, consisting of four trefoil-headed lights surmounted by tracery with the arch above. This is much more suitable for the Stretton Sugwas glass, which was originally made for a four-light window. The glass was restored and inserted in the new window by Thomas Baillie and George Meyer of the London firm, Thomas Baillie and Co.

The east window at the church of St Mary, Ross-on-Wye

Although there is some restoration to the main figures depicted in the window, they are mainly mediaeval and are a fine example of 15th-century work. Reds, blues and yellow stain predominate and the figures stand under soaring and elaborate architectural canopies. In the outer lights are St Ethelbert, whose shrine was at Hereford and who holds a church in his hand, and St Thomas of Hereford. Curiously the scroll next to the St

Ethelbert figure, inserted at the 1873 restoration, identifies it as St Edward the Confessor, but modern antiquarians are sure that this is an error, presumably caused by the church being misidentified as Westminster Abbey. The two inner lights depict the Virgin Mary with her mother, St Anne, and her father Joachim. Bishop Spofford, with his mitre and crozier, appears as a donor figure, and is shown offering his heart up to St Anne and the Virgin as a token of his devotion.

The Ross window is taller than that at Stretton Sugwas, so Baillie and Meyer inserted at the bottom an angel's head in each light set within quarry panels. The inner pair are mediaeval, but the outer are by the restorers. The tracery lights feature Baillie and Meyer's angel musicians in pale colours, anaemic in contrast to the mediaeval figures below, but at least they are 'good mannered' and do not detract from the effect of the main lights.

In addition there are at Ross a few mediaeval fragments, including the initials 'TS' set within one of the south windows of the nave, and it may be assumed that these were also installed by Baillie and Meyer, making use of some leftovers.

Elsewhere there is some mediaeval glass to be seen at **St Weonard's** again restored by Baillie and Meyer, this time in 1875. This is the east window of the Mynors Chapel depicting in the four main lights St Catherine, St John the Baptist, the Crucifixion with Mary Magdalene and St Weonard. Only parts of the glass are mediaeval, notably St Catherine with her attributes of a wheel and a sword in the left hand light. Her predominately yellow dress is set off with a purple robe and coloured jewels round the border of her cloak. St Weonard in the right-hand light, shown as a hermit with a book and a mighty axe, is clearly wholly Victorian. The window is more of a jumble than that at Ross, but overall the restoration is effective and enjoyable. A panel in the chapel provides the visitor with a full description of everything depicted in the glass, and gives Baillie and Mayer's attribution of the mediaeval glass to the end of the 14th century.

Otherwise all we have of mediaeval origin in the Ross area are fragments. The best of these are in the east window at **Hentland**, where parts of three figures, probably 15th century, are set in Victorian quarry patterns. The outer figures are nimbed, the male on the left carrying a book of music and the female on the right with her hands clasped in prayer. The smaller centre figure is more secular looking, possibly a donor.

At Goodrich there are some nice 15th-century angels in the tracery lights of the east window of the north aisle. Some are carrying instruments of the passion and some hold shields with heraldry associated with the Talbots, Earls of Shrewsbury and Lords of Goodrich Castle. In a nave window at **Sellack** a small panel of a 15th-century crucifixion along with a few extraneous pieces has been installed. There are fragments above a Victorian window in the Lady Chapel at **Kings Caple**, while those at **Sollers Hope** include heraldry of the Whittingtons, the family that supplied the Lord Mayor of London of pantomime fame.

The Sixteenth and Seventeenth Centuries

During these centuries when, after the Reformation, little new stained glass was installed in British churches, it continued to be made in some quantities in Flanders, Germany and Switzerland. Mostly this glass was pictorial in style and created by the application of enamel paints, rather than the use of pot-metal. In the 19th and 20th centuries benefactors sometimes gave pieces of such glass to decorate churches, and there are two examples in the Ross area.

In the surprisingly large church of **Christ Church, Llanwarne**, built in 1864 to replace the ruinous mediaeval church over the road, two nave windows contain several 16th-century Flemish roundels set within circles of Victorian coloured glass against a field of patterned quarries. The roundels are pictures painted on clear glass without leading in tones of grey, black and yellow, depicting biblical scenes and allegories. There are some that look suspiciously like Victorian reproductions, but many are undoubtedly genuine and of good quality — see for example the fine Allegory of Justice, which is conveniently at eye level (Plate 17).

At **St Weonards** there is an early 16th-century panel of Flemish glass set in one of the nave windows, donated by Roger Mynors of Treago in 1952 (Plate 16). The Faculty (i.e. the Diocesan authority to install the glass) is in the Hereford Record Office and in the associated papers Mr Mynors mentions that he and his wife bought it very cheaply in Hereford Cattle Market and that it had come from the recently demolished Goodrich Court. One would dearly like to think that it was part of the collection of the famous antiquarian Sir Samuel Rush Meyrick, the builder of the Court. In Mynors' words the panel depicts 'The calling of Andrew and Peter, who are fishing in most unlikely costumes, with a town something like ancient Rome in the background, but the colours are all right.' Although the panel is only small, it has great vigour, with Peter's cloak billowing out behind him as he strides through the water and their curious green-painted boat bobbing on the sea behind. Permission was given for the panel to be put in the lower half of a small window on the south side of the nave, but it is now in the middle of a larger window of clear glass on the north and looks a little lost.

Whilst these pieces were installed in their respective churches at a much later date than their manufacture and are post-mediaeval in style, at **Sellack** the east window was made and installed in the 17th century and is consciously designed to evoke the mediaeval spirit. In the period leading up to the Civil War there was a strong faction in this country, led by the Archbishop of Canterbury, William Laud, which sought to reverse some aspects of the Reformation by re-introducing a greater emphasis on the sacraments, ritual and decoration into the Church. This included the re-introduction of stained glass, which is chiefly to be seen in some of the Oxford colleges. This trend did not have time to pervade much of the country by the time the Civil War put a stop to it, but it did reach Herefordshire, thanks to the friendship between Archbishop Laud and John, Viscount Scudamore.

The east window in Sellack carries the date 1630 and the initials 'RS' for Rowland Scudamore, who lived at nearby Caradoc Court until his death in January 1631. In the past Rowland Scudamore has therefore been identified as the donor of the window, but local historian Joe Hillaby has more recently made the case that it was the work of his great-nephew John Scudamore, friend of Laud, as a memorial on the death of his great-uncle. 1630 would be the date of this event in Old Style reckoning when the year was taken to begin on Lady Day, March 25th. Certainly it was John who was responsible for the great re-ordering of Dore Abbey in 1634, including the installation there of glass in a similar style to that at Sellack. At Sellack also there was a general remodeling of the chancel in a Laudian style with new communion rails and an altar table with panelling behind it. Overall the Sellack window looks a little odd. It was clearly Scudamore's intention to create something in a 14th-century gothic style and it incorporates some pieces of mediaeval glass, but the colours — predominately yellow, blue and orangey-brown

The east window at Sellack

— do not look quite mediaeval, and the composition of the window is rather naïve. In the upper row of the main lights two of the Magi occupy the outer lights with Joseph and the Virgin and Child in the inner ones. Below are two female figures, who may be Mary Magdalene and St Catherine, the third one of the Magi separated from his fellows above, and the place of the Nativity represented by just a portion of the stable with half an ox and half an ass. Each of the upper figures is under a simple canopy bearing three pinnacles, while the canopy of those below consists of a foliated ogee arch. Each light has elaborate borders of lozenges and foliage scrolls. It is not known who made this strange composition, but whoever it was he perhaps learnt from the experience because the windows Scudamore gave at Dore Abbey are much more sophisticated in design.

One person who was impressed by the Sellack window was John Abrahall of **Foy**, who in his will of 1640 made provision for a copy of it to be placed in the parish church there. This was eventually done in 1675. Whilst the stone tracery is an excellent reproduction of that in Sellack, the glass itself compares poorly, the colours being more muted and the drawing cruder. This no doubt reflects a decline in glazing skills over the 45 years since the work at Sellack. It has also been suggested that in the interim it was Louis XIII's invasion of Lorraine and the destruction of glass manufactures there that finally cut off the supply of good pot metal glass.

The one other piece of 17th-century glass in the area is to be found in the North Chapel at **Much Marcle**. Although images in stained glass were generally not produced at this time (with the exceptions noted above) it was still sometimes used for heraldry, and the east window of 1889 includes a heraldic panel of 1628 containing the royal arms of Charles I.

Victorian Glass to *c.*1870

There are no surviving examples of 18th-century enamel painted glass in the Ross area, nor any from the period of romantic antiquarianism which flourished in the early 19th century. There were at one time, however, some excellent examples of this at Goodrich Court, where in about 1830 the antiquarian Sir Samuel Meyrick installed glass designed by his friend and fellow antiquarian Thomas Willement, probably the most important designer of this period. Some Willement drawings for these survive in the British Library and two are illustrated in colour in *Sir Samuel Meyrick and Goodrich Court* by Rosalind Lowe.

The earliest 19th-century glass in the area is from the 1840s when it had become virtually a requirement that designs should be in a correct mediaeval style in step with the Anglican Church's move to re-create itself in its pre-Reformation gothic image. This glass is at **Upton Bishop**, where it was originally in the east window, but this was replaced, and it is now on the north side of the chancel. The manufacturer was William Wailes of Newcastle, who started a glass studio just at the time the Gothic Revival in the Church of England was getting under way and was soon producing large amounts of glass for installation all over the country. The window is quite mediaeval in feel, showing Zacharias and Elizabeth under canopies with angels bearing scrolls below. The colours are bold with reds and blues present, but also dark greens and mauves, which are less likely to be seen in a mediaeval window.

Another window of the early Victorian period is also at Upton Bishop on the north side of the nave. This dates from about 1855 and is an early example of the work of Clayton and Bell, who became one of the biggest glass studios and continued well into the 20th century. The small scenes depicting the raising of Jairus's daughter go across the two lights in the upper and lower registers, but each element is quite self-contained in an authentic mediaeval way. The colour palette is similar to the Wailes window. The drawing

Upton Bishop,
raising Jairus' daughter

of the drapery in the clothing and bedclothes is well handled. The subject is a poignant one, because the window is a memorial by her parents to Maude Chellingworth of Grendon Court, who died aged 14. Her mother Matilda was a friend of the painter Joshua Cristall, whose splendid water-colour of her in her garden with Hay Bluff in the background is in Hereford Museum.

A similar style continued into the 1860s, as can be seen in the north window of the chancel at **Peterstow**, dated 1866. The scene of Christ washing the feet of his disciples is made up of small pieces of glass of subdued colours with plentiful use of leading. The figures are grouped in a stylized circular composition, whilst the drawing of the faces has been finely done. Likewise the figure of Christ the Good Shepherd in the chancel at **Ganarew** is in a simple formal early Victorian style. This window is signed by Alexander Gibbs of London, who, as here, used a very bright colour palette in his work.

However by this decade many glass studios were broadening their range of styles. An example is the east window at **Welsh Newton**, dated 1862, by James Powell and Sons, another prolific and long-lasting studio. Bright, even livid, colours are used — greens, red, blues and purples. The scenes are crowded with figures disposed asymmetrically and canopies are dispensed with, only a sort of floral pediment dividing the earthly scenes below from the heavenly scenes above. There is more naturalism in the backgrounds, for instance in the scene of the Baptism of Christ there are what look like flag irises growing, with questionable botanical accuracy, by the River Jordan. The east window at **Lea** of 1865 also breaks from earlier conventions. Although not so boldly coloured as that at Welsh Newton, the figures in this Deposition scene are shown in dramatic poses, with Christ's body slumped in a naturalistic way.

An interesting glass painter of this period, in whose work we can see this growth of naturalism, is Frederick Preedy who practised initially in Worcester and then in London. A number of Victorian architects dabbled in stained glass design, but Preedy was rare in that he was prolific in both these disciplines. In 1863 he designed a window for the Gregory

Chapel at **How Caple**. The scenes showing Christ healing are still in the earlier style of mediaevalism, but some more naturalistic inventions are introduced, such as some flowers and a dog. The faces are beautifully drawn with very individual features.

Preedy's work is also seen at **Little Dewchurch**, where he was both the architect of the new church in 1870 and the designer of some of the windows. There is more realism and inventiveness in this work, for instance in the chancel south window the scene of Christ with the lost sheep contains various kinds of flora, including a palm tree, and a very realistic sheep, whilst the raising of Lazarus dramatically shows the bound body emerging from the tomb. Once again the quality of the drawing is excellent.

From *c*.1870 to the end of the 19th Century

In the last 30 years of the 19th century the range of styles that became acceptable in stained glass design broadened considerably, as was the case in art and architecture generally. Whilst the production of stained glass in a conventional gothic style continued in abundance, other more pictorial forms, often based on Renaissance paintings, were explored. One of the leaders of this movement was William Morris, whose firm, Morris and Co., was founded in 1861. There is a fine, albeit small, example of their

Little Dewchurch,
raising of Lazarus

work at **Hoarwithy**. This is the trumpeting angel to a design by Edward Burne-Jones in the topmost window at the west end. The figure is clad in a robe of gorgeous blue and has bright red wings. Although the angel is Renaissance in feel, it should be remembered that William Morris's inspiration was rooted in the mediaeval period and the window still uses traditional pot metal glass leaded in a way that emphasizes the design of the figure. In the Morris catalogue this window dates from 1879, the time of the rebuilding of the church. Its architect, John Pollard Seddon, was closely connected with the William Morris circle, and the vicar, William Poole, who paid for the rebuilding, transcribed into his commonplace book extracts from Morris's lectures on art.

However the glass in the other ten windows at the west end of the church is very different in style. Designed by Seddon himself they depict ranks of saints, patriarchs and angels

Levi at Hoarwithy

in stiff, hieratic poses and in pale, subdued colours. In one of his travel diaries Poole had declared that some modern glass he had seen in Bordeaux Cathedral was 'the best I have ever seen — very pale in its colouring and subdued'. So the style was no doubt what Poole wanted and it chimes in well with the Byzantine style of architecture and the mosaic of Christ that he commissioned for the east end of the church, but the juxtaposition with the Burne-Jones window is strange. The mystery deepens because in A.C. Sewter's definitive catalogue of Morris glass the Hoarwithy window is listed as 'not found'. Did Sewter just miss it, or had it been temporarily removed when he visited, or could it possibly have been subsequently moved from the schoolhouse/curate's house next door, also designed by Seddon and financed by Poole?

The other window of this period at Hoarwithy is well worthy of mention, the two lights on the north side of the nave depicting Judah (Plate 9) and Levi. It is of about 1885 by Hugh Arthur Kennedy, a protégé of Seddon's. These are splendid, lively figures in costumes that almost pre-figure Diaghilev's Ballet Russe of 40 years later. Poole never had the funds to achieve all his ambitions for Hoarwithy, so one wonders whether he intended to put six of the leaders of the tribes of Israel on the north side as antetypes to six apostles on the south.

The other great name in late 19th-century stained glass is Charles Eamer Kempe, who shares with William Morris the distinction of having a Society devoted to his work today. His inspiration was the lighter English stained glass of the 15th century, using subdued colours such as dull green, yellow and silver. The drawing incorporates intricate detail and expressive faces and often background landscapes in the manner of 15th- and 16th-century Flemish glass. His earlier work is often held to be more successful, stronger and more inventive than later work, which becomes more stereotyped and too fussy and over-wrought in design.

A local early piece, only some five years from the start of Kempe's glass production, is the Annunciation window of 1874 in the north aisle at **Bridstow**. This is a lovely window, showing Gabriel in one light and Mary in the other. The details of faces, dress and background are all excellent. Gabriel has peacock-feathered wings, a device which became almost a cliché in Kempe glass, and the background curtain is held by curtain rings on a rail, another common feature. Mary's gothic prayer desk has a scene of good fighting evil carved on the side and a demonic looking cat perched on the arm.

More early Kempe glass is to be seen at **Much Marcle**. The east window of 1877 is a crucifixion with Mary and Saint John. At this early stage in his career Kempe was more inclined to use bolder colours and here deep reds and blues predominate. Christ's loincloth flies out to either side, another idiosyncrasy of Kempe design. Kempe is well-known for using a wheatsheaf, from his family coat of arms, as a monogram to 'sign' his windows, and this window is believed to carry the earliest use of the motif. It is dedicated to a third cousin of Kempe's, George Kempe Chatfield, and the background quarries in grisaille glass have the wheatsheaf as a pattern.

On the south side of the chancel is an Annunciation window of 1878, which it is interesting to compare with Bridstow's. It is similar in design, but, being a three light window,

The Kempe Annunciation window at Much Marcle

Gabriel and Mary are separated by a pot of lilies in the centre light. Again there are the peacock feathers in the archangel's wings and the background curtain hung on rings, and again the drawing is exceptionally good, for instance Mary's demure face and downcast eyes. In a nearby window is a Nativity scene of the same date, and the large west window of 1882 depicts saints and carries the wheatsheaf mark in a more conventional position on the border of the window. There is also a Kempe Resurrection window of 1889 in the Kyrle Chapel, surmounting the 17th-century heraldic glass noted earlier.

Slightly later, of 1893, is the east window in the small church of St Dinabo at **Llandinabo**. This is a crucifixion with Mary and St John of a similar design to the earlier one at Much Marcle, but 16 years on Kempe has refined his style. The bold blues and reds are eschewed and there is much silver and clear glass. A background representation of Jerusalem looking like a northern European fortified town is introduced. The

The Hardman Crucifixion window at Goodrich

idiosyncratic 'flying loincloth' remains and the facial expressions and musculature of the torso are drawn with great realism. The style of drawing in Kempe glass is often said to be reminiscent of the great German artist, Albrecht Dürer.

In these latter years of the 19th century the demand for stained glass was great, and the big glass studios increased their output. They took on board the innovations of Morris and Kempe to a varying extent and with different degrees of success. Sometimes windows in a more up to date style replaced earlier Victorian glass. One big firm well represented locally is John Hardman and Co. of Birmingham. They started stained glass manufacture in 1845 and are still in existence today. Their east window at **Goodrich** of 1875 is a striking Crucifixion scene spread over all five lights and crowded with figures. The scene is held together by its background of a light blue sky sprinkled with yellow suns. In the Lady Chapel at **Kings Caple** is their window of the 1880s depicting scenes from the life of Christ. The left hand light showing the Flight from Egypt is particularly lively with the head of the Holy Family's donkey disappearing into the window tracery, suggesting movement, and a toppling statue in the background representing the Slaughter of the Innocents. At **Upton Bishop** the Hardman east window depicts Christ appearing to Mary Magdalene in bright colours with plentiful plant life and, behind Mary Magdalene, a structure with a strange conical roof with alternate bands of red and blue tiles.

Other local windows of this period worth a look include the chancel north window of 1874 at **St Weonards** by Baillie and Meyer, the restorers of the mediaeval window there. It shows a Nativity scene and the Adoration of the Magi, the latter overlooked by a couple of smiling camels from the Kings' baggage train. One of the horizontal saddlebars securing the window has been carefully bent in a couple of places to avoid cutting across the heads of two of the Kings. The east window at **Llangrove** (maker unknown) is in bold colours, including deep purples, oranges and reds. In one light, representing Salvation, is a nice vignette of Jonah scrambling onto a rocky shore with his yellow cloak billowing behind him. The east window at **Llanwarne** of 1896 is by a maker who appears to have been influenced by Kempe. The scene of Christ appearing to Mary Magdalene has dramatically placed scenes of Jerusalem and Golgotha in the background and lots of naturalistic foliage in the foreground, all under elaborate canopy work. Another important studio, Heaton, Butler and Bayne, is represented at **Ross** in the middle window of the south chapel of 1900. It depicts two of the Acts of Mercy, visiting the sick and feeding the hungry, in sober colours. In the north chapel at **Whitchurch** is a Resurrection window of 1900 by James Powell and Sons. The central angel is rather in the Burne-Jones style with big orange wings, and all the faces are finely drawn. The window is particularly interesting because it was designed by Ada Currey, an artist who made many designs for Powells, including the mosaic of Christ in the dome of

Hoarwithy Church. The latter's stern Byzantine style is completely different from the Renaissance inspired window at Whitchurch and demonstrates the designer's versatility.

In some cases it is the dedicatee, rather than the window itself, which is the main interest. There are, for instance, two examples at **Goodrich**. A rather ordinary window commemorates Lt Col Basil Jackson of Glewstone Court, who, according to the inscription, served on the Quartermaster General's staff at Waterloo and was one of those in charge of Napoleon on St Helena. Another window (below the fragments of mediaeval angels previously mentioned) is to a County Court judge and has appropriate legal themes. The figure of Christ seated in judgment appears above the figure of Justice, flanked by the lawgivers Moses — with the Ten Commandments — and Solomon. William Poole, vicar of Hentland and rebuilder of Hoarwithy Church is commemorated in both these churches. At **Hentland** it is by a figure of St Dubricius, patron saint of the church, with the hedgehog, symbol of Archenfield, at his feet (Plate 8). At **Hoarwithy** it is the

The Resurrection window at Whitchurch

five windows around the east end apse, designed by Seddon when an old man, which are to his memory. Christ as the Light of the World in the centre is flanked by the four Evangelists. According to Poole's niece the colours Seddon used were influenced by those in the north transept window at Hereford Cathedral, which Poole was known to admire.

The first half of the 20th Century

At the beginning of the 20th century the Arts and Crafts movement was at its height. This was the age of the artist-craftsman who himself saw the production of a window through from the earliest design to installation. The greatest of these was Christopher Whall who not only produced windows from around 1890 to after the First World War, but was also important as a teacher and writer. His book *Stained Glass Work* is still used as a textbook today. Like Morris his work was rooted in the native mediaeval tradition and displayed the naturalistic forms pioneered in Britain by the Pre-Raphaelites. But he also introduced technical innovations — a wider range of colours from the subtle to the sumptuous and the use of specially made glass of varying thickness and gradations of colour.

The east window at Brockhampton

Whall's work can be seen locally at **Brockhampton**, where the whole church of 1901/2 was designed — by W.R. Lethaby — and erected according to Arts and Crafts principles. Lethaby's east window is in a severe, pared down gothic style and Whall's design for the glass reflects this. Each figure, a saint or angel, is surrounded by a simple border of plain white glass, whilst colour is provided by the backgrounds, alternately blue and red, with several different subtle shades employed. At this time Whall was working on his huge and impressive glazing scheme for the Lady Chapel at Gloucester Cathedral, and at least two of the figures at Gloucester, St Edward and St Chad, are replicated here, although on a smaller scale and in different colours. The window at Brockhampton complements the two Morris and Co. tapestries depicting Burne-Jones angels, which are placed on either side of it. The south transept window of 1916 is also from the Whall studios. Four of the lozenges in this strangely shaped window are filled with angel musicians in memory of Ebenezer Jordan, father of Alice Foster, the donor of the new church. As the inscription explains, 'music ever found an echo in his heart'. By this date the figures have become rather self-consciously cute for some tastes. The west window in memory of Mrs Foster's sister is also later and rather sentimental. As well as St Cecilia and St Margaret the scene includes a heavenly choir above, and below a child at play and a cat and kitten.

The Arts and Crafts tradition was carried on well into the 20th century in the West Midlands by the work of the Bromsgrove Guild of Applied Arts. This was founded in 1898 by Walter Gilbert, the headmaster of the Bromsgrove School of Art. Although very

A Bromsgrove Guild window at How Caple

much a commercial organization, the emphasis was on high standards of craftsmanship and traditional working methods. The Guild produced craft work in many media, including metalwork, plasterwork, woodwork and needlework. In 1906 Gilbert secured the services of Archibald John Davies, who already had a studio in Birmingham, to set up a stained glass workshop, and Davies remained there as chief designer for over 40 years. Bromsgrove Guild glass is present in four churches in this area (and in other locations not far away, such as Canon Pyon, Kentchurch and the Stanbury Chapel in Hereford Cathedral).

An early window of 1916 is in the north aisle at **Bridstow**, a memorial to Captain John Ramsay Cox, killed on the Western Front in the previous year. It is a dramatic composition with deep purples and reds predominating, showing St Michael in armour with his sword of light, a host of trumpeting angels above and a romantic castle in the background. Its style is clearly influenced by the work of Edward Burne-Jones. The Faculty papers include a beautifully executed pencil drawing of the design with a Bromsgrove Guild stamp on the reverse.

At **How Caple** the local landowner, Lennox Bertram Lee of How Caple Court, employed the Guild to produce glass in the church over a number of years. He even had the north side of the nave altered, replacing the porch with two new windows to accommodate more stained glass. The Lee family had been responsible for commissioning a window in memory of his father in the Lady Chapel of Gloucester Cathedral. This sits alongside the magnificent Christopher Whall scheme there and has been described as 'an appalling example of late-Victorian trade glass, its sickly tones clashing terribly with the brilliance of the Whall windows'. L.B. Lee's commissioning of high-class glass in the Whall tradition at How Caple certainly goes a long way to reme-dying this family solecism.

The first glass on the north side of the nave dates from 1915 and is in memory of Lee's son, killed in action. As at Bridstow, it adopts a romantic, chivalric style but is much more sombre in mood and colour. A young knight presents his sword before an altar, while an older dark-robed figure, perhaps Lee himself, sits at an organ. In 1916 the two newly built windows were filled with glass. One is a memorial to Lee's brother and nephew, both killed in the carnage of the First World War. Again the scene is very dark and shows a grieving monk-like figure kneeling before an oratory. The other window in memory of Josephine Constance Batten is lighter in tone, depicting a red-robed Christ reaching out to receive the kneeling young woman. A delicate preliminary drawing for this window is in the Faculty papers and shows that it was embellished in the final version, principally by Christ's robe being spangled with a rich silvery pattern all over.

In 1925 Lee commissioned from the Guild some glass in the chancel south window commemorating his mother. It shows an elderly lady, no doubt her, dressed in blues and purples and playing an organ to two plump, silvery cherubs, one of whom plays a harp. The delicate Virgin and Child in the small window over the chancel arch must also be the Guild's work, as probably are the two figures in the east window above the armorial glass.

This leaves the extraordinary window on the south side of the nave dedicated to the men of How Caple who fell in the Great War (Plate 15). It depicts, under a heavenly host, a vast crowd of minutely drawn soldiers of all ages from knights on horseback on the left to First World War tommies on the right. The colour is mainly confined to white, browns and yellows, and baroque columns form the borders of the pictures, all making the ensemble reminiscent of 16th-century Flemish work. The design is attributed to James Hogan, who was the chief designer for James Powell & Sons and was responsible for several windows in the Anglican cathedral in Liverpool.

Goodrich is the location for another Guild window installed in 1928 on the south side of the nave at the west end. It was erected by Dorothy Trafford of Hill Court in memory of her brother Cecil Harold Moffat of Goodrich Court, who died in 1916. In the tracery light some local topography, an increasingly common phenomenon in 20th-century glass,

A local scene at Goodrich

139

is to be seen. The Faculty papers carry a description: 'On the right is the figure of a young man in armour — the spirit of youth — he is looking up at the star held in the angel's hand in the other half of the window. Below both the young man in armour and the angel are thorns — depicting troubles — and small blue birds — depicting happiness — and flowers. The top light has a miniature sketch of the old castle — Goodrich — the Ferry Oak, a pheasant flying, and below red earth and a streak of water, depicting the river Wye, with fish in it'. The window cost £170.

Bromsgrove Guild Nativity at Aston Ingham

The Nativity in the east window at **Aston Ingham** is one of the best of all the Bromsgrove Guild windows. It was installed in 1923 at a cost of £270, reflecting its larger size compared to the Goodrich window. The colours are sumptuous and the draughtsmanship excellent. Two very realistic sheep lie at Mary's feet, and vigour is added by the way the cloak of the kneeling King is allowed to hang down over the inscription and into the scene below. Beneath the main scene are three jewel-like vignettes of scenes in the life of the young Christ.

The other window, the small lancet on the north of chancel, dates from late in the life of the Guild, 1946, and its hovering angel has by now acquired rather an Art Deco look to it. In the 1920s the system of Diocesan Advisory Committees (DACs) had started, whereby eminent local architects, artists and historians advise the Diocese on the appropriateness of proposed works in a church. It was probably as a result of this system that George Marshall and F.C. Morgan, well known local historians and stalwarts of the Woolhope Club, paid the church a visit, 'the light being good'. The subsequent report on the window in the Faculty papers states: 'They are strongly of the opinion that the suggested design is far too elaborate ... they suggest the flowers be omitted ... the colouring should be kept as light as possible in order not to further darken the chancel'. The donor, Kathleen Stubbs, discussed this with the designer, A.J. Davies, who agreed to keep the background colouring as light as possible. However she stuck to her guns about the flowers, writing 'The flowers are meant to represent the spirit of Aston Ingham with the animal and bird life depicted and both he and I feel the meaning of the picture has gone if these are omitted'. However she did agree to change the flowers from blue ones to the yellow daffodils of Aston Ingham 'as always intended' to give more light. And indeed it is daffodils nibbled at by rabbits that appear in the window as installed (Plate 11).

As can be seen from the above survey of Bromsgrove Guild work, many windows were dedicated as First World War memorials. Another such window can be seen at **Walford**, where the west window commemorates two brothers who fell and appropriately depicts David and Jonathan with the inscription 'They were lovely and pleasant in their lives and in death were not divided'. The colours are rather garish and the drawing not particularly distinguished. A window in the chapel at neighbouring **Hom Green** reminds us that the toll of war was felt even in a tiny hamlet such as this. Dedicated by Guy and Dorothy Trafford of Hill Court to the fallen of Hom Green, it lists but two names. The glass depicts St George, St Michael and St Nicholas and is probably by Burlison and Grylls, another important firm of the later Victorian and early 20th century period, whose work is often associated with the buildings of G.F. Bodley, the architect of this chapel. A quite different response to the war is the east window in the north aisle at **Weston-under-Penyard**. The inscription tells us that it was 'dedicated by Singer Barclay in his 88th year to Our Glorious Victory', and the scene shows angels clashing cymbals, banging drums and generally making a joyous noise in celebration.

Many of the long-established firms went on producing windows well into the 20th century, often without much change of style. **Aston Ingham** has a Morris and Co. window of 1916 depicting St John the Baptist to a design by the long dead Edward Burne-Jones, but without quite the vigour of the firm's earlier work. There is also late Morris & Co. glass in the two small windows high above the chancel arch at **Ross**. The design is unusual because it is Joseph who holds the infant Christ in one window, while Mary stands alone in the other. After the death of Charles Kempe his studio was taken over by a distant cousin, Walter Tower, and subsequently the wheatsheaf motif has a black castle tower superimposed. There is one such window of 1922 at **Much Marcle** and two of 1930 and 1931 at Ross. Their designs have become rather fussy and overcrowded, but the detailed drawing is still excellent. The blue and green dragon vanquished by St George in one of the Ross windows has an especially appealing quality reminiscent of an illustration in a child's comic book (Plate 14). Another window in traditional style, of doubtful artistic merit but of historical interest, is on the south side of **Weston-under-Penyard** and is in memory of Edward Burdett Hawkshaw and his wife. He had been a curate to William Poole at Hentland and Hoarwithy and then served as Rector of Weston for an amazing

58 years until 1912. The faces of St Paul and Dorcas are photographic representations of Hawkshaw and his wife.

However, there are also three local windows of the 1930s in a more up to date style. The first is at **Lea** on the north side of the chancel. It dates from 1933 and is by Geoffrey Webb, a prolific maker of the time. He adopts the mediaeval tradition of the rebus, or visual pun, and signs the window with a spider's web in the bottom right hand corner. The depiction of Christ as the Good Shepherd with a sheep draped round his neck is in a pale, refined version of the gothic idiom that was quite popular at the time. The colour is mostly confined to pale blue and yellow and much clear glass is used within the representation of the figure, as well as the background. Another window in a clear linear style, similar to Webb's, is on the north side of the nave at **Ganarew** by an unknown studio. Dating from 1938 it is a large and impressive Nativity with flanking saints spread across four lights. The colours are relatively subdued and the effect is markedly different from the rich Bromsgrove Guild Nativity at Aston Ingham but it is very good of its kind.

At **Hope Mansell** the chancel south window of 1937 by an unknown maker is more colourful, although a lot of clear glass is used here also. It is in memory of 'Nurse Edith', who was in fact a local lady, Miss Edith Gee, and was given by her sisters. Here again George Marshall was brought in to advise, but on this occasion he found no fault, 'As the window cannot be seen at the same time as the other windows, to which it is superior in colouring and design, it will not clash with the older glass.' The case was still referred to the

Official Referee's Court at the Royal Court of Justice, and the vicar became anxious, writing 'I ask that the business may be carried through as expeditiously as may be as one of the sisters who are giving the window may not be able to get about much longer and is anxious to see it in place.' Perhaps what caused official misgivings is the small scene in a quatrefoil below the main figure of St Barnabas, which is an entirely secular subject showing Nurse Edith ministering to an elderly patient in his long johns and carpet slippers.

Glass commemorating Nurse Edith at Hope Mansell

From 1950 to the Present Day

In the 1950s stained glass makers became more experimental in their designs, but the local examples from this decade are still quite traditional in character. In a small lancet window at **Upton Bishop** is a charming Virgin and Child by G. Maile & Son of Canterbury of 1953. Their chief designer had trained with Burlison and Grylls and the design is still in a pre-Second World War style. The DAC were happy with it, but insisted that the date in the inscription be altered to read '18th January' and not 'January 18th'. This small window cost only £45. A larger window is on the south side of the nave at **Weston-under-Penyard**, dating from 1954 and designed by Basil Barber, who worked in Bristol. There is a lot of clear glass, but the draughtsmanship of the figures is very good. The main ones are St George and St Phocas, an obscure early saint and martyr, who was said to be a market gardener. He is depicted in a monk's habit carrying a rake with the tower of Weston Church behind and the green fields of Herefordshire around. As installed, the window carried an

St Phocas at Weston-under-Penyard

inscription at the bottom, but two years later the donor paid for this to be inscribed on alabaster plaques to the sides of the window, and for it to be replaced by two new scenes, a Nativity and a Pieta, the latter after a picture in St Peter's Rome. Once again the DAC were fussy about putting the day of the month before the name of the month in the inscription.

Another excellent window of this period can be seen at **Ganarew**. As noted above, there is an interesting 1938 window here and it is unexpected and gratifying to find two good examples of 20th-century glass in a little known and little visited church. The 1952 window is by Celtic Studios of Swansea, which was a collaboration between Howard Martin and Hubert Palmer Thomas, who both trained at Swansea School of Art. The three lights have Christ flanked by St Luke and St Thomas the Apostle with his attributes of a builder's square and dividers. The saints are appropriate because Monmouth Priory had a chapel of St Thomas on this spot in the 12th century and when the present church of 1849 was consecrated the bishop — according to *Saints in Herefordshire* by D.M.

Annett — accidentally dedicated it to St Luke, although it has always been known by its intended name of St Swithin. The figures do indeed have a Celtic feel to them, deriving from the slightly stylized drawing and their large dark eyes. In the Faculty papers Celtic Studios promised that the colouring would be as delicate as possible, in order to allow the maximum amount of light to pour into the building, and this has certainly been achieved by the use of some subtle and pleasing tones.

By now the tradition of memorial stained glass was dying out and it was not until the 1980s that more local glass was installed, when two different windows depicting St Francis of Assisi came along. This had become quite a popular subject because the saint's association with the natural world affords a good opportunity to portray him with the local flora and fauna. The window of 1980 at the east end of the south aisle at **Hope Mansell** is an interesting design by Geoffrey Robinson, still active today, who was working from the same Bristol premises as Basil Barber (Plate 12). In the bald words of the Faculty description it depicts 'St Francis standing in a bush, in which are birds'. The bush and birds are highly stylized, grass-like strips representing the former and brightly coloured half-round shapes the latter. Behind the saint is a sun and moon. The window successfully introduces a modern style within an overall traditional context that respects the architecture around it. The St Francis in the north aisle at **Weston-under-Penyard** is treated in a much more naturalistic style, but with excellent draughtsmanship (Plate 13). He is by a river surrounded by local birds and butterflies, with a deer browsing and a frog at his feet. A Herefordshire oak and Herefordshire hills are in the background. The glass carries the monogram of H.J. Hobbs & Son, a Hereford firm still in business today as H.R. Hobbs & Sons.

They are also responsible for the next window chronologically, which is in the chapel in **Goodrich Castle**. It commemorates the personnel of the Radar Research Squadron and is in Goodrich because a Halifax aircraft carrying the prototype bombing-aid radar crashed nearby in 1942, killing all 11 people on board. It is a fairly conventional design, featuring military badges and at the bottom an aircraft, a radar screen and radio masts.

To bring the story up to date, there are three Millennium windows in the area. The one in the chancel at **Weston-under-Penyard** is by the stained glass artist Jane Gray, who is based in Shropshire. It is a harmonious design with religious and other symbols contained by a twisting silver border making up figure-of-eight shapes. The predominant colour is blue, which is used in several different subtle gradations of shades.

The other two Millenium windows are by Nicola Hopwood, who then worked locally at Brockhampton. Her work is in a more abstract, free-form style. At **Little Dewchurch** a flame shoots up the central light from which yellow forms branch out across the outer lights, against a green background. These 'branches' echo the branches of the trees outside, which can be seen through the clear glass parts of the window. The design commissioned by English Heritage for the chapel in **Goodrich Castle** is more complex (Plate 18). A river winds back and across the three lights round a central pillar inscribed 'upon this rock'. Etched into the course of the river are various creatures, people and symbols based on children's drawings. In other parts of the window profiles of childrens' faces appear palely in the glass and representations of some local churches are seen towards the edges of the design. The bold reds, blues and oranges give a very colourful effect. Such stained glass has clearly come a long way from its Victorian and mediaeval antecedents, but successfully represents the spirit of an age when religious beliefs are less formalized and conventions less followed.

A Gazetteer of churches referred to in the text

Aston Ingham, St John the Baptist — Excellent Bromsgrove Guild glass, and a late Morris and Co. window.

Bridstow, St Bridget — An excellent early Kempe window, a Bromsgrove Guild First World War memorial window and a good selection of Victorian glass.

Brockhampton, All Saints — Arts and Crafts glass by Christopher Whall.

Foy, St Mary — A gothic style window of 1673, copying that at Sellack.

Ganarew, St Swithin —Mid-Victorian window by Alexander Gibbs, large window of 1938 and good 1952 glass by Celtic Studios.

Goodrich, St Giles — Mediaeval fragments, Hardman east window, Bromsgrove Guild memorial window and a selection of other Victorian and early 20th-century glass, including some interesting dedicatees.

Goodrich Castle Chapel — Radar Squadron memorial window and Millennium window by Nicola Hopwood.

Hentland, St Dubricius — Interesting mediaeval fragments and memorial window to Rev William Poole.

Hoarwithy, St Catherine — Burne-Jones window, designs by Seddon and a lively window by H.A. Kennedy.

Hom Green — First World War memorial window, probably by Burlison and Grylls.

Hope Mansell, St Michael — Entertaining 1937 window to 'Nurse Edith' and interesting 1980 St Francis by Geoffrey Robinson.

How Caple, St Andrew and St Mary — Several Bromsgrove Guild windows, a window by Frederick Preedy and an unusual First World War memorial window by James Hogan.

Kings Caple, St John the Baptist — Mediaeval fragments with good Hardman glass below.

Lea, St John the Baptist — Delicate window by Geoffrey Webb (1933) and dramatic east window of 1865.

Little Dewchurch, St David — Several windows by Preedy (also the architect of the church) and Millennium window by Nicola Hopwood.

Llandinabo, St Dinabo — 1893 east window by Kempe.

Llangrove, Christ Church — Colourful east window.

Llanwarne, St John the Baptist — Flemish roundels and east window in the style of (but not by) Kempe.

Much Marcle, St Bartholomew — Kempe glass of various periods and 17th century heraldic glass.

Peterstow, St Peter — Good selection of Victorian glass from different periods.

Ross-on-Wye, St Mary — 15th-century east window from the Bishop's Palace, Stretton Sugwas, good selection of Victorian glass and late Kempe & Co. and Morris windows.

Sellack, St Tysilio — Rare 17th-century gothic-style east window and mediaeval fragments.

Sollers Hope, St Michael — Fragments of mediaeval heraldry.

St Weonards, St Weonard — Mediaeval glass restored by Baillie and Meyer, who also designed a new window, and a German or Flemish panel from Goodrich Court.

Upton Bishop, St John the Baptist — Excellent selection of Victorian glass from very early onwards, including Wailes, Clayton and Bell and Hardman, and small 1953 window by G. Maile & Sons.

Walford, St Michael — First World War memorial window to two brothers.

Welsh Newton, St Mary — Highly coloured east window by Powells.

Weston-under-Penyard, St Lawrence — Victorian east window, exuberant First World War memorial window, Rev Hawkshaw memorial, 1954 window by Basil Barber, St Francis by H.J. Hobbs & Son and Millennium window by Jane Gray.

Whitchurch, St Dubricius — Powells window of 1900 designed by Ada Currey.

CHAPTER 6

The Old Mill at Hoarwithy

The Old Mill, the millhouse of an extensive range of buildings known as Hoarwithy Mill, is an attractive property enjoying a long and interesting history dating from the late 17th century. It stands in the riverside village of Hoarwithy, which is situated at the northern end of Hentland parish (Plate 19). Hoarwithy was first recorded in the 13th century as La Horewythy, and the name is derived from 'Whitebeam' or 'White Withy'. Willow trees grow along the banks of the beautiful Wye where an important river crossing has existed since ancient times. Two brooks join and flow into the Wye at Hoarwithy, the Red Brook and Wriggles Brook, the latter in the past powering five water mills along its course. In 1858 Hoarwithy was recorded in a Herefordshire Directory as follows:

> HOARWITHY is a populous hamlet of this parish, 1½ miles distant north. There is a chapel of ease here, and a Primitive Methodist chapel.

> A bridge has been erected over the river Wye. The Old Harp Inn, at Hoarwithy, is a comfortable house.

> TREADDOW township is a place in this parish, 1½ miles south from the church.

> ALTBOUGH, Kinastone, and Treysack, are also townships.

At that date the waters of Wriggles Brook were driving the water wheels of New Mills in Little Birch, Prothither Mill at Little Dewchurch, and, in Hentland parish, Middle Mill, Tresseck Mill and Hoarwithy Mill. These were all corn mills apart from the one at Tresseck which served as a paper mill before being used as a 'Bone Crushing Mill'. But all these mills date from a much earlier period.

During the Civil War Hentland parish suffered pillaging amounting to £82 15s. by the Scottish Army in 1645. This must have left the parish in a poor state during the Commonwealth when Herefordshire was ruled by an 'elaborate system of committees'. The irregular entries in the parish records and registers bear witness to the upheaval in the lives of the people. After the restoration of the monarchy in 1660 there was a period of change in politics, social standing, building styles and agricultural methods. In the parish of Hentland the River Wye became a more important feature due to its navigation, salmon fishing, river crossing and its tributaries providing a good source of water power. This led to Hoarwithy emerging as a populated hamlet, with its ferry, inns and water mills, together with the earlier farms at Tresseck, Altbough and Llanfrother.

It is in this more settled period in the late 17th century that the Old Mill began its life as a 'Smith's Shop and Cyder Mill' worked and occupied by Edward Marrett, a blacksmith who married Marion Witherstone in 1684. The premises were owned by the Mynd family who were established at Llanfrother in Hentland from the early to mid 16th century after Thomas Mynd had acquired the Manor of Hentland consisting of 'messuages, 130 acres arable, 12 acres meadow, 139 acres pasture and 30 acres woodland'. An altar tomb in Hentland churchyard bears a weathered inscription in memory of the Mynds:

Away vain World, thou Oceans
of Annoys and Welcome Heaven
With thy Eternal Joy

The Marretts' eldest son, also called Edward, married Blanche. His father died in 1717 and left him the 'Smiths Shop', 'Cyder Mill', an 'old mare', 'Four feather beds', a 'pair of sheets', some 'brass and pewter', a 'fire shovel, tongs, and irons and grate', 'casks of all sorts' and other items belonging to the kitchen, all worth £48 12s. 3d. Edward's own offspring were born after the death of Edward senior and were baptized at Hentland: Edward in 1720, Thomas in 1722 and William in 1725.

The owner of the smith's shop and cider mill, William Mynd of 'Llanfrawther', died in 1729. In his 'Last Will and Testament' he desired his funeral to be private, to have a plain coffin and not have a bell rung. He requested that 'Only six of my nearest Relatives will attend my Body to the Church and lay me in my Grave, and that 'twelve of my own Servants and Workmen may carry me to Church and each of them to have a pair of Gloves and Half a Crown.' He also stated that 'only six Bottles of Wine may be drunk at my funeral and no other Liquor, three of the Bottles for the Minister and my Relatives and the other three for the Workmen and Servants', and that 'neither my Wife or any of my children wear any mourning'. Lastly he provided for his wife and ten children, and 'My house at Llanfrawther where I now dwell with the Estate belonging to it being already settled on my eldest son William'.

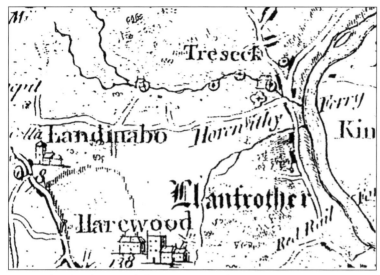

Llanfrother and the Hoawrwithy Ferry as marked on Taylor's map of 1754

This William was running the Llanfrother estate when their tenants at the cider mill and smith's shop, the Marretts, established the water corn mill known as Hoarwithy mill. It stood at the lowest point of the Wriggles Brook in order to secure the maximum water flow, and with easy access from the roads that converged on the Hoarwithy 'horse and small boat' that conveyed goods and livestock across the River Wye. The mill pond stored a plentiful supply of water so that the mill worked effectively to grind corn and animal fodder. From the beginning of the 18th century iron began to be used instead of wood for the gearing, shafts and mechanical parts of the mill, some of which have survived.

A tombstone at Hentland Church records the death in 1770 of 'William Mynd late of Ross, eldest son of William and Helena Mynd of Llanfrother'. After his death the estate passed to his son, William the Younger, including the mill described as 'All that Messuage, Cottage or Tenement and Water Corn Grist Mill with the lands thereto adjoining and belonging commonly called or known by the name of Horewithy Mill situate lying and being at Horewithy in the Parish of Hentland in the county of Herefordshire in the possession of Edward Marrett as Tenant thereof. Together with the Smith's Shop and Cider Mill on part of the said lands erected at Hoarwithy and then in his possession'.

Complicated legal documents reveal that Mynd's will caused financial problems for his son and heir, William the Younger, who was declared bankrupt in 1781. His chosen 'Assigns of his Estate and Effects' were ordered to settle his accounts and pay his creditors from the proceeds of the sale of his properties. As a result, in 1789 the 'Water Corn Mill' and 'Messuage farm and Lands called Llanfrother' were sold for £6,500 to John James for the benefit of George Mynd of Ashe Ingen at Bridstow, younger brother of William the Younger. While these legal transactions were carried out, Edward Marrett was replaced as tenant of Hoarwithy Mill by Thomas Wheeler. After the death of Thomas in 1782 the mill was then occupied by Ann Wheeler, a spinster, who was either a sister or aunt whose tenancy is confirmed in a lease and Release dated 1793:

All that the said Messuage or Tenement Water Corn Grist Mill & the Lands, Tenements and Hereditats thereto belonging situate at Hoarwithy afsd thereinbefore particularly mentd and described or intended so to be and every part and parcel thereof with the appurts then in the possesion of Edwd Wheeler as Tenant thereof — —

In 1795 the cottage and water corn grist mill known as 'Hoarwithy's Mill' together with one acre of land called Gwatkin's Meadow and two acres of arable land called the Laskett were purchased by Edward Wheeler from George Mynd for the 'price or sum of £420'. Edward was a miller from Pencoyd and obviously an unconventional character, who was related to Thomas and Anne Wheeler. Edward's first five children were born before he married their mother, Mary Elliott, in 1798. After the wedding another four sons were baptized in their father's name at Hentland.

Millers of the early 19th century were observed by John Duncumb in his agriculture of County of Hereford published in 1805:

> It is a subject of frequent complaint amongst the lower classes, that they cannot now, as they formerly did, buy their bushel or half bushel of wheat in the market, and employ the miller to grind it, but that they are compelled to purchase the flour already reduced. The millers then (and some of them pursue the same line now,) sent his horse round to collect the corn, which he ground and returned the following day.
>
> This could not be done by the miller without incurring a considerable expense, which was ultimately repaid by the increased quantity of corn which he detained as toll. If he ground, as he then pretended, every one's bushel or peck of corn by itself, much delay was of necessity occasioned; and this delay again enhanced of necessity the price of grinding. The miller had then as good opportunities of mixing the flour as the dealer has now, and will probably be found, that, whenever wheat has been comparatively dearer than other kinds of grain, the practice of mixing different

sorts of flour, was almost as generally formerly, according to the degree of temptation offered, as it has been in later times. Nor is this mixture to be deprecated in seasons of real scarcity; for when the quantity of wheat is not sufficient to afford the requisite supply, a better substitute is not to be found. We may justly lament the necessity, but we cannot arraign the property of the measure. As a dealer in flour, the miller now purchases a load of corn at once from the farmer, and he proceeds in the manufacture without interruption or delay.

This enables him to supply his customers with flour on much lower terms than they could procure it, when the miller sent his horses at a comfortable expense to collect the corn in small quantities, and again to return the flour by the same conveyance.

The wives of the peasantry, it is true, frequently carry their pecks of wheat to the mill, and having waited to see it ground, bring back the flour, and thus seem effectually to guard against all imposition or fraud.

But it often happens, that the miller is too much engaged, to grind it at the time it was brought, and he may sometimes also postpone it with a fraudulent intention. But in every case, and without this expedient, he may impose upon when present. On these occasions the old ladies will generally be found assembled in a group, attending to, and circulating the scandal of the day, and settling the affairs of the nation below, whilst the miller above stairs, takes away or exchanges a portion of their corn, as readily as Jonas and Breslaw could exchange a card in a pack.

In 1807 Edward Wheeler died, a year after the birth of his youngest son. In his will he requested a decent burial and his debts and funeral expenses to be paid. Edward left his property to his 'loving wife Mary Wheeler' until her death, and then to his nine children 'born by me lawfully begotten', words perhaps chosen to explain the first five bearing his wife's maiden name of Elliot. Mary Wheeler continued to occupy and run Hoarwithy Mill paying the annual Land Tax of 4s. until her death in 1831. Under the terms of her husband's will of 1807, the value of the estate had to be divided amongst the surviving members of the family, a lengthy legal process that was resolved in 1833 by the youngest son, John Wheeler. He secured a mortgage of £1,400 to pay his brothers and sisters or surviving spouses their share of the estate, and enable him to remain at Hoarwithy Mill, as set out as follows:

1833
March 15 To Cash paid Edward Elliott his share of purchase money (1200£) after deducting 4.11.0 his share (one ninth) of Bill of Business and Disbursements against the Trust Estate under the Will of Mr. Edward Wheeler ——— 195. 9. —

To Ann Elliott ——— D° ——— 195. 9. —
To John Donne ——— D° ——— 195. 9. —
To Thomas Wheeler ——— D° ——— 195. 9. —
To James Wheeler ——— D° ——— 195. 9. —
To Humphrey Harry ——— D° ——— 195. 9. —

Expenses against the Trust Estate to be divided between the 9 legatees being 4.11.0 each (6 of such shares deducted as above) ——— 40. 18. 5

To Cash paid Mr. John Wheeler ——— 100. —

To Interest to Mr. Garrold on 1200£ from 9 Aug. 1832 (the date of Deposit) to 16 March 1833 (the date of Mortgage) as pr Agreement at 4½ pCent ——— 32. 8. —

Deduct Interest allowed by the Bank ——— 18. 9. 6
13. 18. 6

To Bill for Mortgage and Stamps ——— 24. 5. 8

To Balance ——— 48. 3. 5
————
£ 1400. 0. 0

In the mortgage John Wheeler's property was described as 'All that Messuage or Dwelling House with the two Gardens Malthouse Barn Stables and other outbuildings' and also 'All that Water Corn Mill with the Millhouse called Hoarwithy Mill with the Millhouse and buildings' and 'the Little Meadow', the 'Mill Bank', and the 'Laskett' three acres in the parish of Harewood.

The arrangement of buildings forming John Wheeler's mill, house and outbuildings are clearly shown on the Hentland Tithe Map of 1842. The dwelling house was a smaller L-shaped building with outbuildings where the 36-year-old miller lived with his wife, Mary, their two year old daughter and baby son. John Wheeler employed three agricultural labourers, who also lived on the premises.

Hentland baptism, 1842

In 1851 Wheeler was farming 250 acres and employing 11 labourers including Walter Hyde, Charles Wall and James Smith who lived at the mill with his wife, two children and Sarah Preece, a general servant. Hoarwithy had grown in size and population and supported its own Chapel of Ease erected in 1842, an Independent Chapel built around 1820, a small school run by voluntary contributions and a parish constable. Hoarwithy was then self-sufficient, with a butcher, grocer, dressmaker, shoemaker, tailor, blacksmith, sawyer, haulier, carpenter, stone mason and farmers and fishermen. John Wheeler and Susannah Pymble may have supplied malt to some of the five licensed premises trading in Hoarwithy at that date: the Fisherman's Arms, the Yew Tree, the Odd Fellow's Arms, the Three Salmons and the larger Old Harp Inn.

John Wheeler obviously struggled to pay his mortgage and needed a further loan in 1858, but he continued as a miller and farmer, and in 1871 was employing eight men and two boys as agricultural labourers and one man servant. Eight of his workmen lived at Hoarwithy Mill with him, his wife, five daughters and one son. In 1873 John died followed by his wife in 1875 leaving their young son, John, liable for the debts and the welfare of his unmarried sisters. John junior managed to 'postpone the sale' of the premises by extending the existing loan of £500 to £1,000. Under the terms of the revised mortgage he guaranteed 'not to pull down or remove the said Mill buildings millgear millwright work machinery or fixtures' without permission or unless 'such pulling down or removal shall replace the machinery or articles worn out or replaced by others of at least equal value'. The young Wheeler undertook to keep the mill in 'a good state of repair and also insured against loss or damage by fire in the sum of Eight Hundred Pounds at least in the Law Union Insurance office in London.' The document was signed by all interested parties in 1877.

Unfortunately the finances of John Wheeler did not improve, and in 1883 he was forced by his mortgages to file a 'Petition in the County Court of Herefordshire holden at Hereford for liquidation by arrangement or composition with his creditors under the provisions of the Bankruptcy Act of 1869'. At the first meeting of the creditors a resolution was passed 'that the affairs of John Wheeler should be liquidated by arrangement but not by Bankruptcy'. The outcome of a Further Security dated 1884 was that sisters

Sarah Jane and Emma Wheeler were able to continue at the 'Dwellinghouse with the Two Gardens Malthouse Barn Stables' and the 'Water Corn Mill called Hoarwithy Mill and the millhouse and buildings', together with the pieces of land called Mill Bank, Little Meadow and the Lasketts at a rental of 'Thirty six pounds per annum being a fair and reasonable rent' within the meaning of the Bills of Sale Act 1878.

The 1884 legal documents freed John Wheeler, Ellen Wheeler and his married sister Mary Ann Bennett from the incumbrances caused by their grandfather's request in his will to share his estate equally among his nine children. This left the two spinster sisters, Sarah Jane and Emma Wheeler now in their fifties and sixties to run Hoarwithy Mill during the remainder of the 1880s. This was a difficult task at a time when traditional corn milling by waterpower was being replaced by steampower in larger modern mills with better rail communications.

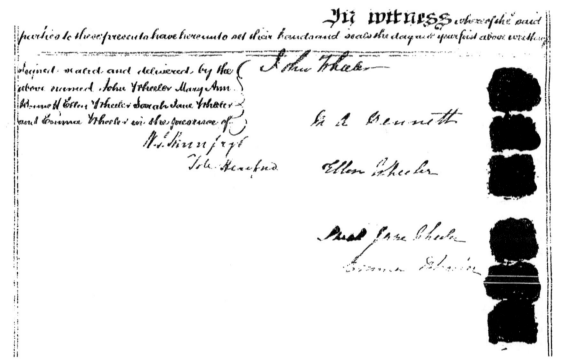

It appears that it was the Wheeler sisters that kept and maybe dispensed various bottles and packets of medications purchased from Williams, a Hereford chemist that traded throughout the second half of the 19th century. At a much later date, a previously hidden cupboard was discovered with numerous narrow shelves containing a medicine bottle and a neat packet containing 'Grains of Paradise'. These were capsules of a West African plant used as a spice, in the preparation of medicines, or the name for malt left over after brewing or distilling.

An advertisement from an 1867 directory

In 1890 'Hoarwithy Mill and lands' was conveyed from the mortgagees with the concurrence of Sarah Jane and Emma Wheeler to James Preece, a hotel keeper from the New Harp, Hoarwithy. Preece paid £660 for the 'dwellinghouse with two gardens malthouse barn stables and other outbuildings', the 'Water Corn Mill called Hoarwithy Mill with the millhouse and buildings' together with 'all machinery', mill gear and millwright's work fixtures and appurtenances, and the three pieces of land including the Lasketts occupied by Thomas Smith. James Preece and his wife, both aged 64 took over the running of the mill with the help of a 16-year-old labourer. The whereabouts of the two spinster sisters is unknown, but it appears that John Wheeler became a corn dealer's agent in Hereford.

James Preece died in January 1900 and was buried at Hoarwithy. In his will Preece bequeathed his 'personal estate' to his executor Henry Jones 'to sell call in and convert into money' to pay his 'funeral and testamentary expenses and debts', and to pay the 'residue arising' to Kate, the wife of Henry Jones.

Hoarwithy Bridge c.1900

The mill workings (Coates & Tucker, 1983)

Preece's other properties in Hoarwithy were left to his brother George, Daniel Hopkins and Eliza Edwards, but his 'grist millhouse and Orchard thereto belonging situate in the said parish of Hentland and also my cottage and garden' were inherited by Kate Jones subject to a payment of £20 to Preece's married sister. By November 1900, James Preece's will had been untangled which enabled his brother George to purchase 'All that Grist or Water Corn Mill called Hoarwithy Mill and All that messuage or dwelling-house known as Mill House Together with the Mill house and malt house barn stables and other outbuildings', in order to sell the premises in 1903 on to Alfred Earnest Lock who already ran and occupied the mill.

During the early years of the 20th century Locke's need for further advances and mortgages indicate a decline in milling at Hoarwithy. Maybe to compensate for the lack of business Alfred

Entries in a directory of 1902

Locke converted the former malt house into a shop, and in 1908 the 34-year-old married a 47-year-old spinster schoolteacher from London called Louisa Clarke. They had been acquainted a year earlier when Louisa was the mortgagee of Alfred's loan.

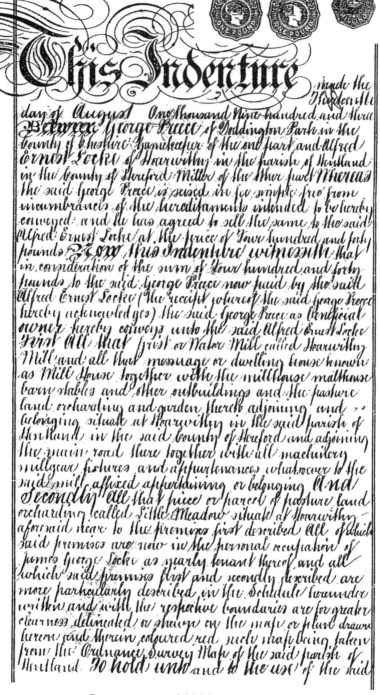

This Indenture made the Thirteenth day of August One thousand Nine hundred and three **Between** George Preece of Doddington Park in the County of Chester Gamekeeper of the one part and Alfred Ernest Locke of Hoarwithy in the parish of Hentland in the County of Hereford Miller of the other part **Whereas** the said George Preece is seised in fee simple free from incumbrances of the hereditaments intended to be hereby conveyed and he has agreed to sell the same to the said Alfred Ernest Locke at the price of Four hundred and forty pounds **Now this Indenture witnesseth** that in consideration of the sum of Four hundred and forty pounds to the said George Preece now paid by the said Alfred Ernest Locke (the receipt whereof the said George Preece hereby acknowledges) the said George Preece as Beneficial owner hereby conveys unto the said Alfred Ernest Locke **First All that** Grist or Water Mill called Hoarwithy Mill and all that messuage or dwelling house known as Mill House together with the millhouse malthouse barn stables and other outbuildings and the pasture land orcharding and garden thereto adjoining and belonging situate at Hoarwithy in the said parish of Hentland in the said County of Hereford and adjoining the main road there together with all machinery millgear fixtures and appurtenances whatsoever to the said mill affixed appertaining or belonging **And Secondly All that** piece or parcel of pasture land orcharding called Little Meadow situate at Hoarwithy aforesaid near to the premises first described **All** of which said premises are now in the personal occupation of James George Locke as yearly tenant thereof and all which said premises first and secondly described are more particularly described in the Schedule hereunder written and with the respective boundaries are for greater clearness delineated or shewn on the map or plan drawn hereon and therein coloured red such map being taken from the Ordnance Survey Map of the said parish of Hentland **To hold unto** and to the use of the said

Conveyance of 1903

157

CERTIFICATE OF MARRIAGE.

190*8* Marriage solemnized at *St Johns Church* in the *Parish* of *Paddington.*
in the County of *London*

No.	When Married.	Name and Surname.	Age.	Condition.	Rank or Profession.	Residence at the time of Marriage.	Father's Name and Surname.	Rank or Profession of Father.
84. 1.	August 4th 1908.	Alfred Ernest Locke	34	Bachelor	Miller	Mill House Hoarwithy Hereford	James Locke	Miller.
		Louisa Clarke	47	Spinster	—	School House Itchborne St	James Clarke	Bootmaker.

Married in the *St Johns Church* according to the Rites and Ceremonies of the Established Church, after Banns, by me, *S. P. Anderson dca*

This Marriage was solemnized between us, { *Alfred Ernest Locke* / *Louisa Clarke* } in the presence of us, { *George H. ... / Helen M. Fuller* }

I Certify, that the foregoing is a true Copy of an entry in the Register Book of Marriages of the *Parish of St John* in the Parish of *Paddington*, and Register Book is now lawfully in my keeping. Witness my hand this *4th* day of *August* 190*8*.   *S. P. An...*   Designation   *Vicar.*

* NOTE.—Strike out that which does not apply.

Marriage Certificate of Alfred Locke & Louisa Clarke, 1908

With he help and support of his wife, Alfred managed to extend his boundaries in 1910 by purchasing a 'piece or parcel of land known as the Weir' occupied by Thomas Dance who kept the New Harp at Hoarwithy. This addition to his property cost Locke £86 acquired by yet another mortgage. A year later Locke was anxious to sell Hoarwithy Mill, and placed an advertisement in *The Miller.*

Unable to sell the mill the Lockes moved to Pound Farm at Tadley in Hampshire, and Hoarwithy mill was let to P. Chapman & Son, 'millers, coal merchants, bakers and grocers'. Unfortunately Locke struggled with his farm at Tadley, and in 1917 mortgaged the 62-acre farm together with Hoarwithy mill, the Weir and Little Meadow which he continued to own until he retired from farming and moved to Reading. In 1920 Locke sold his

HENTLAND, HEREFORDSHIRE.
CORN MILL, HOUSE AND LAND.

MESSRS EDWARDS AND RUSSELL will offer for sale by AUCTION at the LAW SOCIETY'S ROOMS, East Street, HEREFORD, on

WEDNESDAY, NOVEMBER 22ND, 1911,

at 3 o'clock, a Stone Built and Slated Four Storey WATER CORN MILL, known as "Hoarwithy Mill," and containing Iron Water Wheel, two pairs of Stones, Flour Dressing Machine, Driving Wheels and Hoisting Tackle, together with a commodious Stone Built DWELLING HOUSE, Grocer's Shop, Blacksmith's Workshop, Bakehouse, Stables, Cowhouses, Yard and Garden.

Also a piece of MEADOW LAND, of about 1 a. 3 r., and a SMALL ORCHARD. The Property is situate in the Hamlet of Hoarwithy, in the Parish of Hentland, six miles from Ross and two miles from Ballingham and Fawley Railway Stations.

For further particulars apply to the Auctioneers, 67, Newmarket Street, Hereford, or to Messrs. LAMBE, CARLESS AND SON, Solicitors, Hereford.   (5683)

Sale advertisement of 1911

158

Herefordshire mill and land at Hoarwithy for £1,000 to Thomas Dance of Quarry Bank, the former landlord of the New Harp at Hoarwithy. Dance was the last miller at Hoarwithy mill to grind corn by water power as described by Coates and Tucker in *Water Mills of the Middle Wye Valley*:

> **On Wriggle Brook. SO 545293. Still stands with almost complete machinery on north-east side; ceased working c1930. Has provision for two waterwheels, one on each side of the building, with each driving two pairs of stones, but no machinery remains on south-west side. NE wheel remains, derelict, 12ft x 4ft 1½in, overshot; iron boss, rim and buckets; wooden axle, arms and soleplates. Conventional layout of gearing driving two pairs of French burr stones, tubular cast-iron vertical shaft 10in diam. Building still used for milling with electric motor on trolley belt-driving disc grinder.**

Thomas Dance was also a corn dealer, coal merchant and haulier before he died in 1940. His widow, Annie, inherited his estate which passed to Thomas Henry Oldis by an agreement dated 1941. This included a 'Ford motor lorry registered Number VJ5611 formerly the property of Thomas Dance and used by him in his business of a Miller Corn and Coal Merchant and Haulier and now used by Thomas Henry Oldis, always known as Jim, who purchased an additional four acres from Albert Mailes, boarding house proprietor of the Old Harp at Hoarwithy'.

Conveyance of 1943

In 1953 the writers of the Women's Institute of Hoarwithy wrote 'in the centre of the village you will find the Old Mill, which is still in use. Like the previous two mills this was also worked by a Water Wheel, but has now been modernised, and is driven

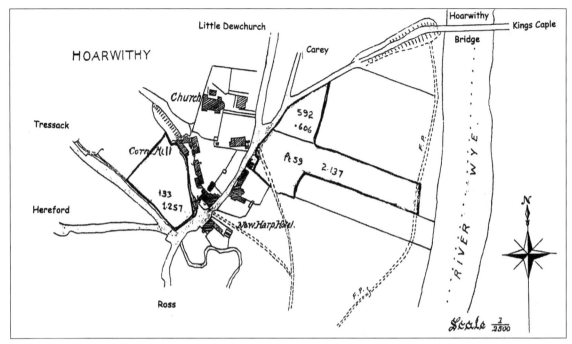

Plan of 1943 accompanying the conveyance

by electricity'. Although the mill building was recorded in the 1970s as being 'used for milling with electric motor' it ceased working before 1978, when the whole property was acquired by the present owner. A year later Hoarwithy mill and its buildings were sold and converted into an attractive dwelling house, and the mill house became a popular guest house offering a 'warm welcome', 'comfortable surrounds' and 'good food'.

Old Mill building before conversion (Coates & Tucker)

160

CHAPTER 7

Henry Southall 1826-1916

Introduction
In the autumn of 2001 I was invited to research and write a 'Pink Publication' for the Ross-on-Wye and District Civic Society. I agreed, on condition that I could write a biography of someone interesting and for whom sufficient primary resource material was available for study. Henry Southall (1826-1916), 'The Grand Old Man of Ross', was the suggested subject for my writing and my preparatory investigations commenced. I soon discovered that an enormous collection of Southall-family letters had been deposited at Herefordshire Record Office by Henry's great grandson, Mr Colin Michael Southall, and my research began in earnest. I spent many months reading hundreds of letters and gradually formed a picture of the Southall family. As I became more familiar with their individual styles of writing, Henry and his wife, Louisa, and their four children, Henry John, Charles, Mary Louisa and Thomas, began to emerge from their letters as real people. They were prolific letter writers and, as they set forth their thoughts and feelings to each other and their numerous relatives, the Quaker world of the 19th century began to be revealed. It was not just the Quaker world of Herefordshire which appeared. The Southalls travelled a great deal and had many business, social, religious and political connections throughout the country. In their politics they were radical and mixed with some of the most radical political thinkers of their day. I asked for an interesting person for the subject of my research and in Henry Southall and his family I was not disappointed.

An Eloquent Speaker at 85
In March 1911, the Ross Traders' Association held its first annual dinner and the *Ross Gazette*[1] provided its readers with a detailed report of the evening's events. The dinner was held at the Royal Hotel and Mr Henry Southall, the oldest trader present, was the guest speaker. He had been a Ross trader for 60 years, was well-known, well-liked and, quite clearly, very well respected, because the hundred or so people present received him

warmly and with prolonged cheering. He had given many lectures and made numerous public speeches during his long association with the town and there can be little doubt that his reputation for pithy remarks, gentle teasing and wise advice, all delivered with wit and good humour, had gone before him. He did not let his audience down, for his was, indeed, an eloquent speech. It included a little of his own personal history, some mild chiding of Ross Urban Council and some wise advice to traders, punctuated throughout with frequent applause.

He reminded everyone just how much traders could contribute to the prosperity of the town and urged all those present to do their very best for it. He admitted that, at his age, there was now little more that he could do, but declared that 'he had served on every public Board in Ross,' adding, a little mischievously, 'except that of church-warden.'[2] Indeed, Henry Southall had served his adopted town very well for decades and continued to do so until his death in 1916.

Henry Southall in his later years
(by kind permission of C.M. Southall)

Ironically, the public offices to which he had so generously and proudly given much of his time and energy had been closed to his father's generation. Henry's father, John, was keenly interested in politics but, at the time of Henry's birth in 1826, Quakers and all other nonconformists were barred from holding public office, irrespective of their abilities or their willingness to serve.

In 1820, John Southall (1788-1862), a prosperous wool and linen draper of Leominster had married Hannah Burlingham (1788-1841), the daughter of a Worcester glove manu-facturer. They had seven children but only four survived infancy: John Tertius born in 1822; Elizabeth in 1823; Henry in 1826; and Hannah in 1828. This high level of infant mortality was quite usual at that time even in the most caring of homes. Their surviving letters suggest that John and Hannah sustained a kind and loving relationship throughout their marriage and their children were brought up gently in a well ordered household. They could afford to keep domestic servants and, in particular, a resident nurse to look after the children. Although Hannah was a tender and attentive mother, she was never to enjoy really robust health and the nurse was probably essential to the smooth running of the house.

There was always a very strong bond between Hannah and her sons, particularly John Tertius who was described as 'the dearest of her children'.[3] She was perhaps trying to compensate, just a little, for what she perceived as their father's strictness with them. In later years, John Tertius was prone to say that his father 'was inclined to be severe with his sons, but spoilt his daughters, especially Hannah'.[4] All in all, though, they appear to have been a happy family and the children developed strong bonds of kinship, affection and loyalty which they all sustained into very old age.

The presence of a family nurse and other domestic servants allowed John and Hannah to participate in the life of Leominster and, particularly, in the work of the small Quaker society which flourished there. At that time Quakers did not learn to dance or learn to play musical instruments. It was thought that such activities might take too much time from the more serious aspects of life and, of particular importance, the pursuit of excellence could engender pride and thus endanger the spirit. They would, however, happily spend money on other aspects of education, on travel and on good works. They took their religious beliefs and duties very seriously, regularly attending weekly and monthly local meetings, regional quarterly meetings and the all important London Yearly Meeting too. Attendance at meetings was clearly quite a costly matter in terms of time and travel and this meant that it was impossible to be working class and Quaker unless individuals were sponsored by more affluent Friends. It cannot have been very easy, either, for John and Hannah to hold to these commitments when the children

From Lascelles & Co Directory & Gazetteer of Herefordshire, *1851*

were very small, even with the assistance of a nurse. Their daughter, Lucy, who had been born in June 1829 and was to die in infancy, had been unwell and it was probably for this reason that in 1830 John travelled to the London Yearly Meeting on his own. Until very late in the 19th century, women attended their own meetings which ran in parallel with the men's meetings. The London Yearly Meeting was at the apex of the power structure of the Society of Friends and, of course, the real power rested with the men.

Despite the fact that he was not of particularly robust health, John Southall travelled quite extensively whilst helping members of his extended family, dealing with matters concerning the Society of Friends and, of course, in pursuing his own business interests as a draper. He was, however, never away for more than a day or two before he wrote home to Hannah and later, when they were older, to his children. In May 1830, John said goodbye to Hannah and the children and set out on the long journey to London in order to attend the Quakers' Yearly Meeting. The journey to London would seldom have been taken by many of the inhabitants of Leominster and would have been beyond the means of most of them.

By 1830, a complex web of coaching routes had been established which made it possible for determined travellers to leave even a remote Herefordshire market town early in the morning and, depending on the time of year and the weather, to arrive in the capital by late evening or, perhaps, the next day. Coaching timetables printed in the Pigot's *Trade Directory* of the time indicated that John Southall could have taken a morning coach from Leominster and travelled on to London on the same day, but his first letter to Hannah confirmed that he broke his journey at Worcester. It is likely, therefore, that he took either The Telegraph Coach from Ludlow which called at Allen's Coach Office in Leominster at eleven o'clock in the morning or, the Royal Mail Coach from Kington which called at the Red Lion at half past eleven. He attended a Quaker meeting in Worcester that evening, stayed overnight with relatives and joined the Sovereign Coach which left the city at 6.30 in the morning after calling at both the Unicorn and the Hop Pole hotels.

The 111 mile journey from Worcester to London would have been exhausting even though it was punctuated by stops at coaching inns or agents' offices in Pershore, Evesham, Chipping Norton, Woodstock, Oxford and High Wycombe. Passengers needed to stretch their legs, take some refreshment and, of course, if speed was to be maintained, fresh horses were needed at regular intervals. Even in good weather, however, coach travel was not without its discomforts and its dangers. The poor state of the roads meant that coach rides could be very bumpy and travellers needed to be in fairly good health in order to undertake a lengthy journey. It was not unknown for coaches to collide on narrow roads or to overturn if the driver was careless or tipsy. There was also the worrying possibility of encounters with highwaymen. Although incidents of highway robbery have almost certainly been exaggerated, they were a very real fear in some parts of the country and

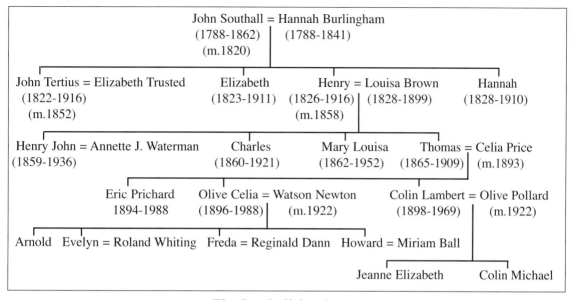

The Southall family tree

particularly on the approaches to London. Fortunately, although very tired, John Southall arrived safely and immediately met up with friends and relatives.

Soon after his arrival in London John sat down to write to Hannah in Leominster to tell her of his journey and to assure her of his safety. It was a gentle and affectionate letter and said much about the nature of their relationship. Writing from the Guildhall Coffee House[5] he explained that on the first three stages of his journey from Worcester there had been heavy rain and he had been able to travel inside the coach, but soon the weather had brightened up and he was pleased that he had not reserved an inside seat for the whole journey. Despite his indifferent health and quite secure financial position, like most Quakers, he would not spend money on luxuries. At 42 years of age he probably saw no reason why, at the end of May, he could not travel quite comfortably on top of the coach in the open air. He commented that the coach driver had been good and the journey had proceeded without mishap.

On arrival he had taken tea with three of his four brothers. He did not mention them by name, but they were probably Edward, Thomas and Samuel. His other brother, William, had been 'disunited' from the Society in 1824 when he had married Elizabeth Baker in accordance with the rites of the Established Church. He was, however, received back into the Society of Friends with his wife and three children, but not until March 1830, so perhaps it was a little early for him to attend the Yearly Meeting again. John finally arrived at his lodgings at 9 o'clock, where he met the brothers Joseph and Charles Sturge whose sister, Priscilla, was married to John's brother, Samuel. The Sturges were staying at the same house as John and he was delighted when they invited him to make use of their private sitting room if he wished to do so. They would have known of John's sometimes less than vigorous health and were perhaps aware that he was looking particularly tired after his long journey from Leominster. They would also have known that Hannah would have been anxious about him. John, for his part, appreciated their invitation as a great act of kindness.

Until the 1830s, Quakers' participation in politics had been limited to forming pressure groups for social change, but in the late 1820s new legislation had allowed religious Dissenters to emerge from the political wilderness they had endured for so long. In 1828 the Test and Corporation Acts were repealed, which paved the way for Dissenters to hold public office. The way was, however, not entirely clear; the declaration required by the new Act did not accord with Quaker consciences. It was a step in the right direction but it was not until the late 1830s that a reworded declaration was deemed acceptable to the Society of Friends. In earlier times it had been one of the tenets of the Society of Friends that they did not participate in politics and there were those Friends who still held firmly to that view. The crucial factor was that, from a legal point of view, Quakers were now free to decide for themselves; that is, whether to become involved in politics at local level or as Members of Parliament. It was John Southall's generation which had led the way and his two sons embraced every opportunity which presented itself to serve their community throughout their adult lives. John Tertius worked tirelessly to achieve improvements in Leominster, just as Henry did for so many years in Ross. Despite their increasing political freedom at home, however, the Friends did not lose sight of other political objectives in the wider world and the subjects debated at the Yearly Meeting of 1830 reflect that vision.

In his letter to Hannah, John related that he had attended lectures and debates on the evils of slavery and on 'carrying the knowledge of the Gospel to Heathen nations'.[6] He had listened to some of the most prominent

An advertisement from 1862 (Hereford Library)

166

speakers of the Quaker world; namely, Sarah Grubb and William Forster. He had also listened to a lengthy, well received, speech given by Joseph Sturge on the emancipation of slaves. Sturge had, long ago, embraced the anti-slavery cause and had been a founder member of the Anti-Slavery Society. In his speech he had strongly advocated the principle of immediate, rather than gradual, emancipation for slaves. No doubt these subjects were eagerly debated amongst the Southall brothers and the Sturges back at their lodgings, as well as within the wider family in Leominster.

John's children were born into a rapidly changing society. The Industrial Revolution was still gathering pace and the enormous urban development which it brought was largely unfettered: there were no planning regulations with which to effect even the most modest control. The notion of control flew in the face of the idea of laissez-faire and the result was that industrialisation created enormous wealth for some people and social degradation for others. The need for reforming legislation to control hours and conditions of work for those employed in mines and factories was urgent, but the law was lagging behind and change was slow to arrive.

The growing number of Nonconformists had their own particular focuses for political change. They were no longer prepared to accept that they should have to pay tithes towards the support of Church of England clergy or a church rate towards the mainte-nance of buildings they did not use, simply because they owned property and were rate payers in the general sense. Indeed, for Quakers this was a particular problem, because as members of the Society of Friends they were firmly enjoined not to pay tithes which, of course, was strictly illegal. These issues were, without a doubt, discussed amongst the Southall brothers who all had commercial interests and property in Leominster. In 1830, Samuel was a grocer and tea merchant with premises in Broad Street; John was a wool and linen draper in the Corn Market; William was a chemist with a shop in Draper's Lane; and Edward was a wine and spirits merchant with a business in Broad Street. The refusal to pay tithes or church rate or contributions to the Militia could result in the distraint of goods and records[7] show that Edward suffered in this way in June 1828. Two Deputy Lieutenants of the Militia, Frederick Allen and Edward Evans, went to his premises and removed wine and spirits to the value of £4 11s. 4d., leaving 9s. 8d. unpaid. It is not clear whether they returned at a later date to collect the deficit, but it is quite clear that holding steadfastly to one's religious beliefs took great humility and a lot of courage.

John and Hannah suffered the distraint of goods for the non-payment of the church rate in 1838 and again in 1841. Writing to her son, John Tertius, whilst he was away serving his apprenticeship as a draper, Hannah gave details of a very distressing event which had taken place and of the goods removed. She stated: 'We have at length had the long expected seizure for church rates, and it proved quite as trying, or more so, than I had expected.'[8] She went on: 'They came last week on market day. The Superintendant of the police with one of his men entered the house, producing the warrant, and then proceeded to perform his office.' Despite her feelings about the matter, Hannah seems to have been very cool about the event. 'They first took a round mahogany table out of the counting house. Next four of the parlour chairs which were in that room.' It seems likely that John was not at home when the seizure was made, but Hannah did not hesitate to investigate what was going on when she heard raised voices coming from the kitchen. She continued the story saying that then they '... walked into the kitchen and seized my nice copper stew pan and the small round table which the servants need in the evenings. Altogether [these goods] amounting in value to about four pounds.' She added, too, that they had actually taken much more than their warrant had demanded. On the same day goods were also seized from Samuel Southall and probably from other members of the Society of Friends as well. The following day the goods were auctioned at a well attended sale in the town hall which had been announced to all by the town crier ringing his bell.

Until the year 1868, Church of England churchwardens of every parish were empowered to declare a church rate for the maintenance of the church building and also empowered to impose it on all householders irrespective of their religious beliefs. Not unreasonably, Dissenters, who did not use the parish church, saw the church rate as very unjust. Hannah Southall seems to have taken the seizure of her property with fortitude and, while she realised that many other local people also accepted that the church rate was unfair, there was very little real support for those who suffered the removal of some of their household possessions.

Later, in 1841, again in a long letter to John Tertius,[9] Hannah poured out her thoughts and feelings about the religious views of the Friends and the awkward position in which they found themselves. 'As occasion has presented I have endeavoured to make it understood that we consider ourselves individually bound to obey the law in our own consciences which forbid any forced maintenance of religious observance and of a hireling ministry.' She clearly understood, though, that however much sympathy there was for their plight, many people were frightened to show their support openly for fear of putting themselves out of favour with their parish priest. Hannah was obviously a clear thinking woman and a realist for she continued: 'Many do appear so far to enter into our views or to acknowledge that the thing is wrong and ought to be done away. But whilst they suffer themselves to be so priest-ridden, I fear but very few will affectually set their faces against it.' Hannah was clearly a very well educated lady who could think for her self and form her own opinions.

The Southalls were prolific letter writers and the content, style and expression of much of their correspondence suggest that by the 1830s they were very interested in the politics of the day. In the letters which passed between John and his sons, John Tertius and Henry, whilst they were away from home serving their apprenticeships, serious political issues were discussed as well as personal and domestic concerns. The Southalls were largely Whigs, except John Southall's spinster sister Mary who was seen as 'something of a Tory'[10] and who viewed the radical reforming ideas and opinions of her nephews as quite 'subversive'.

Although John and Hannah brought up their children in the small market town of Leominster and in an even smaller Quaker community, it was almost certainly not as claustrophobic as it might at first appear. As small children they were educated at home by their mother on a day to day basis and greatly encouraged by their father in a wide range of interests as they grew older. They all went away to school: Elizabeth and Hannah to Worcester and John Tertius and Henry to Birmingham. Within their own generation there were some 55 first cousins amongst the Southalls, Burlinghams, Pritchards, Newmans and the Darbys. They wrote to each other and visited various branches of these families in Worcester, Birmingham, Godalming, Kings Lynn, Bristol and Coalbrookdale quite frequently. They were all well educated and literate young people and their lives were, in many ways, privileged. They were encouraged to think and to question and, particularly, to work for the community as well as themselves. On the 14th November 1912, the *Ross Gazette* reported an address given by Mr Henry Southall to the Men's Own Brotherhood on the subject of 'Life's Work and Duty' in which 'he besought his hearers to put aside all low ideals, and so to follow Christ that they might enlighten the neighbourhood in which they dwelt.'[11] All John's children endeavoured to follow Christ and also embraced public duty throughout their long lives.

Education and Apprenticeship

John and Hannah Southall were literate people. In an age when the hand-written letter was the only means of communication over long distances, it was an important social skill which permeated almost every aspect of their lives. They were in constant communication with their numerous Southall, Burlingham, Pritchard, Newman and Darby relations and took great pains to see that their own four children learned to be sound correspondents too.

At first the children were taught by their mother at home, but from about ten years of age they were sent away to school. They were, however, very fortunate in having relatives who lived in areas near to their schools. The girls, Elizabeth and Hannah, attended Mrs Letitia Impey's school in Worcester where some of their Burlingham relatives lived. The boys, John Tertius and Henry, attended a Quaker school run by one William Lean in the Camp Hill district of Birmingham. By this time their uncles, Thomas and William Southall, both chemists, were working in partnership with premises at 17 Bull Street in the old part of the city. Writing from Camp Hill School in February 1842, Henry told his father that my 'Uncles here are exceedingly kind to me, I might almost say unceasingly kind to me.'[12] The Southall children were clearly very well placed to make the best of their education and John and Hannah were not without expectations. The children were required to write to them very regularly and, although kindly in tone, their parents' replies indicate that the letters they received were considered carefully and comments were made about content, length and style. This was a very good parenting approach and clearly intended to ensure that the children got the best possible start in life.

In late November, 1833 John wrote a long and affectionate letter[13] to Elizabeth at school in Worcester. There were, however, some crisp points made about a recent letter home: 'Thy last letter we thought written neatly. Please to observe that we shall consider thy letters the longer the better.' She was, of course, at school on her own because her sister Hannah was at that time only five years of age. Indeed, in his letter John commented: 'Mamma, I may inform thee continues to keep school every day, and Henry & Hannah are I believe sometimes attentive scholars and sometimes, I fear the contrary altho' I hope we have no great reason to complain of them.' It was evident that although Henry and Hannah were only seven and five years old respectively, their application to learning was an important matter and not considered lightly. It was obvious, too, that the education of John Tertius, then 11 years old, had been under review. In the same letter John told Elizabeth that her brother would shortly be returning from school at Thornbury and, after a week or two at home, he would accompany him to Birmingham, presumably for the beginning of the spring term at William Lean's school at Camp Hill. In later years John Tertius was to speak scathingly of his time at Thornbury and his removal from it underlines, once again, the seriousness with which John and Hannah considered their children's education and its importance in their future progress in life.

Later in his letter John asked Elizabeth if she had been to any Temperance Meetings recently and made the point that there were some very eminent Temperance Characters in Worcester saying: 'I may notice Henry Stone as an eloquent orator & Edward Brewin as a zealous advocate of the cause.' He also added rather dismally that their efforts were, however, unlikely to result in the closing of many gin shops and beer houses. One wonders how he reconciled these thoughts with the fact that his brother Edward had for some years been engaged in the wine and spirit trade in their home town of Leominster.

The tone of John's letter was, by modern standards, quite adult for a 10-year-old girl to receive from her father whilst away at school and the terseness of some of his remarks perhaps calls into question the claim made by John Tertius in later life that his father spoilt his sisters. Older brothers and sisters have, perhaps, always thought that younger ones were spoilt or over-indulged, whatever the truth of the matter. Despite his terseness, however, John ended his letter to Elizabeth: 'With dear love I remain thy truly affectionate Father, John Southall' and the reader is not left with any lingering doubt that he really did mean what he said.

In many of his letters John Southall appeared as a rather intense, perhaps, a highly strung, man who took life very seriously. It had, after all delivered him and his adored wife, Hannah, some very bitter blows. Although parents were perhaps forced to adopt a rather fatalistic attitude to high infant mortality in the early 19th century, the fact remained that they had lost three children in infancy. John was a kind and considerate husband and clearly had continual worries about Hannah's health. He often commented anxiously about his own health, too, and mentioned feeling very tired, but never conveyed the notion that he might have been a hypochondriac. It seems more likely that he was not particularly strong in the physical sense and there was evidence that he worked very hard in many walks of life. It was quite reasonable to suppose that, at times when he was feeling exhausted and particularly low in spirits, his bark was worse than his bite. There was a hint of this in a letter he wrote to John Tertius in April 1842, the year after Hannah Southall, his wife, died. The effect of his wife's death was clearly and understandably profound and the source of much unhappiness, resulting in some sharpness towards his nearest and dearest. His letter conveyed the sense that he realised that he had perhaps been a little severe and regretted speaking sharply and wished to reassure his son of his support and lasting affection.

After he had completed his formal education at William Lean's school in Birmingham, John Tertius was apprenticed to drapers, May and Strange, in Ampthill in Bedfordshire. In 1842, he was a young man of 20 and probably nearing the end of his apprenticeship. His father seemed to be at a very low ebb and, perhaps, a little hurt by his son's failure to write to him. He began, 'My very dear John'[14] and continued rather anxiously: 'It seems some time since any communication has passed between us and I am become rather desirous to hear from thee. In the first place however with regard to money I think when thou wert at home I made some observations to thee about economy in thy expenses.' This was, perhaps, the reason why he had not heard from John Tertius and he was well aware of this for he continued: 'I should by no means wish to straiten thee however, and as I have thought thou mayest perhaps be wanting a further supply by this time thou hast only to mention it and it will be forwarded to thee.' This, perhaps, suggested that John Tertius was also feeling a little bruised by his father's advice about economy and would not ask. Father was feeling guilty; son was feeling aggrieved.

By 1842, Henry was well established at school in Birmingham but perhaps, initially, he found settling into Mr Lean's strict regime rather difficult. In an undated letter, probably from 1835, he told his mother honestly: 'I have not been a very good boy in school' and later 'I am sorry I have other confessions to make besides not being a very good boy which can be better told when I see thee.'[15] Nothing more was mentioned about the confessions but there was the suggestion that Mamma was not at all satisfied with the presentation of his letters and would be looking for an improvement. In subsequent letters

Henry demonstrated a mature hand for a boy of 10 or 11 years of age and, although it sometimes degenerated towards the end of a letter, it would seem that Mamma had made her point. Henry had wisely taken notice of his mother's comments because soon after she was delighted to write: 'We were much pleased to receive thy letter which we thought a great improvement on the last. It was not only better written, but contained so much more intelligence.'[16] Henry had obviously realised that he had to work harder and did so, because Mamma continued: 'It pleased me greatly my dear boy that thou hadst attended my wishes in this respect — and hope thou wilt endeavour to do so in every thing which may be for thy good.'

Much of what remained in Hannah's letter to Henry displayed her motherly anxiety about the possible dangers involved with his imminent journey back to Leominster during very snowy weather. Arrangements had been made for Henry to travel from Birmingham to Worcester where he was to stay over night with relatives and then accompany Elizabeth home. They would all have understood that the journey from Worcester to Leominster would have been the more difficult part of the journey and Hannah explained that in Leominster it had been snowing fast for some time and that there could be a deep fall before they got home. She did not like the prospect of their travelling in such wintery weather and said that they must both travel inside the coach and see that they were warmly dressed and wearing good boots.

Later letters from Henry reveal that he had adapted to life at boarding-school and was not strictly confined; in fact, he appeared to have had a good deal of freedom. He went for long walks and studied bird song. He visited Wombwell's Circus in the Bull Ring and was very impressed with the beautiful giraffes he saw there. Henry and other boys from his school were invited to tea with Joseph Sturge at his house in Birmingham. He attended Friends' Meetings at the large Meeting House in Bull Street and there he heard Elizabeth Fry and also her brothers, Samuel and Joseph John Gurney, address the assembled Friends. Later, Elizabeth Fry visited the boys at their school and Henry also reported that she had visited Uncle Thomas at his house. Since Thomas and William Southall had their business premises in Bull Street and possibly lived there as well, it was quite likely that Henry was present on that occasion too. Considering their kindness to him, Henry's uncles would probably have made sure that he met some of the foremost figures in the Quaker world whenever opportunities arose. The Southalls used their contacts well and their private meetings with prominent Quakers provide some evidence of the family's social standing and influence.

In old age Henry related that on one special occasion whilst he was at school in Birmingham he was invited to dinner at Richard Tapper Cadbury's house in Calthorpe Street because Sarah Grubb was to be present and she had particularly asked to meet Henry. It seemed that she often expressed a closeness to his Southall grandparents and a great affection for his Burlingham grandparents, too. John Burlingham had been very supportive of Sarah Grubb when she had addressed a street crowd in Worcester many years earlier. At that time many people would have considered it very unseemly for a woman to speak publicly and she may well have faced some hostility from members of the general public. It was a very courageous thing to do and John Burlingham, Henry's grandfather, had recognised this and had supported her. He had fetched a chair for her to stand on so that she might be seen and heard and stood next to her whilst she was speaking. Sarah Grubb never forgot this act of kindness and held John Burlingham and his family in great affection for the rest of her life.

Henry seemed to have thrived on the activities and social connections which presented themselves during his stay in Birmingham and began to develop a wider perspective on the world than might have been possible in Leominster. Clearly, he did settle down to apply himself to his school work. His half yearly report in June 1839,[17] was excellent and must have been very pleasing for John and Hannah to read. William Lean reported that

Wedding of Thomas and Celia Southall in 1893. Henry and Louisa Southall are seated on the left with Samuel and Caroline Price on the right. Mary Louisa Southall is standing behind her father (by kind permission of C.M. Southall)

Henry had made good progress in almost every subject and had also maintained his place amongst boys much older than himself. This was praise indeed from a man whom Henry described in later years as 'a classical scholar and a strict disciplinarian but showing perhaps too little tolerance for dull or spoiled children.'[18]

Included with Henry's report was William Lean's account.[19] For a half year's education and board the charge was 20 guineas with an extra guinea for Latin and another for French. There was also the sum of £3 8s. 4d. for sundry items which included: shoe repairs, mending of clothes, drilling master, use of library, haircutting and travelling expenses. This account gave some indication of John Southall's financial standing, particularly when considered in relation to similar expenses he would have sustained in respect of John Tertius in Ampthill and Elizabeth and Hannah at school in Worcester. He was possibly expending £3 to £5 per week on the education and training of his children at a time when the average farm labourer in Herefordshire was earning no more than 7s. to 9s. per week. John and Hannah were probably not rich, but they evidently sustained a good income and a comfortable lifestyle. They were well known in their own community and had many business, social and family connections in Ross as well.

In his speech at the Ross Traders' Dinner in 1911 Henry stated that he had first visited Ross in the summer of 1843 when he had accompanied his father to the funeral of one of the town's leading bankers. The banker in question was, almost certainly, Thomas Prichard who was a first cousin to Henry's paternal grandmother, Mary Southall, who was also born a Prichard. Thomas was not only a prominent banker and businessman, but also a central figure amongst the Quaker community in Ross. Thomas and his close friend Nathaniel Morgan often played hosts to well known Quaker speakers as they travelled about the country. The passing of Thomas Prichard would, without doubt, have been an occasion when numerous Quakers gathered in Ross to pay their last respects to a very kind and generous old gentleman. It was also an opportunity for the renewing and reaffirming of important social connections.

Henry also remarked that his fondness for the town had begun on that August day in 1843. He had just had his 17th birthday and, with his formal schooling over, he was perhaps becoming more aware of the realities and responsibilities of the adult world. It seemed very likely that John Southall would have taken the opportunity to reintroduce his son to numerous relations, friends and acquaintances who had not seen him since early childhood. He may also have introduced him to useful business contacts now that he was becoming a young man. At that time Henry's future course in life was still uncertain, but what was quite certain, was the fact that before many more years had passed he would have to find a means of earning his own living.

At the beginning of 1844 John Southall began to consider placing him as an apprentice draper with one Edward West who had a substantial business in Sankey Street in Warrington in Cheshire. This was probably an attempt to determine how Henry would proceed in life and, indeed, whether life as a draper would suit him. Negotiations were very amicable but rather protracted and correspondence passed backwards and forwards between Edward West and John Southall for some months before arrangements for a trial period were complete. In the meantime John and Henry travelled together to Manchester, ostensibly on business, but possibly with the idea of seeking an alternative apprenticeship place for Henry should the negotiations with Edward West come to nothing. Whilst they were there they attended political meetings held at the Free Trade Hall and listened to several well known, indeed, eminent Free Trade advocates including John Bright and Richard Cobden. It says something of the strength of John Southall's interest in politics that both of these politicians were already quite well known to him. Indeed, John had participated at a Free Trade meeting held at Hereford Town Hall in July 1843, at which it was estimated that there were two to three thousand people present. Richard Cobden had been the main speaker on that occasion and they were on sufficiently familiar terms for John to introduce Henry to him personally. Henry was being encouraged to think about the politics of trade. He was being prepared, if not groomed, for the world of business.

In the autumn of that year, 1843, Henry travelled north to live as part of Edward West's household and his letters suggested that he soon settled in with the family. West was a Quaker which, no doubt, was one of the reasons why John Southall had approached him, in order to ease Henry's transfer into a new situation. He would be moving from one Quaker household to another Quaker household run on very similar lines. It is perhaps significant, too, that John Southall and Edward West knew each other sufficiently well not to go to the bother, or the expense, of making Henry's apprenticeship formal or binding. After several weeks in Warrington, however, an opportunity arose for Henry to follow an apprenticeship at home and he was given the choice as to whether he stayed where he was or returned to Leominster. Several more weeks elapsed during which Henry sought the opinions of John Tertius and Elizabeth, as well as his father. They in turn wanted to know about his hours of work and general living conditions to which Henry replied that 'I still find nothing to complain of in the treatment I receive & I am pretty well.'[20] Henry decided to stay in Warrington. It is more than likely that John Southall and Edward West were known to each well before 1844, through business and through attendance at the London Yearly Meeting. In their correspondence there were suggestions that they might find an opportunity to talk at the Yearly Meeting in May 1845.

During his time in Warrington the flow of correspondence between Henry and the individual members of his family did not slacken. In Leominster they were eager for news of the nature of the drapery business in Cheshire, of Henry's general well being and of his social activities. At one point there had been some concern about his health and the fact that he often seemed very tired, but Edward West assured John Southall that he would monitor Henry's health and said that he thought that the tiredness was simply because he was growing so rapidly. In a letter dated 21st December 1844, West announced that in a few months time a new boy should be in place at his premises which would free Henry of some of his more menial tasks and allow him 'more opportunity for becoming better acquainted with the woollen and fustian trade.'[21] It was possible, perhaps, that Henry's tiredness was as much attributable to the boredom of menial work as it was to a growth spurt.

In January 1845, however, Henry seemed to be well and taking an interest in Friends' meetings and in politics too. He reported[22] that he had attended monthly meeting in Warrington and would attend the next monthly meeting which would be held in Manchester. In the same letter he expressed his delight that Uncle Edward had taken the time to make an impromptu call to see him on his way to Liverpool and also that he had attended a 'Free Trade Tea' in Warrington. He had listened to several speeches and had enjoyed listening to John Bright's long speech in particular. Everything had gone well; the event had been a success and Henry had enjoyed himself. He had also had the opportunity to learn by example from an orator he had found engaging; adding oratory to his own letter writing and to his skills as a public speaker in later life.

Three months later, in April 1845, Edward West wrote[23] to John Southall bewailing the fact that some 900 fustian cutters were out of work in Warrington alone and that the trade in Lancashire was in a very depressed state. It was, perhaps, the slackness in trade that prompted Henry to plan a visit to Leominster. He wrote to his father requesting to be allowed to return home via Chester, because he particularly wanted to see the city. He explained that he had planned the route and could meet all expenses himself if his father could let him have £1 10s. to settle his washing bill.[24] At the end of the month Edward West wrote to John Southall saying that Henry's presence in his house and amongst his family was 'quite agreeable'[25] and that he was impressed by his general knowledge. He also indicated that Henry's influence on the other apprentices in his house had been very positive because both Hewitson and Edmondson wished to acquire more knowledge themselves. Henry sustained an intense curiosity about the world all his life and had something of the teacher in him too. Over a period of six or seven decades he gave numerous talks and lectures on a variety subjects of general interest.

John Southall, too, was a man of many interests and, in particular, he never lost his interest in politics at local and national levels. Vestry records[26] show that he and his brother Samuel attended Vestry Meetings at the Priory Church in Leominster, although they did not worship there, but had a right to be present in their capacity as ratepayers. The prime function of Vestry Meetings was to make decisions about requests for poor relief and their role was later subsumed by the Poor Law Guardians under the Poor Law Amendment Act of 1834. After that date John and Samuel served as Poor Law Guardians for the Borough of Leominster for many years. The Minute Books of Leominster Poor

Law Union show that Samuel Southall was Chairman of the Board in 1852[27] and that John was Chairman in 1856[28] and kept up his attendance at Guardians' meetings to within a few weeks of his death in 1862. The presence of Quakers at Church Vestry Meetings and also the Meetings of Boards of Guardians almost certainly caused some very lively debate, both religious and political, because Boards were generally Anglican dominated. An eloquent Quaker, experienced in public speaking, might well change the whole course of a meeting, particularly if he happened to be the chairman of the meeting too. At Leominster meetings, the Anglican view could probably not be taken for granted.

In April 1842, John wrote to John Tertius whilst he was still at Ampthill explaining that he and Uncle Samuel had been actively involved in generating local opposition to income tax because those in power 'indulge in lavish expenditure and in unnecessary wars — adding largely to the amount of human miseries.'[29] He travelled to attend Free Trade Meetings held in Hereford, Manchester and possibly other towns as well. In April 1847, he was in London for an Education Conference and the following month he was back for the Friends' Yearly Meeting. Writing from London[30] he explained to John Tertius that there had been much discussion about the continued importation of slave grown sugar and Joseph Sturge had urged the government to stop admitting it to the country. There were those present, John added, who tried to avoid the question 'but John Bright would not let them off.' In February, 1850 he attended a Tithe Conference in London. There were many Friends in attendance and most expressed great concern about the distraint of goods for refusing payment of charges. In the past Friends had been expressly forbidden to pay tithes, but now they were recommended to strike bargains with landlords and tithe owners in order to avoid distraint.

The particulars of the Tithe Conference were reported to his children in a letter which was addressed to 'My Dear Four'[31] since they were all now resident in Leominster. Elizabeth, had left Mrs Impey's school in Worcester just before her mother's death in 1841 to manage the house and proved to be a very good housekeeper and hostess. Later she was joined by Hannah when she left school. John Tertius eventually took over the drapery business in Leominster and Henry moved to Ross. In his letter from the Tithe Conference John went on to say: 'I think of Henry so soon likely by moving to break up our house party.' John Southall had been a good father and was, no doubt, pleased to have all his children with him at home again. He was probably dreading the break up of his family and, with his beloved wife Hannah already gone, feared loneliness in old age. He need not have been concerned because neither Elizabeth nor Hannah married, but devoted themselves to his care and, although they travelled extensively, John Tertius and Henry were never far away for very long and could probably be summoned home within a few days.

The Ross Census for 1851 recorded Henry Southall as a 25-year-old bachelor residing at a house in St Mary's Street and described him as a master draper, the word 'master' confirming that he had completed an apprenticeship and was an employer. He was employing two people; these were Richard Preece, a draper's assistant aged 20 and Frederick Potter, a 14-year-old errand boy. Henry's long association with the town had begun.

Ross and Henry's Public Persona

John Southall may have had some slight misgivings about the prospects of Henry's departure for Ross, but he had always brought up his children to be independent and to think for themselves. It was very unlikely that Henry would have decided to set up in business on his own without his father's financial support or without discussing the matter thoroughly with his brother and sisters too. He certainly asked them all for their advice and opinions when he was deciding where he should do his apprenticeship; that is, in Ross or in Warrington. If he had joined the family business in Leominster at the end of his apprenticeship, he would have realised quite quickly that such an arrangement might not have worked for very long. He might always have felt that he was living in his older brother's shadow with little scope for making decisions for himself. For a young man of independent mind and spirit, as Henry certainly was, such a situation would have been very difficult, if not intolerable. There was, too, the simple but crucial question as to whether the business would support John Tertius and Henry and their wives and families if they should both decide to marry. Alternatively, Henry could have set up his own business in Leominster, but that, of course, would have meant trading in opposition to his father and his brother. There was also the issue as to whether a small market town like Leominster could actually generate sufficient trade to support another draper. In 1835, Pigot's *Trade Directory* listed ten wool and linen drapers in Leominster, but only six in Ross. On balance, Henry might well have thought that striking out with his own business was the more interesting and, hopefully, the more lucrative and satisfying alternative.

Whatever Henry's feelings were about entering the business world in a new venture, he received very little encouragement from some of the established drapers in Ross, who quite understandably saw Henry as opposition. Some of them went so far as to predict that within two years he would have given up the effort to make his business work and would have returned home to his father. Initially, Henry may have found trading conditions in Ross very difficult, but his business soon began to prosper. Luckily he received much kindly encouragement and some orders from family and friends, including his much loved Aunt Elizabeth. She was John Southall's sister and the wife of Henry Hunt of Bristol. Elizabeth, who was affectionately known within the family as 'Aunt Hunt', wrote Henry a very kind and encouraging letter[32] and also requested material samples for a new great coat for her husband. This, no doubt, was the sort of practical help Henry needed: kind words are comforting, but they 'butter no parsnips'. Despite the attempts of existing traders to sap Henry's enthusiasm for his first business venture and general concerns about trading conditions, it says much for Henry's ambition and energy that his business did so well. He proved the competition wrong. He did not pack up and go home to Leominster: he stayed for almost 65 years.

It was unclear exactly where Henry's first business was located, but an advertisement of that time confirmed that it was in St Mary's Street, where he also lived. He moved his establishment, however, to the property known as Friends' Place in the middle of the 1850s. These were the premises owned by James Morgan, but previously occupied by Nathaniel Morgan who died in 1854. Henry lived in the rooms above the shop and, while his father, John, accepted that the accommodation they provided might be suitable for a bachelor, they would, in his opinion, be very inconvenient for a wife. His criticism was that: 'It would be next to an unbearable thing to bring a wife to a place where the business and domestic departments are so jumbled together as they are at Friends' Place.'[33] It was, however, the home to which Henry brought his bride, Louisa, the daughter of Henry Brown of Luton, in August 1858 and where they lived until The Graig, the house they planned together and built in Ashfield Crescent in Ross, was ready for occupation in 1864 (Plate 21).

The entrance to The Graig

In August 1857,[34] Louisa wrote to Henry apologising for the delay in answering his letter but explained that its subject being of such deep importance to them both that it must be given her most serious consideration. It seems obvious that Henry had proposed marriage but that Louisa had still not made up her mind. Later that year, however, they became engaged and John Southall travelled to Luton to meet his prospective daughter-in-law. He already knew her father, Henry Brown, from the London Yearly Meetings of The Society of Friends and had probably met some of the other family members too. He readily approved of Henry's choice and Henry and Louisa were married at the Friends Meeting House in Luton in August 1858. They both signed the marriage certificate[35] and, in accordance with Quaker custom, it was also signed by the 59 Friends, men and women, who were present at the ceremony. In the six years between moving to Ross and his marriage to Louisa, Henry had clearly worked hard to build up his business. At the age of 32 he obviously felt that his business could generate sufficient income to support a wife and family in reasonable comfort.

Letters from those years indicate that as well as trying to establish himself in a new situation, he had remained on very good terms with friends he had made during his time at Edward West's establishment and was happy to help them where he could. Even as a comparatively young man Henry seems to have been the kind of person who was a good listener and one who would proffer sound advice when he was asked for it. This, perhaps, says much about his maturity and strength of character and reflects the thoughtful upbringing of a serious Quaker household.

He had also been developing interests in the town which he sustained for many, many years. One of the most important of these was his attachment to The British and Foreign Bible Society which he supported in Ross, alone, for well over 60 years. Indeed, the edition of the *Ross Gazette* dated 24th November, 1910, included details of the Society's Annual Report which was presented by Mr Henry Southall on behalf of Miss Southall, his daughter Mary Louisa, who was secretary of the Ross Branch. Henry was quoted as saying that it was the 60th such annual meeting he had attended in Ross, which suggested that he must have started attending meetings as soon as he moved to the town. In the same article Henry was quoted as saying that 'the older he grew the more he seemed to love the Bible' and it is clear that his religious convictions formed the core of his beliefs through a very long life. He attended meetings with unfailing regularity and also endeavoured to put his beliefs into practice. He was always ready to help the genuinely needy and ever ready to give support to charitable societies whose efforts were directed towards improving the general well being of mankind, particularly in education and understanding of the Bible.

In 1835 a building fund had been started to erect a new school building in Wye Street, then known as Dockhill Pitch and, in 1836, it received the patronage of Her Royal Highness the Princess Victoria.[36] The School was named the Ross and Archenfield Royal Victoria British and Foreign School and Henry became a keen and loyal supporter very soon after the setting up of his business in the town. It seems likely, too, that his support of the school was not just as a committee member, but as a regular and popular visitor because in September 1859 the boys at the school wrote to Henry to congratulate him on the first anniversary of his marriage and wishing him well for the future.[37]

Many of Louisa's letters to Henry have survived and they suggest that although they were very happily married, Louisa found it very difficult to settle to life in Ross and made frequent visits to her parents in Luton. Whilst apart, however, Henry and Louisa wrote to each other every day and the contents of Louisa's surviving letters suggest that they enjoyed a very open, honest and tender relationship. It is quite clear that Louisa's difficulty in settling in Ross was not helped by her father's unhappiness about her leaving home. A letter from Luton dated 1st December 1858,[38] shows that Henry was missing his wife and found the house lonely without her. Louisa expresses the hope that as he became more involved with his business affairs and other engagements he 'mayst be able better to endure my absence' and later 'Papa still speaks of thee as my "Friend" which rather amuses me — I believe my leaving home has been to him a great trial.' Indeed, when Louisa visited Luton her father often tried to persuade her to stay for another week or two. This was perhaps understandable and a problem experienced by many fathers when their daughters marry and leave home, but it was also rather selfish considering that he had clearly approved of the marriage. It must have caused some difficulties for the young couple, yet despite it all, Henry appears to have remained both tolerant and extremely understanding. Louisa's letters were full of family news and general concerns, letters she happily assumed would arrive the following day, although most of them were addressed simply to 'Henry Southall, Ross'. This was not quite as unusual as it might seem; at that time letters were still relatively rare and in a small town addresses were well known.

Henry and Louisa had their first child, Henry John, the year after their marriage. In an undated letter[39] Louisa wrote to Henry in London whilst he was attending the Yearly Meeting reassuring him that both she and the baby were well. She explained that she had enjoyed a mutton chop for dinner; had dressed properly for the first time since the birth; that the nurse had allowed her walk into the next room; and that she had been pleased to look out of the window at the groups of purple iris, narcissus and daisies in the garden. She went on to say: 'We have been very mercifully and tenderly dealt with, and have indeed abundant cause for gratitude and well may we put the query, "What shall I render to the Lord for all his benefits towards me?"' It may seem odd to later generations that Henry was not with Louisa at such a time; that is, attending a meeting at which he was not obliged to be present. For Henry and Louisa, however, their religious beliefs were the very core of their existence and it is quite likely that Louisa encouraged Henry to go to The London Meeting as usual or, perhaps, Henry John arrived sooner than expected. It perhaps throws some light, too, on the priorities expected of a Quaker activist who took religious matters very seriously.

Henry and Louisa had four children: Henry John in 1859; Charles in 1860; Mary Louisa in 1862; and Thomas in 1865. As the family grew it may be that John Southall's critical words about the suitability of the rooms over the shop for a wife and family may have been ringing in Henry's ears and were becoming all too true. In 1862 or 1863 Henry and Louisa planned the building of The Graig in Ashfield Crescent, the house which was to be their home for the rest of their lives. The Census taken in 1871 indicates that by that time

Henry was, indeed, a man of substance, employing 25 people. The household on the day of the Census included: Henry, aged 44; Louisa, aged 42; Mary Louisa, aged 8; Thomas, aged 6; Sophia Sutton, aged 20 (cook); Jane Moore, aged 23 (housemaid); and Mary Ann Bailey, aged 21 (nurse). It may be presumed that Henry John, aged 12 and Charles, aged 11 were away at school. The family moved into their new house in 1864, and in doing so the family was clearly marked out as comfortably middle-class. It had been planned very carefully to provide space for an expanding household and to allow Henry and Louisa scope to indulge their many interests. Henry particularly enjoyed astronomy, meteorology and botany; namely the pastimes of a middle-class Victorian gentleman.

John Southall had sustained an intense interest in astronomy; an interest which he successfully passed on to his sons. He taught Henry and John Tertius to observe the stars whilst they were small boys and, in doing so, he generated a curiosity in the heavens which Henry enjoyed for the rest of his life. In his own recollections of his life, written in 1911,[40] he commented on the 'brilliant display' of the Aurora Borealis in 1833 and in a letter to the editor of the *Ross Gazette* dated 11th February 1907 he stated that: 'One of the finest and most remarkable displays of Aurora Borealis, or "The Northern Lights" that has been witnessed for several years was well seen here on Saturday last, February 9th." He went on to say that it started just after sunset and continued until almost 11 o'clock and described it in some detail: 'Its principal features were a large illuminated arch in the northern sky, extending from about W.N.W to E.N.E., from which streamers of coloured light were continually shooting in various directions towards the zenith.' In October 1912, it was reported by the *Ross Gazette* that Mr Henry Southall had given a lecture to The Young People's Institute at the Congregational Schoolroom entitled 'Celestial Phenomena' in which he recalled his delight in seeing the appearance of Halley's Comet in 1835; the brilliance of Donati's Comet in 1858; and his renewed pleasure in seeing Halley's Comet again in 1910, after an interval of 76 years. His interest in astronomy was such that when Henry and Louisa built their new home in Ashfield Crescent, the plans for The Graig included a tower for observing the stars. This suggests that by the 1860s Henry had proved himself as a businessman and was sufficiently affluent to be able to indulge an interest which he sustained for many decades.

It is not clear from the material available whether Louisa shared Henry's fascination for astronomy, but it seems clear that she enjoyed botany and did much of the planning for the new gardens at The Graig. Henry was very proud of the garden they created and delighted in showing visitors the many rare plants and flowering trees it contained. In Victorian times Alpine Gardens were very, very popular and Henry made a number of visits to The Alps in search of suitable plants and developed a remarkable knowledge and understanding of Swiss botany. He often travelled with fellow enthusiasts Alfred Bennett of London and Henry Tuke Morrell of Croydon and remarked that in search of plants, 'with the latter I have had many a botanical scramble in Switzerland.'[41] He counted among his friends a number of locally eminent botanists: his cousin, Edward Newman; and two clergymen, the Reverend William Purchas and, distant cousin, the Reverend Augustin Ley, who worked together to produce a book entitled *The Flora of Herefordshire*.[42] Henry sometimes threw open his gardens to the public and crowds gathered to see plants from all over the world. His gardens were, of course, also a mark of his social standing and of his wealth.

Many of the interests which Henry developed as a boy remained with him always; none less than his meticulous record keeping of weather conditions. The consistency of his interests is demonstrated by the fact that every morning punctually at 9 o'clock he recorded the maximum and minimum temperatures and the rainfall in his own garden for some 50 years. In her book about the records of the Southall Family, Henry's daughter-in-law, Celia, wife of his youngest son Thomas, stated that: 'These records were considered so valuable that after his death a meteorological station was opened near by in order that continuity of record might be preserved.'[43] As a result, Ross appears in the meteorological forecast right through to today.

By the middle of the 1860s Henry had established himself as a very successful businessman with enough time and money to indulge his interests. In doing so, either deliberately or coincidentally, he also developed his public persona; that is, as a man of some intellect and as a man who took seriously the Victorian notion of public duty. In a small market town in 19th-century Herefordshire these two aspects of life were inexorably linked. A prominent businessman in Ross would need to be seen to do his public duty: in being seen to do his public duty he enhanced his standing as a businessman. If he was known to involve himself in the commercial, political, religious, social and cultural affairs of the town, his public persona would blossom and the public's respect for him and his family would also be assured. Not all businessmen, successful or unsuccessful, took the trouble to develop such a persona, but Henry did and in doing so he established a power base. He had an interest in helping Ross to prosper.

In 1834, parliament passed The Poor Law Amendment Act which was intended to bring uniformity and greater efficiency to the regulation of workhouses and the administration of poor relief throughout England and Wales. This legislation provided the opportunity for able men to participate in public affairs in a way not previously possible. So long as they were ratepayers, men from a variety of social backgrounds could be elected Guardians on an annual basis and as a result drapers, wine merchants, barge owners, timber merchants, farmers, lawyers, doctors and clergymen might sit at the board-room table with equal right to be there. It will be remembered from earlier passages that John Southall and his brother Samuel were Guardians of Leominster Poor Law Union and continued to hold office into the 1860s. In 1866, Henry became a Guardian for the first time and was re-elected in subsequent years. He was one of four elected Guardians for the town of Ross and the Guardians' minute books show that he was very diligent in his attendance at meetings.

The meetings were held in the purpose built board room which had been included in the plans of the new workhouse constructed in Alton Street and opened in 1838. They were called on a weekly or fortnightly basis and usually commenced at about 10 o'clock in the morning. The duties of Poor Law Guardians were not unlike the duties of School Governors today: time consuming and unpaid. Henry was, however, very fortunate in that he did not have to ride into Ross on horseback in all kinds of weather to attend meetings, because his new house was no more than a brisk ten minute walk from the new workhouse itself. Although most of the workhouse was pulled down in 1996, the part in which the Guardians met for their meetings has survived and has been successfully incorporated into the new community hospital.

In Henry's day, Magistrates were allowed to sit as ex-officio or, unelected Poor Law Guardians, as of right. Many of the ex-officio Guardians were men of some social standing, landowners and clergymen, but to be elected as a Guardian, however, also said much about a man's social standing and his financial position. It said that other ratepayers thought him to be an appropriate person to be involved in administering poor relief and, perhaps, even more crucially, thought him sufficiently careful to safeguard their interests as ratepayers as well. Being a Poor Law Guardian said that he was somebody; a man of some substance who could afford to give time to do his public duty. It said that he was a man of probity: it indicated that he had 'arrived' as a man of significance in the locality.

In addition to being a Poor Law Guardian and a Magistrate, Henry was also a Town Commissioner. The Commissioners were appointed under the terms of two Ross Town Improvement Acts passed in 1830 and in 1865. These Acts were passed, as their title suggests, to allow the town's inhabitants the authority to make provision for the improvement of street cleansing and paving; gas street lighting; the effective treatment of sewage; public access to clean water; and other provisions which we all now take for granted. The men who were appointed as Town Commissioners were generally the more prominent businessmen of Ross and, in 1867, Henry Southall was their chairman. In many cases those who served as Poor Law Guardians were the same men who were involved in enterprises such as the building of the Corn Exchange, the Cottage Hospital and the Ross Dispensary. They were the town's business elite. The recognition they gained from the time they gave to such projects explained, perhaps, why men like Henry Southall were willing to fulfil their 'duty'.

In 1866, Henry was elected a member of The Woolhope Naturalists' Field Club and remained an active participant for the rest of his days. At its inception in 1851, membership was limited to 30 or 40 gentlemen; that is, gentlemen of some social standing and wealth. Each member paid an annual subscription of 10 shillings. The club's membership list for the first year indicates that Henry had joined a group which included names from many of the most wealthy and powerful families in Herefordshire and numerous clergymen. Indeed, in 1852, of the 30 members recorded, 10 were clergymen and that ratio had not changed a decade or so later. In 1865, the membership had grown to 61, but approximately a third, 21, were still clergymen. These were men of influence and wealth who had time enough on their hands to indulge their interests. They included two of Henry's clerical friends; the Reverend Augustin Ley and the Reverend William Purchas of Ross. One wonders, however, just how comfortable Henry felt in a society so dominated by Anglican clergymen but, since he remained a member for half a century, it might be supposed that he was not uncomfortable in the company of such men.

The general interests of the club at that time were botany, geology and mycology. Rule 11 of the constitution stated: 'That the Woolhope Naturalists' Field Club undertake the formation of and publication of correct lists of various Natural productions of the County of Hereford with such observations authors may deem necessary.'[44] In 1866, his first year of membership, Henry was invited by the club's president, Dr Henry Graves Bull, to write and present a paper on the plants growing on 'The Doward'. This refers to Little Doward Hill in the parish of Ganarew, which lies between Ross and Monmouth. His paper was published in the club's *Transactions* for that year and was followed by a stream of articles over the next four decades. As a member of the Woolhope Naturalists' Field Club, Henry enjoyed the company of like minded gentlemen; that is, they had strong interests in science, but it is not clear whether they shared an ideology about science. He was, however, moving in an elite circle which included some of the most intellectual and influential members of Herefordshire's gentry. In addition, he had the opportunity to listen to and converse with the society's honorary members; often university lecturers, or renowned professors, but all experts in their fields of study.

It is clear that by 1870, when Henry was in his mid-40s, he had established himself very well in his adopted town. He was a successful businessman and did much to help the people of Ross in his capacity as a Poor Law Guardian, a Town Commissioner and a Magistrate. He also participated in the management and running of numerous charities. As a Quaker he was a loyal supporter of the Friends Meeting House in Brampton Street and was the Friends' honorary treasurer for many years and served as secretary as well. He appears to have been a model of the Victorian self-made man. He had a wife and four children and a fine house in which to live. His public persona speaks for itself: his private persona is more difficult to define.

Henry's Private Persona
At the beginning of the 19nth century, members of The Society of Friends were forbidden, by law, to have any involvement in politics. Participation was also forbidden by the

Society's own rules, so much so that Quaker ministers denounced such activities in their epistles at Yearly Meetings. The observance of the ban, however, was not uniform. The repeal of the restrictive Test and Corporations Acts in the late 1820s cleared the way for a wider view of the world and allowed Friends to participate more freely in public affairs. In the 1830s Quakers were much involved in the movement for the abolition of the slave trade, but were often derided for this; that is, they were accused of hypocrisy and reminded of the white slaves in Britain's mines and cotton factories. They were frequently radical in their political views and embraced the notion of Free Trade. They excelled in business and made money. They were, however, very generous with it too.

In her book, *Victorian Quakers*, Elizabeth Isichei stated that: 'There can be no doubt that the part played by Quakers on the philanthropic scene was wholly disproportionate to their limited numbers.'[45] Their critics accused Quakers of having a great love of money and of deriving great satisfaction from the public's acknowledgement of their giving. This, however, was not very fair, because some of the wealthiest Quakers were not at all ostentatious about their charitable giving. Indeed, men such as Richard Reynolds, Joseph Storrs Fry, George Sturge, William Wilson and John Horniman often went to great lengths to maintain secrecy.

By the middle of Queen Victoria's reign, the late 1860s, The Society of Friends was a predominantly affluent middle-class group comprising merchants, landowners, agents, surveyors, brewers, millers, clerks, bookkeepers, craftsmen and retailers. Above this group was a very small number of exceptionally rich ship-owners, manufacturers and bankers; below the largest group was an equally small group of foremen, skilled and semi-skilled workers, shop assistants, unskilled workers and labourers.

In 1866, when Henry Southall was a mature man of 40, the prohibition against Quakers marrying other than Quakers was still strong. The reality of this stricture was that many of the leading Quaker families were very closely related. One positive aspect of this situation was that it made business connections and networks very advantageous to them. It also meant, however, that when calls were made for donations in support of a particular charity, many Quakers were in a good position to know what might reasonably be expected of their relatives and business connections. Charitable giving in the Quaker world was, almost certainly, much more transparent than in other sections of society. Elizabeth Isichei makes the point that 'Many Quakers probably cared less for their reputations in society at large than for their standing in their own community.'[46] This was probably never more true than in a small town like Ross; the members of the Quaker community would have known, fairly accurately, how much money individuals could afford to give and whether they were being generous or mean. This was the world of Henry and Louisa Southall and their young family at The Graig. Henry had invested a great deal of time in developing his public persona and would not have wished to appear mean. He was, indeed, generous

The Friends Meeting House in Ross-on-Wye, 2004, and see also Plate 22

in his charitable giving irrespective of religious denomination.

In previous passages it has been seen that in some ways Henry was a prime example of a successful self-made man with many interests and many public and private roles to perform. Each of these roles had its own circle of acquaintances and influence, some of which overlapped into others, but few of them featured directly in his family life. His public duties as a Magistrate, a Town Commissioner and as a Poor Law Guardian were, at that time, performed in adminis-trative circles that were, of course, exclusively male. So, too, were many of his other intellectual, religious and recreational interests: The Woolhope Naturalists' Club; the botanical expe-ditions in The Alps; The Men's Own Brotherhood; and Ross Cricket Club, to name but a few. He travelled widely in pursuit of his private interests and his business affairs and made great use of the quickly developing railway system.

One wonders, however, just how much time he actually had to spend with his wife and young family. He was, perhaps, the typical middle-class Victorian husband and father; having a general concern for the health, educa-tion and welfare of his family, but leaving the day-to-day management to Louisa, the children's nurse and the servants. He was, however, kept in constant touch with family affairs by a stream of daily letters which followed him from place to place and hotel to hotel as he progressed from one business contact to another. Louisa did know about some aspects of Henry's business affairs and often reported in her letters from Ross about correspondence she had dealt with or asked for instructions before she proceeded with other matters needing attention. As an employer of 25 one wonders who really ran the business whilst Henry was away. It remains unclear just how much Louisa was involved, but it may have been the case that she merely acted as an agent passing information backwards and forwards between Henry and his senior assistant or manager. She was, however, an able woman who could write clearly and precisely and take decisions.

It may seem a little odd in the 21st century that a husband and wife should be apart so much, but it was not at all unusual for affluent Victorians to do this, particularly if the wife had control of money of her own. A gentleman might travel alone, apart from his own manservant, whilst his wife made visits in the company of her maid, or her children and their nurse. Wives appeared to have a society of their own. The frequency of correspondence between Henry and Louisa suggested that in some years they spent relatively small amounts of time together and, when they did, the time was often taken up with attendance at religious meetings, local social calls, holidays and family visits.

In the weeks before Christmas 1858, a flurry of letters passed between Louisa in Luton and Henry in Ross. Although Henry's letters are not available to gauge his precise responses, Louisa's acknowledgements and comments indicate that they corresponded on a daily basis. Louisa was obviously enjoying being at her old home again, but was also missing Henry and he apparently felt very lonely without her. Louisa wrote very spontaneously and her letters were filled with a mixture of domestic generalities and sometimes her most personal feelings and private thoughts. The general tone of the letters made clear that their relationship was both loving and open. Indeed, in a rather emotional letter, reflecting for a moment on her changed perception of her home in Luton since her marriage, Louisa stated: 'thou likes me to write freely to thee'[47] suggesting that Henry quite understood that at times his wife was still torn between feelings for her old home in Luton and her new one in Ross. Henry appeared to be very understanding about her long absences from Ross, perhaps only too well aware of her parents' desire to keep her with them as long as possible. He did not appear to hold any grudge against his Brown relatives; nor did he appear to be jealous of their possessiveness towards Louisa.

In the same letter she stated: 'I incline most I think to leaving Luton [at] the end of next week, as proposed at first. I do not like the idea of being here at Christmas without thee, and it is a long way for thee to come again even if thou hast the time.' She added that Christmas 'makes but little difference here to any other time.' There was a suggestion that she might travel directly from Luton to Evesham, probably to the home of her brother William, before going home to Ross, but had realised that she would have then been away from Ross for five weeks. Her return had been delayed, partly, because of a recent outbreak of smallpox in Ross. Louisa was also concerned that although they had been invited to Leominster for Christmas, she wondered whether they would really be wanted because of the fear of spreading smallpox. On 18th December, still in Luton, she wrote 'Thou must be the ... judge as to our going to Leominster as regards business, but I think on these universal holidays we should make way for the young people we employ.'[48] This suggested that the Southalls employed people who were not Quakers and that Louisa felt strongly that they should be free to celebrate Christmas in their own way. Although Louisa usually left Henry to make final decisions, she voiced her own opinions quite firmly, particularly where her children were concerned.

Throughout the 1860s and the 1870s Henry was travelling constantly; his business contacts took him to Warrington, Neath, Penzance, Darlington, Evesham and frequently to London, Manchester, York and Bristol. It was not then so very surprising that Louisa made so many visits herself. The constraints which polite society imposed on Victorian women were undoubtedly very frustrating for them all, but, perhaps, particularly for Quaker women. Quakers did not attend orchestral concerts or theatres, and music, dancing, drawing, painting and many card games were also forbidden to them even in private homes. Inadequate lighting, as later generations would view it, even in the best of houses made reading, letter writing or sewing very difficult after dark and consequently the evenings must have seemed very long without company and conversation. Frequent visits to relatives was one solution to the problem which compromised no one.

In June 1875, Louisa was obviously feeling very lonely in Ross whilst Henry was travelling on the Continent and made the point that '... it is very dull for ladies to live alone — those who do suffer great loss.'[49] Many able Quaker women found an outlet for their abilities and great satisfaction in the administration of charities such as schools, hospitals, coal clubs and soup kitchens. Indeed, the pious advice given at one Yearly Meeting was that 'The best recreation of a Christian is the relief of distress.'[50] There must have been a limit, though, to how much time could be spent in this way, even for the most pious of women. Louisa was, indeed, a pious woman and from the time of her marriage she attended the preparatory meetings at the Ross Friends' Meeting House in Brampton Street whenever she could, but at times she almost certainly longed for other interests and distractions. Indeed, her daughter-in-law, Celia, said of her that 'Louisa ... was an interesting and intellectual woman, of great charm and refinement.'[51] Visits to her family and holidays with friends or in the company of her children and their nurse were the only respectable alternatives open to her. This must, without doubt, have been typical of many women in her position.

Louisa was, however, very fortunate in one important respect: she had money of her own. She could, therefore, travel with her children; for interludes in Malvern walking

189

Elizabeth, John Tertius, Henry and Hannah Southall when all over 80
(by kind permission of C.M. Southall)

on the hills; for seaside holidays of two or three weeks at a time. Weston-super-Mare, Dawlish and Llandudno seem to have been particular favourites and her letters indicated that she and all the children always enjoyed these adventures. Henry, too, would join them for a few days whenever his business affairs allowed him to do so, but he never seemed to stay for very long.

Henry was clearly a man of great physical and intellectual energy with interests in many things, but his family holidays seem always to have been fitted in around his business. Louisa fully understood the demands of business, but at times appeared to be concerned about the number of things he did and for his health, particularly when he was away on long business trips. At the beginning of August 1870,[52] when Henry was on business in York, Louisa wrote to him to tell him of her stay in Leominster. She was writing while the children were at a party arranged for them to meet their Newman cousins and she was shortly to go to the house of John Tertius to meet older relatives. When he was away Henry expected to receive a steady stream of letters informing him of all they had done. Almost three weeks later, on 21st August, she wrote to him at his hotel in Manchester and urged him 'to take the opportunity to explore the area around "Scarboro" — stay a few days and enjoy himself.' Not having been well for some time she thought the fresh sea air would do him good. A little later she added, 'Do get a nice coat before thou leaves Manchester.'[53] In other letters Louisa reminded him to think about his clothes and to wear nice things, perhaps feeling that a draper should look neat and smart. On 24th August, Louisa had returned to Ross and wrote a letter for Henry who was by then back in York, but soon to move on to Darlington.[54] By the time he got back to The Graig, Henry would have been travelling on business for well over a month.

Early in 1869, Louisa made the first of many visits to London, using her parents' home in Luton as a base, to take the advice of a Mr Bigg in his consulting rooms in Wimpole Street. It was not her own health that was in question, but that of their daughter, Mary Louisa, or Louie, as she was generally known within the family. Sadly, Louie had been born with a deformed hip and numerous trips were made to see Mr Bigg who designed apparatus to stretch one leg in order to improve her mobility and posture. Henry was kept informed of every stage of the treatment; the initial fitting of the apparatus; numerous adjustments and improvements; and, of course, the frequent alterations which became necessary as Louie grew. The visits and supervision were, however, left very much to Louisa and Henry himself appeared to take very little part in any of the consultations or treatment. One wonders whether Henry was really at ease with children, even his own.

Many Victorian and Edwardian men were, in some senses, very remote from their children until their offspring were entering adulthood and decisions had to be made about their future; that was, deciding on appropriate employment for their sons and on suitable marriages for their daughters. It is perhaps significant, too, that Henry was aged 32 when he and Louisa were married and he had already developed a new life for himself in his adopted town; a bachelor life, with space for his many interests as well as his business. It may also have been the case that while Henry clearly loved his wife and children, they were part of his life and not all of it. They were added to the life he had established for himself whilst he was on his own, but he was sufficiently self contained to be able to detach himself from them when it suited him. It is not clear from the correspondence available for study whether Henry's Continental travels were for business, for botany or for recreation or a mixture of all three, but they obviously did not include Louisa or the children. It was possible, of course, that Louisa did not wish to travel abroad with or without the children, but this seems unlikely considering the fact that she showed no reluctance to travel about England. It is certain, too, that a lady of her intellectual temperament would have enjoyed the geographical, botanical and cultural sights of Europe. It was likely, however, that although the family was quite wealthy, it was not rich enough for the whole family to do the Grand Tour.

In May 1875, Louisa, Louie, Tom and Miss Hanmer, the nurse, were again in Luton; the main reason for their visit being further appointments at Mr Bigg's consulting rooms in Wimpole Street. At that time orthopedic techniques were improving for those who could afford treatment and, from correspondence details, it would seem that Louie's treatment was under constant review. On 10th May, Louisa wrote to Henry in Ross concerning his expected visit and the safety of his travelling. She was alarmed that he might be thinking of travelling on an excursion train on Whit Monday and hoping very much that he would not do so, though she was really looking forward very much to seeing him. Excursion trains would certainly have been associated with lower status individuals who might be carriers of many diseases.

By 22nd May, Tom had been taken off to stay with Brown relatives for a little holiday on his own and Louisa and Louie were on holiday in Dawlish. By the middle of June that year it is clear that Henry was about to embark on a trip to Europe and had left detailed instructions with Louisa about forwarding letters to him whilst he was away. It is not clear, however, whether he was travelling alone or in the company of some of his botanical friends.

The boys, Henry John (Harry) and Charles (Charlie) were due home for the school holidays and although Henry sometimes invited them to join him for breakfast at his hotel when he was on business in York, he clearly did not see them very often. It seems likely, perhaps for that reason, that Louisa was not completely happy with the timing of Henry's trip, because on 16th June 1875, she wrote to him at his hotel in London and there was more than a hint of exasperation, if not annoyance, in her letter. She assured him that she was well, that Louie was a better colour than when he left and described Tom as 'saucy'. She also confirmed that she would send letters ahead for him to read in Montreux, Leukersbad and Piedmont and then added: 'Please do not trouble so about letters. I will write according to order — but I think if thou make up thy mind to go away, thou must also [try] to trust those thou leaves behind — we are all under the same loving care as always.' There is in these words almost an accusation of selfishness; something not encountered in previous letters. She went on to say: 'Louie thinks there is more need to hear from "Papa than for me to write much to him".'[55]

In subsequent letters Louisa reported on the children and general domestic matters. She reported that Harry and Charlie had arrived home safely from school; that Harry had gained weight and that Charlie seemed to have lost weight and his voice had changed. Harry and Charlie, 16 and 15 respectively, attended the prestigious Boothams School in York and were to be followed later by their little brother Tom. She also remarked on how well Harry worked with Tom in the garden and played with him despite the difference in their ages; one a boy of 10 and the other almost a young man. Indeed there seems to have been a great bond of affection between all four children and their holidays with

Louisa at the seaside and at home were very happy and relaxed. They spent their time on very normal childhood activities such as making and flying kites, or collecting moths and butterflies and, in the summer of 1875, in tracing their father's journey on the map and, perhaps, wishing they could have gone with him. Louisa always appeared to be at ease with her children and enjoyed having them around her and they undoubtedly enjoyed their excursions and adventures with her.

The 1880s and the 1890s brought both happiness and sorrow to the family. As the years rolled on Louisa's delicate health began to deteriorate, but she somehow managed to keep up a relentless progression of family visits and seaside holidays. Harry had married a lady called Annette Waterman and was establishing himself in Leominster as a successful solicitor. His professional and personal success as a solicitor, however, was greatly marred by the birth of a stillborn son just before Christmas 1884. There were, though, other children who survived: Arnold, Evelyn, Freda and Howard.

In 1878 Charlie had been admitted to the degree of Bachelor of Arts and his examination results, in both sciences and classics, were very impressive. At some point after leaving London University Charlie had set up in business with a partner, but by 1884 his business affairs were in crisis, to some extent as a result of the deceitful practices of others. It was not clear from family letters quite what manner of business it was, but Louisa's concern for Charlie's health suggested that the work was heavy and physically demanding. In a flurry of letters during this very difficult time Louisa did everything she could to support Charlie: impressing on him the need to take good care of himself; not to neglect his creature comforts; to see that he has good boots; and to take good advice in Liverpool about treatment for his very debilitating hayfever, for which she would meet the expense. Writing to Charlie from The Graig in December, 1884 Louisa again expressed a mother's blend of sympathy and practical help. 'I am very sorry for you in all your business difficulties and am glad that your Papa & Uncle are going to you this week'.[56] She went on to say: 'Next week I am looking forward to seeing you at home — and hope nothing may prevent your coming in good time — and staying as long as possible, it will do you good.' Ever practical, she also urged him to bring his mending for her to do. Letters suggest that Charlie did, indeed, come home for Christmas and returned to Liverpool soon after. In a letter dated 20th January 1885, Louisa wrote to Charlie: 'I am very very sorry for you to have been so deceived.'[57] Fraud appeared to be quite common in business at that date.

Whilst supporting and consoling Charlie, at about the same time Louisa wrote to Henry, then in Liverpool, expressing her views about the sad state of Charlie's affairs very firmly. Her words demonstrate a very clear perception of the situation and a complete and unsentimental understanding of her son. They also express, perhaps, a suggestion of a little recrimination towards Henry himself. There was more than a hint of 'I told you so'. After a few generalities and expressing her concern for both father and son 'in this troublesome business,'[58] Louisa continued: 'Of the three courses open I am disposed most to disposing or closing of the whole concern at once — and entirely agree that Charlie is not strong enough for the place or fitted for the management of so many men.' Later, she remarked on the fact that the hayfever he has all summer makes him unfit for hard physical work and that he looked jaded and exhausted and in need of a change and a rest. 'I cannot fancy he will get on with any partner — and only marvelled that he even wished for one — I shall be glad to hear that the whole thing is dropped — got clear of. It was scarcely likely that C could manage such a large concern himself.'

John Southall, father of Henry (by kind permission of C.M. Southall)

In 1885 Charlie was just 25 years old; a shy, innocent, trusting young man, perhaps encouraged to go in to a business for which he had very little aptitude and even less worldly cunning. Louisa's privately held fears for her son's prospects had seemingly come true, but she was not in despair for him or for the loss of his business. Towards the end of her letter to Henry she added: 'Do not think too much of the pecuniary loss — we must try and save it up again and hope the dear boy will do well yet — as I quite expect he will.' Charlie did, indeed, do well. He became an accountant and was sent by his firm to work in Buenos Aires in Argentina and his letters home suggest that he enjoyed a comfortable life there for many years before returning to Ross. Writing to his Aunt Elizabeth (Trusted) Southall, the wife of John Tertius Southall, in 1888,[59] he said that in Buenos Aires there were plenty of opportunities for making money and that the main aim of most people there was to do just that; make money, live well and enjoy themselves. He also added that people at home in England would be surprised by the number of comforts available to the expatriate community and that life as a strict Quaker would be quite impossible. One wonders how such a comment would have been regarded within the family, but Charlie knew his aunt well and she may well have thought it better not to pursue the matter.

In the early 1880s, Thomas Southall was intent on studying medicine and becoming a doctor. Henry financed his studies for a year but then decided that Tom should give up his studies to return to Ross to run the family firm. By any standards this was a very unkind course to take and caused enormous resentment in Tom. No doubt he envied his two brothers who were free to follow their own chosen paths, whilst he had to apply himself to work for which he had little training and no interest at all. It was likely that by the 1880s Henry's time was so taken up with his public duties and private interests, that there was little left for his business affairs. If a Southall was to remain in control of the family firm after Henry had gone, it could only be Tom. Since Tom was financially dependant on his father, he was manoeuvred into the position against his will. Although Henry put Tom in overall charge of the drapery and furniture businesses, he always retained the crucial control over financial decisions. As the years passed, this was a further source of resentment which ultimately led to events which were to dislocate some family relationships in a way that could never be healed. It may be that after the failure of Charlie's business venture, Henry felt that he must keep control of his own business affairs himself, but, if he really felt that way, it would have been far better to let Tom follow his chosen course to become a doctor and to employ a manager to run his shops. Although Henry had gone his own way as a young man, it was not to be so for Tom.

In August 1893, Tom married Celia Price who was a member of an old established Quaker family in Birmingham. Henry provided them with a house, Ashfield Lodge, which was next door to The Graig, but the house was never conveyed to the couple. Tom and Celia and their three children, Eric, Olive and Colin, lived there by Henry's grace and favour. By most people's standards, Henry did not treat his youngest son well. It may have been the case, however, that in the true manner of the dominant Victorian father, Henry saw it as Tom's duty to obey his father and abide by his wishes however much they were at odds with his own thoughts and inclinations. Mary Louisa (Louie) was similarly under her father's control. She was denied a proper education, but there is no reason to think that she would have benefitted less from a formal education than her very able brothers. Her disability may have been an issue, but it did not appear to be such that she had to remain at home. She did attend school for a while, possibly The Mount School for Quaker girls which was well established in York when Louie's brothers were attending Boothams School. For the most part, however, she remained at home most of her life, and Henry maintained his control over her life, even to the point of reading letters sent to her before she was allowed to see them.

It was not so very uncommon for Victorian fathers to treat their unmarried daughters in this way; it was something they just had to accept until they married. Henry's reading of Louie's letters was, however, a source of great annoyance to Tom, and father and son had words about it. In September 1887, writing to his sister from The Graig, Tom stated: 'Dear Louie, Notwithstanding my protests Papa insists on opening all your letters & then, when he finds there is nought to Interest him he hands them over to me to forward to you. Please write [to] him requesting him not to do it again'.[60] In 1887 Louie was 25 years old, but still firmly under her father's control. Her life was spent keeping her mother company and, in her advancing years, nursing her until her death in 1899. After her mother's death she presided over the household management for Henry and looked after him until his death in 1916. It was a daughter's duty.

Henry's public life and his private life formed two distinct entities and he appeared to have been very successful in keeping them separate. There were few occasions when these two aspects of his life overlapped except at the Friends Meeting House. It would seem that he was a very self contained man who lived two different lives: one which included family visits and short family holidays and one from which his family was excluded. It might be argued that the conventions of polite Victorian Society made this inevitable but, in Henry's case, it appeared to have been a deliberate decision. There were occasions when his two worlds might have been brought together to everyone's satisfaction. He could, for example, have included Louisa and his children in his travels abroad once the children were in their teens, but this never seems to have happened. He could have encouraged his sons to join him in his interest in the Woolhope Club. They were just as capable of writing papers for the club as he was, but he kept that part of his life to himself just as he did many other activities. It may appear to be a harsh judgement to say that as the years rolled on and his children grew up, Henry's public life became more important to him than his private life. The one interest Henry did share with his family and friends, as well as the public, was his abiding love of observing the night sky. Early in 1888, he had purchased a new telescope but it had proved to be a disappointment to him. Writing from The Graig in March of that year, Tom informed his brother, Charlie, in Argentina of its arrival. He stated: 'The monster telescope has come & it is rather a white elephant to papa who finds it hard to manipulate. It requires two persons to move it about. I have had it this evening on the terrace by [the] drawing [room] window on the moon ...'[61] He went on to say, perhaps a little unkindly, 'Its principal use will be to astonish the ignorant gentry of Ross with Papa's great scientific knowledge & attainments.' Henry, it would seem, lived the life he wanted: his family fitted in around it. Evidently, he was his own man and remained so until the very end.

Conclusion

Henry Southall was a man of impressive stature, both physically and intellectually. He was energetic and lived a very full life until he was almost 90-years old. Born in the reign of King George IV, he lived right through the reigns of King William IV, Queen Victoria, King Edward VII and into the reign of King George V. He lived through a period of momentous change. It was a time of enormous opportunity for educated men of energy and initiative to participate in society in ways of which previous generations could only dream. It was a time of enormous industrial development and for the creation of wealth; for greater religious and political freedoms; and for independent men to make their way in the world. For most of Henry's adult life, Queen Victoria ruled over the greatest empire the world had ever known and, in industrial development and manufacturing, Britain led the world. In many ways, Henry was a man of his time; the archetypal self-made

Victorian. He was self confident, self contained and, at times, self centred. He was independent and determined. He could be generous and selfish; thoughtful and thoughtless; kind and unkind, too. He had many human strengths and weaknesses but, despite his faults, he gave freely of his time and did much to help the inhabitants of Ross for more than six decades.

In some respects Henry was a hard man and, despite his outward generosity, wit and charm, not everyone had an easy relationship with him. It is so often the case that a man who has attained personal success, very largely by his own efforts, is ruthlessly single-minded in fulfilling his aims. It is in this way that he has created his success. Unfortunately, as he grew older, he may have become highly critical, in his own mind if not overtly, of younger generations and have seen them in a poor light. This, perhaps, created circumstances in which those who lived and worked with him and who knew him well, perceived that his public persona and his private persona were very different and, perhaps, that he was quite hypocritical.

He earned himself the title of 'The Grand Old Man of Ross' and, if one considers the influences on Henry's life from his early childhood in Leominster they give an insight into how his character was forged and how he became the man he was. In some senses, Henry might be seen as the middle child; that is, he may have believed that he was treated less fairly than his siblings, even though he was no less loved than his brothers or sisters. We shall probably never know whether Henry was treated differently compared with his siblings but it is, perhaps, largely immaterial if he thought it was so. If it were so, then it might explain his single-minded determination to move to Ross and do well in business on his own. Moving away in this manner appeared typical of second sons in business and, having attained success, Henry could not countenance the idea that his business might not be sustained by his descendants.

From the very beginning Friends had realised the importance of education and the training of their children. John and Hannah were very intelligent parents and much was expected of their children in terms of their making the most of their education. There is little doubt that John and Hannah did their best for Henry in preparing him for adult life. He had to take life very seriously, particularly after the early death of his mother in 1841. It was, perhaps, a mark of his maturity, independence and strength of character that, when given the choice about where to do his apprenticeship, he chose to remain in Warrington rather than come home again. Whilst away from home Henry had time to think about his future and to consider the reality of the life which lay ahead of him. He was developing into his 'own man', which was important to his future. He had been schooled in the thinking of Free Trade and had met and talked with some of the most dynamic and radical Free Trade politicians of the time. John and Hannah Southall were radical, hard working and independent and their children were brought up with the same outlook on life. They were people of principle and, importantly to them, they were very secure in their religious convictions. It will be remembered, too, from Hannah's long letters to John Tertius while he was away doing his apprenticeship, they lost valuable household possessions for sustaining their stance in refusing to pay the church rate. This, too, was important to them, in terms of public recognition of their principles. If they were to be successful in life, Nonconformists had to be resolute and determined. All these influences played a part in forging Henry's character and, perhaps, at times, made him more than a little ruthless, even with his family.

He did, however, do a great deal of good for the town of Ross and its inhabitants. In his capacity as a Magistrate he would almost certainly have been firm and clear thinking in the administration of justice. As a Town Commissioner he worked hard to provide Ross with a reliable supply of fresh drinking water; even paving and good street lighting; and, often in the face of considerable opposition, for funds for constables to patrol the streets. These provisions were achieved well ahead of many other similar market towns. As a Poor Law Guardian he attended regular weekly or fortnightly meetings at the workhouse in Alton Street, to oversee the management of the workhouse, to monitor the conduct of its officers, to scrutinise the books of the Medical Officers and Relieving Officers, and, as a member of the visiting committee, to pay attention to the general welfare of the workhouse inmates.

He also did much to encourage different groups of people, irrespective of religious denomination, in their desire to promote education and knowledge and understanding of the Bible. He gave numerous talks to the Bible Society and the Men's own Brotherhood. He moved freely amongst members of other denominations and appeared to hold their respect. His ability to mix freely with Anglican clergymen and the ministers of other denominations suggested that he had the ability to accommodate other opinions. He did much to support the young people of the town. He freely embraced the importance of adult education and he gave numerous talks on a wide variety of subjects, religious and secular, to clubs and societies well into his eighties, many of which were reported in the *Ross Gazette*.

The Southall family fostered a great love of newspapers. Reference books were expensive and not normally owned by individuals, so newspapers were not discarded after reading as they are nowadays, but were kept for reference and reading again. When Henry was living at Edward West's house in Warrington, the *Hereford Times* was sometimes sent to him by his father if there was an article which he felt Henry should or would like to read, but they were always sent back to Leominster afterwards. When Henry had established his own household at The Graig, newspapers were stored for future reference in the tower which was built for observing the stars. Indeed, in an article dated 27th April, 1908, which Henry wrote on the subject of the very severe Easter weather of that year, he referred the editor of *The Times* back to an account he had sent to the paper on the same subject in 1879.

As well as writing numerous letters to a variety of newspapers, Henry also produced a stream of articles and papers for the Woolhope Naturalists' Field Club, all of which are to be found in the club's published transactions. Most of these were on various aspects of meteorology and included: 'Our English Winters — with special reference to the recent protracted period of cold weather' (1879); 'The Exceptional Character of the Winter of 1883-84' (1884); 'Some Changes in the Natural History of the neighbourhood of Ross during the past thirty years' (1884); Meteorology, Heat and Drought in March' (1893); 'The Great Drought of 1893' (1893); 'Remarkable Thunder on 21st August' (1898); 'Weather in Herefordshire during the Nineteenth Century' (1902); and 'Meteorology, Our English Summers' (1903). Henry was elected President of the Woolhope Club in 1889 and again in 1903 and remained a member for the rest of his days.

Henry was enormously lucky in that he had a strong physical constitution and powerful mental abilities which enabled him to work hard all his life; to build up a business strong enough to support a wife and family; and, to allow him sufficient income and time to be able to indulge his interests. He was very lucky, too, that he was born into a family that enabled him to make the most of his abilities. He was also aided greatly by virtue of the fact that in Louisa he had a devoted wife and mother for his children. They had an open and loving relationship and, unlike many Victorian wives, Louisa could and would speak her mind to him and, importantly, was allowed to do so as her letters prove. She was intelligent and clear thinking; she could see her family's faults as well as their strengths; and she could assess difficult situations and make logical decisions. During his long business trips in England and his botanical adventures on the Continent, he could travel in the knowledge that Louisa was quite capable of dealing with whatever domestic or business circumstances might arise in his absence. Despite her often indifferent health she did not allow it to confine her to her house; she travelled frequently and was clearly quite able to co-ordinate all the arrangements for her journeys with her children and their nurse. Louisa's part in Henry's successes should not be underestimated.

Louisa's Quaker lineage stretched back to the times of George Fox in the middle of the 17th century. Louisa was a pious woman. Scores of her letters have survived and even though they were written over a period of some 40 years they suggest that her religious beliefs remained constant throughout her life. Her unshakable devotion to her religious beliefs, no doubt helped her through difficult episodes in her life and provided stability for her family as well. Although she sometimes quoted scriptures in her letters, she did so sparingly and to good effect; it was as though the words of the Bible should not be wasted on trifles. Louisa died at The Graig on 4th March 1899, aged 70. In the obituary published by the *Ross Gazette* many good things were said about Mrs Louisa Southall; the pleasantries which were so often printed at such times, but read in conjunction with her own letters, the reader feels that the compliments which she engendered were quite justified. The obituary states that for some 32 years Louisa had acted as the Secretary of the Ladies' Branch of the British and Foreign Bible Society and on resigning her post in 1898, she had received from the members of the Committee in London a 'handsomely bound presentation Bible as an acknowledgement of the valuable services she had rendered.' It continued: 'By her many acts of unostentatious kindness and true gentility, Mrs Southall had endeared herself to a large circle of friends, amongst whom the news of her decease was received with unfeigned regret.' Louisa's dedication to the British and Foreign Bible Society was, indeed, worthy of reward, the more so, because she appeared to be a very private person and her work for the Society resulted from her steadfast beliefs rather than for any notions of self glory.

Louisa lived up to her beliefs with many generous acts of kindness. One such gesture concerned the Southalls' cook who was suffering from chronic indigestion. The family doctor was summoned to The Graig to attend her. He concluded that the digestive problem resulted from the fact that the cook had almost no teeth left with which to chew her food. Louisa immediately ordered that she be provided with false teeth as soon as possible, at Louisa's expense. At a time when household servants were often treated very badly, Louisa looked after her servants well and the doctor was called to them if she thought it at all necessary. It will be remembered, too, that she considered it important that employees who were not Quakers should be allowed to celebrate Christmas and other church festivals in accordance with their own customs. Whilst Louisa was true to her own beliefs, she was open minded about the views of others. Louisa's death was a severe blow to all the family and to many outside it.

In his remaining years Henry continued to write articles and give lectures, and he also retained a lively interest in new things as well as notions of the past. In 1906 he continued to participate in the affairs of the town as a member of Ross Urban Council and in 1908 he was still the president of Ross Cricket Club. On 26th November 1908, the *Ross Gazette* reported on the Cricket Club Annual Dinner at which Henry made a speech in his capacity as president. 'He was especially glad to see so many of the young life of the town present that evening, and also so many of the second eleven, because it was to them they would have to look in the future to carry on what had been so interesting a game in the past.' He extolled the virtues of cricket in training a young man to be self-disciplined, to do his best and to be able to 'take defeats as well as victories.' Henry would, doubtless, have seen participation in cricket as good moral training, but his beliefs in pacifism would certainly not have allowed him to extol the virtues of uniformed youth organisations. He considered that the sad state of employment at that time was as a result of 'lack of training in youthful days.' Despite the fact that he was 82 years old he did much to encourage the young people of the town to do their best: for themselves; for their town; and, for their country. Sadly, six years later many of them would, almost certainly, have found themselves embroiled in the Great War of 1914-1918.

In the summer of 1913 Henry was still strong enough, and fit enough, to walk long distances and he continued to attend events arranged by the Woolhope Naturalists' Field Club. The *Hereford Times* of 28th June 1913, carried a detailed report of the Club's summer visit which clearly involved a great deal of walking. A large party, including Henry and his daughter, Mary Louisa, set out from Credenhill and, having visited houses, churches and archaeological sites, ended their walk at The Garnons, the mansion of the Lord Lieutenant, Sir John Cotterell, Bart. On taking their leave the party walked via Mansell Gamage to Moorhampton where they boarded the evening train to take them home. Henry was just a few weeks short of his 87th birthday.

In December 1913, Henry addressed the Men's Own Brotherhood and he took for his text, 1 Corinthians: Chapter XVI: verse 13: 'Quit [acquit] you like men, be strong.' In their edition of the 18th December, the *Ross Gazette* reported his talk in some detail. He described St Paul's connection with the city of Corinth, a city well known for its temptations and its wickedness. He explained that St Paul was well aware that perilous times lay ahead and was anxious that the members of the Corinthian Church should be strong and courageous and exhibit true manliness in any crisis that might arise. Henry described, too, his own visit to Rome where he had seen the miserable underground chamber cut from the rock in which St Paul had been held captive and the Coliseum where impious despots had inflicted such terrible cruelties on their hapless victims. He reminded his listeners of the fall of empires and added the warning note that 'we of the present age must not aim as a people at being great at the expense of others'. These words were strangely prophetic, for the following year began the war which was to sweep away the power of two members of Queen Victoria's family: Tsar Nicholas II of Russia and Kaiser Wilhelm II of Germany. It also weakened the power of a her grandson, King George V, and began the slow break up of the British Empire.

The war was still raging when Henry died in 1916, but a short time before his death he hosted a meeting of local Ministers at The Graig. In February that year the *Ross Messenger*, the paper published by the Baptist Chapel in Broad Street, Ross, printed a tribute to Henry. The pastor taking the service on Sunday 30th January, described him as 'the kind friend of every Christian Church'.[62] He continued: 'At a recent meeting at his house, he gave an address to the local ministers which showed a still vigorous mind, and was marked by his usual exaltation of thought, as well as large tolerance for the views of others.' Henry had clearly not lost any of his mental faculties or his confidence in addressing people or in engaging them in religious debate. The pastor continued by pointing out that in his address Henry 'laid stress upon the truths that unite Christians rather than on the beliefs that divide. His own simple confidence in his personal Saviour and his easy familiarity in the realm of the spirit were manifest; while in his prayer he breathed a tender reverence which deeply impressed us all.' He ended by saying that Henry's death was 'a great loss to the best interests of the town'.

Henry's reputation as a public figure justly warrants his being remembered as 'The Grand Old Man of Ross'.

CHAPTER 8

Dubricius, Celtic Saint of Herefordshire

Several of the many lovely ancient churches around Ross are dedicated to the 5th century saint Dyfrig, which is his Welsh name, (pronounced 'Duvrig') or St Dubricius — his Latin name. He seems to have been of Romano-British descent, perhaps a member of the royal family of Erging — a small buffer principality lying between the Welsh and Herefordshire borders. Elizabeth Taylor says in her *Kings Caple in Archenfield:*

> During the 5th and 6th centuries, four men lived who shine a small light on the darkness of the time. Three of them were saints — Illtud, Dyfrig and Gildas — and the other was a king — Erb, king of Gwent and Erging.

Erging stretched to the Black Mountains west of the River Wye, and possibly at times as far as Much Marcle or even the Malvern Hills on the eastern side. Two small border kingdoms — Ewyas in the Golden and Monnow valleys and Erging — survived through Roman and Romano-British eras. Erging's kings continued to be more-or-less independent until the mid-6th century to the early 7th when it became part of Gwent, and later, in the late 8th century, was included in the Anglo-Saxon kingdom of Mercia, although even then Erging kept some independence by having its own bishop until 914 AD, when the story goes that the bishop was captured by marauding Vikings. This bishop was probably Welsh, located at Welsh Bicknor or near Kenderchurch. The bishopric apparently persisted long after Erging had been absorbed into Saxon Mercia, retained some of its own laws until the 16th century and was Welsh speaking until the 17th century.

What we know about the life of St Dyfrig comes to us through a mixture of legends — both ecclesiastical and political. Much Celtic heritage, legends, cultural and sacred history has been passed down orally since the Bronze and Iron Ages, absorbed into Romano-British life and then Christianity. Early written records were not factual descriptions of who did what and when; they were not historical documents of the 'true facts' presenting a so-called objective record of Dark Age events. The first written records that have survived describing the kings, princes and holy leaders such as saints and martyrs, were written in Latin by early mediaeval monks. These were mainly the *Lives of the Saints* hagiography — a biography idealizing its subject. Initially, these Latin *Lives* were to be used by literate clergy, to be read out loud on special occasions such as festivals — not in churches but to disciples, pilgrims and within monastic communities. These *Lives* were written much like the Gospels, not so much as an historical record but as stories and legends which present the saints as Christian teachers, healers and miracle workers.

The earliest extant relevant *Lives* are about St Dyfrig (Dubricius), St Illtud and their disciples St Samson and St Teilo. These accounts are included in Liber Landavensis (*The Book of Llandaff*, or the ancient register of the cathedral church of Llandaff) which was compiled by Jeffrey, brother of Bishop Urban, to be presented

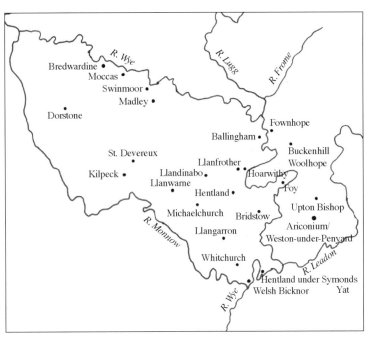

Map of Erging showing the places mentioned in the text

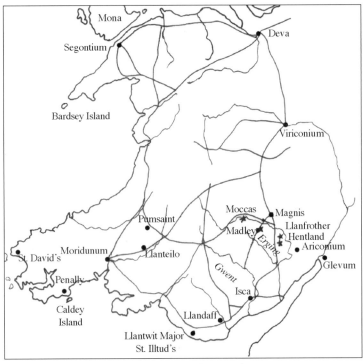

First millenium Wales and Erging

204

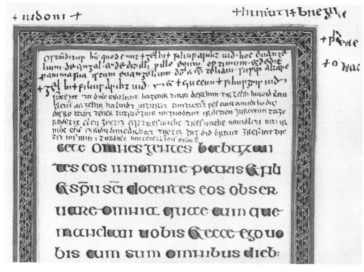

Part of a charter reproduced in The Book of Llandaff

at the removal of the body of St Dyfrig from Bardsey or maybe Caldey Island to Llandaff in 1120. Bishop Urban's political ambitions were to consolidate his Llandaff bishopric at the expense of St David's and Hereford. To this end, the Liber Landavensis claimed the saintly heritage of St Dyfrig and his disciples — bringing St Dyfrig's remains to be placed in a shrine at Llandaff, to create a great pilgrimage centre. For this important occasion, Urban commissioned *The Book of Llandaff* to be written, including the *Lives of the Saints* together with copies of charters — possibly with forged signatures — giving accounts of *llans*/sacred lands, some within the boundaries of Erging, which had been granted to St Dyfrig and his disciples by the kings of Erging and others. Urban wanted to make it clear that all the sacred legends and traditions surrounding Dubricius should be part of his Llandaff heritage.

Dyfrig's Early Life

St Dyfrig was born in the mid 5th century, a hundred years after the end of the Roman Empire, usually measured from the sacking of Rome in 410. According to tradition, St Dyfrig came from the royal family of Erging, of Romano-British descent. Celtic/ Brythonic society was highly stratified; the kings/queens were the top strata, though they were controlled to some extent by the druid priests and priestesses, through magical, sacred duties. For example, the monarch had to be married to the land and its people. As happens now, the coronation included a religious ceremony where the king was anointed and when he pledged to keep his troth to the land and people to preserve security, prosperity, health and fertility. The sovereignty and fertility of the land was symbolised in the form of a goddess representing the people and their homeland.

The druid priests controlled and kept safe the sacred knowledge of the group's tribal oral history, myths of ancestral deities, legends about heroes, heroines, and poetry, which incorporated the tribal values and morality. All these ideas and beliefs were passed on by the druids to following generations through teaching and training their pupils. These societal arrangements fitted well into a Christian framework and hierarchy. The miraculous events in a saint's life — stories of magical happenings — were included in the recorded and oral saintly legends, just as they were in the case of St Dyfrig's birth. St Dyfrig, and some of this disciples too, were presented as members of the Erging ruling class, and the saint was seen in the role of druid/teacher/holder of sacred mysteries.

Little is known of St Dyfrig's early life, except the strange and legendary circumstances of his birth. Tradition has it that Peibio, King of Erging, returned one day from a campaign and noticed, as his daughter Efridyl was washing his hair, that she was expecting a baby. The incensed Peibio ordered her to be put in a sack and drowned in the Wye, but the river washed her alive on to a sandbank. She was then put on a pyre, but did not burn. The next morning she was found nursing her baby, Dyfrig; the daughter was forgiven, grandfather and grandson were united, and legend says that as the baby kissed his grandpa, he healed his grandfather's incurable illness which caused continual dribbling, possibly leprosy.

This story is clearly mythological and designed in true Celtic-style: first, Ynys (Island) Efrddyl was the motherland of Dyfrig, and secondly, how he got his name Dyfrig, meaning water baby, or maybe from the Welsh *dyfrgi* — otter, water creature; the story mentions the sacred elements of fire, water and earth/the tribal land. The place where his mother was supposed to have been thrown in the river was at Madley, but this village is quite a way away from the river. However, Madley does lies close to the Roman road which leads from the village to a ford near Canon Bridge, with a holy well on the other bank; the road then continues on to the nearby Roman town Kenchester/Magnis, so must have been a thoroughfare in the 5th-6th century.

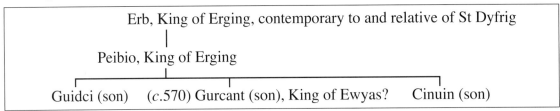

St Dyfrig's family tree from The Book of Llandaff
Traditionally, St Dyfrig appears to have been part of the Erging royal family. If the stories and legends are collected together, a family tree can be composed in which St Dyfrig becomes associated with other noble families — including those of Arthur, Geraint, Tewdric the Martyr, Caradoc Vraich-bras of Sellack, Gawain and Mordred, and the Vaughans of Courtfield. In The Book of Llandaff, *St Dyfrig is placed as a contemporary to King Erb, and Pepiau/Peibio has no daughter called Ebrdil/Efridyl — so that St Dyfrig is a relative but not the king's grandson. We do not know the name of St Dyfrig's father, although there are hints in the legend that he was of illegitimate or even of incestuous birth*

The 5th-6th centuries was a crucial period of change — the end of the Romano-Celtic era on the edges of the dying Roman Empire and the last surviving remnants of the Celtic tribal lands. South-west of the Wye lay the land of the Iron Age Celtic tribe — the Silures; east of the Severn lay the land of the Dobunni; the Latin name of the tribe of Erging and the Forest of Dean may have been the Decangi; to the north of Erging beyond the rivers Lugg and Frome lay the land of the Cornovii Celts.

Despite the problems with the written 'evidence', it is generally accepted that Dyfrig became a well-loved, respected teacher, and leader of the early Christian church — which developed and prospered in post-Roman Herefordshire and in south and south-west Wales. 'Dyfrig's stature, within the early British Church is undisputed' write the Zaluckyjs in their book, *Celtic Christian Sites of the southern Marches*, while Dr Keith Ray links St Dyfrig with Ariconium in the kingdom of Erging: 'The seniority of this Dubric (Dyfrig

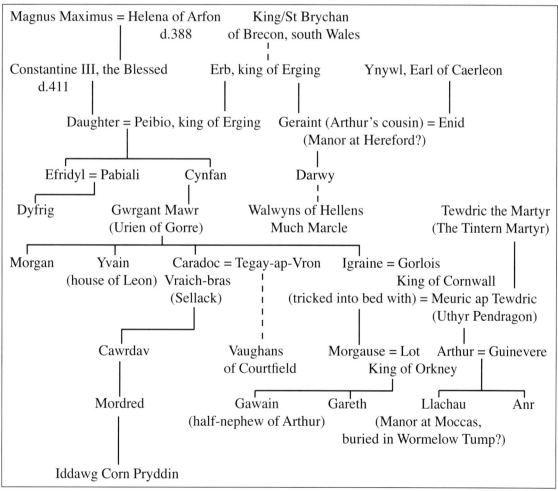

Family Tree of legendary Dyfrig and Arthur (compiled by Margot Miller)

207

or Dubricius) to figures such as St Iltud and St Samson, recorded in several saints' *Lives*, indicates a likely fifth or early sixth century date for his activities ... He is specifically denoted a bishop, his authority was clearly regarded as senior to other saints, and his birth and power were apparently based upon the kingdom of Ercic.' Doble writes in *The Lives of the Welsh Saints*, 'It is clear that Dubricius was one of the chief figures in the creation of Christian Wales.'

We do not know for sure when and where St Dyfrig was born, nor do we know when and where he died. By assuming he was contemporary with St Iltud and that his chief disciple was St Teilo, we can estimate that he lived within the hundred years that spanned 450-550 AD and probably died before the Yellow Plague of 547-9. The day of Dyfrig's death – his saint's day – is 14 November.

Ariconium (Weston-under-Penyard) and early Christianity

Christian communities may have survived in the 5th century in the post-Roman towns — some of which had been previously the cultural, economic and sacred centres of the Celtic peoples. The main identifiable centres of the Decangi in Erging are the hill-top forts or enclosures, and the metalworking, smelting area of Ariconium (Weston-under-Penyard). The Roman invaders took over Ariconium in the 1st century until its closure during recession and political instability in the 3rd century.

Roman towns in the Erging area were:

Roman site	Present name	Celtic tribal centre (Latin name)
Ariconium	Weston-under-Penyard	Ariconium – of the Decangi?
Bravonium	Leintwardine	Decangi or Cornovii tribe?
Epocess	Stratton Grandison	?
Magnis	Kenchester	Decangi?
?	Blackwardine	Decangi?
Viriconium	Wroxeter	Centre of the Cornovii

This list illustrates clearly how little historical information remains in the local area from the Celtic, Roman and post-Roman periods — into the truly Dark Ages. There are almost no 'historical' written works, hardly any archaeology; not even the Romano-Celtic place and tribal names have survived. Scraps of reports by victorious Romans — for example, by Julius Caesar and Tacitus, are the only pieces of written evidence until the appearance of hagiographical writings of St Gildas and early mediaeval monks. St Dyfrig lived during this particularly 'dark' historical era. Myres writes in his book *The English Settlements – English Political and Social Life from the Collapse of Roman Rule to the Emergence of Anglo-Saxon Kingdoms*:

Two centuries lie between the collapse of Roman government in Britain and the arrival of St Augustine in AD 597 — and this time has long been recognized as the most difficult and obscure in British history. Between Roman Britain and Christian England there is a great gulf fixed, a void of confusion which remains a standing challenge to historical inquiry. Within these two centuries changes more profound and far-reaching than in any other corresponding period took place: these changes modified the physical character of the people, altered the fundamental structure of the language, laid the basis of many of our institutions, and made possible an economic exploitation of natural resources on a scale scarcely attempted in prehistoric or even in Roman times.

Unfortunately, physical and literary evidence has been eradicated through time — by Irish invaders in the west, by Saxons from north-west Europe and by Vikings from Scandinavia. In 745 AD the Saxons overran and devastated most of Erging; in 1055 the Welsh sacked Hereford and again destroyed much of Erging; in 1063 the Saxon King Harold won back Erging from the Welsh, but by 1086 the Norman lords of William the Conqueror had taken over.

Erging/Archenfield appears in the Domesday Book as a Welsh district. This Welshness survives in DNA evidence, indicating that many people of the borderlands have kept traces of their Celtic blood, which is relatively unmixed with that of Romans and Saxons. We do not know if the Erging royal family were Romano-Celtic, but St Dyfrig's traditional birth place in Erging is near Madley, just south of the Wye and the Roman town of Magnis/Kenchester.

The carving of a toga-wearing male figure with his hand raised perhaps in benediction, which was found set in the outside wall of Upton Bishop church, could provide evidence of Romano-British Christianity in Erging. Possibly a section of a tripartite stone frieze, it is one of only a handful of Romano-British remains that have so far been found within the area of the principality. Now inside the church in a glass case, the figure may well be a Christian figure of the late Roman period.

St Dyfrig would have been influenced not only by his Romano-British

The carving at Upton Bishop (courtesy of Herefordshire Archaeology)

heritage but also by ideas and developments in post-Roman Christianity. In west and south Wales and the borders, Christianity spread from southern Ireland by settlers and missionaries; these Christians were called the Goidels (from the Welsh for Irishmen: *Gwyddelig*). Some settled in south Wales; holy teachers lived in isolated hermit cells in Wales and in the kingdoms of Ewyas and Erging. These cells are represented in the place names Kil or Cil. St Dyfrig's llans were sometimes set up at the sites of these early cils, e/.g. Kilreague near Llangarron — where the mediaeval church is dedicated to St Deinst or Deiniol, possibly a very early local saint or one of St Dyfrig's disciples.

The cils developed into a wider monastic movement when communities of Christians followed their teacher to set up a small community in an out-of-the-way place, to lead a quiet simple life of learning, study and prayer. In the 5th century, dynamic new ingredients were added to ecclesiastical organisation — these were the cult of saints (which extended and effectively replaced the cult of martyrs), the raising of memorials, and the advent of monasticism. The later monastic form of organisation was eremitical, with groups of hermits living in remote places, following the practices of St Anthony of Egypt, *c*.251-356. St Anthony withdrew from society to follow a religious life, giving away all his worldly possessions. In time he became one of the holy men to whom people made pilgrimage and had so many followers that other settlements had to be established, whilst St Anthony had to go further and further into the desert in order to continue his prayerful life. A later 'desert father' was St Martin of Tours (*c*.316-397) who was given land to set up a sacred settlement. At first a solitary monk, he was inevitably joined by others and became the pioneer of western monasticism. The harsh, ascetic life was moderated in Martin's monasteries, where peasants might be hired to do the heavy labouring, but despite that, St Martin believed the Christian word should be shared equally among rich and poor, urban and rural, and that God made no distinction in class or wealth.

The Pelagian Heresy

St Martin's egalitarianism led to divisions within the church — the Pelagian heresy — that is, the idea that individuals could form their own interpretation and priests could communicate directly with God, and not through the hierarchy. This gave independence of thought and action to individual holy leaders — hermits, abbots and teachers such as St Dyfrig, so that they did not necessarily have to conform to or be ruled by canons laid down by Synod conferences.

The main known leaders of the Pelagian radicals who were seen as heretics came from Britain. One, who is known as the Sicilian Briton wrote:

> One man owns many large mansions adorned with costly marbles,
> another has not so much as a small hut to keep out the cold and

heat ... Inequality of wealth is not to be blamed upon the graciousness of God, but upon the iniquity of man.

Pelagianism continued in Britain longer than in mainland Europe, but appears to have been dead by the time of Gildas in the mid 6th century. Non-hierarchical Pelagian ideas were therefore around during St Dyfrig's lifetime and may well have been supported by him. He seems to have been primarily a father and shepherd close to his people, well-loved and respected. The image of St Dyfrig as a 'bishop' ruling over a large diocese comes from later mediaeval times, as promoted by Urban, 12th-century Bishop of Llandaff.

We do not know if St Dyfrig supported the Pelagian 'heresy', but it seems to me to sit well with his way of teaching and supporting his hundreds of followers. As a Pelagian, he is more likely to have concerned himself with the care and teaching of his many disciples, setting up new teaching centres for those who flocked to learn from him, rather than the building of a local ecclesiastical empire. He does not appear to have been interested in setting up or taking part in a church hierarchy. His busy teaching and administrative work was put aside each Lent to spend quiet time on the Isle of Caldey, off the south coast of Wales (near Tenby), and stay with his friend and disciple St Illtud in some kind of retreat. St Illtud set up his own monastery/teaching and learning centre at Llantwit Major, near Bridgend, Glamorgan. In old age, like St Anthony, St Dyfrig retired to the 'desert' — the Isle of Bardsey on the very edge of west Wales two miles off the Lleyn peninsula, or possibly to Caldey Island where one record states he had 'his own house'.

Connections with St Illtud and St Samson

Illtud was probably a Breton, converted to Christianity as a young man and ordained by Germanus (Garmon) of Auxerre about 445 AD. He came to Llantwit Major about 500 perhaps as a hermit, but as his fame grew, he attracted followers and established a sacred Christian centre — school or monastery. His disciples set up llans dedicated to Illtud — 15 in Wales and seven in Brittany. Illtud is described in the *Life of Samson* as 'the most learned of all the Britons in the knowledge of Scripture, both the Old Testament and the New Testament, and in every branch of philosophy — poetry and rhetoric, grammar and arithmetic; and he was most sagacious and gifted with the power of foretelling events'. Samson also says, 'I have been in his magnificent monastery'.

Mick Sharp says in *Holy Places of Celtic Britain - A Photographic Portrait of Sacred Albion*:

> Llanilltud Fawr [Llantwit Major] ... was an important missionary centre, with a school internationally famous for its Christian knowledge and teaching. Students were divided into 24 groups to enable worship to continue throughout the day and night. The 9th

*Ninth-century crosses in
Llantwit Major Church*

century crosses illustrated here now stand on the site of the old Celtic church.

The west church is a 15th century remodelling of a Norman church built on the site of the Celtic original. Nothing remains of the original monastery beside a stream in this sheltered fertile valley near the coast. The east church was built in the 13th century for the canons of the mediaeval monastery.

For the founder of such an important and long-lived Christian centre, little is known for certain about St Illtud, descriptions of his life being full of wonders and contradictions. He may have been born in Brittany and taught by St Germanus of Auxerre, but there are stories that he was a soldier converted in Wales, who, in a poignant early morning scene, sent away for ever his wife after resolving to found a monastery.

It was St Dyfrig who prepared him as a monk and marked out the monastic enclosure. Illtud drained land for cultivation and introduced an improved form of plough. He was assisted by a tame fawn, and a legend persists that a golden stag [a typical Celtic totem], looking west, is buried on the outskirts of the town. A villa to the north-west of Llantwit, abandoned after a massacre around AD 350, has been suggested as St Illtud's original hermit's cil.

Both St Dyfrig and St Illtud have been credited with founding the first monastic community on Caldey Island. St Samson, pupil of both saints, was probably a monk there and may have been the second abbot appointed by St Dyfrig. The Celtic name of Caldey is Ynys Pyr — the island of Piro; Piro was the first abbot, who, it is said, died one night when he fell into a deep well when drunk. The photograph shows the restored remains of the mediaeval priory which include the gatehouse and tower from the older building. Inside the church is a slab of *c*.500 with an ogham, cross and Latin inscription, which seems to include the names of Dyfrig, Illtud, Cadwgan and Jesus. A stained-glass window depicts St Illtud as a monk and as a knight of King Arthur, told by an angel to return to the holier life of his youth.

A new monastery built between 1910 and 1913 is now home to an order of Reformed Cistercians. Caldey Island is a true holy place, fragrant with spirituality and gorse flowers, used by the monks to make perfume.

As for St Samson, he later established his own centre in Brittany.

On one of Dyfrig's visits to St Illtud, there is a story recorded in his *Life* that he miraculously saved Samson from disgrace in a wine cellar:

Window of St Illtud at Caldey

Caldey Island Priory

St Dyfrig miraculously keeps the wine flowing, a carving by Harry Hems in Hoarwithy Church

... the care of the cellar was granted to St Samson, who, day and night, served the clergy to their satisfaction, and also pleased the common people.

On a certain day, when he had filled the cups of the guests, and all the vessels of the cellar were become empty on the occasion of such great joy as the visit of St Dubricius and his family; it was mentioned by an envious person that the Steward had altogether wasted the drink. ... Hearing the murmuring of the congregation against him, and being ashamed of so much complaint, Samson came

213

to St Dubricius, and related to him all things in order, saying, 'Holy father, flower of thy country, give me thy assistance.' St Dubricius, on hearing his request, prayed to God, that with respect to the distress which Samson suffered, he might liberate him; and being induced by fatherly affection, he went to the cellar, in company with Samson. And as it is said, 'The Lord is wonderful among his saints,' he raised his hand, and pronounced a blessing, which being uttered, marvellous relation! Immediately the vessels overflowed afresh, as if they had been that hour filled with liquor as usual; and the evil effort of envy being got rid of, they were renewed, and what was given away by bestowing bountifully was restored by prayers as remuneration.

In another tale from the *Life*, St Dyfrig heals Argenhell:

As the people were, according to custom, flying for succour to St Dubricius, and recovering the health of their souls and bodies, there came a certain wealthy man, descended from royal ancestor, named Gwyddgeneu, beseeching him on bended knees, that he would release his daughter Argenhell, who was possessed by a demon, and was so far afflicted, that when her hands were bound with cords, one could hardly hold her from being drowned in the river, or burnt in the fire, or from destroying every thing about her with her teeth. O, how excellent a thing it is to serve God, who holds all things by his government, and subjects them to his will! The pious father having heard his entreaty, prayed to the Lord, and falling to the ground with flowing tears, besought God that by the intercession of St Peter the prince of the apostles, and of all the saints, he would succour the diseased. Forthwith, in the presence of her father and relatives, the cords were broken, the evil spirit completely left her, her health and entire reason were recovered, and she received her former state anew, and in every respect improved. She then forthwith acknowledged her own weakness, and being filled with the Holy Spirit, renounced the world; and having preserved the chastity of virginity, and remaining under the protection of the holy man, she led an improved life until she died.

Churches connected with St Dyfrig

There is a 'record' within *The Book of Llandaff* that after the devastation of Erging by the Saxons in 745, eleven churches were returned to the bishop of Erging. This may well have been when local churches were rededicated to patron saints such as Michael, the Virgin Mary, and to local saints especially St Dyfrig. Perhaps, these eleven are the local Herefordshire churches that remain dedicated to St Dyfrig today — including Whitchurch, Hentland, Ballingham and St Devereux.

Madley

Traditionally St Dyfrig was born at Child's Stone (Chilstone) near Madley, from *mad*, good, and *Ile*, place. It has also been said that he was born at Moccas, meaning Pig's Heath, though this is likely to be a confusion with Swinmoor or Swinemoor near Madley, and that the legends have become confused. Most of the church dates from the 1200s, to which was added the Chilstone Chapel in about 1330, its name perhaps recording traditional memories of St Dyfrig's miraculous birth at Child's Stone. Appropriately, the church is dedicated to the Nativity of the Virgin.

Madley Church

Hentland (dedicated to St Dubricius)

Traditionally, St Dyfrig's first *llan* was granted at Hentland (from *henn*, old, and *llan*, church) to him by Erb, King of Erging around 555, but there are several difficulties with this information. Firstly there are two Hentlands in the area, the one near Hoarwithy and another near Symonds Yat and Whitchurch, a church also dedicated to St Dubricius (see Whitchurch below).

Hentland Church (see also Plate 23)

Secondly, the mention of Hentland in the Llandaff Charters: *Hennlann dibric et lann teliau in uno cimiterio* — the old church of Dyfrig and the church of Teilo in one cemetery, suggests there were two churches on the same site or perhaps that one church was re-dedicated — to St Dyfrig and then St Teilo, one of

215

Dyfrig's leading disciples. The reference to two churches could equally refer to the Hentland near Hoarwithy and the nearby site of Llanfrother, the *llan* of the brethren, although there is no evidence here for a teaching centre or *llan*. Silas Taylor says the place was near the river; *The Book of Llandaff* says '*super ripam Gui*' — above the River Wye; and there are old tracks towards Hoarwithy and the Red Rail river crossing, which was probably used from before the Roman period. Certainly the Zaluckyjs suggest that in the 11th century, after the devastation of Erging, pairs of churches were combined into one area church in

The other Hentland below Symonds Yat
(John and Sarah Zaluckyj)

Document by Silas Taylor of 1663 reproduced from The History of the County of Herefordshire, *reproduced here with the kind permission of Hereford Records Office and transcribed below by Sue Hubbard*

Hentland,
a chapple belonging to Lugwrdine
see Mr Barlowe l[ett]er to me of St Dubritius who erected here as he out of Joh[a]n[ni]s Tinmuthensis MS in ye library of Oxford inferrs his podium; a remainder of this yet retained in the name Hentland is Britannice hen llan the ancient church and in a place neare adjoyning on a hill betwixt ye church & ye river called to this day Henfrawdior a corruption of ye British hen ffrauttur w[hi]ch signifies Antinquum monasterium fratrum as Dr Davies in his welsh dictionary doth expound ffrantur.

216

Plate 19 Hoarwithy Mill

Plate 20 Hoarwithy Bridge

Plate 21 The Graig

*Plate 22 The Friends'
Meeting House, Ross*

Plate 23 Hentland Church

Plate 24 Llanwarne, watercolour by Charles F. Walker (Hereford Library)

Plate 25 Moccas, watercolour by Charles F. Walker (Hereford Library)

Plate 26 Llandinabo, watercolour by Charles F. Walker (Hereford Library)

Plate 27 Llanwarne

Plate 28 St Devereux

Plate 29 The Stag

Plate 30 The Crown and Sceptre

Plate 31 Alton Court Brewery dray

Plate 32 Alton Court Brewery labels (HRO)

Plate 33 Alton Court Brewery (HRO)

Plate 34 Sellack Church

Plate 35 Sellack Bridge

troubled times: e.g. Hentland and Llanfrother, Ballingham/ Carey with Llanwarne.

No Romano-British material has been found during fieldwalking next to Llanfrother Farm, but plenty of mediaeval pottery. Similarly, remnants of a mediaeval settlement have been found in the field beside Hentland Church, whilst excavations some 35 years ago to the south side of the churchyard produced sherds of Romano-British pottery dating from St Dyfrig's time. The 2007

Llanfrother Farm 192?

Llanfrother Farm, now part of the Duchy of Cornwall's Harewood Estate (LOWV)

Landscape of the Wye Valley project carried out archeological excavations about a mile away from Hentland, which also dug up Romano-British finds.

The west face of the Hentland cross, with the figures of Mary and John

Hentland is a beautiful church, set in an idyllic spot at the end of a wooded cul-de-sac. The main part of the church, mentioned in 10th-century chronicles, dates from the 13th and 14th centuries, and was a parish on its own until 1291 when it became a chapelry of the parish of Lugwardine. For many years, until 1982, the church had been badly neglected, but thanks to local support and generosity, much restoration has been done, and much more is planned. The churchyard has many interesting old gravestones and monuments, including a 14th-century pink sandstone cross, restored in the 17th century, with the four sides almost worn away. The west side shows the crucifix with Mary and John; the east the Madonna and Child; the south a cleric probably St Teilo; and the north a bishop, perhaps St Dubricius.

Below the churchyard, a lovely spring trickles from an embankment and runs into a sweet pool which is divided into two — one for use by humans, and one for animals. This place would have been wonderful for St Dyfrig to hold baptisms, and is filled with a strong sacred atmosphere.

Moccas (see Plate 25)

Here is another piece of Dyfrig mythology: while looking for a suitable spot to set up his second *llan*. According to his *Life*: 'And during another space of time, St Dyfrig remained with his numerous disciples for many years (some say — seven years at Hentland/Llanfrother), directing their studies, in his native district, namely, Ynys Eurddil, having chosen a place convenient for wood and fish,

Moccas Church (John and Sarah Zaluckyj)

in a corner of that island, on the banks of the Wye, giving it the name of Mochros, that is, *Moch* — hogs, *rhos* — a place in the British language signifying the Place of Hogs. And rightly was it so called, for, during the preceding night, an angel of the Lord appeared to him in a dream, and said, "See that thou, on the morrow, go all round the place which thou has proposed and chosen, and where thou wilt see a white sow lying with her pigs, there lay a foundation, and build it in the name of the Holy Trinity, a habitation and an Oratory."'

There seems to be some confusion with the legend of St Dyfrig's birth near Madley, where there is a place called Swinmoor. This story also includes Celtic lore, where the fertility goddess Ceridwen often shape-shifts into a white sow named Hen Wen with her litter — signifying fertility, prosperity and fecundity. The land of Erging and Dyfrig is associated with the totem hog — hedgehog — and was incorporated into the name Archenfield, through the Saxon name for hedgepig — *urchin*, or *erchu* in the local dialect.

In their book of Celtic sites, the Zaluckyjs suggest that 'in Gaul the cult of St Michael is thought to have replaced the worship of the pagan god Mercury. Mercury was regarded as the guardian of flocks and herds, with hunt and chase in wooded areas. However Mercury can be identified with other deities, for example a pagan god called Moccus — pig — occurred at Langres in Gaul, identified with Mercury. Moccas in Herefordshire, originally Mochros, has a rather uncanny resemblance in spelling to Moccus, and there is a tradition that St Dyfrig was directed by an angel to build a church where he found a white sow suckling. Could it be that a pre-Christian deity was worshipped at Moccas which had links to Mercury/Moccus and which was Christianised through St Dyfrig founding a monastery there?'

This church is dedicated to St Michael and All Angels, and is possibly the site of the first monastery set up by and/or dedicated to St Dubricius.

The Book of Llandaff says: 'the *locus* of Mochros on the bank of the Wye, which in former time the blessed man Dubricius had first inhabited, was given by King Mouric to the church of Llandaff and its pastors for ever, decreed that the former *locus* should always be in subjection to the latter.' (This was part of Bishop Urban's attempts in the 12th century to legitimise the claims of Llandaff to parts of the see of Hereford.)

There is also a potential link with King Arthur, for it is said that Llachau, son of King Arthur, built a palace in an area now part of Moccas Park (see family tree on page 207) and was crowned at the monastery of St Dubricius.

Whitchurch Church

Whitchurch (dedicated to St Dubricius)

There is confusion over whether Whitchurch, or the Hentland site below Symonds Yat, is the original Hentland where St Dyfrig set up his first *llan*. There is no way of knowing, but with almost no archeological excavations, it appears that the positioning of Hentland and Llanfrother might be the more likely site of the saint's teaching centre.

Meanwhile, Whitchurch remains dedicated to St Dubricius, although this dedication may date from the 13th or 14th century, and before that the church may have been dedicated to another early Celtic Saint, Gwynog.

Either way, Whitchurch is a beautiful church beside the Wye, with steps in the graveyard where the ferry boats used to bring the people to church across the river from the historic Huntsham peninsula, where a Romano-British villa site was excavated in 1960 by Elizabeth Taylor (of Sellack Boat, Kings Caple).

Steps from Whitchurch graveyard to the old ferry crossing

*Welsh Bicknor Church. The Rectory on the left now houses Welsh Bicknor Youth Hostel.
Until relatively recently there was a ferry from the English side across the Wye to
Welsh Bicknor (Photograph from the Wye Valley Area of Outstanding Natural Beauty)*

Welsh Bicknor (dedicated to St Margaret)
This church is also confused with Whitchurch and the Symonds Yat Hentland because of
two of the Llandaff Charters which refer to Mainaur Garthbenni:

> Be it known to you that King Peibio son of Erb, granted the Manor
> of Garthbenni, as far as the black marsh beyond the wood, the field
> and water, and the property of King Cystennyn, his father-in-law,
> beyond the Wye, to God, and Dubricius, Archbishop of the See of
> Llandaff, and to Iunapeius his cousin, for his soul, and the writing
> of his name in the Book of Life ...

This is all very confusing, mixing ancestors, names and dates too. Some think the
black marsh refers to the Huntsham peninsula, and the ferry that across to Whitchurch.
It also refers to Romano-British King Constantine III, the Blessed, who might have been
an ancestor of St Dyfrig (see family tree page 207). The *llan* may have been granted
originally to Iunapeius/Junebui — St Dyfrig's disciple & cousin. The small mediaeval
Welsh Bicknor church close to the Wye was taken down and rebuilt, complete with
tower in 1858. The present church of Welsh Bicknor contains a 13th-century effigy
— presumably from the old mediaeval church.

St Dyfrig's Disciples and their Churches
Some of Erging's churches are dedicated to almost unknown early hermits, but some are dedicated to St Dyfrig's disciples:

Samson - Illtud's pupil	Junabui - Dyfrig's cousin	Teilo - David's cousin
Marchwy	Elgwored	Cynwal
Artfod	Aiddan	Cyngar
Anwystyl	Iddnen	Cynfian
Aelhaearn	Gwofan	Gwardogwy
Gwymnyn	Gwernahwy	Ieuan

St Teilo, Dyfrig's heir, went on to work from Llanteilo Fawr near Carmarthen in south-west Wales, where he continued St Dyfrig's pastoral work after his master's retirement. It is said that St Teilo was St David's cousin and grandson of King Ceredigion, born at Penally *c*.AD 500. After an outbreak of the Yellow Plague in 547-9, Teilo took his surviving followers away to St Samson's *llan* in Brittany, returning after seven years to Llanteilo.

In the *Life of Teilo* in *The Book of Llandaff*, it is reported that when St Teilo died, there was a grand argument as to whom should have his sacred remains: Penally where he came from; his church on the banks of the Towy (near Llanteilo) where he retired; or Llandaff — the bishopric which wanted to gather all the saintly relics including St Dyfrig's. The problem was solved by a miracle: 'As in life, so in death of the holy confessor Teilo, miracles should be performed. For, ho! they saw there three bodies, to which there were the same dimensions of body, without any difference. So peace being restored, each with their own corpse returned homewards, and they buried the different bodies in those several places with the greatest reverence.'

Llandinabo (dedicated to St Junabui, St Dyfrig's cousin)
St Dyfrig's disciple's name appears twelve times in *The Book of Llandaff* with several different spellings: Junabius, Iunabui, Iunapius and Iunapeius. His *llan* is identified with Llandinabo; but the Llandaff Charters mention that the '*podum*' (estate) is near the Wye, rededicated to St Dyfrig and the abbot of Moccas in *c*.625, so perhaps it is more likely to be Bredwardine. Maybe with all the different spellings of Junabui his name became confused with that of Hunapui, who was connected with Llandinabo. King Peibio of Erging granted a '*podum Junabui*' with an *uncia* of land (to be dedicated to Dyfrig) in 585 — after the saint's death. This could have been Llandinabo or Bredwardine.

Llandinabo has a very ancient female oak tree which has lasted longer than the old church; the church in the picture (1861) (Plate 26) was rebuilt in 1881 when the architect encased the older, outer walls.

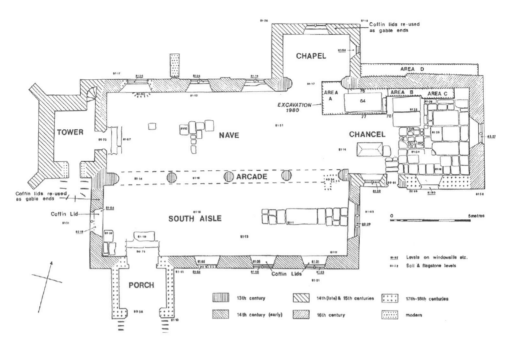

A plan of an excavation at Llanwarne Old Church by Ron Shoesmith reported in the
Transactions of the Woolhope Naturalists' Field Club, *1981*

Llanwarne Old Church (Plates 24 and 27)

In their book on Celtic sites, the Zaluckyjs mention *The Book of Llandaff*'s reference to two churches — one dedicated to St Teilo and another to St Dyfrig — being combined on one site, which perhaps occurred in the 11th century following the devastation of Erging by the Welsh. This also happened at Hentland/Llanfrother and probably at Ballingham/Carey which are both quite close to Llanwarne. They argue that these pairs of churches may have been reduced to a single site in these troubled times.

Llanwarne was deserted once again in 1864 (just after the watercolour [Plate 24] was painted), when its roof was taken off and left as a picturesque ruin, after years of flooding problems. The new church is further up the hill and dedicated to Christ.

Ballingham Church

The old ruined church was surveyed and a small part of the chancel area excavated in 1980 (see plan on previous page, Areas A-D15) but no pre-Conquest evidence was discovered.

Ballingham (dedicated to St Dubricius, and a possible chapel at Carey)

In a charter of *c*.620 'King Gwrgan gave *podum sancti Budgualan* with two and a half *unciae* around it to Bishop Inabwy.' This was regranted in *c*.860 with five other churches to bishop Grecielis when Ballingham is referred to as *ecclesia Lannbudgualan*, and is listed as *Lan budgual* in the churches of Erging listings. The Zaluckyjs suggest that *Badelingahamm* means land in a river-bend belonging to the followers of Badela, and that the *llan* may have been founded by one of St Dyfrig's disciples.

There is a hint that the Lann Budgualan was the *capella de Cari* in 1162 and that there had been two chapels, one at Ballingham and one at nearby Carey, before that time. Like so many of our country churches, Ballingham has been Victorianised with restoration in 1884-5, but there are small pieces of the 13th- and 14th-century church left.

Llangarron

(dedicated to St Deinst)

The earliest parts of St Deinst's church are 14th century, but there is an older carved figure thought to be from the 5th or 6th century, which could be a memorial stone of a priest of the early British church. There appear to have been upwards of 20 cils set up by hermits in the Garron valley, including at Llangarron, Llangrove and Capel Meulog. There is another church dedicated to St Deinst at Itton near Chepstow. He may have been a local saint, or a variant spelling of St Deiniol, a 6th-century abbot-bishop. Maybe this rare carving is of the now-unknown founder of a monastic community at Llangarron, perhaps even St Deiniol?

The church appears in the Llandaff Charters as Lann Garan under a record of *c*.745 when King Ithel returned 11 churches to Bishop Berthwyn 'which had previously belonged to Dyfrig ... after Saxon devastation in the Hereford area'.

St Devereux (dedicated to St Dubricius)

Devereux is the Norman-French version of St Dyfrig's name. This dedication is recorded much later in the 13th century, when the church may have been re-dedicated to St Dubricius on the anniversary of the day he is supposed to have died — 14 November — now the saint's feast day. This lovely church has parts dating from the 13th and 14th centuries, and lies close to the famous church at Kilpeck.

St Dyfrig's lost chapel, Lower Buckenhill, Woolhope

Elizabeth Taylor writes in her book *Kings Caple in Archenfield*: 'There was also a chapel just to the east of Capler hill fort at Lower Buckenhill which has now entirely disappeared. We should know nothing about it if in 1514, Bishop Mayhew had not offered indulgences (absolution for 40 days' sins) for anyone who gave support (meaning money) or made devout visits to:

> The shrine of the Trinity of Hope Wolwith [Woolhope] commonly called St Dubricius, miraculously built by the lord Dubricio below the parish of Hope Wolwith because of an angelic vision; where God, through the merits of his servant, deigned to work many miracles.

Beyond knowing that it was in the parish of Woolhope, the location of the chapel had been forgotten, until in 1954 ploughing brought the piscina and a lot of stone to the surface, and later some walls of a building were found. An ancient hollow way runs beside the site and is known locally as the Pilgrims Way; it is only one of the network of old roads and trackways which converge at Lower Buckenhill. It is difficult to think of any reason other than pilgrimage to St Dyfrig's chapel which would make the place a centre of attraction.'

Foy (dedicated to St Mary or an early Welsh St Moi or Moe)

Foy is mentioned in the Llandaff Charters *c.*866, referred to as *Lann Timoi*. Timoi may have been Tyvoi or Foy, a disciple of St Dyfrig. The church dates from the 12th and 13th centuries, and was previously dedicated to St Faith. The Erging urchin/hedgehog is carved on the heraldic screen on one of nine monuments to the Abrahall family, whose members were lords of the Ingestone manor from 1642 until 1937, with hardly any interruption. In the 15th century, John Abrahall was both law-keeper and law-breaker, buying pardons for his crimes. A much more respectable relative is Ross's John Kyrle, who also has the heraldic hedge pig, which is now on John Kyrle School badge.

Foy Church dedicated to St Mary or St Moi
(John and Sarah Zaluckyj)

CHAPTER 9

The Alton Court Brewery and its Ross Pubs

Introduction

Since the late 1990s I have been collecting information and items of the Alton Court Brewery Company Limited with the intention of writing its history. This was spurred on when the brewery's records together with other documents which form the Whitbread Archive were deposited at Hereford Record Office in 2001. Despite a gap of several years due to researching and writing other publications, I was able to catalogue the archive in 2007, which forms the background of this history of the Ross based brewery.

Apart from examining and recording the Whitbread Archive, other sources have been researched including deeds, conveyances, census returns, directories and newspaper reports. These together with personal recollections, local contacts and brewery and pub publications have enabled the history of the Alton Court Brewery Company Limited to be written. The brewery's pubs in Ross have been fully covered in *The Pubs of Ross and South Herefordshire*, so only their brewery connections and later histories have been featured in this chapter.

Brief History of Brewing

Early man realised that fermented grain, fruit and honey produced alcoholic beverages and these were probably drunk communally during festivals. In the Bronze Age mead was made from hemp and honey, and from fermented lime and honey. In the Iron Age a brew was produced from emmer wheat, and a type of cider made from crab apples, and during the Roman period wine was imported into Britain. Since the liquor called ale was first made by infusing malt, many experiments were tried to improve the brew including the use of hops for flavouring and their preservative properties. Hops were grown in Herefordshire and other counties, and were dried and processed in the familiar looking oast houses.

In the past, towns and villages, most country houses, many farms and the larger inns had their own brew house, where beer was produced for their own consumption, but from the 18th century larger commercial breweries were established. The brewing process was divided into six stages: grinding, mashing, boiling, cooling, fermenting and racking, and best described by Whitbread & Co. in the *Brewer's Art*:

> The Malt is first cleaned and crushed in a mill; the ground malt now called grist, is then mixed with a hot liquor in a vessel called the mash tun, and allowed to stand while the contents are rendered soluble; this is the process of mashing. After mashing the resultant liquid, which is now called wort, is run into coppers where it is boiled with hops, the hopped wort is then passed over coolers until the temperature until the temperature has been reduced to a few degrees above 60° F, when it is dropped into the fermenting vessels and mixed with yeast. Fermentation is allowed to proceed for five or six days; during the latter part of this time the beer, still in the fermentation vessels, is cooled to a temperature suitable for storage. At the end of the fermentation the product which is now beer, is run into casks or storage tanks; this process is known as racking. The subsequent treatment of the beer depends upon whether it is to be sold on draught or in bottle.

Since the above was written in 1948, many new developments have taken place in brewing, packaging, bottling, canning and transportation. New beer styles have been introduced and the small provincial breweries were gradually taken over by larger companies. By 1989 there were six big brewers producing 77 per cent of the nation's beer, which was reduced to four producing 84 per cent in 2003. Fortunately many small local breweries, renowned for their real ale, have been established nationwide during the last few decades.

Brewing in Ross and district before 1865

By Elizabethan times, Ross had emerged as a busy market town, with 'quarterly fairs' and on 'great thoroughfares' from London to south Wales, so it is not surprising that the town earned a good reputation for its inns where wine and spirits were available together with beer and cider produced in the inn's own brew house and cider mill. In the 18th century, Ross had numerous brew houses, malthouses and cider mills including those of Mrs Bellamy, Thomas Hardwick, William Gammon and William Llewellyn. At the beginning of the 19th century there was Thomas Jones's brewhouse and malthouse in Brookend,

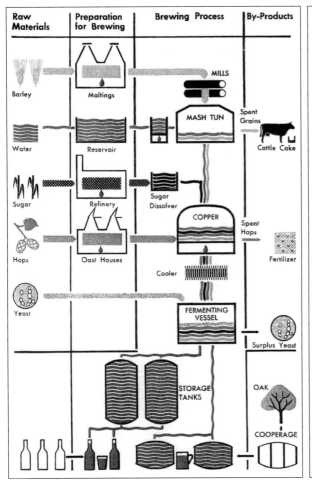

Raw Materials	Preparation for Brewing	Brewing Process	By-Products

MILLS

Barley — Maltings

Spent Grains

MASH TUN

Water — Reservoir — Cattle Cake

Sugar — Refinery — Sugar Dissolver

COPPER

Spent Hops

Hops — Oast Houses — Fertilizer

Cooler

Yeast

FERMENTING VESSEL

Surplus Yeast

STORAGE TANKS — OAK

COOPERAGE

The brewing process, 1948

Advertisement from the 1820s

which in 1813 was 'not used as such', but could have been the 'House, Malthouse, Stable etc.' in Brookend Street where John Hill started his brewery in the early 1820s.

Malting and brewing beer on a larger scale was undertaken at the long established Brookend Tanyard which, at the beginning of the 19th century, consisted of 82 pits with a bark-mill, drying lofts, bark lofts, store-rooms, leather shop, and a dwelling house with a malt house and brew house attached, all belonging to James Frere. In 1827 his son Charles took over the business but ran into financial difficulties, so the 'Excellent Tanyard' was advertised for sale as a premises that 'might easily admit the establishment of a capital Brewery'. When the property was eventually sold in 1836 Charles Frere's 'Furniture, Brewing and washing Utensils' were sold at auction together with 'Mashing Tub, Skeels, Tunpails, 2 Buckets, 6 Tubs, 3 Hogsheads, 5 Barrels, Brewing Sieves, Wood Bottles, Water Tub Etc.'

227

The earliest commercial brewery in the Ross district was established in the early 18th century at Fownhope. In 1771, brandy, rum and other liquors were also for sale at the Brewhouse, which was extended in 1783 when Nathaniel Purchas built his 'new house, Brewhouse Yard, Brewhouse Cellars Etc.' In 1799 George Lipscomb visited the brewery and wrote 'Mr Purchas conducted us through his brewery, and showed us vast repositories of wine: accompanying these attentions with an air of so great good humour, and such a pressing invitation to partake of refreshment, that we took leave of this hospitable gentleman with regret'. From the 1790s Nathaniel's beers, wines and spirits were conveyed by barge or land carriage as far afield as Kington, Bristol and Chepstow.

Although his partner, Robert Whittlesey, had died, Nathaniel continued brewing until his own death in 1817 when his son took over and then entered into partnership with John Reynolds in 1827. From this date the business gradually moved to Hereford under the name of 'Reynolds, Purchas and Reynolds', and a few years later the name Purchas was dropped. In 1834 John C. Reynolds was listed as a brewer, maltster and a wine and spirit merchant in Bewell Street, Hereford. The Fownhope Brewery became known as Rock House and in 1874 the 'commodious Dwelling-house' still contained good spring water, a necessary ingredient for brewing, and extensive cellaring.

At Redbrook in the Wye Valley, at least three breweries once existed, one established by Richard Sims in 1825, another by James Hall around 1830 which was sold in 1855 as an extensive 'Malting and Brewery business', and the Redbrook Brewery. This latter was established by Charles Herbert who sold his premises in 1856 to Thomas Burgham & Son, whose family continued to run the business into the 20th century.

Mitcheldean in the Forest of Dean enjoyed a long history of malting and brewing. In 1839 there were eight maltsters in the town, but this number rapidly declined after Thomas Wintle, an ambitious corn miller of the 1850s, established his Forest Brewery a decade later. By 1833 John Trotter in Coleford had converted a former skinhouse into a 'Brewhouse or Public Brewery with the Counting house, storehouse, furnaces, yard and appurtenances' in Spout Lane. It was later leased as the Coleford Brewery to a succession of brewers including Salmon and Courteen.

Establishment of The Alton Court Brewery Company

John Hill's brewery in the Brookend was taken over during the 1840s by former grocers and brothers, Joseph and Benjamin Turnock from Staffordshire. Known as the 'Ross Brewery' or 'Ross Ale and Porter Brewery' in 1855, it was later moved to Station Street, also known as Queen Street, in a good position to expand with easy access to the Hereford, Ross and Gloucester Railway that opened in 1855. From the documentation it is clear that Turnock purchased parcels of land, orchards, former malthouses, slaughter houses, dwelling houses, barns and gardens on the east side of Brookend

Advertisement (T.S. Smith, 1855)

Street and down Station Street in 1856. Then in 1862 he purchased premises adjoining 'a newly formed street called Henry Street'. Altogether this provided enough land to erect his 'Brewery, Malthouse, Stables and Dwellinghouses' together with 'a Warehouse or Store and retail Department'. Included in the deeds is a strange 'Restrictive Covenants and Conditions' relating to property in Queen Street purchased by Turnock in 1858. It states that buildings should not project into the street and were not to be used as 'slaughter houses, piggery, Blacksmiths Smithy or Tallow or Soap Chandlery' nor house 'any noxious noisy or offensive trade or business', so it is surprising that he was allowed to extend his Ross Brewery and maltings in this street. Turnock was obviously aiming to establish a limited company, but it was not until after the incorporation of the 'Alton Court Brewery Company (Limited)' in 1865 that 'Mr Turnock offered to sell to your Directors upon equitable terms the Ross Brewery'.

The Alton Court Brewery Company was formed under the Liability Act for 'the purpose of supplying its Shareholders, Hotel Proprietors, Inn Keepers, and the Public, generally, with good and wholesome Ales of various description, at moderately remunerative prices: also for the purpose of manufacturing Malt for the Company's own use, and for sale'. Apart from brewing and malting the company also planned to erect steam mills, saw mills, stone quarries and brickworks and to cultivate the Alton Court Estate which they had purchased. At the first meeting of the newly formed company the directors 'considered that it would be much more advantageous to the Shareholders to purchase Mr Turnock's business and premises than to erect works upon the Alton Court Estate, and more especially so, as the Company would then have had to contend not with a single individual, but with a rival Company, having a large and increasing business already established'.

The directors duly purchased the Ross Brewery and installed Mr Turnock as Managing Director of the Alton Court Brewery Company and resolved to sell the Alton Court Estate 'which was originally purchased by the Company as the base of its operations and from which it derived its name and existence'. The estate was sold for £12,000 to Mr Hallum, and the Ross Brewery valued at £6,603 15s. was purchased and extended, but the Brethren's Chapel in Queen Street had to be removed to 'four pieces of land in Henry Street'. This was one of many tasks taken on by the company's secretary, Mr Thomas Blake, a Nonconformist who became a Member of Parliament, a successful businessman and a benefactor to the citizens of Ross.

The setting up of the Alton Court Brewery in Ross was obviously a popular venture as reported by the *Man of Ross* newspaper: 'We learn from good authority that the applications already sent in for Shares in this Company are so numerous that it will be necessary to close the Share List in a few days. The Company is now fully floated, and our friends who wish for shares must make their applications without delay, or they will not get them. We are not a little gratified to find that ours is the only newspaper in which the Directors have thought it necessary to advertise the Prospectus of the Company. Though the Prospectus does not appear in our advertising column to day, it is withdrawn, we understand, for the best of all reasons; namely, that it has answered its end, and because the Share list is now nearly filled.'

In 1867, Ross, with a population of 4,346, was known for its chief manufacturing industries of 'an extensive tannery established in 1837 of Messrs. Smyth and Co., a large brewery (The Alton Court Brewery Company Limited), an iron foundry, agricultural implement and machine manufactory (Messrs Kell Brothers), and several flour mills'. Joseph, as managing director, and James Turnock, the chief brewer, were residing at the brewery premises in Station Street, and Charles Turnock, the clerk to the company, lived in Gloucester Road. With increasing business a new Malt House was completed on 'a piece of land with a frontage facing the Brewery' and 'new plant' had been fixed in the brewery, and new stabling and wagon sheds erected in Henry Street.

After the passing of the second Ross Improvement Act of 1865 there was a growing concern and competition to establish a reliable water supply to the town. For Turnock it was important as an essential ingredient for brewing. Water was taken from the Alton Brook 'where it crossed the road leading to the Railway Station', but there were continual problems including a complaint from Dr Strong who, having allowed the Small Brook to flow into the brewery, had to 'move because of his family's failing health'. Arrangements were made with Mr Samuel Wall of the Ross Water Works 'for a supply of water to the Brewery' and a committee was formed 'to settle the amount to be paid for a water supply'.

Presumably the proceeds from the sale of the Ross Brewery enabled Joseph Turnock to build a large Victorian pile called Purland Chase in 1866 on land originally belonging to Bollin Farm in Walford. The house, which has since been demolished after a fire in 1923, stood on the slopes of Chase Hill known for its springs. From the strange arrangements surviving in the grounds, it appears that Turnock may have attempted to provide a water supply from this site, but by 1874 managed to lease the Town Water Works at the Dock and the 'Water Works, Merry Vale', a property he later purchased.

Advertisement from the Ross Gazette, *1880*

Beer and Mineral Water Production

In 1867 the price of Alton Court Brewery's beer had to be increased due to the high price of barley and hops, but the quantity had increased and £500 was spent on new casks.

The following year it was reported that 'the mouth of the pipe through which the water supplies the Brewery has been repeatedly stopped up with rubble', which caused concern to the directors. It was later revealed that a 'larger hold' was required for the spring water used for cooling purposes and that 'we find that for all purposes every gallon of Beer that is Brewed requires 6 gallons of Water'.

During the 1870s Joseph Turnock was seriously ill and considered retiring, but the brewery was showing a good profit, and he was being paid for the water supply. In 1875 the brewery was flooded, and although the question of water was still a problem, a further supply of casks was needed to replace worn and broken ones. The brewery advertised that they had 'Enlarged their Brewing Plant to meet the increased demand for their justly Celebrated Family Ales and Porter' and were supplying the public with casks of 9, 18, 36 or 54 gallons of XXX (extra strong beer) at 1s. a gallon. A list of their agents covered an impressive area from Swansea to Worcester and Gloucester.

Joseph Turnock acquired the Merryvale estate around 1880 and was supplying the brewery water from there at 'one shilling for each thousand gallons used'. The same year the Chief Brewer James Turnock decided to leave and was replaced by Mr Harryman at £180 a year. He required a microscope to assist him in his duties, two new vats for storing 'Old Beer', and the replacement of two boiling vats in the large brewery. As there had been a decline in profits, an advertising campaign to promote Alton Court brews was started, which included an 'Analysis of Ales' in the local press. The Public Analyst stated that the Alton Court Brewery's Ales 'were exceedingly brilliant, well aerated, and of exquisite flavour and taste'.

It was in 1883 that the company investigated the possibility of manufacturing aerated waters which was in 'great and increasing demand' and had become very fashionable. As space was required, it was decided to use the Foundry Yard for this purpose. Although a Mr Mackenzie from Hereford offered to amalgamate his mineral water company with Alton Court, the offer was not taken up. The

Advertisement from the Man of Ross, *1865*

Aerated Water Factory was completed in 1884, the year that Joseph retired from the company and when his Merryvale water supply ceased to be sufficient. Other sources were found, but the directors were keen to continue with the Merryvale water, and the committee decided that it must be analysed together with the water from the well. At the shareholders meeting in August 1884 it was proposed 'That this being the first General Meeting since Mr Turnock's retirement from the active management of the Company the Shareholders take this opportunity of expressing their thanks to him for his services to the company in past years.' This was proposed by Mr Rootes and seconded by Thomas Blake. At this date Turnock had invented the Merrivale Grate, which he advertised as 'the only open grate which can give the advantage of warmth, comfort, cheerfulness, health, proper and necessary ventilation, with far less than half the coal usually consumed'.

At the brewery new coppers were installed and river water was laid to the boilers, but there were problems. Some brews had gone off possibly due to the water, the casks were in a bad state and enamelling gave the beer a bad taste as complained of by the cellarman in 1885. Also, the retired Mr Turnock was circulating written statements about the financial state of the company that were 'false, unjust, tricky and misleading' to the shareholders. His views were not approved by the Board who at this date were possibly planning to sell the brewery as a valuation was made:

Brewery	£ 9,941	8s	6d
Factory	£ 116	7s	11d
Total	£10,057	16s	5d

During 1885 bad storms had affected the hop harvest, and complaints of 'lack of gravity' in the ales had been made by customers. A new manager, Mr Wooler, was appointed followed by a new brewer in 1886 at a salary of £170. The company was now advertising 'Alton Court Ales' of 'Fine Delicate Flavour' due to the pure and hard water from Merryvale. The same source gave the Aerated Water 'freshness, briskness and piquancy' in their products of Lemonade, Ginger Ale and Soda Water etc. Prices of Ales and Stouts in 1886 varied from 8d. to 2s. a gallon according to type and quality, bottled ales and stout were selling between 3s. 6d. for Diamond Pale to 2s. for Golden Crown per dozen and the mineral waters were available in bottles priced from 1s. 6d. to 3s. per dozen.

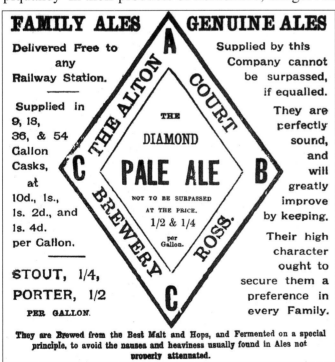

Advertisement from the Ross Gazette, *1888*

The water supply was in short supply again in 1887, the artesian well needed cleaning and repairing, but Thomas Blake came to the rescue. He had managed to purchase the Alton Court Estate and offered a supply from there 'if arrangements could be made with the proprietor of the Merryvale Supply to run the water through their mains'. Turnock agreed and

Advertisement from the Ross Gazette, 1888

allowed a one inch pipe into the main, but the supply was not good, and after a poor analysis of water from Merryvale, the Town Commissioners 'cut off the Supply from Merryvale Waterworks to the Town on the 30th Sept.' In 1887 Joseph Turnock sold Purland, which had been leased, and Merryvale where he had 'erected two reservoirs and a pumping station' to supply the town with water, but many difficulties prevented the Merryvale Water Works from being the success he anticipated'. He retired to south Wales to be near his son.

Although the Alton Court Brewery had a monopoly for providing beer in Ross, there was a nearby competitor at Bill Mills in Weston-under-Penyard for the manufacture of mineral water. The board discussed the sales of their aerated water and the possibilities of selling wine and spirits together with their popular brews.

To improve sales they decided to convert a stable into a Taps in Queen Street, planned a new bottling store and grist mill, and began purchasing and renting numerous inns and pubs in Ross, the Forest of Dean and Monmouth. Since its formation the company had acquired pubs where their beer could be sold and served. However, the three brewery horses used in the yard and for pulling the dray had become 'quite unfit to work' and needed to be replaced. Other horses were initially hired, but this was an unsatisfactory arrangement so two new horses were purchased for £35 in 1888.

The death of Joseph Turnock at the age of 74 years was reported in the *Ross Gazette* on 18th February 1892:

> Another familiar face in Ross will be seen no more. Mr Joseph Turnock, whose death occurred on Saturday night last at 11.30, was a well known man who has played no unimportant part in the history of our town, and the news of his decease, though not unexpected, will be received with general regret. Of late Mr Turnock had become much enfeebled — the wear and tear of business in earlier life having left their mark upon him, which his friends

234

could not help noticing with sorrow. It is 50 years since he came from Stafford — he being a Staffordshire man — to take up his residence in Ross, where he commenced business as a grocer, in the premises now occupied by Mr Charles Preece, butcher, Broad Street; and after a year or two, took to the small brewery in the Brookend, carried on by Mr John Hill, in premises now occupied by Messrs Turner and Co.'s shoe factory.

The obituary continued:

Such was his energy and enterprise that the brewery rapidly grew, and he gradually built up a substantial concern, which ultimately developed into the Alton Court Brewery Company, of which he was managing director for a great many years. We may add that the growth of the brewery was the cause of Station street being opened, when the present extensive brewery buildings and malt-houses are erected ... Mr Turnock, when in the height of his success and popularity, was elected, at the head of the poll, a member of Ross School Board, which office he served with honour and ability for several years. Always ready to take his share of public burdens, he served as Poor Law Guardian for many years.

Station Street, Ross-on-Wye, c.1900 (Tim Ward Collection)

235

Advertisement from 1898 (Brian Thomas Collection)

Joseph Turnock's funeral at Ross Churchyard was attended by old servants, past and present employees at the brewery, his family and friends including James Wylie his son-in-law, Walter Turnock a nephew, Thomas Blake, William Marfell, Alfred Bright and several other notables of the area. Joseph had been left a widower in 1878 when his wife died, and his only son, Rushton, 'was prevented from attending, lying seriously ill at a private hospital in London'.

During the 1890s the Alton Court Brewery underwent complete renovation and was fitted with 'new plant consisting entirely of copper and gun metal' and due to changes made to their Articles of Association the company were able 'to carry on a wine and spirit business in connexion with the brewery'. The artistic adverts for this period show the extent of their business as 'Brewers, Maltsters, Hop Merchants, Wine and Spirit Merchants, Mineral Water Manufacturers' and 'Contractors to Her Majesty's Forces' at Ross-on-Wye, Lydney, Leominster, and Crumlin. Despite various problems with drains, water pollution and arsenic poisoning from the sugar, the brewery appeared to run under the capable management of L.U. Wooler as manager and Frederick Wintle as secretary.

At the beginning of the 20th century a cupola was erected on a new malt kiln. A rather faded advert shows a pipe running across Station Street from the brewery to the malt house, but the water supply from the well and pumps were causing problems. This was resolved in 1914 when a new well was bored deeper and deeper without success until explosives were used to provide the necessary '4,000 gallons per hour', but another £289

Ross Malthouse 1911-12 (Ross Market House Heritage Centre)

6s. 11d. was spent to 'complete the new water supply'. At the end of the First World War the manager of the Aerated Water Manufactory was not available to order supplies, so A.J. Wintle & Sons from Bill Mills provided 'materials, bottles, corks etc.' which led to an increase in prices. From the mid 19th century the smaller breweries had declined in number, many taken over by larger ones which became ever bigger. The Alton Court Brewery had expanded enough by the 20th century for the directors to consider purchasing the City Brewery in Gloucester, Mr Thompson's Brewery at Ruardean, the Monmouth Brewery, and the Redbrook Brewery. The board noted that T.H. Purchas & Sons wine and spirit business in Ross was for sale in 1919, and that Francis Wintle's Forest Brewery was for sale in 1922. After making an offer of £174,500 the Ross based brewery withdrew from that sale.

The Alton Court Brewery was eventually successful in purchasing the Barrel Inn and Brewery in

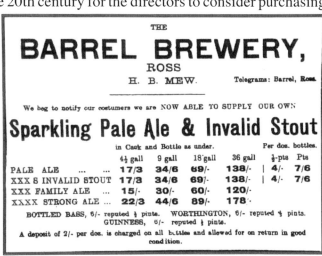

Advertisement from the Ross Gazette, 1921

237

Brookend Street. This brewery started by W.H. Goulding in the late 19th century was acquired by Herbert Mew around 1905 and brewed 'Brilliant Ales' and 'Nourishing Stouts' plus home-brewed ginger beer and lemonade. The asking price for the Barrel Inn and Brewery in 1927 was £14,000 which included an off-licence, a wine and spirit shop and two cottages in Kyrle Street. Offers reached £13,000 and the property was withdrawn and sold as separate premises with Alton Court Brewery buying the inn and the brewery.

Between the two World Wars, a well observed account of the brewery was recorded by Jessie Stonham in her book *Daughter of Wyedean*:

> The only other industry I remember was at Alton Court Brewery, then a flourishing business and occupying most of both sides of the Station road between the bottom of Broad Street and Henry Street. Its malt house also continued up Henry Street and the entrance to the cooperage went from here, eventually coming out on to the Broad Street. It was a very busy place when I was a child and we loved to walk past the windows through which we could see the men treading over and working on the malt. The smell was strong but quite attractive. The cooperage was of course the place in which the wooden barrels for the beer were made. This was a real craftsman's job and as children we were occasionally taken to see the men at work. We enjoyed scuffling our feet through the chippings after the wood had been trimmed ready and watching the hammering of the metal bands on the casks.

> The beer made there was delivered by large drays drawn by shire horses. These lovely creatures were in evidence at the Town carnivals, which commenced when I was much older. They were beautifully groomed and had their manes and tails plaited with coloured ribbons. With their lovely harness shining and their brasses polished they made a lovely sight.

> It was interesting to see them delivering the great wooden barrels to the local public houses and hotels. There were grids, usually square, which would open up upon the pavement and reveal one end of a cellar below. A contraption somewhat like a ladder would be let down and fastened in position and then the barrels, held back by a man holding the rope to which they were attached, would be slowly lowered into the cellar. They were either stored until needed or connected to the hose through which the beer would be pumped to the 'beer engine' in the bar above.

Decline and Take-over

Throughout the 1920s and 1930s the Ind Coope Brewery from Burton-on-Trent were buying numerous breweries, maltings and licensed houses, and were interested in taking over the Alton Court Brewery.

Their interest in the Ross brewery was followed in quick succession by the Stroud Brewery then the Cheltenham Original Brewery both from Gloucestershire. These offers were refused although the brewery and malt house had not been redecorated since 1904 and 'appeared very shabby and needed doing'. The outbreak of the Second World War interrupted any further potential take-overs. Travellers and lorry drivers were taken off the road and many employees departed on active service. This caused an 'acute shortage of beer' in 1941 until the Head Brewer started malting again. During wartime some of the brewery's pubs were damaged by army vehicles, donations were made to the Red Cross, and extra malt did become available. In 1943 the death of a long serving manager of the Alton Court Brewery Company was recorded in a report to the shareholders: 'It is with deep regret that the Directors have to record the death of Mr Louis

*Advertisement of 1920
(Monmouth Museum)*

Upton Wooler. In him they have lost a very valuable colleague and a faithful friend. After more than 46 years' service as Manager of the Company, Mr Wooler retired in the year 1922. He was appointed a Director of the Company in January 1924 and continued to hold that position until his death. In all, Mr Wooler had been connected with the Brewery for 57 years, during which time he had the respect of everyone with whom he came in contact in the Company's business.' When he started with the company he lived beside the brewery in Station Street, but around the 1920s moved to the Firs in Firs Road.

In 1955 a serious offer to purchase the Alton Court Brewery was made by the Stroud Brewery who planned to use the brewery building as a bottle store and use the maltings as a malt house. The matter of transferring shares was discussed by the directors, and on 23rd February 1956 the *Ross Gazette* reported 'Brewing Ends at Ross'. 'The final brew of Alton Court beer has been made and the employment of 37 men and women at the brewery ends tomorrow.' The managing director of the Stroud Brewery regretted the loss of jobs, but the Maltings were kept in operation with part of the premises used as a depot to supply the licensed houses.

According to the late Martin Morris: 'The closure came at a time when the unemployment situation in the town was becoming serious. The drift from the land, the run down at the end of the war of the munitions factory at Hereford and the aircraft factories at Gloucester, and the closure of the oil refinery and other industries that had been brought to Ross as a haven from the bombers, all meant fewer and fewer jobs'. When the manager of the Ross Employment Exchange was questioned about finding other work for those leaving the brewery, he replied 'No fit man who is prepared to travel should be out of work very long'.

In June 1956 the last annual meeting at Ross was held, before further meetings were held at the Stroud Brewery until 1960 when it was suggested that the companies should be leased to Cheltenham and Hereford Breweries Ltd, which a year later was amalgamated into West Country Breweries in Cheltenham, where the final meeting of the Alton Court Brewery Company was held. Before its closure the Alton Court Brewery was advertised as 'Brewers, Maltsters and Mineral Water Manufactures', 'Bottlers of Bass and Worthington's Pale Ales and Guinness's Stout' and 'Established Over a Century'.

When Visiting the Wye Valley

ask for

GOLDEN HOP   QUEENS ALE

SPARKING ALE

brewed and bottled by

The Alton Court Brewery Co., Ltd.

ROSS-ON-WYE

Last Advertisement in 1956

In 1957 the Station Street brewery spread from Brookend to Millpond Street, and consisted of offices, factory premises, brewery tap and other properties. The Maltings with its bottling store, beer store, loading ramp and barley store stood opposite the brewery and ran along Henry Street, and the Mineral Water Factory in Station Street was 'well constructed of stone and brick' with a factory or warehouse space, an office, bottle store and storage space, with an 'Old Lane' to the factory from Henry Street alongside a 'Garage for 3 Lorries with Flat over Service Formerly an old Wool Warehouse'.

The Alton Court Brewery had already sold the brewery, maltings, and mineral water factory for redevelopment before the 1962 Conveyance and Assignment of freehold and leasehold properties to West Country Breweries Limited. The conveyance stated that the 'Company shall be wound up (whether voluntary or otherwise)', and the capital of £79,000 be divided into shares of £1 each. The documentation is confusing with so many vested interests, but it appears that both the Stroud Brewery and West Country Breweries had previously bought and sold certain properties in Ross before 1962.

Since the sale of the brewery and its associated sites in Ross many changes have taken place. The brewery consisting of its factory, offices, brewery tap and premises in Station

Street and Henry Street were sold in 1957 to Mr S. Littler. The brewery building (Plate 33) became derelict and was partly used for storage, and despite an effort made to save the façade of the building it was demolished in 1992 and has been redeveloped. The Maltings were sold to the South Herefordshire Agricultural Society in 1958 and were converted into a supermarket during the 1980s

(Whitbread Archive, HRO)

leaving the outline of the original building. In 1961 the Mineral Water Factory in Station Street with its office and bottle store was sold to Mr Lerego, and since being used as a showroom for stoves and fireplaces has recently been taken over as an antique lighting centre.

Only eight of the brewery's pubs in Ross were open in 2007, the New Inn now the Eagle, the Stags Head formerly the White Hart, the Horse and Jockey, the Drop Inn formerly the Queen's Head, the Vine Tree, the Crown and Sceptre, the Barrel and the re-built Travellers' Rest. Whereas the Castle, True Heart, Saracen's Head, Plough, Royal Oak, Nags Head, Royal Taps, Brewery Taps, Wine Vaults, Railway Inn, Game Cock, and the Harp have been converted into dwellings and retail units. For a fuller history of the Ross pubs see chapters three to six in *The Pubs of Ross and South Herefordshire* (2001) by the author.

Reminders of the past importance of the Alton Court Brewery are the remaining beer and mineral water bottles in private collections and at the Ross Heritage Centre, an engraved glass sign at Alton Court, a superb dray at the Doward Works (Plate 31), numerous adverts in directories, reports in early copies of the *Ross Gazette*, and the Minute Books, labels (Plate 32) and price lists in the Whitbread Archive at the Hereford Record Office. Lastly, shame on Ross for not retaining the name of the 'Brewery' in the Station Street development.

Alton Court Brewery's Pubs in Ross

One hundred and twelve licensed premises in Breconshire, Gloucestershire, Herefordshire, Monmouthshire and Radnorshire were transferred from the Alton Court Brewery to West Country Breweries in 1962. Twelve of these were in Ross, and were either closed,

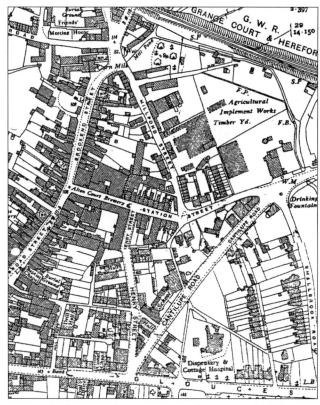

Ordnance Survey map of Ross in 1927

Former Castle Inn

sold or taken over by Whitbread in 1963 who later sold all their pubs and bars in 2001. The Alton Court Brewery purchased or leased a number of inns and licensed houses in Ross between 1865 and 1890 as follows:

CASTLE INN at the top of Wye Street, which the company took 'at a rental of £35 a year and stable for £5' in 1865. The following year it was let to Mr W. Edwards as the 'Castle Wine and Spirit Vaults', but the brewery did not purchase the property until 1908. In 1962 the inn closed and was converted into flats called Malvern House.

TRUE HEART INN was in Kyrle Street, and purchased by the brewery for £400 in 1879. In the 1890s the pub was kept by Benjamin Clark who sold 'The Celebrated Alton Court Ales'. The inn closed before the mid 20th century and was sold in 1962 as 'a dwellinghouse'.

NEW INN on the west side of Broad Street was taken on by the brewery in 1880 under the tenancy of Mr Miller who had a wine and spirit stock valued at 'not more than £150', and in 1886 the company purchased the premises for £1,150. The managers in 1969 decided the name was too common-place, so the pub was renamed the Eagle after the Lunar Module which had landed on the moon.

SARACEN'S HEAD INN stood opposite the Market House in the High Street. In 1884 it was leased by the company who stripped the building of its plaster to reveal timber-framing with interesting carvings depicting Tudor roses, heads and foliage. After passing to West Country Breweries this old inn was closed.

PLOUGH INN at Tudorville was leased by the company in 1884 and was success-fully run during the 1940s and 1950s by 'a very well known pub landlady', but due to lack of business was closed by Whitbread during the 1980s, and has since been converted into residential use.

HORSE AND JOCKEY INN was serving Alton Court Brewery beer from 1886 from the attractive bow-fronted brick building in New Street. Although the skittle alley was removed in the 1990s the pub remains open, and offers a range of beers, real ales and bar food.

Saracen's Head (Whitbread Archive, HRO)

QUEEN'S HEAD INN was a former beer retailers before being named after the street which became Station Street. It was acquired by the brewery in 1888, although an earlier deed exists between Turnock and Lewis in 1858. It now goes under the name of the Drop Inn.

Horse and Jockey

BREWERY TAPS in Millpond Street was a replacement in 1889 for the original taps of the Ross Brewery which Joseph Turnock closed in 1865 before the Alton Court Brewery Company was established. In 1889 the taps was under the supervision of Mrs Woodman. Although it ceased as a licensed premises when the brewery closed the building has survived.

WINE VAULTS was in St Mary's Street and better known in its latter years as the Hole-in-the-Wall. The Ross based brewery took over the Wine Vaults in 1889 more as an off-license. From the beginning of the 20th century the long established Ross wine merchant, T.W. Purchas and Sons ran the shop until Harry Morris opened the premises as a public house which eventually closed in the 1970s.

STAG INN otherwise known as the White Hart in Henry Street was a beer house taken on by the brewery in 1884, but was not purchased from the Kemp family until 1936. It later passed from West Country Breweries to Whitbread and onto Enterprise Inns around 2000 (see Plate 29).

RAILWAY HOTEL was at the bottom of Brookend, and was leased by the company from 1890, and purchased by them in 1935 together with the land at the rear of the property that was once the tanyard. The rather grandly named Railway Hotel catered for 'anglers, cyclists and motorists' during the 1940s. After the railway closed in 1964 the Railway Hotel was converted into retail units.

ROYAL TAPS was attached to the Royal Hotel in Palace Pound. From 1884 the company's brew was available to those not wishing to enter the grand hotel which aimed to attract 'Visitors, Tourists and families', whereas the Hotel Tap was a 'cosy, homely place'.

ROYAL OAK INN stood opposite the Nag's Head at the top of Old Gloucester Road in Copse Cross Street. It was taken over by the Alton Court Brewery in 1884, but only just survived as a pub into the 20th century when

Former Royal Oak

it housed the Conservative Club from 1914, and has more recently served as a licensed restaurant.

GAME COCK was in Brampton Street, and taken over by Alton Court Brewery in 1890. It became a 'busy little pub' with a bar, smoke room and a Jug and Bottle where people could refill their bottles of beer and cider. By 1960 the Stroud Brewery had acquired the premises and sold it as being 'Ideal for use as a private residence', but it was promptly incorporated into a housing development.

VINE TREE INN lies on the road to Walford on the parish boundary, and was taken on by the brewery in 1890, but it was later purchased by Wintle's Forest Brewery from Mitcheldean. In 1923 the Vine Tree with its outbuildings, stalls and stabling was sold to the Cheltenham Original Brewery who were acquired by West Country Breweries then taken over by Whitbread. Fortunately the Vine Tree has survived.

Former Harp Tavern

HARP TAVERN in Alton Street was an Alton Court Brewery Pub from 1891 before Wintle's Forest Brewery acquired the premises with its bar, smoke room and cellarage. It was taken over by the Cheltenham Original Brewery in 1923 and closed by them around 1941.

TRAVELLERS' REST INN 'at the Blackhouse Ross adjoining the road leading from Ross to Ledbury with the outbuildings cottage gardens and land' was a brewery pub from 1890 and taken over by West Country Breweries in 1962. With the transformation of this area due to the construction of the motorway in the early 1960s, the 'Blackhouse, Smithy and Travellers' Rest were demolished and the site redeveloped as a roadside inn and travel lodge.

CROWN AND SCEPTRE INN is still thriving in Broad Street, and was taken on by the brewery in 1891. The property has various conveyances referring to rights-of-way and pieces of land dating from 1898 including one of 1928 when the company purchased the Crown and Sceptre from Bass Ratcliff and Gretton Limited, a Staffordshire brewery. Similar to other Alton Court Brewery pubs it became a Whitbread house in 1963 (see Plate 30).

NAGS HEAD was purchased by the Alton Court Brewery in 1932 when Edward Taylor was the tenant, and although described as 'well furnished throughout' it was redecorated by the brewery. In 1933 a new driveway was made at the rear for easier deliveries.

BARREL INN with 'the brewhouse outbuildings yard and garden' in Brookend, which were acquired by the company around 1927. Although brewery operations ceased at the Barrel, the pub despite being closed for a period, was refurbished and re-opened its doors in 2001.

CHAPTER 10

James Cowles Prichard, 1786-1848

Introduction

Sellack Parish Church, dedicated to St Tysillio, would seem to be an unlikely place in which to search for a memorial to an eminent man of letters whose life began in the Ross Quaker community, but it was, indeed, that remote and peaceful spot which James Cowles Prichard chose for his last resting place. His memorial is there; a wall tablet of white marble edged with black, now somewhat faded with the years and in places difficult to read, but clear evidence of his association with St Tysillio's as a place of worship. The church nestles in a quiet corner close to the river-bank and on a bright spring morning, a sunny summer afternoon or a golden autumnal evening, the views across the Wye to the fields beyond are probably not greatly changed since Prichard ventured there to attend services with other members of his family. Despite the brilliance of his mind he was essentially a quiet, studious, almost timid man who was ill at ease with the pomp and ceremony of public life. It says much about this remarkable man's character, therefore, that he should wish to lie in such a tranquil and modest place of rest.

James Cowles Prichard

James Cowles Prichard was a man of exceptional ability; a linguist, England's leading anthropologist of his day, and also an eminent doctor of medicine with a particular interest in disorders of the mind. He sustained a very successful medical practice in Bristol for many years and later moved to London when he was appointed a Commissioner in Lunacy. He was essentially a man of science, because, despite writing books on his chosen subjects and speaking ten or twelve languages, he appears to have had little time for purely literary subjects. Researchers, past and present, have reluctantly concluded that he left no journals and few personal papers, unless some remain in private hands or lie hidden and yet to be discovered.

He was born into a devout family with a Quaker lineage stretching back to the days of George Fox, the founder of the Quakers, in the middle of the 17th century, but, as a young man he gave up his birthright membership of the Religious Society of Friends and was baptised into the Church of England. He died in London after a short illness and was buried at Sellack parish church where his son-in-law, the Reverend William Henry Ley, was vicar.

Quaker Ancestry: Almeley, Pennsylvania and Ross

Freedom of Conscience, an individual's right to worship as he wishes, or not at all, if that is his choice, is now taken for granted but, of course, it has not always been so, and many people have faced crippling fines or endured long terms of imprisonment or, indeed, given up their lives for their religious beliefs. In the years between the execution of Charles I in 1649 and the restoration of the Stuarts in the elegant figure of his son, Charles II, in 1660; that is, the period when the Commonwealth was declared and England was a republic, the social hierarchy of the country changed and there was a very significant weakening in the power of the Church of England. This led to the rise of radical groups such as the Levellers, the Diggers, the Ranters, the Fifth Monarchists and the Quakers, some of whom saw the removal of the monarchy as a positive step towards social reform. Inevitably, having seen much of their power slip into the control of parliament, both monarchy and church perceived such groups as a serious threat to their authority. The only remedy was to crush them or, at the very least, fetter or restrict their activities in order to strengthen and protect the Establishment. It soon became an offence, punishable by law for any Nonconformist groups to worship in their own way and with the passing of the Quaker Act of 1662 and the Conventicle Act of 1664 it became illegal for more than four people above the age of 17, apart from a family, to meet anywhere for worship if not in accordance with the rites of the Anglican Church. When illegal meetings of worship were discovered heavy fines could be imposed, and in 1670 informers were given an added incentive to spy on their neighbours because, if a case was taken to court and proved, they were entitled to receive one third of any fine imposed by the judge. This measure created a climate of fear and suspicion, but many embraced the struggle for political and religious freedom with bravery and sustained defiance, perhaps none more than Roger Prichard, James Cowles Prichard's great, great, great grandfather, who lived in the remote Herefordshire parish of Almeley.

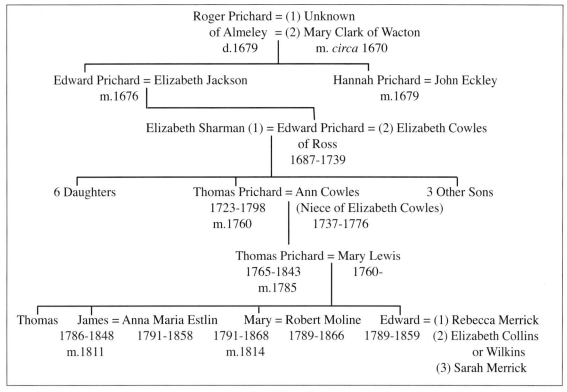

Prichard family tree

Very little is known about Roger Prichard, even the year of his birth remains obscure, but he was clearly a contemporary of George Fox (1624-1691) and was quite evidently, one of his resolute followers and may even have heard Fox preach. By trade he was a glover and a will dated 1679[1] suggests that he was more than comfortably well off, but probably not rich. Church records suggest that he was a determined and very brave man because, despite the legal prohibition against Dissenters gathering for worship, in 1672, he provided the Quakers of Almeley with a cottage-like building in which to hold their meetings. This was a daring thing to do because in a small parish like Almeley, everyone would have known everyone and the church authorities, particularly the parish priest, would have been well aware that illegal religious meetings were taking place. At that time, under an Act of Elizabeth, 1559, it was still compulsory to attend church each Sunday and failure to do so, without very good cause, could result in a summons to attend the Consistory Courts of the bishop or the archdeacon.

The Consistory Courts were, to some extent, the overseers of public behaviour and were sometimes known as the 'bawdy courts' because they dealt with cases of adultery, fornication and slander, as well as disputes about non-payment of tithes and church rate.

The church rate could be levied on all occupiers of property for the upkeep of the parish church, the graveyard and the boundary wall, but since Quakers did not use the parish church they saw no reason why they should contribute towards its maintenance. There is clear evidence in church records, that despite repeated requests from the churchwardens, Roger Prichard and several other Almeley men refused to pay their 'lewn', the local name for church rate. In 1675, for example, it was recorded[2] that Roger Prichard had failed to pay 6s. 6d. and 8s. 5d., William Collier 6s. 10d., John Hall 1s. 6d., Richard Hopley 8d. and Thomas Pembridge 1s. 8d. There is also evidence that on several occasions in the mid 1670s, Roger and his wife, Mary, were summoned before the Bishop's Court convened in the Deanery of Weobley[3] to explain why they had not attended the parish church on Sundays and were excommunicated as a result. The sentence of excommunication, being banished from the Church of England and denied communion, probably worried them little and clearly had little effect in changing their behaviour or their religious convictions. Later, in 1676, however, Roger Prichard, William Collier and Thomas Pembridge were taken to court by the Vicar of Almeley, Samuel Matthews, for refusing to pay tithes and were imprisoned for about two months as a result.[4] Tithes were attached to land, so the people who owned the land had to make payment to the Church of England, irrespective of their own religious adherence, or, face the consequences. Men of principle were quite prepared to go to prison in the fight for religious freedom: the church was quite prepared to send them there. The suppression of religious dissent was vital in sustaining church authority.

As well as the ever looming threat of religious sanctions, Quakers were often savagely attacked because their beliefs were frequently perceived as subversive. Holding firmly to their beliefs, therefore, took courage and fortitude. In September 1676, the Meeting House in Hereford was attacked while Friends were at worship: a noisy rabble broke windows, knocked off the men's hats with staves and one man, John Rea, had his head cut open when a stone was thrown by a young man who was thought to be the mayor's son.[5] It was, almost certainly, with such attacks in mind, that Roger Prichard hoped that an unobtrusive, simple, timber-framed Meeting House, which resembled a modest dwelling might afford the Almeley Quakers some protection when they met for worship. It seems very unlikely, however, that the parish priest would not be well aware of their activities, despite their efforts to avoid notice. As the 1670s passed and the 1680s dawned, Quakers and other dissenting groups still saw little hope of religious toleration and many of them grasped the opportunity to start a new life in America.

In 1681, King Charles II granted William Penn a huge tract of land on the west bank of the Delaware River in payment of a debt he had owed to Penn's deceased father, provided it was named 'Pennsylvania' in Admiral Penn's memory. William Penn set out to create an open community; a 'Holy Experiment', based on Quaker ideals; a community which,

Almeley Meeting House, 2008

guaranteed freedom of conscience to worship according to an individual's own convictions. During the 1680s a steady stream of ships carried many Friends and other Dissenters to Pennsylvania where they would not be troubled by the persecution and anxiety they had endured at home.[6] Many of the first settlers were Quakers and amongst those who sailed with Penn and aided him in developing the settlement were Roger Prichard's son Edward and his son-in-law John Eckley. Edward was one of the 13 signatories to Penn's Charter for Pennsylvania, five of whom were directly connected with Almeley. The Meeting House at Almeley, possibly the oldest in the country, is still a cherished place of worship and has in its possession a copy of a parchment dated 1682 which records the long connection between Almeley and Pennsylvania and perhaps reminds those who read it of the intense struggles of the earliest worshippers. Edward returned to Almeley and later his son, also called Edward (1687-1739) left his native parish to set up his business as a tanner somewhere in the Brookend area of Ross.

By 1700, Ross had an established Quaker community, but this had not been achieved without suffering and considerable bravery. The Quaker belief that anyone could have communion with God without the need for religious texts and ceremonies, or the intercession of priests, if they sought the spirit within themselves, was considered to be blasphemous and put Quakers in danger of prosecution and imprisonment under the blasphemy laws. The first Quakers came to Ross in the 1650s and they were persecuted for their beliefs, suffering the confiscation of goods, attacks upon their person and imprisonment for refusing to take an oath of allegiance to the Crown and, therefore, for disturbing the King's Peace. For the first 20 years Ross Quakers met covertly for worship at the house of James Merrick and his wife Elizabeth, who in 1675, bravely provided land, timber and £40 in money for the building of the Meeting House in Brampton Street. The king, Charles II, died in 1685 and was followed by his brother, James II, a determined Catholic, whose attempts to support the Catholic faith in England resulted in his being forced to flee to France for his own safety, after three short years on the throne. The people had not forgotten the bloodshed of Mary Tudor's brief 45-month reign 130 years earlier, and were not prepared to have another Catholic monarch. James was followed by his daughter Mary who ruled jointly with her husband, William of Orange.

William and Mary were Protestants and their accession paved the way for the passing of the Toleration Act of 1689. This Act brought some relief for Quakers and other Dissenters because it became an offence to disturb another person's worship; freedom of conscience was one step nearer, but many legal restraints remained in force. Quakers and other dissenting groups were prohibited from studying at a university, holding public office or entering the professions and as a result tended to concentrate on being successful in business. Edward Prichard's son, Thomas (1722-1798) followed his father into the tanning business and appears to have done well because, after demolishing an existing dwelling, he erected the substantial property in Brookend Street, still known as Millbrook House. In 1760 Thomas married Ann Cowles and, in 1785, their son, Thomas, (1765-1843) married Mary Lewis, the daughter of William Lewis of Ross. Thomas and Mary had four children: James, Mary, Edward and Thomas.

Childhood and Education
James was born on 11th February, 1786 at Millbrook House just two minutes walk from the Meeting House in Brampton Street where Thomas and Mary worshipped. In 1793, however, Thomas moved his family to the bustling City of Bristol where he had part ownership in an ironworks. James proved to be a boy of exceptional ability, displaying a particular facility for learning and absorbing languages. At that time, the dockland area of Bristol was a vital, colourful and extremely attractive place for a very intelligent boy to ask questions, and James delighted in speaking to foreign visitors and sailors in their own languages. By 1800, however, the city's mercantile prosperity was less secure than in previous decades, if not in decline, and the first signs of social unrest amongst the starving paupers were all too evident, and it may be for that reason that Thomas decided to return to Ross. In 1800, James was 14 years old and for the next two years he studied at home, in particular Latin, Greek and French, under the guidance of a local

Ross-on-Wye Friends Meeting House, 2008
See also photographs on page 187 and Plate 22

clergyman, the Reverend James Mills. Thomas Prichard was, himself, a learned and thoughtful man, but hoped that James would follow him into the iron trade, for fear that a scientific education might alienate him from the Quaker beliefs in which he had been nurtured. James, however, had other ideas and in 1802 he began to attend lectures at the medical school attached to St Thomas's Hospital in London and in the following year entered the University of Edinburgh taking his M.D. in 1808. It is almost certain that James went to Edinburgh because, unlike Oxford and Cambridge, it did not discriminate against Dissenters, and the fees were considerably lower too. In England, Dissenters were still not allowed to enter universities to read for degrees, to hold public office or to enter the professions under laws which were not repealed until the late 1820s. Curiously, there were some eminent Quaker doctors before these laws were repealed, but quite how they managed to accommodate their Quaker beliefs remains unclear. On completing his medical degree, therefore, James was faced with a dichotomy: he could not complete his medical education with postgraduate studies at Oxford and Cambridge, or practise as a doctor and remain a Quaker. In 1808, he took the momentous decision to resign his birthright membership of the Religious Society of Friends, the Quakers, and was baptised into the Church of England.

This must have been a very difficult time for both father and son: for Thomas, because his fears had come true; for James because he knew the pain his father might feel as a result of his decision. James also understood the furore which would ensue at Ross Meeting House when the news had been received and absorbed. He was well aware of the steps the Friends would take: his resignation would be discussed at Ross Meeting House and then referred to Monthly Meeting for further consideration. Monthly Meeting would then appoint two visitors to meet him to discuss the issues leading to his decision, in the hope that they could be resolved and that his resignation might be withdrawn. In his resignation letter[7] James was at pains to make it clear that his decision had not been made lightly or suddenly, but as a result of mature thought and careful deliberation over many years. He had finally resolved that the teachings in the Established Church were more in keeping with the true interpretation of the scriptures than those of the Society of Friends and, for that reason, he felt he must leave the Society. At the same time, however, he earnestly hoped that no unpleasant feelings about him would arise in their minds because he would always entertain the highest respect for them and sincerely desired their esteem. He did not wish to be estranged from his family and had, therefore, chosen his words carefully not to cause any offence, but he had made up his mind and his spiritual life was thereafter set on a new course.

A few weeks later, in September 1809, Thomas Beavington and Nathaniel Morgan of Ross and Leominster Monthly Meeting were appointed to write to the Monthly Meeting at Witney requesting Friends there to visit James who was then residing at Oxford.[8] After something of a chase between Witney and Westminster Meetings, Friends finally managed to talk to him, but reported that he was not prepared to retract any of the sentiments of his resignation letter.[9] After further discussion Ross and Leominster Monthly Meeting

Millbrook House, Ross-on-Wye, in 2008, the birthplace of J.C. Prichard on 11th February 1786

formally disowned James but hoped very much that for the sake of his own peace of mind, he would at sometime return to the Society of Friends.[10] In February 1810, James acknowledged receipt of a copy of the minute of his disownment and the process was complete.

Thomas Prichard must have been a very fair-minded man and a very understanding father, because, despite the heavy financial costs, he obviously continued to fund his son's postgraduate studies at both Oxford and Cambridge. He was well respected as a kind and thoughtful man, and no doubt thought that freedom of conscience was absolute and that James was entitled to express his convictions as much as anyone else. If he had attempted to influence his son's religious views with the imposition of fiscal sanctions, he would have been guilty of hypocrisy in the extreme. It would have been a betrayal of everything that Quakers had sought to achieve for generations; the right to self-determination and the right to worship according to one's own conscience.

It might be assumed that James converted to the Church of England simply to clear the way for him to practise as a doctor, but that might be too cynical a judgement. By that time Quaker thought was divided into two schools; the Quietists and the Evangelicals. The Quietists had an unquestioning, almost reverential, acceptance of the writings of early Friends such as Fox and Barclay in the maintenance of their spiritual purity; the Evangelicals, on the other hand, began to mix in wider circles, largely as a result of evangelism in other religious groups. The Gurneys of Earlham, for example, were at ease in the company of evangelical Anglicans and were beginning to adopt some of their attitudes.[11] It is not clear exactly where James stood in these matters before his resignation, but if he was of an evangelical mind, it is possible that the social, intellectual and religious interactions and influences of university life were also factors in his decision to join the Church of England. Many Quaker Evangelicals began to question the Quietists' strong opposition to evangelical faith and, attracted by the eloquence of some clergymen, left the Society of Friends, and many more considered taking the same step.[12] If leading figures in the Quaker world such as Norwich bankers Joseph John Gurney, his brother Samuel and their sister Elizabeth Fry, were moving in such company, then any other free thinking person might do the same. It will probably never be known exactly why James resigned from the Society of Friends, but his motives may not have been simply those of professional advancement.

Bristol: Doctor and Alienist

By the middle of the 18th century Bristol had grown rich from its participation in the slave trade and the importation of sugar from the West Indies. In 1793, however, when Thomas Prichard took his young family there, Bristol had lost most of its lucrative trade in human cargo to Liverpool where the anchorage was deep enough to accommodate the larger ships needed to keep pace with the ever increasing demand for slave labour. Bristol continued, though, to be a focus for the importation of sugar and, by 1807, when slave trading was abolished in the British Empire, the city had, to a large extent, already adjusted to the loss of that particular trade. In 1810, when Dr James Cowles Prichard returned to Bristol to begin his medical practice it was still a bustling city with many wealthy citizens and prospective patients.

Bristol's medical men, just like those of other towns and cities throughout the country, depended on private patients for their income, so, if they were to be economically successful and well respected in their profession, it was essential for them to cultivate and retain the right families. Social contacts were, therefore, very important for any young man who wished to penetrate this group and build up his own practice. In that respect, James was fortunate in having the confidence of the much-respected Estlin family. John Prior Estlin was a prominent Unitarian minister in the city; his son, John Bishop Estlin, had been a close friend and fellow medical student at Edinburgh University; and in February 1811, his daughter, Anna Maria Estlin, was to become Mrs James Prichard Initially, James shared a medical practice but soon had his own and in 1811, he was appointed as Physician to St Peter's Hospital, which would, without doubt, have assisted him greatly in establishing his own practice. James worked at St Peter's Hospital for over 20 years and it was there that he observed many of the patients who were to be the impetus for his later writings on insanity, because it was, in reality, a parish poor house and a lunatic asylum under the same roof. A few years after that appointment, in 1816, he was elected a Physician to Bristol Infirmary and, although the post was unpaid, it almost certainly raised his professional status in the city. At that time, the affluent members of society did not use hospitals or infirmaries; they were regarded as places for the poor. Admittance to such establishments said much about an individual's social status, because they were generally very overcrowded and bed sharing was common. The way in which poor houses, hospitals and infirmaries were managed varied considerably but, needless to say, some of them were grim places of great sadness and neglect, if not intended cruelty. As far as the mentally ill were concerned, little attempt was made to distinguish between dangerous lunatics and the merely feeble-minded and many, particularly those who appeared to pose no great threat to anyone, were incarcerated in parish poor houses without any kind of treatment for years and years. The following example was probably not particularly unusual.

In 1834, the passing of the Poor Law Amendment Act brought about many changes in the management of poor relief with the establishment of the Poor Law Commission at Somerset House in London and the appointment of Assistant Poor Law Commissioners who liaised between the Commission and the newly elected local Boards of Guardians. In 1835, almost a generation after James began work at St Peter's Hospital, the Assistant Poor Law Commissioner for the south-west made his first inspection of the workhouse in the parish of St Philip and St Jacob in the City of Bristol, and was horrified by the conditions in which he found one particular lunatic. A brief summary of his report[13] indicates a woeful lack of care and paints a very sad and depressing picture of the poor man's existence. Locked in a filthy room which resembled a coal cellar, he was in a pitiful state: dressed in very ragged clothes and shoes long past use; his body unwashed for many a long day; his face and head much bruised from frequent falls; warmed only by the dying embers of a fire; listless, alone and staring vacantly into space. The Assistant Commissioner, obviously much moved by the scene before him, concluded that he tried to rouse the poor man but years of neglect rendered his efforts quite useless. He had existed, much to the shame of the parish officers, in that pitiful and disgusting state for so many years that he was now quite lost to the world.

Doctors involved in the study and treatment of the mentally ill were often known as 'alienists' because they worked with people who appeared to be alienated from general society because of their condition; a mental condition which provided some with an excuse for treating them as little more than animals. In many cases, treatment appeared to amount merely to containment, with no attempt to understand the patient's condition or the reasons for its having arisen. There were people however, like the Quaker tea merchant William Tuke of York who realised that the mentally ill needed a humane and enlightened management regime if there was to be any likelihood of an improvement in their condition. The York Retreat, an asylum which opened in 1796, was the first in England, and perhaps the world, where the insane were treated gently, some attempt was made to diagnose their illness, and an enlightened effort was made to assist their recovery.[14]

In 1822 James Cowles Prichard published *A Treatise on Diseases of the Nervous System*, and in 1831 he placed an article in the *Medical Gazette* giving an account of a new mode of treatment, which by modern standards seems barbaric and was even considered to be rather savage by some of his contemporaries. It involved making an incision in the scalp, filling the wound with peas and leaving it for several weeks or months in order to restore the balance of fluids in the brain's vascular system. James used this mode of counter-irritation on many of his patients and so it might be reasonable to presume that the effects cannot have been too terrible because he remained a very popular and well respected doctor. Indeed, such was his popularity that many of his patients were brought from the Continent for his assessment and his particular style of treatment.

In 1835, after many years of observing his patients at St Peter's Hospital, he published his thoughts in a book entitled: *A Treatise on Insanity and other Disorders Affecting the Mind*. In this book he defined the notion of 'moral Insanity' as a condition in which the patient appeared to retain fairly normal intellectual and reasoning abilities, but seemed unaware that many of his habits, feelings, natural impulses and attitudes to others were unacceptable to society in general.[15] What he appeared to be saying was that he had observed patients who were not insane in the sense that they suffered from impaired mental faculties, but were morally insane in the sense that they were unable to conduct themselves with propriety in the daily interactions of normal life. In present times, they might well be described as patients displaying various forms of personality disorder. It is thought that James's definition of moral insanity had a positive influence on the outcome of numerous court cases and saved many lives. In 1842 he published a book, specifically for the legal profession, entitled: *On the Different Forms of Insanity in Relation to Jurisprudence designed for the use of Persons Concerned in Legal Questions Regarding Unsoundness of Mind*. The notion of moral insanity saved many from the gallows; most notably Edward Oxford and Daniel McNaughton.

In June 1840, Edward Oxford, a frail and rather inadequate young man of 18, fired two shots at Queen Victoria and Prince Albert as they were driving up Constitution Hill. They were not harmed and Oxford was quickly apprehended by onlookers. He was committed to Newgate Prison to await trial and it was widely considered that he would hang for his attempt on the queen's life. He was found guilty, but escaped hanging because he was also judged to be insane. He was committed to the Bethlehem Royal Hospital and later to Broadmoor where he remained for many years. Later he was allowed to travel, under supervision, to Australia where he spent the rest of his life. In 1843, Daniel McNaughton entered the House of Commons and shot and killed Sir Robert Peel's private secretary, Edmund Drummond, thinking that he had killed Peel. The judgement at his trial was codified as the 'McNaughton Rules' which defined the responsibility of the insane and formed a standard for future cases.

By the late 1840s James's careful observation of his patients and his subsequent writings had had a major impact on the thinking of both the legal and medical professions. In 1849, the year after his death, John Addington Symonds, Consulting Physician to the Bristol General Hospital, read a paper on the life and work of James Cowles Prichard to the Bristol Branch of the Provincial Medical and Surgical Association and it is clear from his definition of moral insanity that medical research with regard to such cases was continuing to develop James's original ideas. He stated that 'moral insanity often presents violent anger as its most prominent phenomenon, at other times an inclination to theft, arson or even homicide. Sometimes the most striking characteristic is a sudden change of disposition. There are many instances which show a transition from moral insanity to monomania' (an obsession focused on one interest).[16] In an article to mark the centenary of the death of James Cowles Prichard in December 1948, the *Times* reminded the world of the importance of his work as the most eminent alienist of his day. It also pointed out that James's work on the concept of moral insanity led to modern notions of penal reform and the treatment of criminals as diseased rather than merely wicked.[17] As James was recording his observations of the mentally ill and writing books on insanity, Elizabeth Fry (1780-1845), his almost exact contemporary, was embarking on her crusade for penal reform. In truth, before the advent of the New Poor Law of 1834, it was probably very difficult to see any significant difference in the squalid living conditions which prevailed in many parish poor houses, asylums and prisons and equally difficult to draw any clear distinction between the function of such institutions. The petty criminal, the harmless lunatic and the respectable poor were often housed in the same building. Thus the calls for penal reform and the better treatment of the insane appeared to manifest themselves at the same time and, indeed, there was much for Elizabeth Fry and James Cowles Prichard to do. It is, however, as an anthropologist that he is best remembered today.

The Anthropologist

James's interest in anthropology appears to have manifested itself quite early in life; possibly generating the impetus for his medical studies in Edinburgh. The subject of his student thesis was *De Humani Generis Verietate* which he later extended and published in two volumes in 1813 and entitled: *Researches as to the Physical History of Mankind*. The work was dedicated to his mentor Johann Friedrich Blumenbach (1752-1840) of Göttingen in Lower Saxony. In the early 1800s Blumenbach had made a collection of human skulls which he examined in detail in order to classify the various families of man. There is no suggestion that his studies masked any racist intent, but simply reflected an academic fascination for the history of men and women. It remains uncertain whether Prichard and Blumenbach ever met, but it is certain that they corresponded and exchanged ideas for many years and continued to be good friends until Blumenbach's death.

James continued to develop his theories of human evolution and in 1843 he produced a revised version of his 1813 publication entitled: *Natural History of Man*. It was dedicated 'To His Excellency, The Chevalier Bunsen Envoy Extraordinary and Minister Plenipotentiary of His Majesty the King of Prussia to the Court of Great Britain' and the dedication itself, in the form of a personal letter, says much about the author's friendships and the august circles in which he sometimes moved. He begins:

> My Dear Friend, I gladly embrace the opportunity which your kind permission affords me, of connecting with my new work, on the Natural History of Man, the name of one of the chief ornaments of the most learned nation in Europe – a nation among whom my researches have ever been more favourably estimated than among my own utilitarian countrymen.

Utilitarianism was the name given to the philosophical ideas of Jeremy Bentham (1748-1832) and his followers and was the dominant social theory in England during the 1830s and the 1840s. Utilitarian attitudes, however, were seen by many, James included, as harsh, particularly so with regard to the arrangements for relieving poverty after the passing of the Poor Law Amendment Act of 1834. Almost inevitably, when the guiding principle of social conduct is the greatest happiness for the greatest number, then the individual counts for little and may be lost in the struggle and clamour of human endeavour. Prichard would, without doubt, have greatly disapproved of such a notion, seeing it as unjust and undeniably crushing to the human spirit.

James must have been very secure in his estimation of the King of Prussia's Plenipotentiary, liberal theologian and scholar, Christian Carl Josias von Bunsen, (1791-1860), and the depth of their friendship, because later in the dedication he makes it clear to all readers that His Excellency was a second choice and, had he still been alive, the book would have been dedicated to Blumenbach himself. He continues:

> Since my venerable friend Blumenbach (whose views it was my first object to illustrate and extend) finished his earthly career, there is no one to whom I could so rightly as to yourself dedicate the results of studies which you have promoted by your exhortation and kind encouragement. Accept the tribute of my grateful regard, and believe me to remain, with the highest respect and the most sincere esteem, your obliged friend and faithful servant, James Cowles Prichard.
>
> Bristol, 30th September, 1842

Prichard accepted Blumenbach's analysis of five races of people in the world but had widened his own enquiry to include ethnology and philology as well as anthropology in order to establish a more complete picture of humankind and their beliefs and customs. This combination of study techniques brought together information, as far as was then understood, on evolution, racial characteristics, interactions within and between similar and different communities, the development of languages and literature, and the links to be found between languages. He freely admitted at the beginning of his 1843 publication, however, that his previous anthropological writings had not been well received by everyone. His critics, he stated, fell into two groups. The first accused him of raising doubts where no reason for doubt existed and of creating uncertainty by drawing new inferences from evidence that already appeared to be abundantly conclusive. The second accused him of bigoted adherence to a predetermined opinion and of closing his eyes to all opposing arguments. He answered both accusations very neatly by stating that: 'The author pleads guilty to neither of these accusations, and he trusts that their incompatible and contradictory nature will afford a presumptive proof that he has followed a middle course'.

For those men who built fortunes through the slave trade or owned slaves to work on their sugar plantations in the West Indies and justified their actions on the basis of prejudiced notions of racial superiority and racial inferiority, James's writings must have made uncomfortable reading. Slave trading in the British Empire was abolished in 1807, but slave ownership was not ended until 1833, but even then former slaves were euphemistically called 'apprentices' and in reality their lives probably changed very little until 1838 when apprenticeship ended and they became wage labourers. James's survey was, indeed, wide ranging because as well as considering human physical characteristics, daily life and means of survival, social organisations, moral and intellectual ideas and community government, it also considered internal feelings, social convictions and aversions, notions of good and evil and the worship of gods. Having considered all these things, at the conclusion of his book he declared that: 'We are entitled to draw confidently the conclusion, that all human races are of one species and one family'. Bristol, the city where James had lived and practised medicine for so long, had at one time grown fat on the slave trade and still benefitted from the importation of sugar from the West Indies, so the publication of his book just a decade after the abolition of slave ownership almost certainly pricked a few consciences.

In December 1948, the Royal Anthropological Institute celebrated the centenary of Prichard's death and, in the presence of his last surviving grandson and one of his great grandsons, reminded a forgetful public of the great man's contribution to the world's understanding of physical anthropology. The world remembers Charles Darwin (1809-1882) and the *Origin of the Species*, but less so the fact that all James Cowles Prichard's anthropological writings were complete some 12 years before Darwin's publication appeared in 1859. Prichard's firm, unwavering view of the unity of mankind, of all races being of one family, put him ahead of his time. It should not be forgotten, therefore, that through his writings and establishment of the Aborigines Protection Society, which later became the Royal Anthropological Institute, the foundations of anthropological study in this country were laid down by Doctor James Cowles Prichard of Ross.

The Family Man and Man of Letters

Thomas Prichard, James's father, was a quiet almost timid man, but greatly respected in Ross for his thoughtfulness, his kindness and generosity. He was also possessed of a profound generosity of spirit because he had not sought to obstruct James in his decision to leave the Society of Friends, nor his son Edward and his daughter, Mary Moline, in later taking the same step. He had respected their freedom of conscience, which says much for his personal integrity and his example as a loving father. James appears to have inherited his father's gentle understanding of humankind, a notion enhanced by descriptions of his character dating from 1849 and 1893.

In 1893 Isobel Southall, a distant relative, compiled a book about the Prichards of Almeley and in it she described Dr Prichard as 'in stature rather below the middle height, and of rather slight make. He had light hair and grey eyes, which, though somewhat

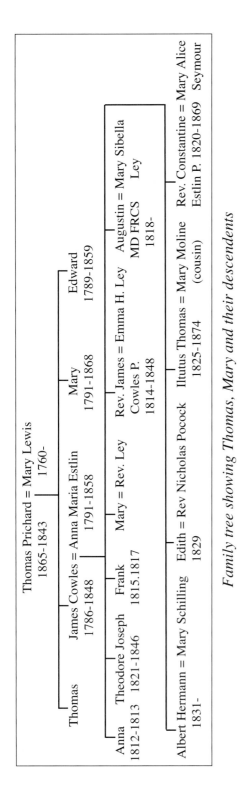

Thomas Prichard = Mary Lewis
1865-1843   1760-

James Cowles = Anna Maria Estlin   Mary   Edward
1786-1848   1791-1858   1791-1868   1789-1859

Thomas

Anna   Theodore Joseph   Frank   Mary = Rev. Ley   Rev. James = Emma H. Ley   Augustin = Mary Sibella
1812-1813   1821-1846   1815.1817   Cowles P. MD FRCS Ley
1814-1848   1818-

Albert Hermann = Mary Schilling   Edith = Rev Nicholas Pocock   Iltutus Thomas = Mary Moline   Rev. Constantine = Mary Alice
1831-   1829   1825-1874 (cousin)   Estlin P. 1820-1869 Seymour

Family tree showing Thomas, Mary and their descendents

small, were of singularly intelligent expression … The countenance, to the most superficial observer, betokened deep thoughtfulness, with something of reserve and shyness, but blended with true kindliness.'[18] It is not clear whether this description was written from personal memory, but it is possible that she met James as a child or young adult. She was the granddaughter of Mary Southall, born Prichard, who was first cousin to James. The description does, however, accord with the precise and revealing observations made by Dr John Addington Symonds, a colleague and friend, in his tribute to James in 1849. He stated that: 'In the moral department of his character, high — nay, highest integrity and honour, and an utter abhorrence of whatever even bordered on the mean and truckling, were united with general benevolence and with strong domestic affections.'[19] James, it seems, was a humble man like his father Thomas and, despite his great learning and superior intellect, he respected and understood humankind.

Domestic life for James and Anna Maria was, however, not without its tragedies, because of their seven sons and three daughters, four of the children predeceased them. Theodore Joseph died aged 25, James Cowles aged 34 and Anna and Frank, their first two children, died in infancy. Iltutus Thomas made a name for himself as the author of books on India; Albert Hermann was Postmaster of Merton College; James Cowles and Constantine Estlin became clergymen in the Church of England and their sisters, Mary and Edith, married clergymen; but Augustin was the only son to follow in his father's footsteps and became a doctor. Despite his heavy workload in medical practice, James appears to have been a dedicated father in providing advice and guidance to his children in their chosen careers. He was also very close to his sister Mary, the wife of Robert Moline, a woolstapler and banker in Godalming, and found time to help and advise their 12 children and, whenever possible, arranged introductions to people who might help in their advancement. In the midst of all his domestic, familial and professional responsibilities he managed to write his books, sustain a huge correspondence and participate fully in Bristol's intellectual life.

James was, indeed, a man of letters, habitually rising early in order to complete three or four hours of writing before embarking on the day's business in his large medical practice. As well as simultaneously writing books on philology, anthropology and the diagnosis and treatment of insanity, he also found time to produce numerous articles and lecture papers on subjects as diverse as Egyptian mythology and the treatment of hemiplegia — paralysis of one half of the body. He was actively involved with the Bristol Auxiliary Temperance Society, the Bristol Medical School, the Bristol Established Church Society and Book Association and the Bristol Literary and Philosophical Institution. In addition he corresponded with other learned Societies in Britain, France, Italy, America and Russia and although the following list of organisations to which he belonged is by no means exhaustive, it does provide a very clear indication of the scope of his interests.

- The American Philosophical Society in Philadelphia
- The Academy of Moral and Political Sciences in Paris
- The Russian Geographical Society
- The Royal Irish Academy
- The Academy of Natural Sciences of Philadelphia
- The Edinburgh Society of Medicine
- The Royal Society of London
- The British Association for the Advancement of Science
- The Royal Academy of Science in Paris
- The Philosophical Society of Sienna

It is almost certain, too, that as well as writing to friend and mentor Johann Friedrich Blumenbach in Göttingen, he regularly corresponded with a number of learned societies in the German states, later unified as Germany, because, in his 1849 paper on the life and work of James Cowles Prichard, Dr John Addington Symonds pointed out that his works on Egyptian mythology and his observations on nervous diseases had been translated into German because the German speaking peoples were much more alive to the merit of his work and far more interested in it than his fellow countrymen.[20] It was not insignificant, therefore, that James's 1813 publication on anthropology was dedicated to Blumenbach and the 1843 edition to the King of Prussia's Plenipotentiary in London and, perhaps, not surprising that in 1837 his treatise on insanity was dedicated to a learned Frenchman,

'Monsieur Esquirol, Physician in Chief to the Royal Hospital of Charenton, Member of the "conseil de salubrité", Chevalier of the Legion of Honor'. In his dedication letter James thanks him for his kindness in allowing him to connect his name with the most distinguished writer of the times on the problems of insanity, and pays homage to him for his service to mankind.

In 1835, Oxford University conferred on James the highest award it could bestow: the Degree of Doctor of Medicine by diploma. It was a rarely given honour, indeed, often after very long intervals, and then only to those whose work was of the highest merit. Despite the great significance of this award, or perhaps because of it and the ever smiling green-eyed monster of academic jealousy, James's work did not receive the widespread recognition and interest from his own countrymen which might have been expected, and this possibly explains why his most important works were dedicated to German and French men of letters. It may also have been the case that recognition was, in part, restricted by his own shy and retiring personality. He did not generally seek the limelight or the company of those people in high society who might have advanced his interests. It is a sad reflection on society, however, that at the beginning of the 21st century few people have any knowledge of James Cowles Prichard, or of his profoundly important work, even in the town of his birth.

The 1840s appear to have been years of relentless travel for James, so it might be presumed that he kept his own carriage and horses and employed a coachman. By that time a complex web of coaching services had been established, but dependence on a public system of transport would have wasted too much time for a man renowned for making wise use of every minute. He had many local visits to make in and around Bristol and, of course, longer journeys to visit his sister, Mary, and her family in Godalming, his father and brother, Edward, in Ross and his daughter, Mary, in Sellack. There were, indeed, many visits to Ross and Sellack, but they brought both joy and much sadness.

In 1839, Mary had married a young clergyman, the Reverend William Henry Ley and, just a few days before Christmas 1841, the Dean and Chapter of Hereford presented William with the joint living of Sellack with Kings Caple. Mary and William already had one baby boy, and a second son, Augustin, was baptised by his father at Sellack Church in May, 1842 (see Plate 34). In July 1843, Thomas Prichard, James's father, died and in November 1844, the family received another blow when Mary died in childbirth or of later complications and in January 1845, the baby, also Mary, died aged just eight weeks. In that same year of 1845, James accepted the post of Commissioner in Lunacy and moved to London. The government had decided to place the administration and regulation of madhouses under the authority of a Commission similar to that devised to oversee the relief of poverty, the Poor Law Commission of 1834. James did not particularly enjoy the work, since it involved almost relentless travelling around the country to inspect the psychiatric establishments, but it was fairly lucrative. In 1846, another blow came with death of his son Theodore Joseph. James's namesake, the Reverend James Cowles Prichard, died in September 1848, and was buried at Sellack and just three months later, after a short illness, James himself died at his home in London and was buried at Sellack. Anna Maria Prichard lived in Bristol for another ten years and was also buried at Sellack, in January 1858.

In 1809, when James wrote his letter of resignation to the Society of Friends in Ross, there were, almost certainly, those who took the view, even if they did not voice it, that his decision was prompted simply by his desire to seek advancement in the medical profession, but theirs would seem to have been too cynical a view. James stated that after mature deliberation of several years he was firmly of the opinion that the profession of religion made by the Established Church of England was more consistent with the true interpretation of the Scriptures and, being of that opinion, he ought not to be a member of the Friends, and he appears to have sustained that view for the rest of his days. Dr John Addington Symonds said of him that he never said anything disparaging about religion and that piety was always a strong influence over his mind and conduct and concluded that: 'His opinions, during the greater part of his life, were in strict conformity with the doctrines embodied in the book of Common Prayer'.[21] As a young man James had insisted on his right to freedom of conscience and, having taken his decision, held to it for the rest of his life. He was a brilliant man, but he never lost his humility.

References and Bibliography

Abbreviations used

ACBC	Alton Court Brewery Company
HAN	Herefordshire Archaeological News
Her Lib	Hereford Library
HRO	Herefordshire Record Office
TBGAS	*Transactions of the Bristol and Gloucestershire Archaeological Society*
TWNFC	*Transactions of the Woolhope Naturalists' Field Club*

Chapter 1 The Ross Union Workhouse, 1836-1914

Anstruther, Ian *The Scandal of the Andover Workhouse* Geoffrey Bles, (London, 1973)

Bagley, J.J. & A.J. *The English Poor Laws* (London, 1966)

Crowther, M.A. *The Workhouse System 1834-1929* Methuen, (London, 1981)

Digby, Dr Anne *Pauper Palaces* Routledge & Kegan Paul, (London, 1978)

Elliott, Nancy *Dore Workhouse in Victorian Times* (Ewyas Harold WEA Study Group, 1984)

Englander, David *Poverty and Poor Law Reform in 19th Century Britain 1834-1914* Longman (1998)

Longmate, Norman *The Workhouse Temple* (London, 1974)

Morrill, Dr Sylvia A. 'Poor Law in Hereford 1836-1851' *TWNFC* (1972)

Morris, M.H. *The Book of Ross-on-Wye* Barracuda Books, (Buckingham, 1980)

Powell, Dr John, C. Map of Ross Union in unpublished MSS (1972)

Webb, S. & B. *English Poor Law History* Vols 1 & 2, Frank Cass & Co Ltd (London, first published 1929) *English Poor Law Policy* Frank Cass & Co Ltd (London, first published 1910)

Records of Clerk to the Guardians

Minute Books 1836-1914 (HRO K42/406 – K42/428)

Minute Books of Finance Committee 1905-1914 (HRO K42/434 – K42/435)

Minute Books of House Committee 1905-1914 (HRO K42/439 – K42/440)

The Ross Gazette

Report by the Royal Commission on the Historical Monuments of England (1992/1994)

Ross Vestry Minutes L78/8

Chapter 2 The Catholic Martyrs of the Monnow Valley

Bradney, Sir Joseph *Monmouthshire. Hundred of Skenfrith* Vol 1 Part 1 (1904)

Cap, Rev. Frank *Two Historic Parishes. Welsh Newton & Llanrothal* (undated)

Clarke, Arthur *Story of Monmouthshire* Vol 1 (Monmouth, 1980)

Church in History Information Centre *King James II and the Glorious Revolution of 1688* Parts 1 and 2

Frazer, Antonia *The Gunpowder Plot* (1996)

Guy, John R. *The Anglican Patronage of Monmouthshire Recusants* (Catholic Record Society, 1981) *Eighteenth Century Gwent Catholics* (Catholic Record Society, 1982)

Hopson, Mary *Roman Catholic Burial Ground and Former Church at Coedanghred, Skenfrith* (1985) *Further to Coedanghred* (1994) *A Wander Round Llanrothal* (1998)

Jenkins, Philip *Monmouthshire Catholics in the 18th Century* (Catholic Record Society, 1980)

Kissack, Keith *Victorian Monmouth* (undated) *Monmouth, The Making of a County Town* (London 1975)

Levett, F.G. *The Story of Skenfrith, Grosmont and St Maughans* Section Two (1984)

Lane, Jane *Titus Oates* (London, 1949)

Murphy, Paul 'The Jesuit College of the Cwm' in *Severn & Wye Review* (1971/72) 'Catholics in Monmouthshire 1688-1850' in *Presenting Monmouthshire* No 29 (1970)

O'Keefe, Madge *Four Martyrs of South Wales and the Marches* (Cardiff, 1970)

Pugh, F.H. *Monmouthshire Recusants in the Reigns of Elizabeth and James I* (South Wales and Monmouth Record Society Publication No 4 1957)

Pilley, Walter 'Notes on Suppressed College of Jesuits at Coombe, Llanrothal' *TWNFC* (1900)

Smith, T.S. 'Herefordshire Catholics and rites of passage 1560-1640' *TWNFC* (1978)

Thomas, T. *The Welsh Elizabethan Catholic Martyrs* (Cardiff, 1971)

Vaughan, Mary *Courtfield and the Vaughans* (London, 1989)

Whelan, Dom Basil *History of Belmont Abbey* (London, 1959) *Narrative of Discovery of a College of Jesuits* (HRO Reference X61/1)

Newscutting (HRO Reference K38/F/S1)
Monmouthshire Beacon 1838, 1846, Monmouth Museum

Chapter 3 The Beautification of Hoarwithy Church

Annett, D.M. *Saints in Herefordshire* (Logaston Press, 1999)

Barlow, A. & K. Kissack *Blue guide to Churches and Chapels* Herefordshire Section (1991)

Darby, Michael *John Pollard Seddon* (1983)

Dixon, Roger & Muthesius, Stefan *Victorian Architecture* (1978)

Harrison, Martin *Victorian Stained Glass* (1980)

Howell, Peter & Sutton, Ian *The Faber Guide to Victorian Churches* (1989)

Jenkins, Simon *England's Thousand Best Churches* (1999)

Leonard, John *Churches of Herefordshire & their Treasures* (Logaston Press, 2000)

Newman, John *The Buildings of Wales – Gwent/Monmouthshire* (2000)

Pevsner, Nikolaus *The Buildings of England – Herefordshire* (1963)

Port, M.H. *Six Hundred New Churches* (1961)

Reid, Peter *Burke & Savill's Guide to Country Houses – Vol II* (1980)

Seaton, Prebendary *History of Archenfield with a Description of The Churches in the Old Rural Deanery* (1903)

Tyack, Geoffrey *Oxford – An Architectural Guide* (1998)

Verey, David *Collin's Guide to Parish Churches* Hereford and Worcester Section (1990)

Webster, J. Roger *Old Church Aberystwyth* (1995)

Various *Victorian Church Art* – Catalogue of an exhibition at the Victoria and Albert Museum (1971)

Wyatt, Daphne 'Angel Found at Hoarwithy' in *PAX Church Magazine*

Hoarwithy Church Guide Leaflet

Hentland Church Guide Leaflet

Archenfield Magazine

Hereford Times William Poole Obituary 15.3.1902

Hereford Journal William Poole Obituary 15.3.1902

Hereford Times Rev S. Scarlett Smith's recollections of Prebendary Hawkshaw 21.7.1950

Directories: Kelly's, Jakeman & Carver, Littlebury's (Various dates)

Building News 22.6.1833

Builder 5.7.1884

Builder J.P. Seddon Obituary 10.2.1906

Department of Environment Official Listing 1975

Script of Barbara Fleming Talk, Broadcast on the Home Service 25.5.1960

Herefordshire Record Office – Poole Papers C95/B/4

Herefordshire Record Office – Annual Box 1843 HD8/18

Herefordshire Record Office – Hopton photo album J67/1

Herefordshire Record Office – Hentland Parish Records J66/1

Hereford Reference Library – Hopton collection

Chapter 4 Domesday Book entries for the district around Ross-on-Wye

Ballard, A. *The Domesday Inquest* (Methuen, 1906)

Bradley, A.G. *Herefordshire* (1915)

Darby, H.C. and Terrett, I.B. *The Domesday geography of Midland England* (CUC, 1954)

Denman, D.R. *Origins of ownership. A brief history of land ownership and tenure* (George Allen & Unwin, 1958)

Dyer, C. *Standards of living in the later Middle Ages* (CUC, 1993)

Everyday life in Mediaeval England (Hambledon Press, 1994)

Ellis, H. *A general introduction to the Domesday Book* (1883)

Galbraith, V.H. and Tait, J. *Herefordshire Domesday* (Pipe Roll Society, 1950)

Galbraith, V.H. *The making of Domesday Book* (Clarendon Press, 1961)

Domesday Book - Its place in administrative history (Clarendon Press, 1974)

Hillaby, J.G. 'The origin of the Diocese of Hereford' *TWNFC* Vol XL11, pt. 1 (1976), pp.16-52

Hart, C.E., 'The metes and bounds of the Forest of Dean' *TBGAS* Vol. 66 (1947), pp.166-207

Hart, C.E., *Between Severn (Saefern) and Wye (Waege) in the year 1001* (Sutton, 2000)

Jackson, J.N. 'The historical geography of Herefordshire from Saxon times to the Act of Union, 1536' in *Herefordshire … Chapters written to celebrate the centenary of the Woolhope Naturalists' Field Club* (British Publishing Co., 1954)

Jolliffe, J.E.A. *The constitutional history of Mediaeval England from the English settlements to 1485* (A & C Black, 1937)

Maitland, F.W. *Domesday Book and Beyond* (1897)

Moore, J.S. 'The Gloucestershire section of the Domesday Book: geographical problems of the text' *TBGAS* Vol. 105 (1987), pp.109-132

Roffe, D. *Domesday – The inquest and the book* (OUP, 2002)

Round, J.H. *Feudal England* (Sonnenschein & Co., 1895)

Rowley, T. *The Norman heritage 1066-1200* (Paladin Books, 1983)

The landscape of the Welsh Marches (Michael Joseph, 1986)

Seebohm, F. *The English village community* (Longman & Co., 1883)

Thorn, F. and Thorn, C. *Domesday Book; 17 Herefordshire* (Phillimore, 1983)

Welldon Finn, R. *Domesday Book, A Guide* (Phillimore, 1973)

Winchester, A. *Discovering parish boundarie*s (Shire Publications, 2000)

Chapter 5 Stained Glass in the Ross-on-Wye area

Annett, D. *Saints in Herefordshire* (Logaston Press, 2000)
Barlow, A. & K. Kissack *Blue Guide to Churches and Chapels,* Herefordshire Section (1991)

Collins, P. (ed.) *The Corpus of Kempe Stained Glass in the United Kingdom and Ireland* (2000)

Cormack, P. *The Stained Glass Work of Christopher Whall* (1999)

Cowen, P. *A Guide to Stained Glass in Britain* (1985)

Crewe, S. *Stained Glass in England 1180-1540* (1987)

Goedicke, A. & M. Washburn (eds.) *Stained Glass Marks and Monograms* (2002)

Hadley, D. 'Ada Currey: A Forgotten Artist' in *The Journal of Stained Glass* (ed.) S. Coley Vol. XXIV (2000)

Harrison, M. *Victorian Stained Glass* (1980)

Harrison, Martin 'Stained Glass' in *By Hammer and Hand – The Arts and Crafts Movement in Birmingham* (ed.) A. Crawford (1984)

Hillaby, J. '"Beauty of Holiness": The East Window' in *A Definitive History of Dore Abbey* (eds.) R. Shoesmith & R. Richardson (Logaston Press, 1997)

Kerney, M. *The Stained Glass of Frederick Preedy* (2001)

Leonard, J. *Churches of Herefordshire and Their Treasures* (Logaston Press, 2000)

Lowe, R. Sir Samuel Meyrick and Goodrich Court (Logaston Press, 2003)

Mowl, T. '"The Wrong Things at the Wrong Time", 17th century Gothic Churches' in *Gothic Architecture and its Meanings* (ed.) M. Hall (2002)

O'Connor, D. 'Bishop Spofford's Glass at Ross-on-Wye' in *Mediaeval Art, Architecture and Archaeology at Hereford* (ed.) D. Whitehead (1995)

Pevsner, N. *Buildings of England, Herefordshire*

Sewter, A. *The Stained Glass of William Morris and His Circle* (1974)

Watt, Q. (ed.) *The Bromsgrove Guild* (1999)

Faculties for Stained Glass in the Diocesan Annual Boxes in The Herefordshire Record Office

Chapter 6 The Old Mill at Hoarwithy

Bannister, Rev. A.T. *The Place Names of Herefordshire* (1916)

Coates, S and Tucker, D. *Water Mills of the Middle Wye Valley* (1983)

Coplestone-Crow, B. *Herefordshire Place-Names* (1989)

Duncumb, J. *Agriculture of the County of Herefordshire* (1805)
Continuation of the History of Herefordshire Vol 6 (1913)

Herefordshire Directories 1851-1941

Hurley, H. *The Pubs of Ross and South Herefordshire* (Logaston Press, 2001)
The Story of Bill Mills (Logaston Press, 2001)

Major, K. *Watermills and Windmills* (1986)

Raistrick, A. *Industrial Archaeology* (1972)

Taylor, E,. *Kings Caple in Archenfield* (Logaston Press, 1997)

The Miller (1911)

Woman's Institute, Hoarwithy Village mss (1953)

TWNFC, vol XLIV (1983)

Hentland Notes 1916, Her Lib

Hentland Parish Registers 1688-1837, HRO

Hentland Tithe Map and Apportionment 1842, HRO

Hoarwithy Mill deeds and documents 1775-1943, now deposited at HRO

Land Tax of Hereford 1776 -1831, HRO

Land Valuation Tax 1910, HRO

Marriage Index 1742-1769, HRO

Marriage Settlement 1691, HRO

Pencoyd Parish Register printed 1900

Taylor's Map 1754, Her Lib

Wills, William Mynd 1729, Edward Marrett 1717, HRO

Chapter 7 Henry Southall, 1826-1916, Ross-on-Wye

1. *Ross Gazette*, 23rd March, 1911.
2. *Ibid.*
3. Southall, C., *The Records of the Southhall Family,* p.66.
4. *Ibid.* p.60.
5. HRO BG99/2/4 John's letter to Hannah from Yearly Meeting, May 1830.
6. *Ibid.*
7. HRO BG99/2/86 - Edward Southall - goods distrained.
8. HRO BG99/4/111 letter dated August, 1838 from Hannah to her son John Tertius.
9. HRO BG99/4/113 letter dated 1.2.1841. from Hannah to her son, John Tertius.
10. Southall, C., *The Records of the Southall Family,* p.49
11. *Ross Gazette*; 14th November, 1912.
12. HRO BG99/3/48 letter dated 21.02.1842 from Henry to his father John.
13. HRO BG99/12/13 letter dated 15.11.1833 from John to his daughter Elizabeth.
14. HRO BG99/2/14 letter dated 13.04.1842 from John to his son John Tertius.
15. HRO BG99/3/47 letter (undated) from Henry to Hannah, his mother. (probably 1835)
16. HRO BG99/2/26 letter 1830s from Hannah to her son Henry.
17. HRO BG99/2/8 Henry's School Report - June, 1839.
18. Southall, C., *The Records of the Southall Family,* p.139.
19. HRO BG99/2/8 William Lean's Account. June, 1839

20. HRO BG99/3/48 letter dated 08.12.1844 from Henry to his father, John.
21. HRO BG99/2/22 letter dated 21.12.1844 from Edward West to John Southall.
22. HRO BG99/3/48 letter dated 06.01.1845 from Henry to his father John.
23. HRO BG99/2/22 letter dated 19.04.1845 from Edward West to John Southall.
24. HRO BG99/3/48 letter dated 21.04.1845 from Henry to his father, John.
25. HRO BG99/2/22 letter dated 29.04.1845 from Edward West to John Southall.
26. HRO AK3/72 Leominster Vestry Minutes 1796-1844.
27. HRO K42/388 Leominster Union Minutes (1852).
28. HRO K42/389 Leominster Union Minutes (1856).
29. HRO BG99/2/14 letter dated 03.04.1842 from John Southall to his son John Tertius.
30. HRO BG99/2/14 letter dated 27.05.1847 from John Southall to his son John Tertius.
31. HRO BG99/2/15 letter dated 22.02.1850 from John Southall to all his children.
32. HRO BG99/3/65 letter dated 18.3.1851 from Elizabeth (Southall) Hunt to nephew Henry.
33. Southall, C., *The Records of the Southall Family,* p.128
34. HRO BG99/3/8 letter dated 8.8.1857 from Louisa Brown to Henry Southall.
35. HRO BG99/3/1 Marriage Certificate dated 18.8.1858: Henry Southall and Louisa Brown.
36. HRO AP72/1 letter dated 7.10.1836 from Sir John Conroy to Captain Adams.
37. HRO BG99/3/2 letter dated 5.9.1859 from The Ross British and Foreign School to Henry.
38. HRO BG99/3/9 letter dated 1.12.1858 from Louisa to Henry.
39. HRO BG99/3/9 undated letter from Louisa to Henry after the birth of Henry John in 1859.
40. Southall, C., *The Records of the Southall Family,* p.139.
41. *Ibid.* p.138.
42. *Ibid.* p.138.
43. *Ibid.* p.130.
44. *TWNFC* (1852-1865).
45. Isichei, E., *Victorian Quakers,* p.212.
46. *Ibid.* p.216.
47. HRO BG99/3/9 letter dated 4.12.1858 from Louisa to Henry.
48. HRO BG99/3/9 letter dated 18.12.1858 from Louisa to Henry.
49. HRO BG99/3/18 letter dated 16.6.1875 from Louisa to Henry.
50. Isichei, E., *Victorian Quakers,* p.217.
51. Southall, C., *The Records of the Southall Family,* p.131.
52. HRO BG99/3/17 letter dated 4.8.1870 from Louisa to Henry.
53. HRO BG99/3/17 letter dated 21.8.1870 from Louisa to Henry.
54. HRO BG99/3/17 letter dated 24.8.1870 from Louisa to Henry.
55. HRO BG99/3/18 letter dated 16.6.1875 from Louisa to Henry.
56. HRO BG99/3/83 letter dated 16.12.1884 from Louisa to Charlie her son.
57. HRO BG99/3/83 letter dated 21.1.1885 from Louisa to Charlie her son.
58. HRO BG99/3/20 letter dated 1885 from Louisa to Henry.
59. HRO BG99/3/82 letter dated 1888 from Charlie to Aunt Elizabeth (Trusted) Southall.
60. HRO BG99/3/93 letter dated 13.9.1887 from Tom to Louie.
61. HRO BG99/3/86 letter dated 18.3.1888 from Tom to Charlie.
62. HRO BG99/4/49 Ross Messenger (Baptist Chapel Paper) February, 1916.

Bibliography

Curtis, S.J. *History of Education in Great Britain,* (University Tutorial Press Ltd., 1948)

Hey, D. *The Oxford Companion to Local and Family History* (BCA and Oxford University Press, 1996.

Hughes, P. and Hurley, H. *The Story of Ross,* (Logaston Press, 1999 & 2009)

Isichei, E. *Victorian Quakers,* (OUP, 1970)

Morgan, C.A.V. *Nathaniel Morgan 1775-1854 of Ross-on-Wye, Herefordshire* (Ross-on-Wye and District Civic Society, 1995)

Neave Brayshaw, A. *The Quakers, Their Story & Message* (Sessions Book Trust, York, 1982)

Sessions W.K. and E.M. *The Tukes of York* (Sessions Book Trust, York. 1987)

Southall, C. *Records of the Southall Family* (printed for private circulation, 1932)

Stewart, K.A. *The York Retreat* (William Sessions, York, 1992)

*Pigot's National Commercial Trade Directory, (*Norwich, 1835, Facsimile Edition, Norwich, 1996)

Punshon, J. *Portrait in Grey: A Short History of the Quakers* (Quaker Books, 1984)

Reeves, N.C. *The Town in the Marches: A History of Leominster and its Environs* (Orphans Press, undated)

Southall, C.M. *Eric Pritchard Southall: A Biography* (1994)

TWNFC (1852-1865) (Jakeman and Carver, 1907)

The Southall Collection: HRO Ref: BG99

Leominster Vestry Minutes, (1796-1844) HRO Ref: AK3/72

Leominster Union Minutes, (1852) HRO Ref: K42/388
Leominster Union Minutes, (1856) HRO Ref: K42/389

Ross British and Foreign School Records (1836) HRO Ref: AP72/1 Whiting, E. *Quakers in Ross,* HRO Ref: BL28.

The Ross Gazette
The Times
The Hereford Journal
The Hereford Times
The Leominster News
The Ross Messenger (Baptist Chapel Publication)

Chapter 8 Dubricius, Celtic Saint of Herefordshire

Andere, Mary *Arthurian links with Herefordshire* (Logaston Press, 1995)

Doble, G.H. *Lives of the Welsh Saints* (ed.) D. Simon Evans (University of Wales Press, 1971)

Fenn, R.W.D., 'Early Christianity in Herefordshire', in *TWNFC*, (1968) pp.333-347

Jones, Mary *The Life of St Dubricius* trs. from 12th century Latin, the *Liber Landavensis* (2005) website: www.maryjones.us/ctexts/dubricius.html

Kelly, Vivian *St.Illtud's Church, Llantwit Major*, (D. Brown & Sons, 1993)

Knight, Jeremy K. *The End of Antiquity - Archeology, Society & Religion AD 235-700* (Tempus, 1999)

Leonard, John, (ed.) *Herefordshire Churches through Victorian Eyes: Sir Stephen Glynne's Church Notes for Herefordshire, including Water colours by Charles F. Walker* (Logaston Press, 2006)

Myres, J.N.L. *The English Settlements - English Political and Social Life from the Collapse of Roman Rule to the Emergence of Anglo-Saxon Kingdoms* (Oxford University Press, 1989)

Nash Ford, David *Early British Kingdoms – St Teilo* (2001). website: www.earlybritishkingdoms.com

Ray, Dr. Keith 'Archaeology and The Three Early Churches of Herefordshire' in *The Early Church In Herefordshire* (Leominster Historical Society, 2001)

Rees, Rev. W.J. (trs.) *The Liber Landavensis/The Book of Llandaff or the ancient register of the cathedral church of Llandaff; from mss. in the libraries of Hengcort, and of Jesus College, Oxford; with an English translation and explanatory notes* (The Welsh Manuscript Society, 1860).

Salter, Mike *The Parish Churches of Herefordshire* (Folly Publications, 1998)

Sharp, Mick *Holy Places of Celtic Britain - A Photographic Portrait of Sacred Albion* (1997)

Shoesmith, Ron 'Llanwarne Old Church' in *TWNFC* Vol XLIII (1981) pp.267-29

Taylor, Elizabeth *Kings Caple in Archenfield* (Logaston Press, 1997)

Walters, Bryan *The Archaeology & History of Ancient Dean & the Wye Valley* (Thornhill Press, 1992)

Zaluckyj, Sarah & John *The Celtic Christian Site of the central and southern Marches* (Logaston Press, 2006)

Chapter 9 The Alton Court Brewery and its Ross Pubs

Brown, Meredith *The Brewer's Art* (Whitbread & Co., 1948)

Hackwood, Frederick *Inns, Ales and Drinking Customs* (*c.*1904)

Herefordshire Directories 1840-1941

Hughes, Pat & Heather Hurley, *The Story of Ross* (Logaston Press, 1999 & 2009)

Hurley, Heather (ed.) *Landscape Origins of the Wye Valley* (Logaston Press, 2008)

The Pubs of Monmouth, Chepstow and the Wye Valley (Logaston Press, 2007)

The Pubs of Ross and South Herefordshire (Logaston Press, 2001)

The Pubs of the Royal Forest of Dean (Logaston Press, 2004)

The Story of Bill Mills (Logaston Press, 2001)

Hurley, Jon 'Thomas Blake, The Pious Benefactor', *Historical Aspects of Ross* (2000)

Morgan, Virginia & Bridget Vine, *A History of Walford and Bishopswood* (Logaston Press, 2002)

Morris, Martin *The Book of Ross-on-Wye* (1980)

Putman, Roger *Beers and Breweries of Britain* (2004)

Richmond, Lesley & Alison Turton, *The Brewing Industry* (1990)

Ritchie, Berry *An Uncommon Brewer, The Story of Whitbread* (1992)

Shoesmith, Ron & John Eisel, *The Pubs of Hereford City* (Logaston Press, 2004 ed.)

Stonham, Jessie *Daughter of Wyedean* (1977)

Wye Valley Guides 1898, 1920, 1936, 1950, 1956

Brookend Tanyard Sale Notice and Plan, 1820s, Hurley Collection

Furniture Sale Notice 1836, Hurley Collection

ACBC Schedule of Deeds 1857-1942 Hurley Collection

Statutory Declaration 1866, Hurley Collection

Restrictive Covenants 1858, Hurley Collection

Registration of Mortgage 1865, HRO BT63

ACBC Minute Books 1-12, 1865-1961, HRO BT63/1-12

Purland Deeds 1841-1887, privately owned

Stroud Brewery Documents 1934-1961, HRO BP78/1-119

ACBC Advert 1910, HRO BW87/5

ACBC and Stroud Brewery Deeds misc., Hurley Collection

Conveyance and Assignment of ACBC 1962, Hurley Collection

Conveyance and Assignment of Stroud Brewery 1962, Hurley Collection

Castle Inn list of deeds 1838-1961, Hurley Collection

The Royal Hotel Company, 1987 Hurley Collection

Whitbread Key Dates 2007, www.whitbread.co.uk
Census Returns 1851, 1871, 1881, HRO
HAN No 52 1989, H. Hurley The Brookend Tanyard
Ross Gazette, 10 Jan 1884, 10 April 1884, 18 Feb 1892, 23 Feb 1956
Hereford Times, 24 Feb 1956
Man of Ross, 6 April 1865
The Brewing Trade Review 1 Feb 1893, 15 April 1897
HRO Friends Newsletter no. 48, 1997, H. Hurley The Alton Court Brewery

Chapter 10 James Cowles Prichard, 1786-1848

1. HRO BG99/2/126 Roger Prichard's will dated 1679
2. HRO BO3/7 Almeley Parish Register 1595-1752
3. HRO HD4/1/200 Consistory Court Record, Weobley Deanery, 1673-1676
4. Southall, I. *The Prichards of Almeley* (1893), p.12
5. *Ibid.*
6. Punshon, J. *Portrait in Grey: A Short History of The Quakers* (1984), p.100
7. HRO A85/5 Leominster and Ross Monthly Meeting Minutes, p.25
8. *Ibid.*, p.26
9. *Ibid.*, p.29
10. *Ibid.*
11. Punshon, J. p.166
12. Isichei, E. *Victorian Quakers* (1970), p.11
13. Longmate, N. *The Workhouse*, p.210
14. Brayshaw A N. *The Quakers, Their Story and Message*, p.212
15. Prichard, J.C. *A Treatise on Insanity and other Disorders affecting the Mind*, p.16
16. Symonds, J A. *Some Account of the Life, Writings and Character of the late James Cowles Prichard MD, FRS, MRIA*, p.42
17. *The Times*, 23rd December 1948
18. Southall, I. p.61
19. Symonds, J A. p.48
20. *Ibid.*, p.10
21. *Ibid.*, p.51

Bibliography
Brayshaw, A.N. *The Quakers, Their Story and Message* (Sessions Book Trust, 1987)
Bronowski, J. *The Ascent of Man* (BBC, 1973)
Driver, F. *Power and Pauperism: the Workhouse System, 1834-1884* (CUP, 1993)
Evans, EJ. *The Contentious Tithe, 1750-1850* (Routledge and Kagan Paul, 1976)
Gardiner, Juliet (ed.) *The History Today Who's Who in British History* (Collins and Brown and Cico Books, 2000)

Geiter, M K. *Profiles in Power: William Penn* (Pearson Education, 2000)
Hey, D. *The Oxford Companion to Local and Family History* (BCA and OUP, 1996)
Hibbert, C. *Queen Victoria, a Personal History* (Harper Collins, 2000)
Hughes, P. and Hurley, H. *The Story of Ross* (Logaston Press, 1999 & 2009)
Isichei, E. *Victorian Quakers* (OUP, 1970)
Lamont-Brown, R. *John Brown, Queen Victoria's Highland Servant* (Sutton Publishing, 2000)
Longmate, N. *The Workhouse* (Pimlico, 2003)
Marshall, P.J. (ed.) *Cambridge Illustrated History – British Empire* (CUP, 1996)
Milligan, E H. *Biographical Dictionary of British Quakers in Commerce and Industry 1775-1920* (Sessions Book Trust, 2007)
Morgan, CAV. *Nathaniel Morgan 1775-1854 of Ross-on-Wye, Herefordshire* (Ross-on-Wye and District Civic Society, 1995)
Pigot's *National Commercial Trade Directory* (1830, Facsimile edition, Norwich, 1994)
Prichard, J.C. *The Natural History of Man* (H. Bailliere, 1843)
    A treatise on Insanity and Other Disorders Affecting the Mind (Haswell, Barrington and Haswell, 1837 and Arno Press, 1973)
Punshon, J. *Portrait in Grey: A Short History of The Quakers* (Quaker Books, 1984)
Sessions, WK & EM. *The Tukes of York* (Sessions Book Trust, 1987)
Southall, C. *Records of the Southall Family* (printed for private circulation, 1932)
Southall, I. *The Prichards of Almeley* (printed for private circulation, 1893)
Stewart, K.A. *The York Retreat* (William Sessions, 1992)
Symonds, J A. *Some Account of the Life, Writings and Character of the late James Cowles Prichard, MD, FRS, MRIA (*privately printed, 1849
Weintraub, S. *Albert, Uncrowned King* (John Murray, 1997)

Roger Prichard's will, dated 1679, HRO REF. BG99/2/126
Almeley Parish Register, 1595-1752. HRO REF. BO3/7
Consistory Court Records, Weobley Deanery, 1673 -1676. HRO REF. HD4/1/200
Leominster and Ross Monthly Meeting Minutes, 1809. HRO REF. A85/5
The Times
The Hereford Times
The Manchester Guardian
The Ross Gazette

Index

(entries in italics refer to illustrations)

273

baby & toddler food

baby & toddler food

Recipes and practical information for
feeding babies and toddlers

Introductory text by Carol Fallows
Additional text by Karen Kingham (nutritionist)

MURDOCH BOOKS

contents

A good start to life includes a variety of tasty, healthy foods. By making an effort with your child's meals from when you start at 6 months you will establish the good habits your child will take with them into their future — a precious thing considering the number of diet-related diseases that face us in adulthood. Of course there is not always time for lengthy preparation but this does not have to be the hallmark of a good meal.

starting out

the essentials

At first you may find it hard to believe that all your precious little newborn needs for nourishment is breast milk. An amazing food and drink in one, breast milk not only provides the ultimate nutrition, it is packed with antibodies and other properties important to the health and development of your baby. Infant formula has been devised as a substitute for breast milk when breast-feeding is not possible. Specially modified to meet a baby's needs, it is the only alternative; other milks are totally unsuitable.

For the first few months all your baby will need is breast milk. Then sometime around the middle of the first year your baby will start to show an interest in food other than breast milk or formula — which will continue to remain a very important part of baby's nutrition. The guidelines for introducing your baby to family foods are not set in stone. Every baby is different and some babies will show an interest in food before 6 months and some later. A few years ago the advice of health authorities was that babies could start eating solid foods after 4 months, but it is now recommended that parents wait until closer to the 6-month mark when babies' digestive systems are able to cope with new foods and their ability to taste is developing. By this age they are also likely to have lost a reflex that makes them push out the food the moment it meets the tongue.

introducing food

It is easiest to introduce your baby to food in four stages:

1) Begin with purées. Many parents start with rice cereal, then move onto fruit and vegetable purées. Follow your baby — eating cereal as a first food is not essential.

In many other cultures weaning recipes are handed down from grandmother and mother to daughter. In Asian diets, rice is the basis of foods such as congee, which is fed to babies from around 5 months of age. At first it is sieved and mixed with lentil juice. Gradually baby will be introduced to vegetables, fresh herbs such as coriander (cilantro) and milk products such as yoghurt. In Africa, maize porridge or rice is baby's first food and in South America first foods are based on corn and potatoes.

2) After 3–5 weeks (or once your baby is happily eating puréed food from a spoon) you can introduce lumpy foods. Baby may love his rice cereal but he needs to learn about new tastes and textures. Gradually include food which has a lumpier consistency. You should also combine different foods together as well as introducing new flavours.

3) Finger foods come next. From around 8 months baby may start to show more interest in being involved in feeding. You can now add foods for chewing practice — rusks and toast are the obvious ones, but there are many more.

4) The last stage, which should have arrived by your child's first birthday, is regular food with some modifications. This means your baby will be able to eat many of the foods that the rest of the family regularly eats, with some changes and exceptions.

introducing baby to drinking from a cup

You can start to introduce your baby to a cup as early as 6 months old. If you decide to start using a cup at this age you might like to buy a baby cup that has a lid and a spout or straw. This makes it easier for you as baby is less likely to spill the contents. It will take some time for baby to get used to sucking from the cup, just as it has been for him to get used to swallowing food.

By around the age of 9 months, if you are breast-feeding and your baby has never got used to a bottle, you can go straight to the cup — and if this is the case, an ordinary plastic beaker or mug is perfectly fine; you don't have to buy a special cup. Baby needs time and opportunity to practise whatever cup he is using and he will get the hang of it. Provided you continue to offer him the breast or the bottle, he will not be thirsty while he is learning.

It is worth noting that giving a child a spout cup or a bottle to carry around most of the time is not a good idea. Children who carry these will fill up on fluid, be it water, milk or diluted juice, and even a belly full of water will stop a toddler feeling hungry at snack or meal time.

what to drink

After breast milk or formula, the most important drink for babies is water. In the first year it needs to be cooled boiled water, but once your baby reaches his first birthday, tap water is perfectly acceptable. It is worth noting that bottled water does not contain fluoride (which is important for the healthy growth of your baby's teeth) and can be high in sodium (salt). If you choose to filter your water, check that this process does not remove the fluoride.

Around 50 years ago mothers were told to introduce their babies to rose hip syrup, as it is a naturally rich source of vitamin C, at the same time as their first cereal. By the beginning of the 21st century there were dozens of 'baby' fruit juices available that contained more vitamin C than other juices, had no colourings and were usually diluted. Yet the fact remains that babies don't need rose hip syrup and they don't need juice. The main source of fluid in the first 6 months should be either breast milk or infant formula. Babies over 6 months will still enjoy breast milk or formula as their main drink, however the introduction of a cup at this time means that water, and very occasionally, diluted fruit juice, will also contribute to their total fluid intake.

reasons babies don't need juice:

- It contains fructose. Too much of this natural sugar can cause diarrhoea.
- Juice is filling — it can satisfy a baby's appetite when food or milk are more important, but it won't satisfy the body's need for nutrients.
- Too much juice can contribute to excess weight gain.
- Juice can cause tooth decay. Even diluted fruit juice can pool around baby's first teeth and cause decay. Never give your child juice at bedtime after his teeth have been cleaned.

There will come a time when your child will ask for juice and when that happens be sure to dilute it to at least 50/50. Avoid using a bottle and give it to him in a cup, but not one that he can suck from; this way it will only be a small quantity. Children between the age of one and six need no more than 1 cup of diluted juice a day. Encourage them to have a piece of fruit instead and, if they are thirsty, they can drink a cup of water.

Carbonated drinks of all kinds — even soda water added to juice or cordials — are also not suitable for babies or toddlers. Sports drinks are definitely out since they contain a cocktail of flavourings, colours and preservatives, as well as sugar, sodium and potassium and often stimulants.

your family's food

You can include shopping for baby when you shop for the family's food. Baby food sold in tins, jars or that is frozen can be expensive and baby will not learn about eating family foods if he does not eat home-made food most of the time.

Baby's nutrition needs are high so every food needs to count towards his overall nutrition needs. Foods high in sugar and fat such as chips (fries), sweet biscuits (cookies) or lollies (candy) contribute very little in the way of vitamins and minerals and take the place of foods that are more 'nutrient-dense'.

Use the following tips when you are shopping and cooking for all the family as well as for baby:

- Think fresh. It is best to have really fresh fruit and vegetables on hand. If you have a vegetable patch or fruit trees, you will have a great source of really fresh food — even a few pots of fresh herbs on the window sill will be a bonus. Shopping for fruit and vegetables every two or three days is ideal.
- Make your own. It is easy and cheaper than buying to make many of the basics such as soups and salads — and you know exactly what they contain.
- Read the labels. Some foods can contain ingredients that you would not normally suspect. For example some breakfast cereals have more salt than potato chips (crisps).
- Use little or no salt and buy low-salt products. Adults can always add salt or condiments if they find a dish needs it, but it is not possible to take it out. Babies and children do not need salt and their sense of taste is more heightened than that of adults. Cook without salt and let the adults add their own — out of sight of inquisitive little eyes.
- Don't sweeten any food with sugar or honey. Sugar is another flavour enhancer. It adds kilojoules (calories) without nourishing and can also cause tooth decay. The same goes for honey, and it is also potentially dangerous for babies under 12 months.
- Use foods that are low in animal fat — but don't give your baby or toddler low-fat foods. This may sound like a contradiction, but it isn't. The under-twos need fat in their diets, unless they are overweight (in which case they need a diet designed by a dietitian). Foods that are low in animal fat include chicken, minus the skin, lean meat and full-fat dairy products.

AGES & STAGES

BABY'S AGE	SKILLS	TYPE OF FOOD
0–6 months	Suck, suckle, swallow	Liquids
6–7 months	Begins to chew, stronger sucking ability, gag reflex disappearing	Purées
8–12 months	Bites and chews, takes all the food off a spoon, can move food in mouth	Mashes; chopped food; finger food
From 12 months on	Can move food around mouth; jaw is stronger	Family food

important nutrients

It can be worrying and confusing trying to work out if your baby is getting the right amounts of all the important nutrients he needs in order to have a healthy diet. The baby's stores of iron and zinc deplete at around the age of 6 months and milk feeds are unable to support increased requirements from this age. Commercial, iron-enriched baby rice cereals are usually one of baby's first foods and so help to top up falling iron stores.

If you introduce fruit and vegetables next, you will be giving your baby new textures and tastes as well as important vitamins and minerals; and if meat, poultry and fish follow soon after you will be ensuring that your baby receives the protein and minerals he needs. Ensuring your baby spends some time exposed to gentle indirect sunlight will provide enough vitamin D to meet his requirements.

It is now commonplace to hear that babies need vitamin supplements to ensure their intake is adequate. However, unless these have been prescribed by a doctor or a dietitian the food you are preparing and providing will give baby all the vitamins and minerals he needs. For an overview of the food sources of important nutrients, refer to the chart on pages 14–15.

There are basic guidelines you can follow that will help to ensure you are meeting baby's nutritional needs. These are:
- breast-feed
- provide a variety of nutritious foods
- avoid low-fat diets
- be careful not to over or underfeed
- offer water as the first drink
- do not add sugar to baby's food
- choose low-salt foods and do not add salt to baby's food
- serve foods that contain calcium
- serve foods that contain iron

including nutrients

There are many practical ways to ensure important nutrients are included in your family's diet, such as:

- Eating a wide range of breads, including wholegrain and wholemeal (whole-wheat), and plenty of cereals, rice, pasta and noodles. From these foods come fibre, vitamins, minerals, carbohydrates and protein.
- Choosing a wide variety of fresh vegetables and legumes. Tinned and frozen are an alternative when fresh are not available. Important vitamins, minerals, dietary fibre and carbohydrate are found in vegetables, beans, lentils

and legumes. When planning a family meal a simple way to include a wide variety of vitamins and minerals is to think one white, one red or yellow and one green vegetable.

- Eating plenty of fruit and choosing whole fruit instead of fruit juice. Dried fruits are a nutritious alternative, as are tinned and frozen fruit without any added sugar. Fruit provides vitamins, including vitamin C and folate, carbohydrates and fibre.
- Offering milk, yoghurt and cheese, all of which are valuable sources of calcium, protein, riboflavin and vitamin B12. You don't have to drink milk and eat cheese — you can add milk to soups, casseroles and sauces; include cheese in dishes such as omelettes and vegetable dishes; and use yoghurt in curries and dips. Low- and reduced-fat dairy products are not suitable for babies and toddlers under the age of 2 years. Other sources of calcium include tinned fish, soy milk, lentils, almonds, brazil nuts and dried apricots.
- Including a variety of lean meat, fish, poultry, eggs and legumes in the diet. These foods provide protein, iron and zinc; and red meat is particularly high in these nutrients. Nuts are also an important source of these nutrients, but whole nuts must never be given to children under 5 because they are a choking hazard. Smooth nut butters or crushed nuts are fine for children to consume, as long as they don't have a nut allergy.
- If you are vegetarian, legumes, seeds and nuts as well as wholegrain cereals and breads are important and need to be eaten at the same meal as fruit in order to maximize the absorption of important minerals such as iron.

the vegetarian or vegan baby

Families who do not eat meat will often want their babies to follow the same diet as they do. Vegetarian babies can be weaned in much the same way as babies whose families eat meat. Milk, cheese and eggs will provide first-class animal protein. Dried beans, peas, lentils and ground nuts are good sources of vegetable protein. As you do with your own diet, if you are vegetarian you will soon begin to combine vegetable protein with whole-grain cereals in order to get a complete protein. For example, you might combine soya beans with brown rice, or wholemeal (whole-wheat) bread with peanut butter. Fruit and vegetables will be a good source of many of the important nutrients and cereals and green vegetables will provide iron, which will be more useful as a nutrient when it is combined with a vitamin C-rich food. A vegan diet cannot provide all the nutrients a baby or toddler needs and is not recommended for small children. Refer to the chart on the following pages for the sources of important nutrients.

SOURCES OF MAJOR NUTRIENTS

NUTRIENT	FOOD SOURCES	IMPORTANT FOR
Protein	Breast milk, infant formula, lean meats, fish, seafood, poultry, eggs, dairy foods, legumes, grains, nuts, seeds	Growth and repair of all body cells. Children have a proportionally greater need for protein than adults because they are growing and protein is needed for the formation of new cells
Fat	Breast milk, infant formula, oils, margarine, lean meats, fish, eggs, dairy foods, whole grains, olives, avocados, nuts, seeds	General health and the absorption of fat-soluble vitamins A, D, E and K. Fats are also an important stored source of energy/fuel for growing babies and toddlers. This is because of their small stomachs and high needs for energy
Essential fatty acids (omega-3 fats)	Breast milk, some infant formula, lean meats, fish, canola, sunflower and safflower oils and margarine, linseeds (flax seeds), walnuts, pecans, egg yolk	Brain and visual development, plus the production of hormone-like substances. Unlike other fats, these can't be made by the body so must come from food
Carbohydrates	Breast milk, infant formula, grains such as wheat, rice, oats, barley and the foods made from them such as bread, pasta, breakfast cereals, flour, semolina. Sugar, sweet corn, potato, root vegetables, fruit, milk	Supplying the body with its major source of energy. In their unprocessed forms, they are good sources of fibre
Fibre	Wholegrain breads and cereals, vegetables, fruits, legumes (dried peas and beans), nuts, seeds	Healthy, regular functioning bowel
Vitamin A (retinol)	Breast milk, infant formula, dairy foods, liver, eggs, fortified margarine, oily fish	Well developed vision and healthy skin and hair
Beta-carotene	Orange and green fruit and vegetables such as sweet potatoes, carrots, orange-fleshed melon, apricots, spinach, broccoli	Supply of vitamin A (beta-carotenes are converted into vitamin A in the body)
Thiamin (vitamin B1)	Breast milk, infant formula, wheat germ and wholemeal (whole-wheat) foods such as breads and cereals, yeast extracts, nuts, fortified breakfast cereals, lean pork	Release of energy from carbohydrate foods
Riboflavin (vitamin B2)	Breast milk, infant formula, dairy products, yeast extracts, meat extracts, eggs, fortified breakfast cereals, mushrooms, wholemeal (whole-wheat) flour and bread	Healthy skin and eyes and the release of energy from food

SOURCES OF MAJOR NUTRIENTS

NUTRIENT	FOOD SOURCES	IMPORTANT FOR
Niacin (vitamin B3)	Breast milk, infant formula, lean meats, peanuts, fish, legumes, fortified breakfast cereals, eggs, milk	Growth and release of energy from food
Vitamin B12	Breast milk, infant formula, lean meats, chicken, fish, seafood, eggs, milk, fortified vegetarian products	Formation of nerve cells, genetic material (DNA) and red blood cells
Folic acid	Breast milk, infant formula, green leafy vegetables, whole grains, legumes, nuts, fortified breakfast cereals	Healthy growth; development; formation of red blood cells
Vitamin C	Breast milk, infant formula, potato, parsley, brussels sprouts, cabbage, capsicum (pepper), citrus fruits and juices, mango, berries, papaya	Healthy skin, bone and gums; helps the body absorb iron from foods other than meat
Vitamin D	Breast milk, infant formula, oily fish, eggs, butter, margarine, cheese	Absorption of calcium and phosphorus and for strong and healthy teeth and bones. The body also makes this vitamin in the skin when it is exposed to sunlight
Vitamin E	Breast milk, infant formula, wheat germ and wheat germ oil, nuts, seeds and the oils of nuts and seeds	Development and maintenance of healthy body cells — especially in the blood and nervous systems, due to its antioxidant properties
Iron	Breast milk, lean meats, chicken, fish, eggs, legumes, fortified baby cereals, wholegrain cereals, dark green leafy vegetables, dried fruits	Healthy blood and muscles. It is estimated that more than one in three young children don't receive their recommended needs for iron*
Calcium	Breast milk, infant formula, dairy foods, calcium-fortified soy products, tinned sardines and salmon (including bones)	Growth of strong and healthy bones and teeth. Almost 50 per cent of toddlers don't get enough of this mineral*
Fluoride	Fluoridated drinking water, fish	Strengthening teeth and reducing the risk of dental decay. Although not essential, the inclusion of fluoride in the diet is recommended by the World Health Organization (WHO)
Zinc	Breast milk, infant formula, lean meat, chicken, seafood, milk, legumes, nuts	Healthy growth, wound healing and immune system. Young children often don't get enough of this mineral

* Statistics from the 1995 Australian National Nutrition Survey

When born, 14 per cent of a baby's body weight is fat, at 6 months it is 25 per cent and at 2 years, it has dropped back to 20 per cent of body weight.

Healthy children will generally grow to a height between their mother's and father's height. To work out a boy's height, add the parents' heights together, divide by two and add 7.5 cm (3 in). To estimate a girl's height, subtract 7.5 cm (3 in) from the parents' heights. This is only an approximation as other factors, such as health and nutrition, will play a part in the final result.

genetically modified food

Genetic modification of food has been around for centuries with the selective breeding of animals and food crops, but the genetically modified (GM) foods of today include ingredients that have been modified by gene technology. This has enabled many crops to be modified to make them resistant to insects and viruses and more tolerant to herbicides. Crops that have been modified in some countries include soya bean, rape seed (canola), chicory, corn, squash and potato and genetically modified food ingredients are present in some foods. Soy flour in bread, for example, may have come from modified soya beans. In some countries food labels are required by law to show if a food has been genetically modified and this may apply to baby food. While there are distinct advantages to GM foods in increased quality and quantity of food with longer shelf life, their safety is still being debated. It is impossible to predict all the potential effects, including the risks.

Making food for your baby and toddler at home means that if you want to you can avoid GM foods by being selective about which products you include in your shopping.

organic food

Organic foods have been produced without the use of synthetic fertilizers, pesticides or other chemicals. They are not genetically modified and irradiation is prohibited. Only free-range animals are can be considered organic. When a food is organically certified it means that not only has it been organically grown but also harvested, prepared and transported using systems that guarantee the produce is not contaminated by synthetic chemicals.

Organic baby food is one of the biggest growth areas for organic farmers in many countries.

When you prepare your own food you know exactly what the ingredients are and how it has been prepared. You can buy commercial baby foods that are organically certified. However, you need to be aware that these foods may contain small amounts of non-organic ingredients and these will be specified on the label.

For families on a tight budget organic food can be expensive. Much organic food is more expensive than regular food because it costs more to produce. Looking for bargains, using your freezer, buying food when it is in season, buying frozen organic vegetables if they are cheaper than the non-frozen variety, growing some of your own food and creating a compost heap or worm farm are some of the ways you can provide your family with a diet based on organic foods.

FOODS NOT SUITABLE FOR CHILDREN

FOOD TYPE	DANGER
Honey (under 12 months)	Honey can contain botulism spores which can cause serious health problems in babies — fortunately this is rare. It is not known why this only affects babies under the age of 12 months, but older children and adults are not affected. You should also not include honey in any cooking for babies under the age of 12 months
Tea, coffee or herbal teas	Tea and coffee, including decaffeinated coffee and some herbal teas, contain caffeine. Herbal teas can also contain other substances not suitable for children
Raw or undercooked eggs	Egg allergy is most common in babies under the age of 12 months. Cooked eggs are better tolerated
Nuts	Children cannot chew whole nuts such as peanuts. It is possible for children to choke on or inhale whole nuts. It is therefore advised that children do not eat whole nuts until they are 5 years old. They can eat smooth nut butters or crushed nuts if they are not allergic to them
Hard foods	Young children can easily choke on foods such as raw and cooked peas, raw carrot, popcorn, hard cheese chunks, large pieces of raw apple, lollies (candy), whole nuts and whole grapes
Cow's milk (under 12 months) and soy beverages (under 2 years)	These are poor sources of iron and should not be substituted for breast milk or formula in the first 12 months. They can be added to foods in cooking. Both are potential allergens. Their use as a main drink is acceptable from 12 months for cow's milk and from 2 years for soy beverages
Snack foods	Babies need maximum nutrition because every food counts and these foods are high in kilojoules (calories) but low on nutrition
Soft drinks or alcohol	Soft drinks offer no nutritional benefits and can affect a child's growth and ability to gain weight. Alcohol is totally unsuitable and must never be given to a child
Raw or uncooked meat products	Delicatessen meats such as salami are not suitable for babies or children

Listeria is bacteria that can
cause serious illness in some
people if they eat food
contaminated with listeria
bacteria. In the early days of
starting new foods, babies are
particularly susceptible.

Your child has plenty of
years ahead in which to eat
the foods listed below, so for
now it is wise not to include
them in his diet. Foods that
have a high risk of containing
listeria are:

• ready-to-eat, sliced cold
meats from delicatessens

• cold, cooked takeaway
chicken

• pâté and meat spreads

• ready-made salads from
salad bars

• raw shellfish and smoked
seafood

• soft, semi-soft and unripened
cheeses — camembert, brie,
fetta, ricotta, blue

• soft-serve ice cream

• unpasteurized dairy products

foods to take care with:

soy milk: Unless a soy milk infant formula has been prescribed for your baby or toddler because of an intolerance to lactose (the natural sugar found in breast milk and cow's milk), it is not a recommended food for your child. Soy milks and drinks which are not specially designed for babies must not be given to a baby, and are not suitable as a drink for children under 2 years old.

These soy milks are not a complete food and do not have enough iron, calcium or vitamins to be a substitute for breast milk or infant formula. They also do not contain vitamin B12 (an essential vitamin for growth and development), they are too rich in minerals and they have too much protein, but not the protein containing essential amino acids that growing children need (these are added to soy infant formula).

Soy milk and soy milk formulas have a natural aluminium content that is higher than cow's milk, cow's milk formula or breast milk. Soy products also contain phyto-oestrogens. Though many babies have been consuming soy milk formula for some years it is not known what the long-term effects might be. So unless your baby has a diagnosed intolerance to dairy products it is best to offer dairy milk products instead until he is at least 2 years old, when soy can be introduced as part of a varied diet.

cow's milk: Breast milk is of course ideal at any time, though take care not to overheat expressed breast milk as important nutrients and immune factors can be destroyed. For the first 12 months, breast milk or a cow's milk-based infant formula is the ideal milk for your child to drink, but you can include cow's milk in cooking or yoghurt or custard after about 7 months. Cow's milk, as a regular drink, is too high in sodium for baby's kidneys. Cow's milk, goat's milk and sheep's milk are very poor sources of iron and also lack many of the other important nutrients — including vitamins A, C and E — that are found in breast milk and which are added to infant formulas; they are not suitable for babies in the first year. Unpasteurized milk from any animal can carry salmonella which causes food poisoning, so it should never be given to babies or toddlers.

eggs: Eggs are a very good food. If your family has no history of allergy such as eczema or asthma, you can introduce egg yolk to your baby's diet from around the age of 8 months. Egg white can be added a month or two later, if there were no problems with the egg yolk. There is no research to suggest that cholesterol is a problem at this age. It is better not to give undercooked or raw eggs to children before they are 1 year old.

healthy not fat

It is estimated that between 25 and 30 per cent of children under the age of 5 are overweight — some of these are obese. Some health experts are classing obesity as an epidemic because there are so many related health problems. How and what you feed your baby in the early years will determine whether he has a weight problem. Babies who are breast-fed have the best start — they are less likely to become obese and babies who are breast-fed for a year or longer are five times less likely to be obese than babies who are not; babies who are breast-fed for 3–5 months are half as likely to be overweight when they are older.

how to ensure your baby is fit and healthy — and not fat:

- Don't introduce solid foods before baby is ready. Ideally solid food should not introduced before 6 months of age.
- Stick to small portions of food — if baby doesn't want to eat, don't force it. Keep meal times relaxed and let your child decide how much he will and won't eat, being sure to provide healthy choices at all times.
- Don't introduce sugary, fatty or fast foods at all. One day someone will give your child something you would rather he didn't have, like a doughnut or hot chips (fries) — but until then, avoid these foods.
- Never give your baby or toddler soft drinks. Make milk and water the main drinks and water down drinks of juice to at least 50/50.
- Give your baby or child the space to exercise. From the time he is crawling, he needs to practise using his muscles as much as possible. Once he can walk he will love running and playing outdoors. Family exercise, such as ball games, walking to the shops, trips to the park or the beach ideally should happen every day.

commercial baby food

Baby food in tins or jars or that is frozen can be a saviour when you are in a hurry, things are not going to plan, you have to go out or you are away from home, but it is best saved for these times and not given to your baby every day.

Unlike foods you prepare at home, commercial baby food is of a very uniform consistency. Purées are smooth regardless of the vegetable from which they are made and different from what you would prepare at home. The smoothness of puréed pumpkin (winter squash) is nothing like the grainy texture of puréed broccoli or green peas and it is these subtle differences in foods that help to prepare baby for the stages to come.

Commercial foods for older toddlers have similar problems. Though they may have lumps, the type of cooking they are subjected to makes them very soft, offering little resistance and variation in texture compared to that provided by a mashed home-cooked food.

Taste is another factor to consider. Try the food you offer your baby and you will soon discover that with some brands chicken and vegetable tastes much the same as beef and vegetable and probably has little similarity to something that would come from your own kitchen.

Using your own home-prepared meals also means you know exactly what your baby or toddler is eating. While this may still be the case for high-quality commercial baby foods which provide ingredient lists with percentage amounts for each ingredient, others don't and can 'pad out' the contents with extra water and thickeners. It is not unknown to find only 10 per cent chicken in a chicken baby food which leaves you wondering what the rest of the meal contains.

Thickeners are not necessarily a bad thing for babies and toddlers and are usually needed to hold a product together and stop it from separating. It is when they are used to take the place of 'real' ingredients that the nutrition of the meal becomes diluted.

Once your baby moves on to toddler food there exists another range of commercial foods designed to make your life easier. As with baby foods, they can be a great convenience when time is short. However, unlike baby foods which have very strict guidelines about what can be added to them, food for toddlers don't have the same restrictions. Avoid toddler foods that use too much salt, added sugar or contain flavours and preservatives.

Generally, toddlers don't need to eat specially formulated and marketed children's food. Provided you are choosing healthy convenience options for the whole family they can eat what you are eating.

For more information on how to get the best for your baby and toddler ready prepared and off the shelf, check the section on reading labels (page 21).

quick meal solutions

Trying to feed hungry young children and babies when they want food that very instant is never easy. Think of the quick options you might already have to hand:

• Team mashed fruits with a spoonful of ricotta cheese or thick plain yoghurt for a more nourishing meal.

• No-added-salt or reduced-salt baked beans and creamed corn are excellent stand-by meals; serve them with toast fingers for older toddlers.

• Reduced-salt or water-packed tinned fish (salmon, tuna, sardines, mackerel) all mash and flake really well — just crush or remove any bones (which are usually very soft anyway).

• Avocado, banana, mango, papaya, pear or kiwi fruit take very little time to prepare and no cooking.

• It also takes no time at all to beat an egg and make an omelette — see our recipe for this basic and nourishing meal on page 70.

read the label!

A lot can be learned from reading the ingredients list on a product's label. The ingredient in the greatest quantity will come first and so on down to the last ingredient. If you find ingredients that you wouldn't normally put into your own version of a baby food, such as ground rice or other cereals, it is likely they are being used to bulk the meal out so consider another brand. You should also consider the following:

• If the food's name is based on ingredients such as 'sweet corn and chicken', then the manufacturer is obliged to state what percentage these ingredients are of the final food. High-quality baby foods will do this with all their ingredients so you know exactly what you are feeding your baby.

• In most countries the information panel will tell you about the energy, fat, protein, carbohydrate, sugar and sodium content of the food 'per serve' and/or 'per 100 g'. Using the 'per 100 g' column, if it is present, makes comparing food products easy. Other nutrients may also be on the panel but those listed above will usually always be there. For more information on food labels and how to use them contact your local government food authority.

• When shopping for young children consider the amount of sodium and sugar in food. As well, fat might be an issue for the family as a whole, but low-fat foods are not appropriate for young children

• Sodium is part of sodium chloride or salt. Many commercial foods can be high in salt. The easiest way to keep salt to a minimum in your family's diet is to look for products labelled no-added-salt, reduced-salt or low-salt. The other way is to compare products and choose the one with the lowest amount of sodium. As a guide, a low-salt food will have a sodium content of about 120 milligrams (mg) per 100 g or around 6 per cent of your recommended daily value (RDA) per serve.

• Sugar is not bad for children when it comes to them naturally, as it does in fruit and milk. You can keep extra sugar out of your family's diet by choosing foods with no-added-sugar, reduced-sugar or low-in-sugar on the label.

Because sugar might occur naturally from fruit-based ingredients, using your judgement based on the ingredients list and the nutrition label is often best. For example, it is unlikely a fruit-based food will ever be labelled 'low sugar', but this doesn't mean that it won't be healthy if it has no added sugars and just contains the natural sugars from the fruit.

- 'No artificial colours, flavours or preservatives' is something that you may find on the labels of food marketed for children. Be aware that it is not only the artificial ones that can cause problems for children. That said, the majority of the additives used in the world's food supply are necessary to ensure food is safe for us to eat. If you are concerned about additives in your child's diet see the allergy and intolerance section in this book (page 198) for information.

food safety

Bacteria and viruses can cause food-borne illness in children and adults and it is not always possible to tell by the way food looks, smells or tastes whether it contains pathogens. Being careful and hygienic will help you to prevent food poisoning which can be a very serious illness in babies. This care begins when you shop for food.

- Shop for non-perishables first and put cold foods in an insulated container.
- Put raw meats in separate bags from other foods.
- Do not buy foods in damaged packaging.
- Avoid chilled food or frozen food that are stacked high in cabinets, since they may have been there for some time.
- Be sure that staff at the delicatessen counter are using separate tongs for each food and wearing gloves to handle food. Ask for meats to be cut freshly.
- Only buy hot foods if you will be home in half an hour, then reheat the food as soon as you arrive home, or refrigerate it.
- Refrigerate all cold foods as soon as you arrive home.
- Unpack perishables straight away.
- Before you do anything in the kitchen and in between tasks wash your hands in warm soapy water.
- Cover cooked food.
- Cool hot food quickly — put it into the refrigerator as soon as the steam has stopped rising.
- Make sure your refrigerator is between 4–5°C (39–41°F); and your freezer is between 15–18°C (59–65°F).
- Thaw frozen food in the refrigerator or microwave rather than on the kitchen bench or chopping board.
- Do not prepare family food if you have vomiting or diarrhoea.

- Use separate chopping boards and utensils for cooked and raw foods and wash them in hot soapy water.
- Be sure the food you cook is completely cooked through. This is particularly important for poultry and minced (ground) meat — juices should run clear when poultry is pierced with a skewer.
- Always reheat food to steaming hot. If you are using a microwave be sure to stir the food during reheating — and if it is for baby, taste it with a separate spoon. It is not recommended that you heat a baby's bottle in the microwave because of the way the milk heats unevenly.
- Don't use the same plate for raw and cooked food.
- Thoroughly wash and dry all fruit and vegetables.
- Wash all working surfaces with warm soapy water.
- Change tea towels (dish towels) and dishcloths regularly — every couple of days at least. Disposable paper towels are a good alternative.
- Wash baby's hands before — and after — he eats.
- Never mix pet dishes with your own — wash and dry them separately.

babies with colic

When a baby cries uncontrollably and seems irritable and uncomfortable the diagnosis is usually colic. There is no one cause for colic and in most cases a cause cannot be determined. By the time a baby is ready to start eating solid foods he has usually outgrown colic. There is no reason to give solid food early in an attempt to relieve the condition. As baby's gut matures he will outgrow the colic.

babies with reflux

Reflux (gastro-oesophogeal reflux) is one of the most common problems that can make feeding difficult. Most babies bring up a little food at some stage, and some do it after every feed. This is not reflux, it is called possetting. Possetting is perfectly normal and as your baby's digestive system matures it will stop. Reflux is more serious and can be mild or severe. A baby with reflux will either vomit easily and often or be very distressed after a feed because he is in pain. This pain is caused by acid from the stomach irritating the oesophagus, which is the tube that connects the mouth with the stomach. Children with reflux usually grow out of it between 6 and 18 months of age.

If your child is distressed after feeds, vomits frequently or in large amounts, or if there is blood present, and he is not gaining weight you need to talk to your doctor.

	1 MONTH	2 MONTHS	3 MONTHS	4 MONTHS	5 MONTHS	6 MONTHS
Breast milk and/or infant formula	All baby needs in the first 6 months is breast milk, no other solids or fluids. If breast milk is not available offer infant formula					Offer breast milk or formula before food
Cereals and bread						Baby rice cereal, steamed rice
Fruits & vegetables						Cooked/stewed apple, pear, pumpkin (squash), potato, sweet potato. Fresh avocado, banana
Meat, chicken, fish, egg, legumes, lentils and tofu						
Dairy products						
AMOUNTS / TEXTURE	Breast milk or formula according to baby's need					1–2 teaspoons puréed

7 MONTHS	8 MONTHS	9 MONTHS	10 MONTHS	11 MONTHS	12 MONTHS	13+ MONTHS
	Introduce cooled boiled water as an occasional drink from a regular rimmed or spouted cup		Offer breast milk after food	Continue to offer breast milk. Aim to breastfeed for at least 12 months — 2 years is ideal		
	Other baby cereals, oats, corn, pasta, couscous, polenta	Unsweetened adult cereals, wholemeal (whole-wheat) and wholegrain breads, unsalted crackers			Include baby in family foods and snacks, starting with very small amounts	
Gradually introduce a wide variety of fruits and vegetables. Melon, peaches, plums, apricot, papaya, beans, broccoli, carrot, zucchini (courgette), parsnip, cauliflower		Offer water as the main drink in addition to breast milk or formula. Fruit juice should be diluted to at least 50/50 and only offered occasionally and never in a bottle, only in a cup			Avoid offering fruit cordials and soft drinks, limit fruit juices to half a diluted cup per day	
Chicken, lamb, fish, beef, legumes, lentils, tofu	Egg yolk (cooked)		Whole egg (cooked)			Nuts, crushed or as smooth butters
Full-fat plain yoghurt, custard, mild cheddar cheese, small amounts of cow's milk if cooked						Full-cream cow's milk as a drink. If still breast-feeding less cow's milk needed
2–4 tablespoons, increasing according to baby's needs. Mashed soft food and finger foods		2–4 tablespoons according to baby's needs. Grated, minced (ground) and finely chopped.			Vary textures and quantities according to baby's appetite. Offer a variety of foods in small amounts.	

The real food journey begins here. The first weeks are a chance for baby to discover the new tastes, smells and textures of solid foods. As weeks become months, the purées become mash and your spoon is replaced by eager fingers keen to practise their motor skills. This is the time to allow food to be a form of play as well as nourishment. Cover the floor and don't fret about the washing!

baby food

first foods

Obviously, you want your baby to enjoy eating, and also to enjoy meal times. It is important, therefore, that you don't force your baby to take solids if she is not yet ready for them; this makes meal times difficult. Instead, keep feeding your baby the usual amounts of nourishing breast milk or infant formula until she exhibits the signs that she is ready.

In the early days, food is a new learning experience and your baby is still getting all her vitamins, minerals and protein from milk, while the new foods are providing valuable kilojoules (calories). The main aim in the early days is to avoid foods that could cause allergies. Theoretically you can feed your baby almost any food that you are eating, if you avoid those that could cause an allergic reaction, and which baby likes the taste of and which is the right consistency — a purée or liquid. Most people, however, start their baby on a cereal, often rice, as these are less likely to cause an allergic reaction than a wheat cereal.

some signs baby may be ready for solids:

- Baby holds things and puts them in her mouth. She may try to grab food you are eating. If the food is bland you can test her readiness by dipping a clean finger into it and letting her suck off the food. If she enjoys it, try her out with some rice cereal.
- Baby is able to sit supported and hold her head up.
- She has lost the tongue-thrust reflex. If the moment a spoon or your finger touches baby's tongue it 'thrusts' the spoon or finger out, then baby is not ready. This reflex is important as it protects a baby from choking.
- Baby seems to still be hungry after a milk feed and is not gaining weight. Younger babies will go through periods, usually at around 6 weeks and 3–4 months, when they seem to be hungry after feeding, but this can be solved by offering them more breast milk or formula.

don't feed baby before she's ready because:

- It won't make her sleep better or sleep through the night. That happens with maturity. Babies need to learn to sleep at night.

- She is more likely to develop allergies as her system is not mature enough to cope with food other than milk.
- She is susceptible to infections or tummy upsets.
- She may not drink as much breast milk or formula as she needs for optimum growth.
- Constipation is more likely as her system cannot cope with solids yet.
- If you feed solids too early, feeding can be a messy business, especially with a baby who has not lost the tongue-thrust reflex. Why make more work for yourself and baby?

how baby learns to swallow

Up until now baby has only needed to suck to get the sustenance she needs. Now she must learn that nourishment also comes from food and to do this she must learn to swallow and chew as well. Watching you eat, sitting at the table while others eat and being able to touch, finger and play with food is all part of this learning process. Baby needs time to learn these new skills so make her first feeds at a time when she is not ravenous. If baby regularly falls asleep after a milk feed you may find that the best time for other foods is in the middle of the milk feed.

When you first put food on baby's tongue she won't know what to do with it. She may move it around until much of it dribbles out of her mouth. You can't overcome this by putting the food at the back of her mouth, as this may cause her to gag. One method that often works is to allow your baby to simply suck it off the spoon. Using this method will help you to know when baby has had enough because she will usually turn her head away or close her lips.

making life easy

When you prepare baby's food do so in batches and freeze it — this cuts down on the preparation time needed for the next time you make the meal. Make enough baby food to fill up half an ice cube tray — each cube is around 1 tablespoon. When you have done this a few times with a variety of different purées, you will have a well-stocked range of foods that you can thaw easily and mix together.

When you thaw and reheat baby food make sure it is very hot, then cool it down — if you are using the microwave, stir the food before you test it on the inside of your wrist. Like formula, left-over baby food must be discarded because it will contain bacteria-carrying saliva. Never re-freeze it or store it for later use.

from 6 months

When first introducing solids to your baby, choose a time of day that suits you best. It might be after breakfast or before dinner, but you need to have time to take it gently and slowly. Over the next month you will introduce other meal times.

Always give baby her milk before you offer other foods — milk is still the most important source of nutrition for baby; it will not be replaced by food for another couple of months.

For her first meal offer her 1 teaspoon of one food, for example rice cereal. If she enjoys this, you can mix up another teaspoon for her next 'meal'. You can mix the cereal with expressed breast milk, formula or cooled boiled water. Remember, her first feed needs to have a runny consistency.

Use a clean bowl and spoon. Be sure to wash baby's bowls and cutlery in hot soapy water and to rinse thoroughly before drying with a clean tea towel (dish towel), if you don't have a dishwasher. Start by feeding baby on your lap which is covered with a towel or a nappy (diaper) and be prepared for a mess. You can move to a highchair when you think baby is ready.

After a couple of days with one food, try a new food. In the beginning it is important to offer new foods one at a time so baby can learn about different tastes and textures and you can determine if there are any foods that do not agree with baby. If baby does not like a particular food, try another and try again at a later date.

Don't add any salt or sugar — even if the food tastes bland or tasteless to you. Babies have 'new' tastebuds that taste flavours much more sharply than adults.

Once baby is eating solids you will notice a change to the smell of her urine and the look and smell of her bowel movements. Also any possetting (see page 23) will have a stronger smell. If your baby has been breast-fed until now, the change to the smell will be more noticeable as breast milk does not cause the strong smells that formula does.

After a couple of weeks baby will have tried a few new foods and you can mix them together for variety. Baby has to learn that food can be as satisfying as milk — she does not know this yet. You may find that sometimes baby will cry because she is hungry but giving her purée does not seem to work. It may be because she didn't have her milk feed first.

ground rice cereal

Rice cereal (either home-made or ready-made) is the best food to begin with because it is one of the foods least likely to cause an adverse reaction.

40 g (1½ oz/¼ cup) short-grain polished rice

125 ml (4 fl oz/½ cup) water

Prep time: 5 minutes

Cooking time: 5 minutes

Makes 6 serves

Grind the rice to a smooth powder in a spice grinder or use a mortar and pestle.

Put in a small saucepan and stir in the water. Stir over low heat for 2–3 minutes, or until the mixture becomes thick and creamy.

bulk rice cereal

Grind 220 g (7¾ oz/1 cup) short-grain polished rice to a smooth powder in a spice grinder or in a mortar with a pestle. Put in a small saucepan and stir in 625 ml (21½ fl oz/2½ cups) water. Stir over low heat for 2–3 minutes, or until the mixture becomes thick and creamy. Pour into ice cube trays and freeze.

puréed vegetable

Try pumpkin (winter squash) as a first vegetable for your baby. Its smooth, creamy texture and naturally sweet flavour make it enjoyable for new palates.

150 g (5½ oz/½ cup) vegetable such as finely chopped pumpkin (winter squash), potato, carrot, sweet potato, parsnip, peas, English spinach, broccoli or zucchini (courgette)

breast milk, formula or cooled boiled water

Prep time: 5 minutes
Cooking time: 15 minutes
Makes 6–8 serves

Put the chosen vegetable into a steamer basket over a saucepan of gently simmering water. Cover tightly and steam until tender.

Finely purée the vegetable pieces with a fork or press through a sieve. Add a little breast milk, formula or cooled boiled water to the mixture to achieve a smooth consistency.

After feeding, spoon the (untouched) remainder into ice cube trays and freeze or store in the refrigerator for up to 3 days.

variation: If using tomatoes, peel and deseed them before passing them through a fine sieve.

puréed avocado

Rich in healthy monounsaturated fats, avocado is also a good source of vitamin E and many of the B vitamins. This good nutrition, combined with its smooth, easy-to-prepare texture, means you have a perfect first food for babies.

Choose a small, soft avocado. Mash or purée one-eighth of the avocado with breast milk, formula or cooled boiled water to achieve the desired consistency.

stewed fruit

Babies are born with an innate taste for sweet foods; the natural sweetness of fresh stewed fruits makes them great favourites with babies.

I medium apple, peach or pear, peeled, cored and sliced

Prep time: 5 minutes
Cooking time: 5 minutes
Makes 6–8 serves

Put the sliced fruit into a small saucepan with 2 tablespoons water. Bring to the boil, reduce the heat and simmer until soft and pulpy, adding more water as required.

Purée with a little boiled water to make about 125 ml (4 fl oz/½ cup) stewed fruit.

variations: You can also use a variety of other fruits such as rhubarb or peeled and cored plums or apricots.

mashed banana

Bananas are rich in vitamin C, an important nutrient to help boost baby's iron absorption.

Choose a ripe banana. Mash or purée the banana with breast milk, formula or cooled boiled water to achieve the desired consistency.

pear & sweet potato purée

Once baby has tried a range of single fruits and vegetables, expand her repertoire. Combine fruits, vegetables and even rice cereal to create a new food experience.

80 g (2¾ oz/⅔ cup) chopped sweet potato

80 g (2¾ oz/⅔ cup) peeled, cored and chopped pear

breast milk, formula or cooled boiled water

Prep time: 5 minutes
Cooking time: 12 minutes
Makes 1–2 serves

Put the chopped sweet potato and pear pieces in a steamer basket over a saucepan of gently simmering water. Cover tightly and steam for about 12 minutes, or until very tender.

Finely purée the pieces with a fork or press through a sieve. Add a little breast milk, formula or cooled boiled water to the mixture to achieve a smooth consistency.

After feeding, spoon the (untouched) remainder into ice cube trays and freeze or store in the refrigerator for up to 3 days.

COMBINATION IDEAS:

- *Parsnip and carrot*
- *Baby pea and apple*
- *Avocado and pear*
- *Broccoli, carrot and potato*
- *Dried apricot and rice cereal*
- *Avocado and ricotta cheese (from 7 months)*
- *Potato and leek*
- *Pumpkin (winter squash) and apple*
- *Broccoli and sweet potato*

The combinations are only limited by your imagination!

from 7 months

COPING WITH THE MESS

Learning to eat can be a messy process. You can make this time easier on yourself if you think of it as an important and necessary learning experience for your baby. It helps to know that your child — usually before her fourth birthday — will be able to eat with a spoon and fork without making a mess.

Once baby is used to eating from a spoon, has tried a few different purées and is having two or three feeds a day, it is time to start making the food more lumpy. This stage usually comes around 7–8 months.

Don't worry if she doesn't have any teeth. Babies have very hard gums, as any breastfeeding mother will know, and are able to chew. If baby doesn't start eating mashed food at this stage, her cheek and jaw muscles will not get the workout they need and it will be more difficult when she is older.

a growing apetite

Though milk is still important, you may like to start giving food before the milk and start getting into more of a routine for meal times. Breast milk or formula can be given when baby wakes up and for morning, afternoon and evening 'snacks'.

Baby is growing quite quickly and you may find her appetite is growing too. She may be having around 2 tablespoons or she may be hungry enough to eat around half a cup of food. Never force baby to eat. It is better to have too little food and have to make her something else than to feel unhappy that baby has not eaten all the food you have prepared so carefully.

You can start giving your baby finger foods sometime soon. Babies love rusks (home-made or ready-made). Even if they are not teething, babies enjoy chomping on them. Foods which dissolve easily when they are sucked or chewed make ideal finger foods — foods which are bitten off in hard lumps (such as carrot, apple or celery) do not, because of the possibility of choking.

At this age baby will be able to sit up and will enjoy sitting in a high chair or a hook-on chair. She will enjoy eating with you sometimes — try to do this at least once a day since she will learn a great deal about eating and food by eating with the family.

Expect a mess. Learning about texture does not just happen with the tongue. When baby plays with her food she is also learning about food and, maybe surprisingly, some of it will end up in her mouth. Some babies are strongly independent and want to feed themselves everything. The best way around this is to have two spoons, one for baby and one for you.

Don't feel that in order to be a good parent you need to make all baby's food. Ready-made baby foods can make a great stand-by, and are useful when you are out and about. They are also hygienic and can provide good nutrition.

baby oat porridge

Oats provide all the goodness of a whole grain, as well as giving baby long-lasting energy throughout the day. Oats are also an excellent source of fibre.

25 g (1 oz/¼ cup) rolled (porridge) oats

185 ml (6 fl oz/¾ cup) milk

Prep time: 5 minutes

Cooking time: 5 minutes

Makes 3–4 serves

Grind the rolled oats to a fine powder in a spice grinder or a small food processor.

Put the oats in a small saucepan and gradually whisk in the milk and 60 ml (2 fl oz/¼ cup) water until well combined. Slowly bring to the boil and cook for 1–2 minutes, stirring constantly, or until the mixture thickens. Remove from the heat.

cauliflower soup

Cauliflower, along with broccoli, brussels sprouts and cabbage, belongs to the Brassica family of vegetables, which are all excellent sources of vitamin C.

2 teaspoons olive oil

1 small onion, chopped

1 small garlic clove, crushed (optional)

300 g (10½ oz/2½ cups) cauliflower, cut into small florets

500 ml (17 fl oz/2 cups) salt-reduced vegetable or chicken stock

Prep time: 10 minutes

Cooking time: 15 minutes

Makes 6–8 serves

Heat the oil in a saucepan over medium heat. Add the onion and garlic and cook for 2–3 minutes, or until softened. Add the cauliflower and stock, cover and bring to the boil. Reduce the heat to low and simmer for 10 minutes. Cool slightly and process in a blender or food processor until smooth.

The soup keeps for up to 3 days in the refrigerator or can be frozen in serving-size portions for up to 2 months.

lentils & vegetables

A rich source of vegetable protein, lentils are an excellent food for babies. Ensure they are well cooked and consider including a little garlic and onion.

2 tablespoons lentils or split peas

2 tablespoons mashed mixed vegetables

milk or cooled boiled water

cottage cheese (optional)

Prep time: 5 minutes
Cooking time: 25 minutes
Makes 1 serve

Rinse the lentils or split peas under cold running water and drain. Bring a saucepan of water to the boil, add the lentils or split peas and cook for 20–25 minutes, or until tender.

Drain, then process in a blender or small food processor with the vegetables and a little milk or cooled boiled water to give a smooth consistency. Add a little cottage cheese if desired and mix well.

As baby gets older, simply mash the cooked ingredients together with a fork to produce a lumpier consistency.

chicken, lentils & vegetables

Steam 1 boneless, skinless chicken tenderloin until cooked through. Add to the food processor with the lentils and vegetables and blend until smooth. As baby gets older and is starting to eat lumpier food, finely chop the steamed chicken and mash the cooked lentils and vegetables with a fork until lumpy, rather than pureé them.

spinach & potato mash

Potatoes are not only rich in energy-giving carbohydrates but also in vitamin C. Try using the creamy texture of potato mash in combination with other vegetables.

1 potato, peeled

1 tablespoon finely chopped English spinach

milk or cooled boiled water

Prep time: 5 minutes

Cooking time: 10 minutes

Makes 1 serve

Cook the potato in boiling water for about 10 minutes, or until tender. Put the chopped spinach into a small saucepan with 2 teaspoons water. Cook over low heat for 2 minutes, or until the spinach is wilted. Keep the saucepan tightly covered during cooking, then drain to remove any excess liquid.

Mash the potato and stir in the English spinach, adding a little milk or cooled boiled water if necessary to give a smooth consistency.

variations: Peas or broccoli can be easily substituted for the spinach. Ensure that the peas are well blended as whole peas are a choking risk for very young children.

poached fish with potato & peas

White fish has a soft texture and mild flavour that baby should enjoy. Fish is rich in high-quality protein plus vitamins and minerals such as vitamin D and iodine, which are important for growth and development.

60 g (2¼ oz) piece white fish

milk

1 small new potato, cut into cubes

2 teaspoons frozen peas

Prep time: 10 minutes
Cooking time: 5 minutes
Makes 1 serve

Put the fish in a small saucepan and add enough milk to cover. Simmer, covered, for 3–5 minutes, or until tender.

Meanwhile, add the potato and peas to boiling water and cook until tender. Drain. Mash the potato and peas, adding a little milk from the fish.

Remove any bones from the fish, then flake and serve with the mashed vegetables or mix through the vegetables.

INTRODUCING FISH

Fish is a highly nutritious food rich in vitamins, minerals, good-quality protein and omega-3 fats. Choosing the right types of fish for your baby or toddler is important because their small body size means they are more susceptible to the high mercury levels of some types of fish.

Babies and young children who eat fish regularly should avoid shark (flake), billfish (swordfish/broadbill and marlin) orange roughy (deep sea perch) and catfish. For more information, contact your local food authority.

stewed beef & vegetables

Iron is an important nutrient for babies and toddlers. Meals with iron-rich meats should be on the menu regularly to keep iron stores topped up.

90 g (3¼ oz) lean round or chuck steak or veal steak

1 new potato

1 small carrot

1 baby onion

½ garlic clove, crushed

small piece of bay leaf

sprig of parsley

Prep time: 5 minutes

Cooking time: 40 minutes

Makes 2 serves

Put the steak, potato, carrot and onion in a small saucepan. Add the garlic, the piece of bay leaf and parsley sprig, then cover with water. Cover, bring to the boil, then simmer gently until the meat is tender. Add more water as needed.

Discard the bay leaf and parsley. Blend the ingredients with a little of the cooking liquid.

steamed chicken & apple

The mild flavour of chicken teams well with the sweetness of fruit. Using a fruit that baby is familiar with helps to introduce her to a new flavour.

½ red cooking apple, peeled and cored

2 boneless, skinless chicken tenderloins

Prep time: 10 minutes
Cooking time: 5 minutes
Makes 1 serve

Thinly slice the apple and cut the chicken into small cubes. Place the chicken tenderloin pieces in a steamer and arrange the apple slices over the chicken. Set over a saucepan of boiling water and steam for about 5 minutes, or until tender.

Purée or finely chop the chicken and apple, together with a little of the cooking liquid.

steamed chicken & pumpkin

Cut 100 g (3½ oz) pumpkin (winter squash) into 5 mm (¼ inch) thick slices and steam with the chicken for 5 minutes, or until the pumpkin is tender and the chicken is cooked. Pureé or finely chop the pumpkin and chicken and mix with a little ricotta cheese if desired.

homemade rusks

As your baby discovers her hands she will want to use them to get everything within reach to her mouth. Offering a rusk when this happens will launch your baby into the world of finger food.

1 loaf unsliced wholemeal (whole-wheat) bread

Prep time: 10 minutes

Cooking time: 1 hour

Makes about 80

Preheat the oven to 130°C (250°F/Gas 1). Cut the bread into 2.5 cm (1 inch) thick slices. Remove the crusts and cut each slice into strips about 1.5 cm (½ inch) wide.

Bake the strips on an ungreased baking tray for about 1 hour, or until the rusks are dry and crisp. Turn them occasionally.

Cool and store in an airtight container for up to 7 days.

yeast extract & cheese rusks

Preheat the oven to 150°C (300°F/Gas 2). Spread slices of day-old bread with yeast extract and cover with a thin layer of grated cheddar cheese. Cut into fingers and bake for 1½–2 hours until really hard. Store these rusks in an airtight container.

semolina pudding

The grainy texture of this nourishing pudding helps with the introduction of more textured foods to baby's diet.

2 tablespoons semolina

1 teaspoon unsalted butter

250 ml (9 fl oz/1 cup) milk or cooled boiled water

Prep time: 5 minutes

Cooking time: 5 minutes

Makes 1 serve

Put the semolina in a small saucepan, then add the butter and milk. Simmer, covered, until the semolina is completely tender.

variation: Stir in 1 tablespoon each of finely chopped sultanas (golden raisins) and dried apricots with the butter and milk.

INTRODUCING TEXTURE

While baby's first solids should have a smooth texture, she will soon need variety in the preparation. This will come naturally from the type of fruit, vegetable or cereal you give her – compare the silky smoothness of puréed pumpkin (winter squash) to the grainy feel of puréed broccoli or cauliflower – but you will also need to start to 'process' her foods less.

So, once she is competently managing puréed foods move her along to foods with lumps and bumps in them. Do this by not blending foods for as long, using a fork to mash where you can and allowing her to have a go at finger foods like the rusks on page 45.

from 9 months

AS BABY LEARNS TO EAT:

• *Continue to offer milk. If you are breast-feeding, baby can feed as often as she (and you) like. If baby is bottle-fed, keep feeds to under 800 ml (28 fl oz) a day, as the milk can affect the quantity of other food baby eats.*

• *Chop rather than mash food, even if baby has no teeth.*

• *Watch out for hard foods. Babies can easily gag or choke.*

• *Teach your baby to wash her hands before and after eating.*

• *Always be on hand, since babies can have trouble with the softest of foods.*

This stage can start at anywhere from 8 to 9 months. Once baby is eating three times a day you may have difficulty thinking of what to feed her at times. By now baby may already be eating little snacks or finger foods. Some babies are determined to feed themselves; others are content to sit back and let you do it most of the time. It is worth encouraging the reluctant finger food eater, as it gives you a bit of time off to eat your own meal when you are eating together.

By the time your child reaches her first birthday she will be eating many foods that the family normally eats. She needs a healthy variety of foods and will be able to chew many of them, though it is still important to avoid hard foods, such as raw vegetables.

choking

Babies learn by putting things into their mouths. They will put anything that fits into their mouths, from burst balloons to tiny batteries — and consequently choking is a major hazard for the under-twos. We want them to put food in their mouths, but pieces of hard food are potential choking hazards, which is why experts advise against giving babies and toddlers certain foods (refer to the 'hard foods' chart on page 17 for specific examples).

Don't let the thought of your baby choking put you off giving her finger foods and other foods such as apples and carrot. Your baby will learn to eat these foods, but in the process may gag. A baby can gag on any food while she is learning to swallow and chew. In fact, babies have a gagging reflex which activates when they swallow too much, whether it is soft or hard.

When baby has teeth she may bite off a piece that is too large and because she is still learning to chew she may try to swallow it. This can cause gagging, but mostly baby will cough it up. If not you can hook the food out with your finger. Because this can happen it is important that baby is never left to eat alone.

While baby is learning to chew you can give her soft finger foods and cut up other foods or grate foods like carrot and apple.

simple scrambled eggs

Eggs are a good source of protein and fat plus valuable vitamins and minerals. In fact, they contain every nutrient except vitamin C, making them an important part of a growing baby's diet.

1 whole egg
1 egg yolk
1 tablespoon milk
1 teaspoon unsalted butter

Prep time: 2 minutes
Cooking time: 4 minutes
Makes 1 serve

Lightly beat together the whole egg and egg yolk with the milk. Melt the butter in a small non-stick frying pan over low heat and pour in the egg mixture. Cook, stirring occasionally, until the egg begins to set underneath. This will take about 3–4 minutes. Stir lightly and cook until just set. Serve the scrambled eggs with lightly toasted bread.

variations: Try adding grated cheese and chopped cooked chicken for a more substantial meal. Alternatively, fold through finely chopped wilted baby English spinach leaves and finely chopped tomatoes.

INTRODUCING EGGS

Allergy to egg is the most common food allergy among children. Fortunately, most children grow out of it by the time they go to school. Egg white is the most likely offender in egg allergy and this is the reason why the yolk rather than the whole egg is introduced to babies first, at around 8–9 months. If all goes well with this, then the white or whole egg can be introduced at around 10 months. When introducing either part of the egg make sure it is well cooked — allergy-causing proteins in food can cause a stronger reaction if they are not cooked.

carrot & pumpkin risotto

This recipe uses vegetables your baby knows and is her start on family foods. Blend it in the beginning stages of baby's feeding development if necessary.

90 g (3¼ oz) unsalted butter

1 onion, finely chopped

250 g (9 oz) pumpkin (winter squash), cut into small cubes

2 carrots, cut into small cubes

1.75–2 litres (61–70 fl oz/ 7–8 cups) salt-reduced vegetable stock

440 g (15½ oz/2 cups) risotto rice

90 g (3¼ oz/1 cup) freshly grated parmesan cheese

¼ teaspoon ground nutmeg

Prep time: 15 minutes

Cooking time: 35 minutes

Makes 4 serves

Heat 60 g (2¼ oz) of the butter in a large, heavy-based saucepan. Add the onion and fry for 1–2 minutes, or until soft. Add the pumpkin and carrot and cook for 6–8 minutes, or until tender. Mash slightly with a potato masher. Put the stock in a separate saucepan and keep at simmering point.

Add the rice to the vegetables and cook for 1 minute, stirring constantly. Ladle in enough hot stock to cover the rice; stir well. Reduce the heat and add more stock as it is absorbed, stirring frequently. Continue until the rice is tender and creamy (this will take about 25 minutes).

Remove the pan from the heat, add the remaining butter, cheese and nutmeg and season with freshly ground black pepper. Fork through. Cover and leave for 5 minutes before serving.

HINT: Left-over risotto is great the next day formed into balls and deep-fried. Ensure the balls are cool before serving them to baby.

cheesy stars

Pasta is a great quick-cook food for kids of all ages and with more than six-hundred named shapes of pasta, this meal need never be the same!

60 g (2¼ oz/⅔ cup) small, star-shaped pasta (see hint)

1 teaspoon unsalted butter

1 tablespoon grated cheese

1 tablespoon milk

chopped parsley

Prep time: 5 minutes
Cooking time: 10 minutes
Makes 1 serve

Cook the pasta in boiling water for about 8–9 minutes, or until tender.

Drain, return the pasta to the saucepan, then add the butter, cheese and milk. Mix well and stir over low heat for 1 minute, or until the butter and cheese have melted. Stir in a little parsley. If necessary, mash to serve.

variation: You could substitute the star-shaped pasta for any number of other small pasta shapes. Use larger spirals and bow-shaped pasta for babies as they show more interest in finger foods.

HINT: Small star-shaped pasta is about the size of a split pea.

steamed fish & diced vegetables

It's not just babies that need to eat fish, health authorities recommend we all have at least one or two fish meals a week.

60 g (2¼ oz) piece boneless white fish, cut into cubes

2 tablespoons finely diced vegetables (asparagus, broccoli, carrot, frozen peas)

milk (optional)

Prep time: 10 minutes

Cooking time: 8 minutes

Makes 1 serve

Put the fish with the vegetables in a steamer and set over a saucepan of boiling water. Steam for about 8 minutes, or until tender.

Mash the fish and vegetables together to form a smooth consistency, adding a little of the cooking liquid or milk if necessary. Otherwise, flake the fish and chop the accompanying vegetables, adding a little milk or cooking liquid.

cauliflower in creamy sauce

When well cooked, this dish makes a creamy meal for younger babies. With less cooking, the firm florets makes an ideal finger food for the older baby.

60 g (2¼ oz) fresh or frozen cauliflower, cut into small florets

2 tablespoons milk

1 teaspoon dry milk powder or ricotta cheese

¾ teaspoon cornflour (cornstarch)

Prep time: 5 minutes

Cooking time: 8 minutes

Makes 1 serve

Cut the cauliflower into small florets and boil or steam until tender. Drain well.

Put the milk, milk powder or ricotta cheese and cornflour in a small saucepan. Cook, stirring, until thickened.

Finely chop or mash the cauliflower and stir into the sauce.

HINT: This recipe can also be used for diced carrots, tiny florets of broccoli, diced asparagus or pumpkin (winter squash).

dal

Lentils are a powerhouse of nutrition. Excellent as a source of protein, iron and zinc, they provide a valuable alternative to meat.

310 g (11 oz/1¼ cups) red lentils

30 g (1 oz) unsalted butter

1 medium onion, finely chopped

2 garlic cloves, crushed

1 teaspoon grated fresh ginger

1 teaspoon ground turmeric

1 teaspoon garam masala

Prep time: 15 minutes
Cooking time: 20 minutes
Makes 4–6 serves

Put the lentils in a large bowl and cover with water. Remove any floating particles and drain the lentils well.

Heat the butter in a saucepan. Fry the onion for about 3 minutes, or until soft. Add the garlic, ginger and spices; cook, stirring for another minute.

Add the lentils and 500 ml (17 fl oz/2 cups) water and bring to the boil. Lower the heat and simmer, stirring occasionally, for 15 minutes, or until all the water has been absorbed. Watch carefully towards the end of cooking time, as the mixture could burn on the bottom of the pan.

Transfer to a serving bowl and serve warm or at room temperature with pitta toasts or with naan or pitta bread.

pitta toasts

Preheat the oven to 180°C (350°F/Gas 4). Cut 4 rounds of pitta bread into wedges and brush lightly with oil. Arrange on a baking tray and cook for 5–7 minutes, or until lightly browned and crisp.

lamb shank & barley casserole

Rich with flavour, this dish is well worth the time. It is also big on protein, the minerals iron and zinc and soluble barley fibre (the gentle type).

1 tablespoon olive oil

1 small onion, finely chopped

1 garlic clove, crushed (optional)

50 g (1¾ oz/⅓ cup) diced carrot

2 tablespoons finely diced celery

2 teaspoons finely chopped rosemary

2 French trimmed lamb shanks (about 600 g/1 lb 5 oz)

plain (all-purpose) flour, for dusting

2 tablespoons pearl barley

500 ml (17 fl oz/2 cups) salt-reduced beef stock

Prep time: 15 minutes

Cooking time: 2 hours 10 minutes

Makes 3–4 serves

Heat the oil in a small flameproof casserole dish or heavy-based saucepan. Add the onion, garlic, carrot, celery and rosemary and cook over medium heat for about 5 minutes, or until soft.

Dust the lamb shanks in flour, shaking off any excess. Add to the dish, turning to brown all sides. Add the barley and stock and bring to the boil. Reduce the heat to low and cook, covered, for 2 hours, or until the meat is very tender and falling away from the bone.

Remove the shanks, allow to cool slightly, then remove the meat from the bone, discarding any sinew. Cut the meat into small pieces and return to the casserole, stirring to combine. For a smoother texture put in a food processor and lightly process. This meal can be frozen for up to 3 months. Thaw, then reheat to serve.

vegetable casserole

The foundations of healthy eating are now laid. By making vegetables a regular part of baby's menu, you will guarantee they are enjoyed in the future.

I tablespoon olive oil

½ onion, finely chopped

I garlic clove, crushed (optional)

½ celery stalk, finely diced

½ carrot, diced

50 g (1¾ oz/¼ cup) brown lentils

200 g (7 oz) tinned diced tomatoes

185 ml (6 fl oz/¾ cup) salt-reduced vegetable or chicken stock

150 g (5½ oz) pumpkin (winter squash), deseeded and cut into 1 cm (½ inch) cubes

½ zucchini (courgette), quartered lengthways and cut into 1 cm (½ inch) slices

Prep time: 15 minutes

Cooking time: 1 hour

Makes 3–4 serves

Preheat the oven to 200°C (400°F/Gas 6).

Heat the oil in a flameproof casserole dish over medium heat. Add the onion, garlic, celery and carrot and cook for 5 minutes, or until softened. Add the lentils, tomato and stock and stir to combine. Cover and bake for 40 minutes. Add the pumpkin and zucchini and cook for a further 10–12 minutes, or until tender.

Mash lightly with a fork to serve if necessary.

rice pudding

Good rice pudding takes time — make this recipe as a special dessert for the whole family. Add some sultanas (golden raisins) to boost its fibre and sweetness.

110 g (3¾ oz/½ cup) risotto rice

1 litre (35 fl oz/4 cups) milk

2 tablespoons caster (superfine) sugar

1 teaspoon natural vanilla extract

1 teaspoon unsalted butter (optional)

pinch of cinnamon (optional)

fresh berries, to garnish (optional)

Prep time: 10 minutes
Cooking time: 1½ hours
Makes 4 serves

Preheat the oven to 180°C (350°F/Gas 4).

Place the rice, milk, sugar, vanilla and butter and cinnamon, if using, in a baking dish and stir.

Bake for about 1½ hours, stirring every 15 minutes to make sure it doesn't stick to the dish. Remove the pudding from the oven when it has the consistency of creamed rice. Do not overcook or it may dry out. Cool slightly and top with fresh berries.

fresh fruit salad

Soft chunks of ripe seasonal fruit make baby's first fruit salad a delightful exploration of taste and texture. For younger babies, simply mash the fruits.

100 g (3½ oz) seedless watermelon, cut into 2 cm (¾ inch) cubes

100 g (3½ oz) orange-fleshed melon, cut into 2 cm (¾ inch) cubes

60 g (2¼ oz) strawberries, hulled and cut into quarters

½ kiwi fruit, peeled and cut into pieces

50 g (1¾ oz) seedless white grapes, halved

¼ banana, sliced

1–2 tablespoons unsweetened fruit juice or orange juice

Prep time: 5 minutes

Cooking time: Nil

Makes 2–3 serves

Place the fruits in a bowl, pour over the orange juice and toss to coat. Serve as finger food or cut up into smaller pieces for spoon feeding.

HINT: You can substitute any seasonal fruits for the above suggestions. Avoid fruits with seeds, though, unless you can remove them first.

fruit jelly

Jelly (gelatine dessert) is a tasty textural delight for toddlers. This recipe is also a vitamin- and fibre-packed alternative to ready-made varieties.

1 tablespoon gelatine powder

375 ml (13 fl oz/1½ cups) unsweetened fruit juice

200 g (7 oz/¾ cup) puréed fresh or drained, tinned fruit in natural juice

Prep time: 10 minutes

Cooking time: 5 minutes

Makes 6 serves

Sprinkle the gelatine over 125 ml (4 fl oz/½ cup) cool water in a small saucepan. Heat through, then add the fruit juice and heat through again. Pour into a mixing bowl and leave until it begins to thicken. Stir in the puréed fruit until well combined.

Transfer to small dishes and refrigerate until set.

yoghurt jelly

This is a good source of vitamin C plus the important minerals calcium and phosphorus. Use a Greek-style yoghurt for an extra creamy version.

1½ tablespoons gelatine powder

375 ml (13 fl oz/1½ cups) unsweetened fruit juice

250 g (9 oz/1 cup) plain yoghurt

Prep time: 10 minutes

Cooking time: 5 minutes

Makes 6 serves

Sprinkle the gelatine over 125 ml (4 fl oz/½ cup) cool water in a small saucepan. Heat through, then add the fruit juice and heat through again. Pour into a mixing bowl and leave until it begins to thicken. Stir in the yoghurt, then beat with electric beaters until fluffy.

Transfer to small dishes and refrigerate until set.

Independence is a feature of toddlers' behaviour and meal times are a perfect time to show it. Appetites will wane and fads and fussiness will come and go. Stay relaxed with food and your toddler will too. Cleaning up a plate is not what it is all about. Instead, trust your toddler to tell you when they are full. Make sure the food they get is good and healthy *most* of the time.

toddler food

1 year & on

By the time your child reaches his first birthday he will have tried a wide range of foods and you will be able to include him in many of the meals you make for yourself or the rest of the family.

During their second year children start to assert their independence and parents can become frustrated when they find their child being finicky about food. Toddlers can clamp their mouths shut or tip their food on the floor, just to get your attention.

tricks for trouble-free meal times

If you find that your toddler is being stubborn at meal times there are strategies you can employ to help avoid meals turning into battles. If you have a child who is taking a stand over meal times be assured that you are not alone. By offering him a wide range of wholesome foods he will not starve. It will also help if you follow these suggestions:

• Try to eat as a family as often as you can. This may only be possible at the weekends, or only at breakfast time, but it is important. When your toddler sees you eating something he will want to copy. At this age children are natural copycats and this is an easy way to educate children about food and table manners. Children who eat alone often develop bad habits. If you can't eat together then at least sit with your child, put his chair up to the table and make it a special time. You need to to be there to supervise.

Plonking your child down in front of the television set with a bowl of finger food or a favourite meal may seem like an easy way out. However, in the long run it is not adding to your toddler's enjoyment of food or meal times and it may actually lead to fussy eating. Television can also be a problem if the program includes advertisements for junk foods or food that is high in fat, sugar or salt.

• Feed your child the same foods that you normally eat. If you taste commercial baby or toddler food you will be amazed at its blandness — and its sameness. Some home-made dishes will need to be presented to your toddler over and over again before he eats them — and a few he may never eat. But if he sees you eating the same food he may decide he is missing out on something and try it himself.

• Keep challenging his food horizons. Continue to present him with new variations on the food he is eating. If you eat the same foods every night of the week, and so does he, he will never learn about new foods. If you are eating a Thai meal or a curry try him out with a little bit of mild food. Some children take to lightly spiced food more quickly than others.

• Give him the freshest, most nutritious and best-quality food that you can buy and make.

• Set a good example. If you don't eat fruit and vegetables you can't expect your child to want them. If you haven't been in the habit of eating four or five vegetables and two or three pieces of fruit a day, then start today.

• Avoid food battles. If your child refuses to eat something one day offer it again another day — and another day again. Don't get into an argument.

• Cheat. You can hide vegetables in meat sauces, meatballs or casseroles. You can hide milk in sauces, custards or ice cream. Be creative. You can serve fish and chips (fries) on paper towels or in a clean takeaway food box, or wrap up a burger. You can use a pastry cutter to make cheese into star shapes or turn a salad into a face by cutting a cheese circle, popping on a cherry tomato nose, two sultana (golden raisin) eyes, a cucumber mouth and lettuce hair! You can make iceblocks (popsicles/ice lollies) out of frozen bananas on a stick, or milkshakes from milk blended with fruit.

• Let him help get the meal ready. There are many simple things toddlers can do — fetch and carry anything unbreakable, wash vegetables or fruit, stir simple mixes and shake dressings.

• Feed him at around the same times each day. Toddlers are creatures of habit so they like a routine.

• If he is having a bad day and you feel he won't eat anything, put together a plate with a choice of foods, such as dried apricots, cooked chicken, cooked pasta, a slice of banana, a cube of cheese, a couple of stoned olives or cherry tomatoes, two or three cooked beans or snow peas (mangetout), or a piece of wholemeal (whole-wheat) bread with his favourite spread.

• Don't reward with desserts or sweets (candy) to make your child eat a particular food he doesn't like. This can actually make children dislike the food in question even more. Bribing your child with sweets only raises their importance in his eyes. Only give him dessert if he is still hungry after he has eaten his other food. Children are more likely to want a food when they are told they can't have it or if it is used as a reward. That said, it is important to allow treats sometimes.

It won't hurt your child if he refuses the occasional meal. Nagging, cajoling or shouting is not going to help.

breakfast

Your toddler needs breakfast, just as you do. Skipping breakfast has been found to be behind poor concentration and forgetfulness — and this applies to children as well as adults. After hours of fasting while you were asleep, your brain needs fuel in order to function properly. If your toddler sees you skipping breakfast he will want to copy you — and that is not good for either of you.

Research has also found that children who eat breakfast have better overall diets than those who skip this meal. They are also more likely to achieve the recommended daily amounts of vitamins and minerals than those who don't eat breakfast.

Breakfast is a good time to consume a range of nutrients including fibre in cereal and bread; protein and calcium in milk and yoghurt; and vitamins, minerals and fibre in fruit.

It is important to give yourself enough time for breakfast as well as getting lunches and snacks ready if you have to take them to childcare. Being prepared the night before is always a good start. You can pack some of the snacks, put lunchboxes out, get out cereal bowls, cereal and cutlery and have the kitchen ready.

breakfast on the go

Mornings can be a challenge when everyone has to be ready on time. Consider these quick breakfast suggestions:

- Home-made muesli (granola) with yoghurt and fruit
- Quick-cook microwave oats (porridge)
- Fresh fruit salad with yoghurt
- Baked beans and toast fingers
- Fruit toast spread with ricotta or cream cheese
- Fruit and yoghurt smoothies
- Omelettes or scrambled eggs

home-made muesli

While adult commercial cereals can be used for a toddler's breakfast, some are high in sugar and salt. This muesli (granola) has all the goodness of whole grains and dried fruits without any unwanted extras.

150 g (5½ oz/1½ cups) rolled (porridge) oats

2 tablespoons wheatgerm

30 g (1 oz/¼ cup) raw oatmeal

20 g (¾ oz/¼ cup) bran

60 g (2¼ oz/½ cup) sultanas (golden raisins)

30 g (1 oz/⅓ cup) dried apple, chopped

90 g (3¼ oz/½ cup) dried apricots, chopped

Prep time: 10 minutes

Cooking time: Nil

Serves 8

Combine all the ingredients together and store in an airtight container for up to 4 weeks. To serve, pour over a little milk, place in a saucepan and stir over medium heat for 30–60 seconds to soften; or place in a microwave for 20–30 seconds.

Alternatively, blend the dry muesli in a food processor until almost fine. Serve with other dried fruits, fresh fruit, yoghurt or a drizzle of honey (only for children over 12 months) or fruit purée.

banana porridge

A wholegrain cereal like oats is rich in energy-giving carbohydrates, essential fats and minerals. Team it with banana and it becomes a great source of B vitamins including folate, as well as vitamin C and potassium.

1 tablespoon quick-cook oats
1 tablespoon cold water
1½ tablespoons hot water
2 teaspoons mashed banana
milk or cooled boiled water

Prep time: 5 minutes
Cooking time: 2 minutes
Serves 1

Combine the quick-cook oats with the cold water in a small saucepan. Add the hot water and bring to the boil, stirring. Reduce the heat and simmer for 30 seconds or until the mixture is thick and creamy.

Remove the porridge from the heat and stir through the mashed banana. Mix with enough milk or cooled boiled water to produce the required consistency.

fluffy omelette

The ultimate in convenience food, eggs make a perfect meal at any time of the day for a growing toddler — don't just save them for breakfast!

I egg yolk
2 egg whites
I teaspoon unsalted butter

Prep time: 5 minutes
Cooking time: 5 minutes
Serves I

Lightly beat the egg yolk with I teaspoon water. Beat the egg whites to soft peaks and stir in the yolk mixture.

Melt the butter in a small frying pan and pour in the egg mixture. Cook quickly on one side, then turn and cook until just firm.

variations: Fillings of flaked fish such as red salmon, finely chopped sautéed zucchini (courgette) and onion, mushrooms, tomato or grated cheddar cheese can be used. Place along the centre of the omelette on the uncooked side, then fold over to enclose the filling. Cook until the omelette is cooked through, turning once.

eggs en cocotte

Research shows that a healthy diet is encouraged when children eat with their family regularly. Enjoy this recipe with your toddler as a special breakfast.

TOMATO SAUCE

1 tablespoon olive oil

1 garlic clove, crushed

3 vine-ripened tomatoes (about 300 g/10½ oz), peeled, seeded and chopped

½ teaspoon olive oil

4 eggs

2 tablespoons snipped chives

4 slices thick wholegrain bread

15 g (½ oz) unsalted butter

Prep time: 15 minutes

Cooking time: 30 minutes

Serves 4

Preheat the oven to 180°C (350°F/Gas 4). To make the tomato sauce, heat the oil in a heavy-based frying pan. Add the garlic and cook for 30 seconds. Add the tomato and season with salt and freshly ground black pepper. Cook over medium heat for 15 minutes, or until thickened.

Grease four 125 ml (4 fl oz/½ cup) ramekins with the olive oil, then carefully break 1 egg into each, trying not to break the yolk. Pour the tomato sauce evenly around the outside of each egg, so the yolk is still visible. Sprinkle with chives and season lightly with salt and freshly ground black pepper.

Place the ramekins in a deep baking dish and pour in enough hot water to come halfway up the outside of the ramekins. Bake for about 10–12 minutes, or until the egg white is set. Toast the bread and lightly spread the slices with the butter, then cut into thick fingers. Serve immediately with the cooked eggs.

french toast

Bread is an important staple food for the growing toddler. Vary the types of bread you use for this recipe by using wholegrain, rye or even fruit bread.

I egg, lightly beaten

2 teaspoons milk

2 thick slices wholemeal (whole-wheat) bread

unsalted butter or oil, for frying

pinch of cinnamon (optional)

Prep time: 5 minutes

Cooking time: 2 minutes

Serves 2

Beat the egg with the milk. Cut two slices of the wholemeal bread into different shapes, using shaped biscuit (cookie) cutters. Dip the bread into the egg mixture. Cook in a non-stick frying pan, brushed with a little melted butter or oil, until golden on both sides. Sprinkle with a little cinnamon, if desired.

cat toast

Cut the bread into the shape of a cat face by trimming away the lower corners of the slice to make a rounded chin and cheeks. Shape the top edge into a rounded head with two pointed ears. Dip into the egg mixture and fry in butter to make french toast, then add halved dried apricots for eyes, a raisin for the nose and a thin strip of orange zest for the mouth.

scrambled eggs with sweet corn sauce

The combination of eggs, with their high-quality protein, and corn, rich in carbohydrate, makes this meal a great start to the day for energetic toddlers.

250 g (9 oz/1 cup) tinned creamed corn

15 g (½ oz) unsalted butter

2½ teaspoons cornflour (cornstarch)

250 ml (9 fl oz/1 cup) milk

6 eggs

1 tablespoon milk, extra

1–2 teaspoons unsalted butter, extra

Prep time: 10 minutes
Cooking time: 10 minutes
Serves 4

Put the corn and butter in a saucepan. Combine the cornflour and 1 tablespoon of the milk in a bowl, then add the remaining milk, stirring well. Pour into the saucepan and bring to the boil. Simmer, stirring, for 2–3 minutes, until the sauce thickens. Keep warm.

Beat the eggs and extra milk together and season with freshly ground black pepper. Melt the extra butter in a frying pan and pour in the egg mixture. Cook gently, stirring occasionally, for 2–3 minutes, or until just firm. Transfer to a plate and pour on the sweet corn sauce.

home-made baked beans

Soya beans are the perfect size for tiny fingers to practise their fine motor skills. They also provide vitamins, high-quality protein, iron and zinc.

550 g (1 lb 4 oz/3 cups) dried soya beans

400 g (14 oz/1⅔ cups) tinned diced tomatoes

250 ml (9 fl oz/1 cup) salt-reduced vegetable stock

1 bay leaf

2 tablespoons chopped parsley

pinch of dried thyme

1 tablespoon vegetable oil

Prep time: 5 minutes
Cooking time: 4 hours 40 minutes
Serves 4

Cook the soya beans in plenty of water for about 4 hours, or until tender. Drain. Preheat the oven to 180°C (350°F/Gas 4).

Put the soya beans in a casserole dish and add the tomato, stock, herbs and oil. Bake, covered, for 40 minutes.

HINTS: If you want a thicker consistency, remove the lid of the casserole dish and cook for a further 10–15 minutes, or until reduced to the desired consistency. Instead of using dried soya beans, you can use the same amount of drained tinned soya beans.

blueberry pancakes

A source of vitamins A, C and the B group, blueberries make these pancakes a much healthier breakfast for toddlers than pancakes with maple syrup.

250 g (9 oz/2 cups) plain (all-purpose) flour

2 teaspoons baking powder

1 teaspoon bicarbonate of soda (baking soda)

90 g (3¼ oz/⅓ cup) sugar

2 eggs

80 g (2¾ oz) unsalted butter, melted

310 ml (10¾ fl oz/1¼ cups) milk

310 g (11 oz/2 cups) blueberries, fresh or frozen

Prep time: 10–15 minutes

Cooking time: 18 minutes

Makes 6

Sift the flour, baking powder and bicarbonate of soda into a large bowl. Add the sugar and make a well in the centre. Using a fork, whisk the eggs, melted butter and milk together in a bowl and add to the dry ingredients, stirring just to combine (add more milk if you prefer a thinner batter). Gently fold in the blueberries.

Heat a frying pan and brush lightly with melted butter or oil. Pour 125 ml (4 fl oz/½ cup) batter into the pan and spread out to make a pancake about 15 cm (6 inches) in diameter. Cook over low heat until bubbles appear and pop on the surface.

Turn the pancake over and cook the other side (these pancakes can be difficult to handle so take care when turning). Transfer to a plate and cover with a tea towel (dish towel) to keep warm while cooking the remaining batter. The pancakes are delicious served warm with blueberry coulis (see recipe below) and Greek-style plain yoghurt.

HINT: If you use frozen blueberries there is no need to thaw them.

blueberry coulis

Put 310 g (11 oz/2 cups) fresh or frozen blueberries in a blender or food processor and blend until puréed. Strain through a fine sieve to remove the skin and to make a smooth sauce. Stir in 2 teaspoons icing (confectioners') sugar. Stir the coulis through plain yoghurt or serve plain with pancakes, ice cream, fruit salad or breakfast cereal. Store any left-over coulis in the refrigerator for up to 3 days. Makes 150 ml (5 fl oz).

mushrooms with toast fingers

Mushrooms are as rich in the B vitamin niacin as red meat. They provide a flavoursome breakfast that can be enjoyed by the whole family.

MUSHROOM SAUCE

1 tablespoon olive oil

800 g (1 lb 12 oz/8 cups) mixed mushrooms (flat, button, open-cap), chopped

2 garlic cloves, crushed

1 teaspoon finely chopped thyme

125 ml (4 fl oz/½ cup) salt-reduced vegetable stock

1 large handful parsley, finely chopped

4 slices thick wholemeal (whole-wheat) bread

baby English spinach (optional)

shaved parmesan cheese (optional)

Prep time: 10 minutes

Cooking time: 20 minutes

Serves 4

Heat the olive oil in a large frying pan. Add the mixed mushrooms and cook over high heat for 4–5 minutes, or until soft. Add the garlic and thyme. Season and cook for 2–3 minutes. Add 185 ml (6 fl oz/¾ cup) water. Cook until it has evaporated. Add the stock, then reduce the heat. Cook for a further 3–4 minutes, or until the stock has reduced and thickened. Add the parsley.

Grill (broil) or toast the bread until golden on both sides. Slice into fingers, if desired. Divide among the serving plates and top with the mushrooms. Top with baby English spinach leaves and parmesan shavings, if desired.

dried fruit compote with yoghurt

This fruity breakfast is full of flavour and is a great source of fibre, calcium and potassium with small but important amounts of iron and beta-carotene.

50 g (1¾ oz/⅓ cup) dried apricots, quartered

50 g (1¾ oz/¼ cup) stoned prunes, quartered

50 g (1¾ oz/⅔ cup) dried pears, chopped

50 g (1¾ oz/⅔ cup) dried peaches, chopped

185 ml (6 fl oz/¾ cup) orange juice

1 cinnamon stick

plain yoghurt, to serve

Prep time: 5 minutes

Cooking time: 10 minutes

Serves 4

Put the fruit, orange juice and cinnamon stick in a saucepan and stir to combine. Bring to the boil, then reduce the heat to low, cover, and simmer for 10 minutes, or until the fruit is plump and softened. Discard the cinnamon stick. Serve drizzled with the cooking liquid and a dollop of the plain yoghurt.

Store in an airtight container in the refrigerator for up to 1 week.

mixed berry couscous

Fruit-based breakfasts are rich in vitamins, minerals and fibre, and are a quick and yummy way for kids to start the day. If berries aren't in season use a medley of whatever happens to be ripe and tasty in your fruit bowl.

185 g (6½ oz/1 cup) instant couscous

500 ml (17 fl oz/2 cups) apple and cranberry juice

1 cinnamon stick

250 g (9 oz/2 cups) frozen raspberries, thawed

250 g (9 oz/1⅔ cups) frozen blueberries, thawed

2 teaspoons orange zest, plus extra, to garnish

250 g (9 oz/1⅔ cups) strawberries, halved

185 g (6½ oz/¾ cup) Greek-style plain yoghurt

fresh mint leaves, to garnish

Prep time: 15 minutes
Cooking time: 5 minutes
Serves 4

Put the instant couscous in a bowl. Pour the apple and cranberry juice into a saucepan and add the cinnamon stick. Cover and bring to the boil, then remove from the heat and pour over the couscous. Cover the couscous with plastic wrap and leave for about 5 minutes, or until all the liquid has been absorbed. After this time, remove the cinnamon stick from the bowl.

Gently pat the thawed berries with paper towels to absorb the excess juices. Separate the grains of couscous with a fork, then gently fold in the orange zest and most of the berries. Spoon the couscous mixture into four serving bowls and sprinkle with the remaining berries. Serve with a generous dollop of the yoghurt. Garnish with mint leaves and orange zest and serve.

lunch

The type of lunch your child has will depend on whether he is at home with you, out with you or at childcare, preschool or kindergarten. If he is in childcare it will depend on whether he needs to take his own lunch or whether the centre prepares the midday meal.

If you are packing the lunch, you will know what he has had for breakfast and will be able to prepare different types of food for lunch. If your child is served lunch at childcare check the menu to be sure that you don't give your child the same type of food for dinner as he had at lunchtime.

One of the most fun lunches to have with a toddler is a picnic. You can pack a picnic and take it with you to your own backyard, the nearest park, to a bench while you are out shopping or to the beach. It can be an opportunity to get together with other parents or just to get out. Remember that if it is a warm or hot day the safest way to travel with food, even sandwiches, is for it to be in an insulated bag.

lunch in a hurry

When kids are hungry they often need food immediately. Consider these suggestions for a quick solution to a fast lunch:

- Microwave or bake a potato, cut it in half and serve it topped with a tin of baked beans or creamed corn.
- Keep left-over pasta in the refrigerator to team with a tin of tuna or salmon plus any combination of the following: quartered cherry tomatoes, cooked frozen peas, tinned sweet corn, grated cheese or avocado.
- Mash up some avocado with cream cheese and serve with toast fingers for dipping.
- Scrambled eggs or omelettes — don't just reserve these for breakfast.
- Cheese and ham or tomato on toast.

chicken meatballs in soup

Be it laziness or just tired little jaws, toddlers often don't manage meat well. Meat needs to be presented in a way toddlers can manage (without puréeing). Minced (ground) meat, as in this recipe, is the perfect solution.

1 spring onion (scallion)

375 g (13 oz) minced (ground) chicken

875 ml (30 fl oz/3½ cups) salt-reduced chicken stock

1½ tablespoons frozen peas

1½ tablespoons finely diced carrot

1 tablespoon alphabet noodles or other small pasta

Prep time: 20 minutes
Cooking time: 20 minutes
Serves 4

Finely chop half the spring onion and thinly slice the remainder. Combine the chicken and finely chopped spring onion until thoroughly mixed, then form into small balls, about the size of walnuts. Bring the chicken stock to the boil in a saucepan and add the peas, carrot and noodles. Simmer until the vegetables are tender, then add the reserved sliced spring onion.

Drop the chicken balls into the simmering soup. Cook until the meatballs float to the surface and turn white.

variation: You can substitute the chicken with the same amount of boneless, skinless chicken breast. Simply cut the chicken into thin slices, place it between two sheets of baking paper and gently pound with a rolling pin to make almost transparent slices. These will cook in seconds in the hot soup.

tomato soup

Soup is a great way to get vegetables into toddlers. Make sure it is cool enough to eat and then let them dunk toast fingers for a nourishing 'hands on' meal.

20 g (¾ oz) unsalted butter
1 celery stalk, finely chopped
1 onion, finely chopped
1 carrot, finely chopped
1 garlic clove, crushed
700 g (1 lb 9 oz/2¾ cups) tomato-based pasta sauce
750 ml (26 fl oz/3 cups) salt-reduced chicken or vegetable stock
1 teaspoon sugar
1 parsley sprig
1 bay leaf
250 ml (9 fl oz/1 cup) milk
2 teaspoons chopped parsley
toast, to serve

Prep time: 10 minutes
Cooking time: 20 minutes
Serves 4

Melt the butter in a saucepan and sauté the celery, onion and carrot for 3–4 minutes. Add the garlic and cook for 30 seconds. Add the pasta sauce, chicken or vegetable stock, sugar, parsley sprig and bay leaf. Bring to the boil, then simmer for 10 minutes. Remove the parsley and bay leaf.

Purée the soup in a blender, then return it to the pan. Stir through the milk and heat until hot.

Garnish with the parsley and serve with toast.

salmon & basil fish cakes

These tasty cakes make a great meal or even a nutritious snack served cold. They are packed with energy-giving carbohydrate, as well as vitamins, minerals (especially calcium if you mash in the salmon bones) and important fats.

2 medium all-purpose potatoes, quartered

415 g (14¾ oz) tinned pink salmon, drained, skin and large bones removed

½ teaspoon grated lime zest

4 spring onions (scallions), finely chopped

1 handful basil leaves, roughly chopped

1 tablespoon capers, rinsed, drained and roughly chopped

1 egg yolk

1 egg, lightly beaten

1 tablespoon milk

40 g (1½ oz/⅓ cup) plain (all-purpose) flour

70 g (2½ oz/¾ cup) dry breadcrumbs

oil, for shallow-frying

Prep time: 20 minutes + 30 minutes refrigeration

Cooking time: 20 minutes

Makes 8

Cook the potatoes in a large saucepan of boiling water until just tender. Drain and lightly mash, leaving some large pieces. Allow the potatoes to cool.

Meanwhile, in a bowl, gently flake the salmon into large pieces. Add the lime zest, spring onion, basil, capers and egg yolk. Mix lightly then stir in the mashed potato. Season with freshly ground black pepper.

Combine the egg and milk in a shallow bowl. Spread the flour and breadcrumbs out on separate plates. With wet hands, shape the salmon mixture into eight patties about 6 cm (2½ inches) in diameter, pressing the mixture firmly together. Dust with flour, and shake off any excess. Dip the fish cakes into the egg mixture, then coat in the breadcrumbs. Place the patties on a tray and refrigerate, covered, for 30 minutes, or until firm.

Add enough oil to come one-third of the way up a large, deep frying pan. Heat over high heat. Cook the patties for 3–4 minutes each side, or until golden and heated through. Drain on paper towels. Serve with mashed sweet potato and minted peas.

HINTS: The patties can be made several hours ahead and refrigerated. You can substitute tinned tuna for salmon if desired.

macaroni cheese

This creamy, cheesy pasta meal always seems to be a firm favourite with toddlers. And the dairy it contains is good for young children, being rich in calcium needed for growing teeth and bones.

30 g (1 oz) unsalted butter

1 tablespoon plain (all-purpose) flour

250 ml (9 fl oz/1 cup) milk

60 g (2¼ oz/½ cup) grated cheese

350 g (12 oz/2¼ cups) macaroni, cooked

1 tomato, cut into wedges

Prep time: 5 minutes
Cooking time: 10 minutes
Serves 4

Melt the butter in a small saucepan. Blend in the flour and cook for 1 minute.

Remove the pan from the heat and gradually blend in the milk. Return to the heat and cook, stirring, until the sauce boils and thickens.

Reduce the heat and simmer for 3 minutes. Add the grated cheese and stir until melted. Mix the macaroni through the sauce and season with freshly ground black pepper to taste. Serve with the tomato wedges.

minestrone

Kidney beans, vegetables and pasta combine to make this a hearty and nutritious lunch for the whole family. Prepare this recipe ahead of time and keep it in the refrigerator for warming winter lunches through the week or on weekends.

2 tablespoons olive oil

1 onion, chopped

1 slice rindless bacon, finely chopped

3 carrots, halved lengthways and chopped

3 zucchini (courgettes), halved lengthways and chopped

2 celery stalks, sliced

2 potatoes, chopped

425 g (15 oz/1¾ cups) tinned diced tomatoes

300 g (10½ oz/1½ cups) tinned 4-bean mix, drained and rinsed

30 g (1 oz/⅓ cup) small pasta shapes

125 g (4½ oz/1 cup) green beans, trimmed and sliced

grated parmesan cheese

chopped parsley

Prep time: 15 minutes
Cooking time: 1 hour 20 minutes
Serves 20

Heat the oil in a large saucepan and sauté the onion and bacon until the onion is soft. Add the carrot, zucchini, celery, potatoes, tomatoes and 4-bean mix and cook, stirring, for 1 minute.

Add 2.5 litres (87 fl oz/10 cups) water to the pan and season with freshly ground black pepper. Bring to the boil, then reduce the heat and simmer, covered, for 1 hour.

Stir in the pasta and green beans and simmer for 12 minutes, or until tender. Sprinkle the minestrone with parmesan cheese and chopped parsley and serve with crusty bread.

creamy chicken & corn soup

This recipe needs only to be assembled and heated — perfect for hungry toddlers. And, it is good for protein, energy-giving carbohydrates and the B vitamin niacin.

1 litre (35 fl oz/4 cups) salt-reduced chicken stock

40 g (1½ oz/½ cup) small pasta

175 g (6 oz/1 cup) finely chopped cooked chicken (see Hint)

125 g (4½ oz/½ cup) tinned creamed corn

1 tablespoon chopped parsley

Prep time: 10 minutes
Cooking time: 20 minutes
Serves 6

Put the stock and pasta in a saucepan. Bring to the boil, then reduce the heat and simmer for 10–12 minutes, or until the pasta is very tender. Add the chicken and corn and simmer for 5 minutes.

Stir in the parsley and cool slightly. Process in a blender or food processor until smooth. Reheat to serve or refrigerate in an airtight container for up to 3 days or freeze in portion sizes.

HINT: For the cooked chicken, use skinless barbecued (grilled) chicken or chopped boneless, skinless, raw chicken breast. If using uncooked chicken, add to the stock with the pasta.

mini drumsticks

Toddlers enjoy managing their own food at meal times. This recipe will certainly let them do that — just remind them to eat the chicken and not only the sauce!

12 chicken wings, tips removed

cornflour (cornstarch), for dusting

2 egg whites, lightly beaten

175 g (6 oz/1¾ cups) dry breadcrumbs

oil, for deep-frying

TOMATO MAYONNAISE

90 ml (3 fl oz) tomato sauce (ketchup)

90 ml (3 fl oz) mayonnaise

½ teaspoon finely chopped dill or parsley

½ garlic clove, crushed

Prep time: 30 minutes

Cooking time: 5 minutes

Makes 12

Use a small sharp knife to separate the meat from the bones at the meaty end of each wing bone. Push the meat along the bone and fold it over the end of the bone to form a ball shape. Coat each piece lightly with cornflour, shaking off any excess, then dip into the egg white and coat with the breadcrumbs.

To make the tomato mayonnaise, combine the tomato sauce, mayonnaise, dill or parsley and garlic in a bowl until well combined.

Fill a saucepan two-thirds full with oil and heat to 170°C (325°F), or until a cube of bread dropped in the oil browns in 20 seconds. Cook half the drumsticks at a time in the hot oil for 2–3 minutes, or until golden and cooked through.

Drain on paper towels and serve with the tomato mayonnaise.

HINTS: Look for chicken drumettes in your supermarket to save time preparing the chicken wings. These mini drumsticks can also be served cold and make great picnic food.

quiche lorraines

These tasty little quiches make a filling meal. They are also a good source of calcium and phosphorus plus they provide vitamin A, D and the B vitamins.

2 sheets frozen ready-rolled shortcrust (pie) pastry, thawed

1 tomato, chopped

60 g (2¼ oz/½ cup) grated cheddar cheese

40 g (1½ oz/¼ cup) chopped ham or bacon

1 spring onion (scallion), finely chopped

125 ml (4 fl oz/½ cup) milk

1 egg

Prep time: 10 minutes
Cooking time: 15–20 minutes
Makes 12

Preheat the oven to 200°C (400°F/Gas 6).

Cut the pastry into 12 rounds using a 8 cm (3¼ inch) cutter. Line 12 shallow patty pans or mini muffin tins with the pastry.

Mix together the tomato, cheese, ham and spring onion and spoon the mixture into the pastry cases.

Whisk together the milk and egg. Pour enough into each pastry case to cover the filling.

Bake in the oven for 15–20 minutes, or until the filling is set and golden. Transfer to a wire rack to cool. Store in the refrigerator in an airtight container for up to 2 days.

variations: There are many different combinations of ingredients you can use to create your toddler's favourite quiche. Try semi-dried (sun-blushed) tomatoes, feta and thyme; chopped black olives, ricotta and chicken; and tinned salmon, capers and cream cheese.

fruit & vegetable salad
with creamy cottage cheese

Getting toddlers to eat vegetables can be difficult. Mix vegetables with fruit and a tasty dressing and your toddler may surprise you. Don't despair if he only eats fruit, as both fruit and vegetables are rich in fibre and have similar vitamins.

50 g (1¾ oz/⅔ cup) dried fruit (apples, prunes, apricots, sultanas/golden raisins and raisins)

1 celery stalk, diced

1 orange or 2 mandarins, segmented

mixed salad leaves

DRESSING

125 g (4½ oz/½ cup) cottage or ricotta cheese

2 tablespoons cream (whipping)

Prep time: 15 minutes + 5 minutes standing

Cooking time: Nil

Serves 4

Cut the dried apple rings into quarters and the prunes and apricots into halves. Put the apples, prunes and apricots into a bowl and cover with boiling water. Leave to stand for 5 minutes. Drain, rinse under cold water and drain again.

Combine all the fruit with the diced celery and orange segments. Put the salad leaves in a bowl and arrange the fruit and vegetable mixture on the leaves.

To make the dressing, combine the cottage or ricotta cheese with the cream. Toss the dressing through the fruit and vegetable mix and serve.

instant mini pizzas

These pizzas are a quick lunch that your toddler can help you prepare. Let him spread on the tomato sauce or sprinkle over the cheese — this makes the pizzas an even more anticipated meal.

3 English muffins, split in half

unsalted butter or olive oil

3 tablespoons chunky tomato-based pasta sauce

90 g (3¼ oz) cooked ham, bacon or chicken, cut into strips

60 g (2¼ oz/½ cup) grated cheddar cheese

Prep time: 5 minutes
Cooking time: 10 minutes
Makes 6

Preheat the oven to 240°C (475°F/Gas 8). Lightly spread the muffin halves with butter or oil. Spread the tomato-based pasta sauce over the muffins, top with the strips of ham and cover with the cheese. Place onto a baking tray and bake for 8–10 minutes, or until the muffins are crisp and the cheese has melted and turned golden.

variations: Adult and older children's servings can be garnished with pineapple pieces, avocado chunks or olives before heating in the oven. Small sized pitta bread (pockets) can be used instead of muffins.

leek, zucchini & cheese frittata

This frittata combines the vegetables in a nourishing cheese and egg base, which is a great — if slightly sneaky — way of upping your toddler's vegetable intake.

2 tablespoons olive oil

3 leeks, thinly sliced (white part only)

2 zucchini (courgettes), cut into matchstick pieces

1 garlic clove, crushed

5 eggs, lightly beaten

4 tablespoons freshly grated parmesan cheese

4 tablespoons diced Swiss cheese

Prep time: 20 minutes

Cooking time: 40 minutes

Serves 4

Heat 1 tablespoon of the olive oil in small ovenproof pan. Add the leek and cook, stirring, over low heat until slightly softened. Cover and cook the leek for 10 minutes, stirring occasionally. Add the zucchini and garlic and cook for another 10 minutes. Transfer the mixture to a bowl. Allow to cool, then season with freshly ground black pepper. Add the egg and cheeses and stir through.

Heat the remaining oil in the pan, then add the egg mixture and smooth the surface. Cook over low heat for 15 minutes, or until the frittata is almost set.

Put the pan under a preheated hot grill (broiler) for 3–5 minutes, or until the top is set and golden. Allow the frittata to stand for 5 minutes before cutting into wedges and serving. Serve with a fresh green salad.

spanish omelette

This recipe is a great way to serve up potatoes, a little known source of vitamin C. It also makes a great picnic food that can be sliced up cold into bite-sized pieces for little ones or larger wedges for grown-ups.

1 kg (2 lb 4 oz) potatoes

2 large red (Spanish) onions, coarsely chopped

50 g (1¾ oz) unsalted butter

2 tablespoons olive oil

1 garlic clove, crushed

2 tablespoons finely chopped parsley

4 eggs, lightly beaten

Prep time: 20 minutes

Cooking time: 35 minutes

Serves 4–6

Cut the potatoes into small cubes and place in a large ovenproof saucepan. Cover with water, then bring to the boil and cook, uncovered, for 3 minutes. Remove the pan from the heat and allow to stand, covered, for 8 minutes, or until the potato is just tender. Drain well.

Heat the butter and oil in a deep, non-stick frying pan over medium heat. Add the onions and garlic and cook for 8 minutes, stirring occasionally. Add the potato and cook for another 5 minutes. Remove the vegetables with a slotted spoon and transfer them to a large bowl, reserving the oil in the frying pan. Add the parsley and eggs to the potato and onion and mix until well combined.

Reheat the oil in the frying pan over high heat and add the mixture. Reduce the heat to low and cook, covered, for about 10 minutes, or until the underside of the omelette is golden. Brown the top of the omelette under a hot grill (broiler).

corn & capsicum fritters

As with spanish omelette, this recipe can also be served up cold as part of a picnic. Try serving them with your toddler's favourite dipping sauce and see how much he enjoys these vegies!

1 large red capsicum (pepper)

2–3 cobs fresh corn kernels (about 300 g/10½ oz) or 300 g (10½ oz/1½ cups) tinned corn kernels, drained

oil, for frying

2 tablespoons chopped parsley, coriander (cilantro) leaves, chives or dill

3 eggs

Prep time: 20 minutes

Cooking time: 10 minutes

Serves 4

Cut the capsicum into large pieces, discarding the seeds and membrane, then chop into small pieces. Cut the kernels from the fresh corn, using a sharp knife. Heat 2 tablespoons oil in a frying pan. Add the corn and stir over medium heat for 2 minutes. Add the capsicum and stir for another 2 minutes. Transfer the vegetables to a bowl. Add the herbs and stir well to combine. Beat the eggs in a small bowl with a little freshly ground black pepper. Stir the egg gradually into the vegetable mixture.

Heat a non-stick frying pan over medium heat. Add enough oil to cover the base. Drop large spoonfuls of the vegetable mixture into the oil, a few at a time. Cook the fritters for 1–2 minutes, or until brown. Turn and cook the other side. Drain on paper towels and keep warm while you cook the remainder.

HINTS: These fritters may be served with sour cream and a green salad for lunch or as an accompaniment to a main course. Take care as these fritters contain no flour, so they cook quickly. You want them to still be a little creamy in the middle when done.

chickpea & parsley salad

Chickpeas are popular with toddlers because of their small size and yummy nut-like texture and taste. Chickpeas make a perfect meal, as they are a great source of vegetable protein, many vitamins and minerals, especially iron.

440 g (15½ oz/2 cups) tinned chickpeas

3 large tomatoes

2 tablespoons chopped parsley

2 teaspoons chopped mint

2 tablespoons lemon juice

2½ tablespoons plain yoghurt

Prep time: 10 minutes
Cooking time: Nil
Serves 4

Drain the chickpeas, rinse under cold running water and drain again. Chop the tomatoes into 1 cm (½ inch) pieces and put in a bowl with the drained chickpeas, parsley and mint.

In a small bowl, combine the lemon juice and yoghurt. Pour over the salad and mix until well combined.

vegetable filo pouches

This recipe makes a good meal for vegetarian toddlers, being rich in vegetable protein, vitamins and minerals. You can also add a variety of other vegetables.

oil spray

8 sheets filo pastry

80 g (2¾ oz/½ cup) sesame seeds

FILLING

450 g (1 lb/3 cups) grated carrot

2 large onions, finely chopped

1 tablespoon grated fresh ginger

1 tablespoon finely chopped coriander (cilantro) leaves

225 g (8 oz/1⅓ cups) tinned water chestnuts, rinsed and sliced

1 tablespoon white miso paste

3 tablespoons tahini paste

Prep time: 45 minutes

Cooking time: 35–40 minutes

Serves 4

Preheat the oven to 180°C (350°F/ Gas 4). Spray two baking trays with oil.

To make the filling, combine the carrot, onion, ginger, coriander and 250 ml (9 fl oz/1 cup) water in a large pan. Cover and cook over low heat for 20 minutes. Uncover, cook for a further 5 minutes, or until all the liquid has evaporated. Remove from the heat and cool slightly. Stir in the water chestnuts, miso and tahini.

Place one sheet of filo pastry on a work surface. Spray lightly with oil. Top with another three pastry sheets, spraying between each layer. Cut the pastry into six even squares. Repeat the process with the remaining pastry sheets giving 12 squares in total.

Divide the filling evenly between each square, placing the filling in the centre. Bring the edges together and pinch to form a pouch. Spray the lower portion of each pouch with oil, then press in the sesame seeds. Place the pouches on the prepared trays and bake for 10–12 minutes, or until golden brown and crisp. Serve hot with sweet chilli sauce, if desired.

You can assemble the pouches up to 1 day ahead and cook just before serving. Store in the refrigerator until needed.

bubble & squeak

This is a great way of turning leftovers into a tasty and nutritious meal rich in vitamins A, C and the B group, as well as potassium.

150 g (5½ oz/1 cup) cooked potato

150 g (5½ oz/1 cup) cooked pumpkin (winter squash)

50 g (1¾ oz/1 cup) grated cabbage, cooked

50 g (1¾ oz/1 cup) small broccoli florets, cooked

4 eggs, beaten

2 chives, snipped

20 g (¾ oz) unsalted butter

Prep time: 10 minutes
Cooking time: 5 minutes
Serves 4

Put the vegetables in a bowl and mix well with the egg and chives. Melt the butter in a large frying pan and add the vegetable mixture. Cook over medium heat until the underside is golden, then cut into quarters and turn. Cook the mixture for a little longer until the surface is golden and the egg set. Alternatively, once the underside is cooked, put the frying pan under a hot grill (broiler) for 1–2 minutes, or until the top is set.

HINTS: Any combination of left-over cooked vegetables can be used. Any left-over cooked meat can also be chopped and added to the mixture.

pork & chive dumplings

Tasty little surprise packages are fun to make. The pork makes them a good source of protein and the B vitamin thiamin.

1 teaspoon vegetable oil

2 garlic cloves, crushed

2 teaspoons finely grated ginger

30 g (1 oz/1 bunch) chives, snipped

½ carrot, finely diced

200 g (7 oz) minced (ground) pork

2 tablespoons oyster sauce

3 teaspoons salt-reduced soy sauce

½ teaspoon sesame oil

1 teaspoon cornflour (cornstarch)

24 round gow gee wrappers

Prep time: 45 minutes
Cooking time: 15 minutes
Makes 24

Heat a wok over high heat, add the vegetable oil and swirl to coat the side of the wok. Add the garlic, ginger, chives and carrot, then stir-fry for 2 minutes, or until fragrant. Remove the wok from the heat and allow to cool.

Meanwhile, put the pork, oyster sauce, soy sauce, sesame oil and cornflour in a bowl and mix well. Add the vegetable mixture once it has cooled, mixing it into the pork mixture until well combined.

Put 2 teaspoons of the mixture in the centre of a gow gee wrapper. Moisten the edges with water, then fold the sides together to form a semi-circle. Pinch the edges together at 5 mm (¼ inch) intervals to form a ruffled edge. Repeat with the remaining filling and wrappers. Line a double bamboo steamer with baking paper. Put half the dumplings in a single layer in each steamer basket. Cover and steam over a wok of simmering water for 12 minutes, or until cooked through.

tomato, tuna & white bean pasta

Keep an eye on the big picture when fussiness about the evening meal happens. With a protein and carbohydrate-rich lunch like this pasta under his belt, you have less to worry about if he is too tired for a substantial dinner.

25 g (1 oz/¼ cup) small shell pasta or other small pasta

90 g (3¼ oz/⅓ cup) chunky tomato-based pasta sauce

100 g (3½ oz) tinned tuna in spring water, drained

2 tablespoons drained, rinsed tinned cannellini beans

1 teaspoon chopped drained, rinsed capers in brine

1 teaspoon finely chopped fresh basil

Prep time: 5 minutes
Cooking time: 10 minutes
Serves 2

Cook the pasta in a saucepan of boiling water until *al dente*. Drain and keep warm.

Meanwhile put the pasta sauce, tuna, beans, capers and basil in a small saucepan and stir over medium heat for 1–2 minutes, or until heated through. Toss through the pasta to serve.

tuna, caper & bean sandwich

Children like what they know, so if they only ever get to know white bread that is all they will ever want. Expose them early onto a wide range of breads. Rye, wholemeal (whole-wheat), wholegrain and pitta pockets are all good bread choices.

100 g (3½ oz) tinned tuna in spring water, drained

1 teaspoon finely chopped drained, rinsed capers in brine

3 teaspoons whole-egg mayonnaise

2 teaspoons canned cannellini beans, mashed

bread of your choice

Prep: time: 5 minutes

Cooking time: Nil

Serves 1

Put the tuna, capers, mayonnaise and cannellini beans in a bowl and mix well.

Add to the bread of your choice.

dinner

At the end of the day you may have more time to relax and have some family time together — and this can include dinner. If dinner becomes a time for constant discipline it will not be a pleasurable experience for either your toddler or you. Parents have been known to get anxious about what their children don't eat, so it is important to remember that your toddler is the only one who knows when he has had enough.

Being concerned about your toddler's eating habits is a waste of time and energy — as long as there is a variety of healthy foods presented to the toddler at meal time and he is allowed to eat as much of what he likes, he will be healthy and happy. Tiredness is also an issue at dinnertime. Don't delay dinner if it can be helped, as an overtired and emotional toddler is not likely to eat even if he is hungry.

The evening meal is the beginning of wind-down time. Your toddler may need to have his bath as soon as you have cleared away the plates, or after a short, quiet playtime. Many toddlers need a milk drink and some need a small snack as well before they have their teeth cleaned and snuggle down for the all-important bedtime story.

dinner on the go

Don't be afraid to use convenience foods to make life quicker and easier; just check the label for unwanted extras (see page 21 for more information). Try some of the following suggestions:

• Fresh or frozen fish can be easily microwaved (or steamed) to serve with a cooked frozen vegetable medley.

• Pasta with sliced ham, cooked frozen peas and grated cheese.

• Scrambled eggs and oven-fried potato chips (French fries).

• Boil up some quick-cook noodles with a frozen vegetable medley. Serve with shredded barbecued (grilled) chicken tossed through.

• Boil up the quick-cook noodles and some frozen vegetables in low-salt or home-made chicken stock. Add some shredded barbecued (grilled) chicken for quick chicken noodle soup.

• Couscous with tinned tuna or salmon.

• Macaroni cheese (see the recipe on page 87).

crispy lentil balls

Dried red lentils are excellent as they are the quickest legume to cook. Legumes are a good source of protein and vitamins, minerals and fibre.

125 g (4½ oz/½ cup) red lentils

2 bulb spring onions (scallions), chopped

1 garlic clove, crushed

½ teaspoon ground cumin

40 g (1½ oz/½ cup) fresh breadcrumbs

60 g (2¼ oz/½ cup) grated cheddar cheese

½ large zucchini (courgette), grated

70 g (2½ oz/½ cup) polenta

oil, for deep-frying

Prep time: 20 minutes
Cooking time: 15 minutes
Makes 15

Put the lentils in a saucepan and cover with water. Bring to the boil, reduce the heat to low, then cover and simmer for 10 minutes, or until the lentils are tender. Drain and rinse well under cold water.

Combine half the lentils in a food processor or blender with the spring onions and garlic. Process for 10 seconds, or until the mixture is pulpy. Transfer to a large bowl and add the remaining lentils, cumin, breadcrumbs, cheese and zucchini. Stir until combined.

Using your hands, roll level tablespoons of the mixture into balls and toss lightly in the polenta.

Heat the oil in a heavy-based pan. Gently lower half the balls into medium–hot oil. Cook for 1 minute, or until golden brown and crisp. Carefully remove from the oil with tongs or a slotted spoon and drain on paper towels. Repeat the process with the remaining balls. Serve hot with your favourite dipping sauce.

quick pasta with tomato sauce

This recipe can be reinvented many times over by using various combinations of vegetables and tuna, plus any one of a variety of pasta shapes.

1 tablespoon extra virgin olive oil

1 garlic clove, crushed

400 g (14 oz/2 cups) tinned diced Roma (plum) tomatoes

250 g (9 oz/2¾ cups) penne or farfalle (bow tie pasta)

1 tablespoon shaved parmesan cheese (optional)

Prep time: 5 minutes
Cooking time: 10 minutes
Serves 4

Heat the olive oil in a frying pan over medium heat. Cook the garlic, stirring constantly, for 30 seconds. Add the tomatoes and stir through. Reduce the heat to low and cook for a further 8–10 minutes, stirring occasionally, or until reduced.

Meanwhile, cook the pasta in a large saucepan of salted boiling water until *al dente*. Drain and return to the saucepan.

Add the cooked tomatoes to the pasta and stir them through. Spoon a small portion into a bowl and sprinkle with parmesan cheese, if desired.

variation: Stir through the tomato sauce a spoonful of mashed, drained tinned tuna (preferably in spring water, not oil or brine) and just cooked (not mushy) vegetables such as diced zucchini (courgettes), diced carrot, diced butternut pumpkin (squash), finely chopped English spinach and finely chopped flat-leaf (Italian) parsley.

simple bolognese

Most of us eat far too much salt, even young children. When preparing this dish use salt-reduced or no-added-salt tinned tomatoes, tomato paste and stock.

2 tablespoons olive oil

1 onion, finely chopped

1 garlic clove, crushed

500 g (1 lb 2 oz) minced (ground) beef

25 g (1 oz/¼ cup) chopped mushrooms

2 tablespoons tomato paste (concentrated purée)

425 g (15 oz/1¾ cups) tinned chopped tomatoes

125 ml (4 fl oz/½ cup) salt-reduced beef stock or water

1 tablespoon chopped parsley

cooked pasta of your choice

parmesan or cheddar cheese, grated

Prep time: 10 minutes

Cooking time: 30 minutes

Serves 8

Heat the oil in a heavy-based saucepan and sauté the onion and garlic until tender. Add the beef and brown well, breaking the meat up with a spoon as it cooks.

Add the chopped mushrooms to the saucepan and cook for 1 minute. Blend in the tomato paste.

Stir in the tomato, stock or water, parsley and season with freshly ground black pepper. Bring to the boil and then reduce the heat and simmer, stirring occasionally, for 20 minutes.

Toss the sauce through hot, drained pasta, such as spaghetti or linguine. Sprinkle with grated parmesan or cheddar cheese, if desired, and serve with a crisp green salad.

You can freeze the left-over sauce in portion sizes for up to 3 months.

mini shepherd's pies

The lean minced (ground) beef used in this recipe is not only easy for toddlers to chew, but will make a significant contribution to your toddler's iron intake.

1 tablespoon oil

500 g (1 lb 2 oz) minced (ground) steak

2 tablespoons plain (all-purpose) flour

250 ml (9 fl oz/1 cup) salt-reduced beef stock

2 tablespoons chopped parsley

4 potatoes, cooked

60 ml (2 fl oz/¼ cup) milk

15 g (½ oz) unsalted butter

270 g (9½ oz/2 cups) frozen mixed vegetables (peas, beans, carrots), thawed

60 g (2¼ oz/½ cup) grated cheese

25 g (1 oz/¼ cup) dried breadcrumbs

Prep time: 10 minutes

Cooking time: 30 minutes

Makes 4

Preheat the oven to 180°C (350°F/Gas 4). Heat the oil in a frying pan, add the meat and brown, breaking the meat up with a spoon as it cooks. Stir in the flour and cook, stirring, for 1 minute.

Blend in the stock, parsley and some freshly ground black pepper to taste. Simmer, stirring, for about 5 minutes, or until the mixture thickens.

Mash the potatoes well and beat until smooth with the milk and butter, adding more of each if needed.

Spoon the meat mixture into four small ramekin dishes. Top with an even amount of the mixed vegetables and spread the mashed potato over the top.

Mix together the cheese and breadcrumbs and sprinkle over each pie. Bake in the oven for 10–15 minutes, or until the tops are golden.

bean enchiladas

Make this an interactive meal — let your toddler assemble these himself — making it a fun 'hands on' meal. Don't forget to relax about the mess!

1 tablespoon light olive oil

1 onion, thinly sliced

3 garlic cloves, crushed

2 teaspoons ground cumin

125 ml (4 fl oz/½ cup) salt-reduced vegetable stock

3 tomatoes, peeled, deseeded and chopped

1 tablespoon tomato paste (concentrated purée)

850 g (1 lb 14 oz) tinned 3-bean mix

2 tablespoons chopped coriander (cilantro) leaves

8 flour tortillas

1 small avocado, chopped

125 g (4½ oz/½ cup) light sour cream

1 handful coriander (cilantro) sprigs

115 g (4 oz/2 cups) shredded lettuce

Prep time: 20 minutes
Cooking time: 25 minutes
Makes 8

Preheat the oven to 170°C (325°F/Gas 3).

Heat the oil in a deep frying pan over medium heat. Add the onion and cook for 3–4 minutes, or until just soft. Add the garlic and cook for a further 30 seconds. Add the cumin, vegetable stock, tomato and tomato paste and cook for 6–8 minutes, or until the mixture is quite thick and pulpy. Season with freshly ground black pepper.

Drain and rinse the 3-bean mix. Add the beans to the sauce and cook for 5 minutes to heat through, then add the chopped coriander.

Meanwhile, wrap the tortillas in foil and warm in the oven for 3–4 minutes.

Place a tortilla on a plate and spread with a large scoop of the bean mixture. Top with some avocado, sour cream, coriander sprigs and lettuce. Roll the enchiladas up, tucking in the ends. Cut each one in half to serve.

variations: For beef enchiladas, use only half the quantity of 3-bean mix and add 500 g (1 lb 2 oz) lean minced (ground) beef. Cook the beef with the garlic for 5–6 minutes, or until browned and cooked through, breaking up any lumps with the back of a spoon. Alternatively, for tuna enchiladas, use only half the quantity of 3-bean mix and add 425 g (15 oz) tinned tuna in brine, drained. Add the tuna with the stock.

vegetable & noodle stir-fry

Protein is an important part of a growing child's diet. Main meals for vegetarian children should always include a vegetable protein such as tofu.

50 g (1¾ oz) cellophane or egg noodles

2 teaspoons oil

1 carrot, chopped

1 celery stalk, chopped

1 small zucchini (courgette), halved lenthways, sliced

½ red capsicum (pepper), deseeded, chopped

60 g (2¼ oz/½ cup) cauliflower florets

30 g (1 oz/½ cup) broccoli florets

30 g (1 oz/¼ cup) sliced green beans

½ garlic clove, crushed

2 teaspoons salt-reduced soy sauce

Prep time: 10 minutes
Cooking time: 7 minutes
Serves 4

Place the noodles in a bowl. Cover with boiling water. Leave to stand for 1 minute, or until tender. Drain.

Heat the oil in a wok or frying pan. Add the carrot, celery, zucchini, capsicum, cauliflower, broccoli, beans and garlic and stir-fry for 4–5 minutes.

Toss the noodles through the vegetables with the soy sauce. Stir-fry for 1 minute. Serve immediately.

variation: To make this a more substantial meal, cut 200 g (7 oz) silken firm tofu into 2 cm (¾ inch) cubes or grate 200 g (7 oz) hard tofu and add to the stir-fry after cooking the vegetables. Gently toss through for 1 minute to heat through. If adding tofu, reduce the amount of vegetables.

fried rice

Using frozen foods won't compromise your family's nutrition. That's because their cooking and freezing are so quick that loss of important nutrients is small. This means more vitamins for everyone.

2 tablespoons peanut oil

2 eggs, well beaten

4 slices rindless bacon, chopped

2 teaspoons finely grated fresh ginger

1 garlic clove, crushed

6 spring onions (scallions), finely chopped

50 g (1¾ oz) red capsicum (pepper), deseeded and diced

1 teaspoon sesame oil

750 g (1 lb 10 oz/4 cups) cooked, cold, long-grain white rice (see Hint)

100 g (3½ oz/⅔ cup) frozen peas, thawed

100 g (3½ oz) cooked, chopped chicken

2 tablespoons salt-reduced soy sauce

Prep time: 25 minutes
Cooking time: 10 minutes
Serves 4

Heat a large heavy-based wok until very hot, add about 2 teaspoons of the peanut oil and swirl. Pour in the eggs and swirl to coat the side of the wok. Cook until just set. Remove from the wok, roll up and set aside. Add the remaining oil to the wok and stir-fry the bacon for 2 minutes. Add the ginger, garlic, spring onion and capsicum and stir-fry for 2 minutes.

Add the sesame oil and the rice. Stir-fry, tossing regularly, until the rice is heated through.

Cut the egg into thin strips and add to wok with the peas and the chicken. Cover and steam for 1 minute, or until everything is heated through. Stir in the soy sauce and serve.

HINT: White rice almost triples in bulk during cooking so you will need about 250 g (9 oz/1¼ cups) uncooked rice to give 750 g (1 lb 10 oz/4 cups) cooked rice. Alternatively, you can buy pre-cooked frozen rice. Ensure it is thawed before using it in this recipe.

chickpea curry

Until recently, spicy foods were considered a no no for children. But with the exception of hot spices like chilli and cayenne, there is no reason why your older baby or toddler can't experience the wonderful flavours of the world.

1 tablespoon oil

2 onions, thinly sliced

4 garlic cloves, crushed

1 teaspoon turmeric

1 teaspoon paprika

1 tablespoon ground cumin

1 tablespoon ground coriander

875 g (1 lb 15 oz/4 cups) tinned chickpeas, drained

440 g (15½ oz/1¾ cups) tinned chopped tomatoes

1 teaspoon garam masala

Prep time: 15 minutes
Cooking time: 35 minutes
Serves 4

Heat the oil in a saucepan over medium heat. Add the onion and garlic to the pan and cook, stirring, until soft.

Add the turmeric, paprika, cumin and coriander. Stir for 1 minute.

Add the chickpeas and tomato, and stir until combined. Simmer, covered, over low heat for 20 minutes, stirring occasionally. Stir in the garam masala, then simmer, covered, for another 10 minutes. Serve with steamed rice.

HINT: This curry also makes a delicious meal wrapped inside chapattis or naan bread.

chinese-style steamed fish on vegetables

Iodine is an essential nutrient for humans, both large and small, and both fish and seafood are excellent sources.

1 carrot, cut into 5 cm (2 inch) matchstick strips

½ celery stalk, cut into 5 cm (2 inch) matchstick strips

2 small spring onions (scallions), cut into 5 cm (2 inch) matchstick strips

4 mushrooms, cut into matchstick strips

4 boneless white fish fillets (about 400 g/14 oz), skin on

2 teaspoons salt-reduced soy sauce

2 teaspoons vegetable oil

Prep time: 10 minutes
Cooking time: 10 minutes
Serves 4

Put the vegetable strips on a dish that will fit in a steamer. Arrange the fish, skin side up, on the vegetables. Combine the soy sauce and vegetable oil together, then pour over the fish. Place the dish in a steamer, cover, and steam over simmering water for about 10 minutes, or until the fish flakes when tested with a fork.

HINT: To cook this dish in the oven, arrange the ingredients, as above, on a rack in an ovenproof dish and add 60–125 ml (2–4 fl oz/¼–½ cup) water. Cover and bake in a preheated 180°C (350°F/Gas 4) oven for 15 minutes, or until the fish flakes easily and is cooked through.

beef stroganoff

Stroganoff is a hearty and tasty winter meal that is a good source of protein and the minerals iron and zinc.

500 g (1 lb 2 oz) lean rump steak

2 tablespoons plain (all-purpose) flour

50 g (1¾ oz) unsalted butter

1 large onion, sliced

1 garlic clove, crushed

150 g (5½ oz) mushrooms, sliced

185 ml (6 fl oz/¾ cup) salt-reduced beef stock

1 tablespoon tomato paste (concentrated purée)

185 g (6½ oz/¾ cup) sour cream

1 tablespoon finely chopped flat-leaf (Italian) parsley

Prep time: 15 minutes
Cooking time: 15 minutes
Serves 4

Cut the beef into strips and place it and the flour in a plastic bag and toss to coat, shaking off any excess. Heat half the butter in a large frying pan and cook the onion and garlic for 2 minutes, or until golden. Add the mushrooms and cook for a further 3 minutes, then remove from the pan.

Heat the remaining butter in the same frying pan, add the beef in batches and cook over medium–high heat for 3–4 minutes, or until browned. Return the onion and mushroom mixture and all the beef to the pan with any juices.

Stir in the stock and tomato paste, bring to the boil, then reduce the heat and simmer for 2–3 minutes. Add the sour cream and half the chopped parsley and season to taste with freshly ground black pepper. Mix together well, then serve immediately with steamed rice. Garnish with the remaining parsley.

niçoise salad

Tinned tuna is a tasty, nutritious food, rich in the omega-3 fats that are such good brain food for growing children. The best choices are those packed in a good oil (such as olive, canola or sunflower oil) or spring water.

3 eggs

125 ml (4 fl oz/½ cup) olive oil

2 tablespoons white wine vinegar

1 garlic clove, crushed

325 g (11½ oz) iceberg lettuce, shredded

12 cherry tomatoes, cut into quarters

175 g (6 oz/1½ cups) baby green beans, trimmed and blanched

1 small red capsicum (pepper), deseeded and thinly sliced

1 celery stalk, cut into 5 cm (2 inch) strips

1 Lebanese (short) cucumber, deseeded, cut into 5 cm (2 inch) strips

375 g (13 oz) tinned tuna, drained and flaked

12 stoned kalamata olives, halved

4 anchovy fillets, finely chopped (optional)

Prep time: 20 minutes

Cooking time: 10 minutes

Serves 4

Put the eggs in a saucepan of cold water. Bring slowly to the boil, then reduce the heat and simmer for 10 minutes. Stir the water during the first few minutes to centre the yolk. Drain and cool under cold water, then peel and cut into quarters.

Combine the oil, vinegar and garlic in a small bowl and mix well. Put the lettuce, tomato, beans, capsicum, celery, cucumber, tuna, olives and anchovies in a large bowl. Pour over the dressing and toss well to combine. Serve the salad topped with the egg quarters.

baked chicken & leek risotto

Rice is a great food for kids to demonstrate their developing cutlery technique. It's still a messy business at this stage, so be patient!

60 g (2¼ oz) unsalted butter

1 leek, thinly sliced

2 boneless, skinless chicken breasts, finely chopped

440 g (15½ oz/2 cups) risotto rice

60 ml (2 fl oz/¼ cup) white wine

1.25 litres (44 fl oz/5 cups) salt-reduced chicken stock

35 g (1¼ oz/⅓ cup) grated parmesan cheese, plus extra, to garnish

2 tablespoons thyme, plus extra, to garnish

Prep time: 10 minutes

Cooking time: 40 minutes

Serves 4–6

Preheat the oven to 150°C (300°F/Gas 2). Heat the butter in a 5 litre (175 fl oz/20 cup) ovenproof dish with a lid over medium heat, add the leek and cook for 2 minutes, or until softened but not browned.

Add the chicken and cook, stirring, for 2–3 minutes, or until it is golden on both sides. Add the rice and stir so that it is well coated with butter. Cook for 1 minute.

Add the wine and stock and bring to the boil. Cover and place in the oven and cook for 30 minutes, stirring halfway through. Remove from the oven and stir through the parmesan and thyme leaves. Season with freshly ground black pepper. Sprinkle with the extra thyme and parmesan and serve.

lamb kofta curry

This curry is a great introduction to the tastes of India for your toddler. Just be certain the curry paste you buy is a mild one.

500 g (1 lb 2 oz) lean minced (ground) lamb

1 onion, finely chopped

1 garlic clove, crushed

1 teaspoon grated fresh ginger

1 teaspoon garam masala

1 teaspoon ground coriander

40 g (1½ oz/⅓ cup) ground almonds

steamed rice, to serve

SAUCE

2 teaspoons oil

1 onion, finely chopped

3 tablespoons mild Korma curry paste

400 g (14 oz/2 cups) tinned chopped tomatoes

125 g (4½ oz/½ cup) plain yoghurt

1 teaspoon lemon juice

Prep time: 25 minutes

Cooking time: 35 minutes

Serves 4

Combine the lamb, onion, garlic, ginger, garam masala, ground coriander and ground almonds in a bowl. Shape the mixture into walnut-sized balls with your hands.

Heat a large non-stick frying pan and cook the koftas in batches until brown on both sides — they don't have to be cooked all the way through at this stage.

Meanwhile, to make the sauce, heat the oil in a saucepan over low heat. Add the onion and cook for 6–8 minutes, or until soft and golden. Add the curry paste and cook for 1 minute, or until fragrant. Add the chopped tomato and simmer for 5 minutes. Stir in the yoghurt (1 tablespoon at a time) and the lemon juice until combined.

Place the koftas in the tomato sauce. Cook, covered, over low heat for 20 minutes. Serve over steamed rice.

pea & ham risotto

Green peas are a good source of vegetable protein and fibre. Their sweet flavour and bright colour also makes them a hit with small children.

1 tablespoon olive oil

1 celery stalk, chopped

2 tablespoons chopped flat-leaf (Italian) parsley

70 g (2½ oz) sliced ham, coarsely chopped

250 g (9 oz/1⅔ cups) peas (fresh or frozen)

125 ml (4 fl oz/½ cup) dry white wine

750 ml (26 fl oz/3 cups) salt-reduced chicken stock

60 g (2¼ oz) unsalted butter

1 onion, chopped

440 g (15½ oz/2 cups) risotto rice

35 g (1¼ oz/⅓ cup) grated parmesan cheese, plus extra shavings, to garnish

Prep time: 25 minutes

Cooking time: 45 minutes

Serves 4

Heat the oil in a frying pan, add the celery and parsley and season with freshly ground black pepper. Cook over medium heat for a few minutes to soften the celery. Add the ham and stir for 1 minute. Add the peas and half the wine, bring to the boil, then reduce the heat and simmer, uncovered, until almost all the liquid has evaporated. Set aside.

Put the stock and 750 ml (26 fl oz/3 cups) water in a separate saucepan and keep at simmering point.

Heat the butter in a large heavy-based saucepan. Add the onion and stir until softened. Add the rice and stir well. Pour in the remaining wine; allow it to bubble and evaporate. Add 125 ml (4 fl oz/½ cup) hot stock to the rice mixture. Stir constantly over low heat, with a wooden spoon, until all the stock has been absorbed. Repeat the process until all the stock has been added and the rice is creamy and tender (it may take about 20–25 minutes).

Add the pea mixture and parmesan and serve immediately. Serve with the extra parmesan shavings and some freshly ground black pepper.

HINT: If fresh peas are in season, 500 g (1 lb 2 oz) peas in the pod will yield about 250 g (9 oz/1⅔ cups) shelled peas.

toddler's chilli con carne

Research tells us that the foundations of a child's food preferences are established in the early days of eating. Don't be afraid to allow them to try new and tasty flavours; the experience will pay off when they are older.

2 teaspoons olive oil

1 large onion, chopped

1 garlic clove, crushed

2 teaspoons sweet paprika

1 teaspoon dried oregano

2 teaspoons ground cumin

750 g (1 lb 10 oz) lean minced (ground) beef

375 ml (13 fl oz/1½ cups) salt-reduced beef stock

400 g (14 oz/2 cups) tinned diced tomatoes

125 g (4½ oz/½ cup) tomato paste (concentrated purée)

300 g (10½ oz) tinned kidney beans, drained and rinsed

Prep time: 15 minutes

Cooking time: 1 hour 10 minutes

Serves 6

Heat the olive oil in a large saucepan over low heat. Add the onion and cook for 4–5 minutes, or until soft. Stir in the garlic, paprika, oregano and cumin. Increase the heat to medium, add the beef and cook for 5–8 minutes, or until just browned, breaking up any lumps with a spoon.

Reduce the heat to low, add the stock, tomato and tomato paste to the pan and cook for 35–45 minutes, stirring frequently.

Stir in the kidney beans and simmer for 10 minutes. Serve on its own or over rice.

baked chicken nuggets

This recipe is great competition for its fast food counterparts because it uses premium ingredients that are nutritious, tasty and fun to eat.

40 g (1½ oz/1⅓ cups) corn-based cereal flakes

400 g (14 oz) boneless, skinless chicken breasts

plain (all-purpose) flour, for dusting

1 egg white

Prep time: 15 minutes
Cooking time: 10 minutes
Serves 4

Preheat the oven to 200°C (400°F/Gas 6). Process the corn-based cereal flakes in a food processor, blender or in a mortar with a pestle, to make fine crumbs.

Cut the chicken breasts into bite-sized pieces. Toss in seasoned flour then in lightly beaten egg white. Roll each piece in the cereal-flake crumbs until well coated.

Lightly grease a baking tray with oil and place the nuggets on it. Bake for 10 minutes, or until golden and cooked through.

baked potato wedges

Preheat the oven to 200°C (400°F/Gas 6). Peel and slice 1.3 kg (3 lb) orange sweet potato into 6 x 2 cm (2½ x ¾ inch) wedges. Put the sweet potato wedges in a large roasting tin and toss with 2 tablespoons of olive oil. Bake for about 30 minutes, or until browned and crisp. Serve warm. Serves 4.

battered fish & chunky wedges

Full of the good fats important for brain development, fish should be a weekly part of the family menu. Firm white fish is a good choice for this recipe.

3 all-purpose potatoes

polyunsaturated oil, for deep-frying

125 g (4½ oz/1 cup) self-raising flour

1 egg, beaten

185 ml (6 fl oz/¾ cup) beer

4 white fish fillets

plain (all-purpose) flour, for dusting

125 g (4½ oz/½ cup) ready-made tartare sauce

Prep time: 15 minutes
Cooking time: 15 minutes
Serves 4

Wash the potatoes, but do not peel them. Cut into thick wedges, then dry with paper towels. Fill a large heavy-based saucepan two-thirds full with oil and heat. Gently lower the potato wedges into medium–hot oil. Cook for 4 minutes, or until tender and lightly browned. Carefully remove the wedges from the oil with a slotted spoon and drain on paper towels.

Sift the self-raising flour with some freshly ground black pepper into a large bowl and make a well in the centre. Add the egg and beer. Using a wooden spoon, stir until just combined and smooth. Dust the fish fillets in the plain flour, shaking off the excess. Add the fish fillets one at a time to the batter and toss until well coated. Remove the fish from the batter, draining off the excess batter.

Working with one piece of fish at a time, gently lower it into the medium–hot oil. Cook for 2 minutes, or until golden and crisp and cooked through. Carefully remove from the oil with a slotted spoon. Drain on paper towels, and keep warm while you cook the remainder. Return the potato wedges to the medium–hot oil. Cook for another 2 minutes, or until golden brown and crisp. Remove from the oil with a slotted spoon and drain on paper towels. Serve the wedges immediately with the fish and tartare sauce. If desired, serve with wedges of lemon and garnish with fresh dill.

HINTS: Old potatoes can be used in this recipe. Be sure to wash them well if you don't peel them. The beer can be fizzy or flat.

variation: You can serve the wedges with sour cream and sweet chilli sauce instead of tartare sauce.

chicken pilaf

Barbecued (grilled) chickens are a quick and healthy way to add protein to a meal — especially once you have removed the skin.

1 barbecued (grilled) chicken

50 g (1¾ oz) butter

1 onion, finely chopped

2 garlic cloves, crushed

300 g (10½ oz/1½ cups) basmati rice

1 tablespoon currants

2 tablespoons finely chopped dried apricots

1 teaspoon ground cinnamon

pinch of ground cardamom

750 ml (26 fl oz/3 cups) salt-reduced chicken stock

1 small handful coriander (cilantro) leaves, chopped

Prep time: 15 minutes
Cooking time: 20 minutes
Serves 4

Remove the skin and any fat from the chicken and chop the meat into even, bite-sized pieces.

Melt the butter in a large, deep frying pan over medium heat. Add the onion and garlic and cook for 2 minutes. Add the rice, currants, apricots and spices and stir until well coated.

Pour in the stock and bring to the boil. Reduce the heat to low and simmer, covered, for 15 minutes. Add a little water if it starts to dry out.

Stir through the chicken for 1–2 minutes, or until heated through, then stir through the coriander just before serving.

vegetable couscous

Couscous is a great staple for any family's pantry. It is made from durum wheat and is already pre-steamed, so it needs only a few minutes to cook.

30 g (1 oz) unsalted butter

1 onion, sliced

1 garlic clove, crushed

1 teaspoon ground cumin

2 carrots, thinly sliced

150 g (5½ oz) pumpkin (winter squash), chopped

300 g (10½ oz/1⅓ cups) tinned chickpeas, rinsed and drained

400 g (14 oz/2 cups) tinned chopped tomatoes

1 potato, chopped

1 small eggplant (aubergine), chopped

60 ml (2 fl oz/¼ cup) salt-reduced vegetable stock

150 g (5½ oz/1¼ cups) green beans, cut into short lengths

2 zucchini (courgettes), cut into chunks

COUSCOUS

250 ml (9 fl oz/1 cup) salt-reduced vegetable stock

185 g (6½ oz/1 cup) instant couscous

30 g (1 oz) unsalted butter

Prep time: 20 minutes

Cooking time: 30 minutes

Serves 4

Melt the butter in a saucepan over medium heat. Add the onion, garlic and cumin and cook for 2–3 minutes, or until softened.

Add the carrot, pumpkin, chickpeas, tomato, potato, eggplant and vegetable stock. Cook for 10 minutes, stirring occasionally. Mix in the beans and zucchini and cook for a further 5 minutes, or until the vegetables are tender.

To make the couscous, pour the stock and 60 ml (2 fl oz/¼ cup) water into a saucepan and bring to the boil. Remove from the heat and stir in the couscous and butter. Cover and stand for 5 minutes. Fluff the grains with a fork to separate. Serve the couscous topped with the vegetables, or fold the vegetables through the couscous.

fresh spring rolls

Letting children be involved in preparing and selecting their food can increase their desire to eat it. So for a fun meal, let everyone wrap their own rolls.

½ barbecued (grilled) chicken (see Hints)

50 g (1¾ oz) dried mung bean vermicelli

8 x 17 cm (6½ inch) square dried rice paper wrappers

16 Thai basil leaves

1 large handful coriander (cilantro) leaves

1 carrot, cut into short thin strips and blanched

2 tablespoons plum sauce

Prep time: 30 minutes

Cooking time: Nil

Makes 8

Remove the meat from the chicken carcass, discard the skin and finely shred. Soak the vermicelli in the hot water for 10 minutes and then drain. Dip a rice paper wrapper into warm water until it softens then place it on a clean work surface. Put one-eighth of the chicken in the centre of the wrapper and top with 2 basil leaves, a few coriander leaves, a few carrot strips and a small amount of vermicelli. Spoon a little plum sauce over the top.

Press the filling down to flatten it a little, then fold in the two sides and roll it up tightly like a parcel. Lay the roll seam side down, on a serving plate and sprinkle with a little water. Cover with a damp tea towel (dish towel) and repeat the process with the remaining ingredients. Serve with your favourite dipping sauce or a little extra plum sauce.

HINTS: When buying the barbecued (grilled) chicken, ask for two breast quarters. Rice paper wrappers must be kept moist or they become brittle. If you leave the spring rolls for any length of time and they start to dry out, sprinkle cold water on them.

chicken & mushroom spirals

Recipes that can be prepared ahead, like this one, are a blessing when dealing with small children. As every parent knows, timing is everything.

1 tablespoon olive oil

20 g (¾ oz) unsalted butter

2 slices rindless bacon, cut into thin strips

2 garlic cloves, crushed

250 g (9 oz) mushrooms, sliced

125 ml (4 fl oz/½ cup) dry white wine

185 ml (6 fl oz/¾ cup) cream (whipping)

4 spring onions (scallions), chopped

1 tablespoon plain (all-purpose) flour

2 large cooked boneless, skinless chicken breasts, chopped

500 g (1 lb 2 oz) spiral pasta

50 g (1¾ oz/½ cup) grated parmesan cheese

Prep time: 10 minutes
Cooking time: 20 minutes
Serves 4

Heat the oil and butter in a large, deep frying pan over medium heat. Add the bacon, garlic and mushrooms and cook for 2 minutes.

Add the wine and cook until the liquid has reduced by half. Add the cream and spring onions, and bring to the boil. Combine the flour and 60 ml (2 fl oz/¼ cup) water until smooth. Add to the pan and stir over the heat until the mixture boils and thickens. Reduce the heat and simmer for 1 minute. Fold through the chicken and cook for 1 minute to heat through. Season with freshly ground black pepper.

Cook the pasta in a large saucepan of boiling water, following the packet directions. Drain. Add the pasta to the sauce and toss to mix. Sprinkle with parmesan. Serve with a green salad.

HINTS: Scrub cutting boards thoroughly in hot soapy water to remove all traces of chicken. Make sure wooden boards have a smooth surface. Rough, cracked surfaces can contain bacteria. This sauce can be made 1 day in advance. Reheat the sauce and cook the pasta until al dente, just before serving.

veal schnitzel

Crumb the veal while your toddler is sleeping and this becomes another quick and nutritious meal to serve up with his favourite vegetables.

4 thin veal steaks

100 g (3⅓ oz/1 cup) dry breadcrumbs

½ teaspoon dried basil (optional)

25 g (1 oz/¼ cup) grated parmesan cheese

plain (all-purpose) flour, for coating

1 egg, lightly beaten

1 tablespoon milk

oilve oil, for frying

Prep time: 20 minutes + 30 minutes chilling

Cooking time: 5 minutes

Serves 4

Trim the meat of any excess fat. Place the veal between sheets of plastic wrap and flatten with a meat mallet or rolling pin until 3 mm (⅛ inch) thick. Nick the edges to prevent curling. Combine the breadcrumbs, basil, if using, and parmesan on a sheet of baking paper.

Coat the veal steaks in flour, shaking off the excess. Combine the beaten egg and milk. Working with one at a time, dip the steaks into the egg mixture, then coat with the breadcrumb mixture. Lightly shake off the excess. Refrigerate for 30 minutes to firm the coating.

Heat the oil in a large frying pan and cook the veal steaks over medium heat for 2–3 minutes on each side, or until golden and cooked through. Drain on paper towels and serve.

gado gado

Rich in protein from the eggs, beta-carotene from the carrots and sweet potato and vitamin C from the cabbage, gado gado is a nutritious adventure for toddlers.

3 eggs

2 orange sweet potatoes, cut into 1 cm (½ inch) thick slices

2 potatoes, halved and cut into 1 cm (½ inch) thick slices

125 g (4½ oz) baby (pattypan) squash, halved

250 g (9 oz) cabbage, cut into large pieces

2 carrots, cut into 1 cm (½ inch) thick strips

1 cucumber

125 g (4½ oz/1⅓ cups) fresh bean sprouts, tails removed

Prep time: 20 minutes
Cooking time: 20 minutes
Serves 6

Put the eggs in a saucepan with cold water to cover. Bring to the boil, reduce to a simmer and cook for 10 minutes; stir the water during the first few minutes to centre the yolk. Drain and cool under cold water.

Bring a large saucepan of water to the boil. Blanch each type of vegetable separately in the boiling water; they must be firm and not overcooked. The sweet potato and potato will each need about 8–10 minutes; the squash 1 minute; the carrots 2 minutes; and the cabbage 2 minutes. Remove the vegetables from the water with a slotted spoon and plunge into a bowl of iced water to stop the cooking process and set the colour.

Drain the vegetables from the iced water and dry briefly on paper towels. Shell the boiled eggs and cut them into quarters. Slice the cucumber into thin strips. Arrange all the vegetables in decorative groups and garnish with the sliced eggs and bean sprouts. Top with peanut sauce (see below).

peanut sauce

Heat 1 tablespoon oil in a saucepan and cook 1 finely chopped small onion for 5 minutes over low heat, or until soft and lightly golden. Add 125 g (4½ oz/½ cup) smooth peanut butter, 185 ml (6 fl oz/¾ cup) coconut milk, 1 tablespoon lemon juice, 1 tablespoon salt-reduced dark soy sauce and 60 ml (2 fl oz/¼ cup) water, and stir well. Bring to the boil, stirring constantly, then reduce the heat and simmer for 5 minutes, or until the sauce has reduced and thickened.

lamb cutlets with potato & pea mash

Meat on the bone is tender, tasty and particularly popular with toddlers. Finely chop the meat for those reluctant chewers but leave some meat remaining on the bone for them to gnaw off.

MASH

100 g (3½ oz) small new potatoes, chopped

½ small garlic clove, chopped

40 g (1½ oz/¼ cup) frozen peas

5 g (⅛ oz) unsalted butter

1 tablespoon milk

2 teaspoons oil

2 French trimmed lamb cutlets

Prep time: 5 minutes

Cooking time: 5 minutes

Serves 1

Bring a small saucepan of water to the boil and cook the potato and garlic for 4 minutes. Add the peas and cook for a further 1 minute or until the potato is soft. Drain, return to the saucepan and mash with the butter. Stir through the milk and keep warm.

Meanwhile, heat the oil in a small frying pan and cook the cutlets over medium heat for 2 minutes. Turn and cook for a further 1 minute, or until done to your liking. Serve with the mash.

HINT: Some toddlers will use the cutlet bone as a handle and chew the meat away from the bone. For smaller toddlers remove the meat from the bone, chop into small pieces and stir through the mash.

chicken & vegetable star pasta

Quick pasta meals like this are a good choice when hungry tummies are rumbling. It is also good for beta-carotene, protein and energy-giving carbohydrates.

2 tablespoons small star pasta or other small pasta

2 teaspoons oil

½ small onion, finely chopped

½ small garlic clove, crushed

60 g (2¼ oz) minced (ground) chicken

2 tablespoons grated zucchini (courgette)

2 tablespoons grated carrot

1½ tablespoons ricotta cheese

Prep time: 5 minutes
Cooking time: 10 minutes
Serves 2

Cook the pasta in boiling water for 5 minutes or until *al dente*. Drain and keep warm.

Heat the oil in a small saucepan and cook the onion and garlic over medium heat for 2–3 minutes, or until soft. Add the chicken and cook for 2–3 minutes, breaking up any lumps with a spoon. Add the zucchini and carrot and cook for 2 minutes, or until softened. Stir through the ricotta and pasta until well combined and warmed through.

spinach & ricotta cannelloni

Make an activity of meal preparation to keep toddlers happily occupied — let them stir the filling, peel the onion or wash the spinach.

FILLING

20 g (¾ oz) unsalted butter

1 small onion, finely chopped

2 garlic cloves, crushed

3 bunches English spinach

300 g (10½ oz/1¼ cups) ricotta

1 tablespoon oregano

SAUCE

1 tablespoon olive oil

1 small onion, finely chopped

2 garlic cloves, crushed

440 g (15½ oz/1¾ cups) tinned peeled whole tomatoes

125 ml (4 fl oz/½ cup) tomato-based pasta sauce

1 teaspoon dried oregano

2 teaspoons Dijon mustard

1 tablespoon balsamic vinegar

1 teaspoon sugar

375 g (13 oz) fresh lasagne

70 g (2½ oz/½ cup) grated mozzarella cheese

50 g (1¾ oz/½ cup) finely grated parmesan cheese

Prep time: 45 minutes

Cooking time: 1 hour

Serves 4

Preheat the oven to 180°C (350°F/Gas 4).

To make the filling, melt the butter in a pan and add the onion and garlic. Cook for 3–5 minutes, or until the onion softens. Trim and finely shred the spinach, add it to the pan and cook for 5 minutes, or until wilted and the moisture has evaporated. Remove from the heat. Once cooled, combine with the ricotta and oregano in a food processor or blender. Process until smooth and season.

To make the sauce, heat the oil in a pan, add the onion and garlic and cook over low heat for 8–10 minutes. Add the rest of the sauce ingredients. Bring to the boil, then reduce the heat and simmer for 10–15 minutes, or until the sauce thickens.

Cut the lasagne sheets into twelve 12 cm (4½ inch) squares. Lightly grease a 2 litre (70 fl oz/8 cup) ovenproof dish. Spread one-third of the sauce over the base, then spoon 1½ tablespoons of the spinach mixture onto one side of each square of lasagne, leaving a 5 mm (¼ inch) border. Roll up the pasta to cover the filling and place in the dish seam side down. Repeat with all the sheets, spacing the cannelloni evenly in the dish. Spoon over the remaining sauce and sprinkle with the cheeses. Bake for 30–35 minutes, or until the cheese is bubbling and golden. Allow to stand for 5 minutes before serving.

sausages with parsnip & cauliflower purée

Sausages often get a bad rap but kids always seem to love them. Try to shop for sausages which contain lean meat, little salt and few, if any, additives.

PUREE

125 ml (4 fl oz/½ cup) salt-reduced vegetable or chicken stock

50 g (1¾ oz) parsnip, chopped

50 g (1¾ oz) cauliflower, cut into small florets

½ small garlic clove, chopped

2 teaspoons oil

2 chipolata sausages, or other small sausages

Prep time: 5 minutes

Cooking time: 5 minutes

Serves 1

To make the purée, put the stock in a small saucepan and bring to the boil. Add the parsnip, cauliflower and garlic, cover and cook for 5 minutes, or until the vegetables are soft. Drain, reserving the liquid. Place the vegetables in a small food processor and process until smooth, adding enough liquid to achieve the required consistency. Keep warm.

Meanwhile, heat the oil in a small frying pan and cook the sausages over medium heat for 3–4 minutes, turning until cooked through.

Cut the sausages into slices and serve as finger food with the mash or chop up and stir through the mash to be spoon fed.

potato & egg salad

This delicious salad is an excellent source of protein, fibre and carbohydrate, and also provides useful amounts of most vitamins and minerals. You can also prepare this salad ahead of time and store in the refrigerator.

1 egg

1 new potato, cut into 1.5 cm (⅝ inch) cubes

1½ tablespoons frozen peas, thawed

1 tablespoon drained tinned corn kernels

2 teaspoons finely diced celery

½ teaspoon finely chopped parsley

½ small garlic clove, crushed (optional)

2 teaspoons whole-egg mayonnaise

Prep time: 10 minutes
Cooking time: 10 minutes
Serves 1

Put the egg in a small saucepan of water and bring to the boil. Cook for 2 minutes, then add the potato and cook for a further 8 minutes. Drain. Rinse the egg under cold running water, peel and roughly chop.

Put the potato, egg, peas, corn, celery, parsley, garlic and mayonnaise in a small bowl and mix to combine. Season to taste.

osso buco

Take advantage of daytime sleeps to get this recipe on the stove — come dinnertime, all that needs to be done is the accompaniments. Osso buco is rich in protein, vitamins and the minerals iron and zinc.

8 large veal shanks, sliced

plain (all-purpose) flour, for dusting

20 g (¾ oz) unsalted butter

60 ml (2 fl oz/¼ cup) oil

1 onion, finely chopped

1 carrot, finely diced

1 celery stalk, finely diced

1 bay leaf

2 garlic cloves, crushed

250 ml (9 fl oz/1 cup) red wine (optional)

1 litre (35 fl oz/4 cups) salt-reduced beef stock

400 g (14 oz/2 cups) tinned diced tomatoes

Prep time: 20 minutes

Cooking time: 2 hours 50 minutes

Serves 6

Lightly dust the veal shanks in flour, shaking off the excess. Heat the butter and 2 tablespoons of the oil in a large heavy-based saucepan or casserole dish over high heat. Add the veal and cook in two batches for 2–3 minutes on each side, or until golden. Remove from the pan.

Reduce the heat to low and add the remaining oil to the pan. Heat, then add the onion, carrot, celery and bay leaf and cook over low heat for about 10 minutes, or until softened and golden. Add the garlic and wine, if using, increase the heat and boil for 3–4 minutes.

Add the stock and tomato and return the veal to the saucepan. Bring to the boil, then reduce the heat and simmer for 2½ hours, or until the meat is very tender.

Serve with mashed potato or steamed rice.

HINT: This recipe works with other less expensive cuts such as lamb forequarter pieces. If you are not using red wine, add an extra 250 ml (9 fl oz/1 cup) stock.

Kids of all ages run on snacks but never is it so important for the snacks to be healthy as when the kids are little. Think mini-meal and not plastic-wrapped convenience. Fresh and healthy means you will be ensuring good nutrition and good habits for their future. These snacks don't have to mean hours of preparation either; more often than not a well stocked fruit bowl or vegetable crisper is all that is needed.

simple snacks & drinks

snack time

Little children need to eat little and often. Your toddler needs to eat at least five times a day, so the snacks you give her need to complement the other food she is eating.

With a little bit of planning when you shop you can have some simple, quick snacks on hand for those in-between times. You can also put some snacks into little storage pots or resealable plastic bags and use them in an emergency or when your child goes to kindergarten or childcare.

tips for healthy snacking:

• Offer snacks at regular times each day – just as is done at childcare. Make sure it is at least 1 hour before a meal.

• Serve snacks in the kitchen, or sit down together outside. Try not to serve them in front of the television.

• Aim for at least two different types of food in each snack. For example bread sticks and a piece of cheese, a muffin and a few grapes, or raw vegetables with a dip.

• Be a good role model. Don't eat something in front of your child that you would not give to her, for example a chocolate biscuit (cookie).

• Think creatively. You may have a piece of healthy home-made pizza left over from last night, or a hard-boiled egg in the refrigerator.

• Travel with snacks. When you go out always take at least two snacks and a drink with you. Pop them in an insulated bag for safe keeping.

• Include protein for an extra-satisfying snack. Cheese, peanut butter and egg are all good sources.

• Think about your child's teeth. Encourage your child to have a drink of water after a snack.

• Relax. If she occasionally has a packet of chips (crisps) or chocolate it's no big deal so long as they don't become an everyday thing.

vegetables with tzatziki dip

Snacks for toddlers don't need to be complicated, but they do need to be made from fresh healthy foods. This snack certainly fits the bill.

DIP

2 Lebanese (short) cucumbers, deseeded and grated

185 g (6½ oz/¾ cup) plain yoghurt

2 garlic cloves, crushed

1 teaspoon lemon juice

1 teaspoon chopped dill

½ teaspoon chopped mint

selection of sliced blanched vegetables (see Hints), to serve

Prep time: 15 minutes

Cooking time: Nil

Serves 4

Wrap the grated cucumber in a tea towel (dish towel) and squeeze out the excess water.

Mix the cucumber with the remaining ingredients and serve with the sliced vegetables. If you like, offer some poppadoms or chunks of bread.

HINTS: Choose your favourite vegetables or a selection which might include cauliflower, baby corn, broccoli, spring onion (scallion), beans, snow peas (mangetout), mushrooms, celery, zucchini (courgette), cucumber, capsicum (pepper), carrot and cherry tomatoes. Some vegetables (celery, cucumber, zucchini/courgette, carrot) will be extra crisp if refrigerated in a bowl of iced water before use. Other vegetables may soften if left in water.

sour cream dip

Combine 250 g (9 oz/1 cup) sour cream with ¼ teaspoon snipped dill, a pinch of sugar and 2 tablespoons thickened (whipping) cream. Pour into a small dish and place in the centre of a serving platter. Surround with a selection of blanched vegetables.

crunchy cheese bites

For healthy pastry snacks choose pastry that is made from good oils such as canola, olive or the polyunsaturated fats like sunflower or safflower. This makes these cheese bites a good snack for parents too.

250 g (9 oz/2 cups) grated cheddar cheese

125 g (4½ oz) feta cheese, crumbled

60 g (2¼ oz/¼ cup) ricotta cheese

30 g (1 oz/¼ cup) chopped spring onions (scallions)

1 small tomato, chopped

1 egg, beaten

4 sheets ready-rolled puff pastry

beaten egg, to brush

milk, to brush

Prep time: 15 minutes
Cooking time: 15 minutes
Makes about 20

Preheat the oven to 220°C (425°F/Gas 7). Combine the cheeses, spring onion, tomato and egg in a bowl. Season with freshly ground black pepper.

Cut the pastry into rounds using a 10 cm (4 inch) cutter. Place heaped teaspoons of the mixture onto one half of each round.

Fold the pastry over the filling to make semi-circles, brush the edges between the pastry with a little of the beaten egg and press the edges together firmly with a fork to seal.

Place on a baking tray and brush with a little milk. Bake in the oven for 10–15 minutes, or until puffed and golden. Allow the pastries to cool for at least 10 minutes before serving.

cheesy pinwheels

Alternatively, divide the cheese mixture from the recipe above into two and spread over 2 sheets of puff pastry, leaving a 1 cm (½ inch) border. Roll up firmly and trim the ends. Cut into 1.5 cm (⅝ inch) lengths and place on a lined baking tray. Bake for about 12–15 minutes, or until the pastry is puffed and golden. Cool for 5 minutes before removing from the tray, then serve warm. Makes 24.

pitta bread with hummus

Young toddlers will probably prefer to dip their fingers into the hummus. But as they get older, toddlers will enjoy dipping with pieces of pitta bread or vegetable sticks. Vegetable chips are also a great accompaniment to hummus.

220 g (7¾ oz/1 cup) dried chickpeas

80 ml (2½ fl oz/⅓ cup) olive oil

3–4 tablespoons lemon juice

2 garlic cloves, crushed

2 tablespoons tahini

1 tablespoon ground cumin

pitta bread, to serve

Prep time: 15 minutes
+ 8 hours soaking

Cooking time: 1 hour

Serves 4

Soak the chickpeas in water for 8 hours or overnight. Drain. Put in a saucepan, cover with cold water, bring to the boil and cook for around 50–60 minutes. Drain, reserving 185–250 ml (6–9 fl oz/¾–1 cup) of the cooking liquid.

Place the chickpeas in a food processor with the oil, lemon juice, garlic, tahini and cumin. Blend well until the mixture begins to look thick and creamy. With the motor running, gradually add the reserved cooking liquid until the mixture reaches the desired consistency. Serve with pitta bread, raw or blanched vegetables or vegetable chips (see below) or use as a spread for sandwiches.

vegetable chips

Preheat the oven to 180°C (350°F/Gas 4). Peel the skin of 500 g (1 lb 2 oz) each orange sweet potato, beetroot (beet) and parsnip. Run a vegetable peeler along the length of the sweet potato and beetroot to make thin ribbons. Cut the parsnip into thin slices. Fill a deep heavy-based saucepan one-third full of oil and heat to 190°C (375°F), or until a cube of bread dropped into the oil browns in 10 seconds. Cook the vegetables in batches for about 30 seconds, or until golden and crisp, turning with tongs if necessary. Drain on crumpled paper towels. Keep warm on a baking tray in the oven and cook the remaining chips (fries). Serve with the hummus.

muesli crunch biscuits

Because of their small tummies and high nutrition needs every food in a toddler's diet needs to count — including snacks. These biscuits hit the spot, combining the goodness of rolled oats and dried fruits.

125 g (4½ oz) unsalted butter

90 g (3¼ oz/½ cup) soft brown sugar

a few drops natural vanilla extract

1 egg

75 g (2¾ oz/½ cup) wholemeal (whole-wheat) self-raising flour

400 g (14 oz/3 cups) untoasted muesli (granola), without nuts

125 g (4½ oz/⅔ cup) chopped dried apricots

Prep time: 20 minutes
Cooking time: 15 minutes
Makes 24

Preheat the oven to 190°C (375°F/Gas 5). Lightly grease two large baking trays.

Cream the butter and sugar together, then add the vanilla and egg and beat well. Sift in the flour, add the muesli and stir in the chopped apricots. Shape the biscuit (cookie) mixture into balls, then place on the prepared trays and flatten lightly with a fork. Bake for about 10–12 minutes, or until lightly golden. Cool on a wire cooling rack, then store in an airtight container.

variation: Use corn-based cereal flakes or bran flakes instead of some of the muesli, and mix the chopped apricots with other dried fruits.

easy berry muffins

These delicious muffins couldn't be easier to make, so offer a great opportunity for eager toddlers to lend a hand in the kitchen.

250 g (9 oz/1 cup) plain yoghurt

100 g (3½ oz/1 cup) rolled (porridge) oats

60 ml (2 fl oz/¼ cup) oil

80 g (2¾ oz/⅓ cup) caster (superfine) sugar

1 egg

125 g (4½ oz/1 cup) self-raising flour, sifted

3 teaspoons baking powder

300 g (10½ oz/1⅓ cups) mixed frozen berries, thawed

Prep time: 10 minutes
Cooking time: 25 minutes
Makes 16 muffins

Preheat the oven to 180°C (350°F/Gas 4). Place paper cases into 16 muffin holes. Mix together the yoghurt, oats, oil, caster sugar and egg. Gently stir in the sifted flour and baking powder with the fruit.

Spoon the mixture into paper cases in the muffin tin and bake for 20–25 minutes or until golden brown and a skewer comes out clean when inserted into the centre.

HINT: Muffins can be made with any number of delicious fruit-based combinations. Aside from berry combinations, apple, sultanas (golden raisins) and cinnamon, or pear and date can make a tasty alternative.

corn & ham muffins

Muffins are a good way to get extra fruit or vegies into your toddler's diet. Sweet corn is a good source of beta-carotene and B vitamins — especially niacin.

oil, for brushing

125 g (4½ oz/1 cup) self-raising flour

40 g (1½ oz/¼ cup) chopped ham

60 g (2¼ oz/⅓ cup) tinned corn kernels, drained

¼ red capsicum (pepper), deseeded and finely chopped

2 teapoons chopped parsley

60 g (2¼ oz) unsalted butter, melted

125 ml (4 fl oz/½ cup) milk

1 egg

1 tablespoon sesame seeds

Prep time: 10 minutes
Cooking time: 20 minutes
Makes 24

Preheat the oven to 210°C (415°C/Gas 6–7). Brush two 12-hole mini muffin tins with oil. Sift the flour into a large bowl. Add the ham, corn, capsicum and parsley and stir to combine.

In a small bowl, combine the melted butter, milk and egg. Make a well in the centre of the flour mixture and add the milk mixture. Mix the dough lightly with a fork or rubber spatula until the ingredients are just combined. (Do not overmix; the batter should be quite lumpy.)

Spoon the mixture into the prepared tins. Sprinkle the muffins with the sesame seeds. Bake the muffins for 15–20 minutes, or until golden. Cool on a wire rack.

variations: If you prefer, use wholemeal (whole-wheat) flour instead of white flour. A little extra milk may be required as wholemeal flour absorbs more liquid. Try adding other vegetables instead of the corn and capsicum, such as half a grated carrot and zucchini (courgette). For a vegetarian option, replace the ham with chopped, semi-dried (sun-blushed) tomatoes.

junior pikelets

A universal favourite, these carbohydrate-rich pikelets (griddle cakes) are bite-sized energy food for small children on the go.

125 g (4½ oz/1 cup) self-raising flour

¼ teaspoon bicarbonate of soda (baking soda)

2 tablespoons caster (superfine) sugar

125 ml (4 fl oz/½ cup) milk

1 egg

2 teaspoons oil, plus extra for greasing

60 g (2¼ oz/½ cup) sultanas (golden raisins)

Prep time: 10 minutes
Cooking time: 15 minutes
Makes 24

Sift the flour and bicarbonate of soda together into a bowl. Stir in the sugar. In a small bowl, combine the milk, egg and oil. Make a well in the centre and whisk in the milk mixture to make a smooth batter. Add the sultanas to the mixture and mix well.

Lightly grease and heat a frying pan with oil. Drop teaspoons of the batter into the pan and cook until bubbles form. Turn and cook the other side of the pikelet (griddle cake) until golden. Cool on a wire rack, then serve warm with butter. These pikelets be frozen, layered between sheets of baking paper, for up to 1 month.

banana smoothie

A nutritious drink like this is often all a toddler needs as a snack. Especially when made with bananas, which have twice the vitamin C of apples and pears.

1 banana

1 tablespoon plain yoghurt

1 teaspoon honey (optional, only for children over 12 months)

250 ml (9 fl oz/1 cup) milk

Prep time: 5 minutes

Cooking time: Nil

Serves 2

Peel the banana and roughly chop. Place in a blender with the yoghurt, honey, if using, and milk and blend until smooth, thick and creamy.

Pour into two glasses and serve.

HINT: The secret to the success of this smoothie is the preparation of the banana. The smoothie will be thicker and, as a result, more delicious if the banana is peeled and frozen for at least half an hour before it is used.

variation: Mangoes also work well in this smoothie, either as an accompaniment or added to the smoothie with the banana. Alternatively, you can add tinned peaches or apricots along with the banana for a delightful tangy taste.

vanilla milkshake

For the reluctant milk drinker there is nothing wrong with adding flavouring to encourage enjoyment. Research has shown that children who drink milk are often taller and have healthier bones and body weights than those who don't.

500 ml (17 fl oz/ 2 cups) milk, well chilled

1 teaspoon natural vanilla extract

sugar, to taste

Prep time: 5 minutes
Cooking time: Nil
Serves 2

Put the milk, vanilla extract and sugar into a large bowl or blender and whisk or blend for 20 seconds to combine.

Pour into two long cups and serve with straws for fun.

HINT: Milkshakes can be made using an electric blender, a whisk or a hand-held beater, or the ingredients can be placed in a tall sealed container and shaken until frothy.

variation: Your toddler's favourite fruit can be added to this recipe but it will need to be first processed in a blender to make it smooth.

berry froth

Berries are a good source of vitamin C and, for those with lots of seeds like raspberries, also a great source of fibre.

220 g (7¾ oz/1 cup) fresh or frozen mixed berries
500 ml (17 fl oz/2 cups) milk
2 ice cubes
sugar, to taste

Put the mixed berries, milk and ice cubes in a blender and blend until smooth. Add sugar and blend again until combined.

Pour into two long cups and serve with straws for fun.

Prep time: 5 minutes
Cooking time: Nil
Serves 2

fresh fruit slushy

This recipe for toddlers is a much healthier alternative to fruit juice as it has around four times the fibre of most commercial juices.

90 g (3¼ oz) fresh pineapple, peeled and cored
1 banana
3 kiwi fruit, sliced
250 ml (9 fl oz/1 cup) tropical fruit juice
2 ice cubes

Cut the pineapple and banana into chunks. Put in a blender with the kiwi fruit, fruit juice and ice cubes and blend until smooth.

Pour into four cups and serve.

Prep time: 10 minutes
Cooking time: Nil
Serves 4

Sweets are often a forbidden zone in the world of children's food. However, they don't necessarily deserve their bad reputation. Desserts aren't essential for young children but when you have time to prepare them, any of the fruit-based recipes in this chapter would complement a meal well. The recipes would also make a good snack but never use them as a bribe for the vegetables to be eaten!

something sweet

baked raisin apples

Tough, cooked skin will probably need to be removed for younger toddlers, but this fruit dessert makes a tasty and fibre-rich end to a meal.

4 cooking apples

80 g (2¾ oz/⅓ cup) soft brown sugar

1½ tablespoons chopped raisins

½ teaspoon ground cinnamon (optional)

20 g (¾ oz) unsalted butter

yoghurt or ricotta cream (see recipe below), to serve

Prep time: 10 minutes

Cooking time: 35 minutes

Serves 4

Preheat the oven to 220°C (425°F/Gas 7). Core the apples and score the skin around the middle. Combine the sugar, raisins and cinnamon. Place each apple on a piece of heavy-duty foil and stuff it with the filling. Spread a little butter over the top of each apple, then wrap the foil securely around the apples. Bake for about 35 minutes, or until cooked. Serve with yoghurt or ricotta cream.

HINT: These apples can also be baked on a covered barbecue.

ricotta cream

Whip equal quantities of ricotta cheese and Greek-style plain yoghurt together and sweeten slightly with soft brown sugar. You can use this as a dip for fresh or tinned fruits, as a creamy filling for pastries or in place of whipped cream.

bread & butter pudding

This is a wholesome sweet treat based upon bread, milk, eggs and fruit. It can be made even more nutritious if you use fibre-rich bread instead of white.

butter, for greasing

6 slices wholemeal (whole-wheat) bread

750 ml (26 fl oz/3 cups) milk

¼ teaspoon grated lemon zest

110 g (3¾ oz/½ cup) sugar

4 eggs

125 g (4½ oz/¾ cup) mixed dried fruits (sultanas/golden raisins, raisins, chopped dried apricots, currants, mixed peel/ mixed candied citrus peel)

Prep time: 20 minutes + 10 minutes standing

Cooking time: 35 minutes

Serves 4

Preheat the oven to 180°C (350°F/Gas 4). Grease an ovenproof dish. Remove the crusts and thickly butter the bread.

Heat the milk in a saucepan and add the lemon zest. Bring to the boil, then cover and remove from the heat, leaving to infuse for 10 minutes. Beat the sugar and eggs together, then strain the milk over the eggs and mix well.

Scatter half the dried fruit over the bottom of the prepared dish and arrange the bread, buttered sides down, on top. Pour in half the custard, then repeat with the remaining fruit, bread and custard. Place the dish in a baking tin and add enough water to fill halfway up the outside of the dish. Bake for 35 minutes.

apple sago pudding

Sago is made from the dried starchy granules found in the pith of Indonesian palm trees. Its unique texture will likely spark the interest of young eaters.

80 g (2¾ oz/⅓ cup) caster (superfine) sugar

100 g (3½ oz/½ cup) sago

600 ml (21 fl oz) milk

40 g (1½ oz/⅓ cup) sultanas (golden raisins)

1 teaspoon natural vanilla extract

pinch of ground nutmeg

¼ teaspoon ground cinnamon

2 eggs, lightly beaten

3 small ripe apples (about 250 g/9 oz), peeled, cored and very thinly sliced

1 tablespoon soft brown sugar

Prep time: 15 minutes
Cooking time: 50 minutes
Serves 4

Preheat the oven to 180°C (350°F/Gas 4). Grease a 1.5 litre (52 fl oz/6 cup) ceramic soufflé dish. Place the sugar, sago, milk and sultanas in a saucepan. Heat the mixture, stirring often. Bring to the boil, then reduce the heat and simmer for 5 minutes.

Stir in the vanilla extract, nutmeg, cinnamon, egg and the apple slices, then pour into the prepared dish. Sprinkle with the brown sugar and bake for 45 minutes, or until set and golden brown.

choc-banana bites

Besides being a good source of vitamin C and energy-giving carbohydrates, bananas are a great easy-to-handle fruit for kids.

5 wooden iceblock (popsicle/ice lolly) sticks, cut in half

3 large bananas, peeled and cut into 3 pieces

125 g (4½ oz) dark cooking chocolate, chopped

Prep time: 10 minutes + 4 hours freezing
Cooking time: 5 minutes
Makes 9

Line a 33 x 28 cm (13 x 11¼ inch) baking tray with foil. Carefully push a half-stick into each piece of banana. Place on the prepared tray and freeze for 2 hours or until firm.

Put the chocolate in a small heatproof bowl. Stand the bowl over a saucepan of simmering water and stir until the chocolate has melted and is smooth.

Working with one banana piece at a time, dip each piece into the hot chocolate mixture, turning to fully coat. Drain off any excess chocolate. Place the banana pieces on the prepared tray. Refrigerate until the chocolate has set, then wrap in plastic wrap and place in the freezer for at least 2 hours to harden. Serve frozen.

frozen fruit yoghurt

This sweet snack is a good source of calcium and fibre — try freezing some into iceblock (popsicle/ice lolly) moulds for healthy treats on hot days.

60 g (2¼ oz/½ cup) fresh fruit salad (pineapple, apple, banana, peach, apricot, orange)

125 g (4½ oz/½ cup) plain yoghurt

Put the fruit salad in a blender, add the yoghurt and purée. Pour the mixture into a freezer tray and freeze.

For a lighter texture, remove the mixture from the freezer, return to the blender and whip, then refreeze. Repeat once more.

Prep time: 5 minutes + 4 hours freezing

Cooking time: Nil

Serves 2

strawberry parfait

Jelly and ice cream — what more could a child want, except perhaps some strawberries! This is a sweet that is perfect for an occasional extra.

85 g (3 oz) strawberry-flavoured jelly crystals (gelatine dessert)

250 g (9 oz) strawberries, hulled

500 g (1 lb 2 oz) vanilla ice cream

Put the jelly crystals (gelatine dessert) in a heatproof bowl and pour over 250 ml (9 fl oz/1 cup) boiling water. Stir to dissolve the crystals, then add 250 ml (9 fl oz/1 cup) cold water. Refrigerate until set.

Process half the strawberries in a food processor until smooth. Reserve the remaining strawberries to top the parfait.

Spoon the jelly evenly between six cups. Top the jelly with the puréed strawberries and the ice cream. Finally, add the reserved strawberries and serve immediately.

Prep time: 10 minutes + setting time

Cooking time: Nil

Serves 6

HINT: Halve the strawberries if they are large.

frozen fruit kebabs

New and unusual ways to eat fruit will always appeal to a curious toddler, so these fruit kebabs should be a hit!

140 g (5 oz) fresh pineapple

½ mango

80 g (2¾ oz) fresh seedless watermelon

100 g (3½ oz) fresh rockmelon or any orange-fleshed melon

4 iceblock (popsicle/ice lolly) sticks

Prep time: 10 minutes + 4 hours freezing

Cooking time: Nil

Makes 4

Remove the skin from all the fruit and cut each type into four cubes. Thread onto the iceblock sticks and freeze for 4 hours or until frozen. To serve, remove from the freezer 10 minutes before eating to allow them to soften slightly.

HINT: Extra quantities of this recipe can be made and kept in the freezer for a hot day.

Celebrating doesn't have to mean unhealthy food, as you will find out in this chapter. Foods with crunch, colour and sweetness can all be tasty and good for your child too! Of course there will always be foods that are purely for the joy of the occasion but when the party is on, you will want to know that some of what they are eating is going to count as nutritious!

birthdays & other occasions

chicken nuggets

These nuggets are a tasty, high-protein, low-salt party food that will be as big a hit as their unhealthy fast-food counterparts.

melted butter, for greasing

375 g (13 oz) boneless, skinless chicken thighs, roughly chopped

1 egg

1 tablespoon snipped fresh chives

¼ teaspoon sesame oil

2 teaspoons plum sauce

1 teaspoon salt-reduced soy sauce

30 g (1 oz/1 cup) corn-based cereal flakes

Prep time: 20 minutes
Cooking time: 15 minutes
Makes 34

Preheat the oven to 180°C (350°F/Gas 4). Line a 33 × 28 cm (13 × 11¼ in) baking tray with foil. Brush with melted butter or oil.

Put the chicken, egg, chives, sesame oil and sauces in a food processor. Process for 30 seconds, or until the mixture is smooth.

Shape heaped teaspoons of the mixture into balls. Roll the balls in the corn-based cereal flakes. Place the nuggets on the prepared tray. Bake for 15 minutes, or until golden and crisp.

cheese & bacon tarts

These yummy little tarts are rich with the goodness of cheese and egg and if you choose a shortcrust (pie) pastry made with healthy fats (canola or sunflower oils), then birthday treats are as healthy as they can be.

melted butter, for greasing
2 sheets ready-rolled shortcrust (pic) pastry
2 slices bacon, finely chopped
1 small onion, finely chopped
125 ml (4 fl oz/½ cup) cream (whipping)
1 egg
½ teaspoon mild mustard
60 g (2¼ oz/½ cup) grated cheddar cheese

Prep time: 30 minutes
Cooking time: 15 minutes
Makes 18

Preheat the oven to 180°C (350°F/Gas 4). Brush two 12-hole mini muffin tins with melted butter.

Lay out the pastry on a lightly floured work surface. Cut out rounds with a 7 cm (2¾ inch) fluted cutter. Ease the pastry rounds into the muffin holes. Sprinkle the chopped bacon and onion over the pastry shells. Combine the cream, egg and mustard in a small bowl and whisk until smooth. Spoon 1 teaspoon of the mixture into each pastry case. Sprinkle with the grated cheese. Bake the tarts for 15 minutes, or until golden and crisp. Serve warm.

variation: If you like, you can substitute drained and flaked tinned salmon for the chopped bacon.

sausage rolls

Prepared ahead and frozen, home-made sausage rolls are as convenient as ready-made ones while having the benefit of being lower in salt and fat.

1 teaspoon oil, plus extra, for greasing

1 onion, finely chopped

500 g (1 lb 2 oz) sausage mince (meat)

80 g (2¾ oz/1 cup) soft white breadcrumbs

2 tablespoons tomato sauce (ketchup)

1 egg, lightly beaten

2 sheets frozen ready-rolled puff pastry, thawed

beaten egg or milk, for glazing

Prep time: 35 minutes
Cooking time: 30 minutes
Makes 48

Preheat the oven to 210°C (415°F/Gas 6–7). Lightly grease a baking tray with oil.

Heat the oil in a frying pan. Add the onion and cook, over low heat, for 2–3 minutes, or until soft and transparent. Put the onion, meat, breadcrumbs, tomato sauce and egg into a bowl and mix together.

Lay the pastry sheets on a lightly floured work surface and cut into three horizontal strips. Divide the meat mixture into six equal portions and place across the long edge of the pastry. Roll the pastry up to form long sausage shapes. Brush lightly with a little beaten egg or milk. Cut the rolls into 4 cm (1½ inch) lengths and place on the prepared tray.

Bake for 10 minutes, then reduce the heat to 180°C (350°F/Gas 4) and bake for a further 15 minutes, or until golden.

HINT: These sausage rolls can be frozen for up to 2 weeks before serving. Thaw and reheat them in a 180°C (350°F/Gas 4) oven for around 15–20 minutes, or until hot.

baby burgers

These mini burgers will best suit older toddlers who will be more able to hold and eat them than younger children. However, that doesn't mean that they won't enjoy dissecting them and eating each piece separately!

500 g (1 lb 2 oz) minced (ground) beef

1 small onion, finely chopped

1 tablespoon finely chopped flat-leaf (Italian) parsley

1 egg, lightly beaten

1 tablespoon tomato sauce (ketchup)

2 tablespoons oil

½ lettuce, finely shredded

2 small tomatoes, thinly sliced

10 small bread rolls, halved

5 cheese slices, halved

5 tinned pineapple rings, drained and halved

tomato sauce (ketchup) or barbecue sauce

Prep time: 30 minutes
Cooking time: 10 minutes
Makes 10

Combine the beef, onion, parsley, beaten egg and tomato sauce in a large bowl. Using your hands, mix until well combined. Divide the mixture into 10 portions. Shape into round patties.

Heat the oil in a large, heavy-based pan over medium heat. Cook the patties for 5 minutes on each side, or until they are well browned and cooked through. Remove and drain on paper towels.

To assemble the burger, put the lettuce and tomato on the base of the roll. Top with the meat patty, cheese slice and pineapple slice. Add the sauce and cover with the remaining roll half. Serve immediately.

vegie puffs

These tasty pastries look just like sausage rolls except they are packed with the goodness of vegetables and cheese. Serve them with tomato sauce (ketchup).

1 small potato, diced
1 small carrot, diced
1 zucchini (courgette), diced
1 celery stalk, diced
40 g (1½ oz/¼ cup) diced pumpkin (winter squash)
15 g (½ oz/¼ cup) chopped broccoli
15 g (½ oz/¼ cup) chopped cauliflower
250 g (9 oz/2 cups) grated cheddar cheese
1 sheet frozen, ready-rolled puff pastry, halved
milk, for the pastry

Prep time: 15 minutes
Cooking time: 15 minutes
Makes 12

Put the vegetables in a small saucepan and add enough water to cover. Bring to the boil, then reduce the heat and simmer for 3 minutes. Drain well and transfer the vegetables to a bowl to cool. Add the cheese and mix well.

Preheat the oven to 220°C (425°F/Gas 7). Lay the two pieces of pastry on a work surface, divide the mixture in half and spread it along the long side of each piece.

Roll up the pastry to form a sausage shape, brush the edge with a little milk and press to seal.

Cut each roll into six even-sized pieces. Make a small slit in the centre of each and place on a lightly greased baking tray. Brush with milk and bake for 10 minutes, or until crisp and golden.

HINT: These can be made ahead of time and frozen before cooking. To cook, thaw and follow the recipe above.

money bags

These little parcels are a fun, easy-to-hold food with a great crunch factor. This recipe also gives you the option of a making them more exotic by using Asian flavourings (don't forget that this will add more salt).

1 tablespoon peanut oil

4 spring onions (scallions), finely chopped

2 garlic cloves, crushed

1 tablespoon grated fresh ginger

150 g (5½ oz) minced (ground) chicken

150 g (5½ oz) minced (ground) pork

2 teaspoons salt-reduced soy sauce

2 teaspoons soft brown sugar

2 teaspoons lime juice (optional)

2 teaspoons fish sauce (optional)

3 tablespoons finely chopped coriander (cilantro) leaves

30 won ton wrappers

oil, for deep-frying

garlic chives, for tying

Prep time: 30 minutes + cooling time
Cooking time: 15 minutes
Makes 30

Heat a wok over medium heat, add the oil and swirl to coat. Add the spring onions, garlic and ginger and cook for 1–2 minutes, or until the onions are soft. Add the meats and cook for 4 minutes, or until cooked, breaking up the lumps.

Stir in the soy sauce, brown sugar, lime juice and fish sauce, if using, and coriander. Cook, stirring, for 1–2 minutes, or until mixed and dry. Set aside to cool.

Place 2 teaspoons of filling in the centre of each won ton wrapper, then lightly brush the edges with water. Lift the sides up tightly and pinch around the filling to form a bag. Trim the edges if necessary.

Fill a clean wok one-third full of oil and heat to 190°C (375°F), or until a cube of bread dropped in the oil browns in 10 seconds. Cook in batches for 30–60 seconds, or until golden and crisp. Drain on crumpled paper towels, then tie with the chives to serve.

three cheese & chicken pizza

Time is often of the essence on party day. For a quicker version of this recipe buy a pre-prepared pizza base from your bakery or supermarket.

BASE

250 g (9 oz/2 cups) self-raising flour

30 g (1 oz) unsalted butter, chopped

80 ml (2½ fl oz/⅓ cup) milk

80 ml (2½ fl oz/⅓ cup) water

TOPPING

100 g (3½ oz/⅓ cup) spreadable feta cheese

100 g (3½ oz/⅓ cup) ricotta cheese

1 tablespoon finely chopped basil

½ barbecued (grilled) chicken, skin and bones discarded (see Hints)

80 g (2¾ oz/½ cup) semi-dried (sun-blushed) tomatoes, finely chopped

4 balls bocconcini (baby mozzarella cheese) (about 60 g/2¼ oz each), thinly sliced

Prep time: 15 minutes

Cooking time: 25 minutes

Serves 4

Preheat the oven to 220°C (425°F/Gas 7). Lightly grease a 30 cm (12 inch) round pizza tray with oil.

To make the base, put the flour in a bowl and use your fingertips to rub in the butter until it looks like breadcrumbs. Make a well in the centre and pour in enough of the combined milk and water to mix to a soft dough. Turn out onto a lightly floured work surface and knead lightly to form a ball. Roll out to a 30 cm (12 inch) circle and place on the prepared tray.

To make the topping, combine the feta, ricotta and basil and spread over the pizza base leaving a 1 cm (½ inch) border. Chop the chicken into small pieces and sprinkle over the pizza with the tomato. Cover with the bocconcini slices and bake for 20–25 minutes, or until the base is golden and cooked through and the cheese is melted. Cut into wedges and serve.

HINTS: Half a barbecued (grilled) chicken gives about 185 g (6½ oz) chicken meat or 1¼ cups finely chopped meat. If bocconcini is unavailable, you can use mozzarella.

fish cocktails

Just because it's good for you doesn't mean it can't be party food. Toddlers will get a healthy serve of brain food from these nuggets and enjoy their crunchiness.

250 g (9 oz) boneless white fish fillets

2 tablespoons plain (all-purpose) flour

1 egg white

15 g (½ oz/¼ cup) crushed corn-based cereal flakes

mayonnaise, to serve

Prep time: 20 minutes
Cooking time: 15 minutes
Makes 24

Preheat the oven to 180°C (350°F/Gas 4). Cut the fish into 3 cm (1¼ inch) cubes. Coat the fish pieces in flour and shake off any excess.

Whisk the egg white in a small bowl. Dip the fish, one cube at a time, in the egg white, then coat with the crushed cereal flakes. Place in a single layer on a baking tray. Bake for 15 minutes, or until golden, turning the pieces over after 10 minutes. Serve hot with mayonnaise or your toddler's favourite seafood sauce.

oven chips

Children just love chips (fries) and potatoes are chock full of carbohydrates — just what toddlers need to give them the energy they need for party games.

6 medium potatoes
60 ml (2 fl oz/¼ cup) olive oil

Prep time: 10 minutes
Cooking time: 45 minutes
Serves 6

Preheat the oven to 220°C (425°F/Gas 7). Peel the potatoes, and cut them into slices about 1 cm (½ inch) square.

Soak the chips (fries) in cold water for 10 minutes. Drain well, then pat dry thoroughly with paper towels.

Spread the chips onto a baking tray and sprinkle the oil over them. Toss them to coat well. Bake the chips for 45 minutes until golden and crisp, turning occasionally.

meatballs

Bite-sized and easy-to-eat foods like these meatballs are an important party food, especially when toddlers have so many better things to do than eat.

375 g (13 oz) minced (ground) beef

1 small onion, finely chopped

40 g (1½ oz/½ cup) fresh breadcrumbs

1 tablespoon tomato paste (concentrated purée)

1 teaspoon worcestershire sauce

1 egg, lightly beaten

2 tablespoons oil

Prep time: 15 minutes
Cooking time: 10 minutes
Makes 25

Put the beef, onion, breadcrumbs, tomato paste, sauce and egg in a large bowl. Using your hands, mix until well combined. Shape level tablespoons of mixture into balls.

Heat the oil in a large frying pan. Add the meatballs and cook over medium heat, shaking the pan often, for 10 minutes, or until the meatballs are cooked and evenly browned. Drain on paper towels. Serve hot or cold with tomato sauce (ketchup), if desired.

apple & orange mini cakes

Cakes can always be made healthier for kids by basing them on fruit and using wholemeal (whole-wheat) rather than white flour, as has been done in this recipe.

90 g (3¼ oz) unsalted butter

125 g (4½ oz/⅔ cup) soft brown sugar

1 tablespoon honey

1 egg

270 g (9½ oz/1 cup) apple sauce or puréed tinned pie apples

125 g (4½ oz/1 cup) wholemeal (whole-wheat) self-raising flour

60 g (2¼ oz/½ cup) self-raising flour

1 teaspoon ground cinnamon

pinch of powdered cloves

Prep time: 20 minutes
Cooking time: 20 minutes
Makes 36

Preheat the oven to 180°C (350°F/Gas 4).

Place 36 paper cases on a baking tray. Beat the butter, sugar and honey together until light and creamy, then add the egg and apple sauce and beat until well combined. Sift in the flours and spices and mix well. Spoon the mixture into the paper cases and bake for about 20 minutes, or until a skewer comes out clean when inserted into the centre. Allow to cool and cover with orange glaze icing (see below).

orange glaze icing

To make the icing (frosting), combine 125 g (4½ oz/1 cup) icing (confectioners') sugar, 10 g (¼ oz) butter, 1 teaspoon orange zest and 2 tablespoons orange juice in a heatproof bowl to make a soft pouring consistency. Add a little more orange juice if needed. Stand over a saucepan of simmering water and stir until smooth and glossy. Remove from the heat. Allow to cool slightly, then ice the cakes.

shortbreads

These crisp, crunchy, butter-flavoured biscuits are popular with small children, especially when they come in fancy shapes.

250 g (9 oz/2 cups) plain (all-purpose) flour

2 tablespoons rice flour

115 g (4 oz/½ cup) caster (superfine) sugar

250 g (9 oz) unsalted butter, chopped

Prep time: 15 minutes

Cooking time: 30 minutes

Makes 16

Preheat the oven to 160°C (315°F/Gas 2–3). Lightly grease 2 baking trays. Sift the flours together into a large bowl and mix in the sugar. Rub in the butter using your fingertips and press the mixture together.

Turn out onto a lightly floured work surface and knead gently. Press out into a round about 1 cm (½ inch) thick and cut out with shaped cutters. Put the shortbreads onto the prepared baking trays. Bake for 25–30 minutes, or until golden brown.

Leave to cool on the trays for 5 minutes and then transfer to a wire rack to cool completely. Store in an airtight container.

choc-chip crackles

These crunchy chocolate treats filled with sultanas (golden raisins) and choc chips will be full of surprises for small party goers.

90 g (3¼ oz/3 cups) puffed rice cereal

30 g (1 oz/¼ cup) unsweetened cocoa powder

150 g (5½ oz/1¼ cups) icing (confectioners') sugar

60 g (2¼ oz/½ cup) sultanas (golden raisins)

60 g (2¼ oz/⅔ cup) desiccated coconut

200 g (7 oz) Copha (white vegetable shortening), melted

60 g (2¼ oz/⅓ cup) dark choc chips

Prep time: 20 minutes
Cooking time: 5 minutes
Makes 24

Line two 12-hole mini muffin tins with foil cases. Combine the puffed rice cereal, cocoa and sugar in a large bowl. Mix thoroughly, then stir in the sultanas and coconut. Stir in the melted shortening.

Spoon the mixture into the prepared muffin tins. Sprinkle with the choc chips. Refrigerate until set.

martian biscuits

For any chemical-sensitive party goers, ice a set of biscuits (cookies) as 'snowmen' without the green colouring. This way no one will miss out.

125 g (4½ oz) unsalted butter

115 g (4 oz/½ cup) caster (superfine) sugar

1 egg

210 g (7½ oz/1¾ cups) plain (all-purpose) flour

125 g (4½ oz/1 cup) icing (confectioners') sugar

60 ml (2 fl oz/¼ cup) hot water

4 drops green food colouring

1 packet liquorice allsorts, thinly sliced

Prep time: 20 minutes + 30 minutes refrigeration
Cooking time: 15 minutes
Makes 10

To make the biscuits (cookies), beat the butter, sugar and egg using electric beaters in a medium bowl until light and creamy.

Add the flour to the mixture. Using your hands, press the mixture together to form a soft dough. Turn onto a lightly floured work surface and knead for 2 minutes, or until smooth. Refrigerate, covered with plastic wrap, for 30 minutes.

Preheat the oven to 180°C (350°F/Gas 4). Brush a 33 x 28 cm (13 x 11¼ inch) baking tray with melted butter or oil. Roll the dough, between sheets of baking paper, to 5 mm (¼ inch) thickness. Cut into shapes using a 12 cm (4½ inch) people-shaped biscuit (cookie) cutter. Place on the prepared tray and bake for 15 minutes, or until golden. Leave to cool on a wire rack.

Place the sifted icing sugar in a medium bowl. Add the water and food colouring and stir until well combined. Dip the front of each biscuit into the icing (frosting), holding the biscuits over the bowl to allow any excess icing to drain away. While the icing is still soft, decorate the biscuits with liquorice allsorts. The biscuits can be made up to 7 days ahead and stored in an airtight container.

gingerbread people

If you can handle the 'help' when making your gingerbread characters, offer a small amount of dough to your toddler and let him roll and cut his own shapes.

125 g (4½ oz) unsalted butter

90 g (3¼ oz/½ cup) soft brown sugar

115 g (4 oz/⅓ cup) golden syrup (dark corn syrup)

1 egg

250 g (9 oz/2 cups) plain (all-purpose) flour

40 g (1½ oz/⅓ cup) self-raising flour

1 tablespoon ground ginger

1 teaspoon bicarbonate of soda (baking soda)

ICING

1 egg white

½ teaspoon lemon juice

125 g (4½ oz/1 cup) icing (confectioners') sugar

food colourings

Prep time: 30 minutes + 15 minutes refrigeration

Cooking time: 15 minutes

Makes 15–20, depending on size of cutters

Line two or three baking trays with baking paper. Using electric beaters, beat the butter, sugar and syrup in a large bowl until light and creamy. Add the egg and beat well.

Sift in the flours, ginger and bicarbonate of soda. Use a knife to mix until just combined.

Use a well-floured hand to gather the dough into a ball. Knead gently on a well-floured surface until smooth. Don't over-handle the dough or it will become tough.

Lay a sheet of baking paper over a large chopping board. Roll out the dough on the lined board to a 5 mm (¼ inch) thickness. Preheat the oven to 180°C (350°F/Gas 4).

Refrigerate the dough on the board for 15 minutes, or until it is firm enough to cut. Cut the dough into shapes using assorted gingerbread people cutters. Press any remaining dough together. Re-roll and cut out into shapes.

Bake for 10–12 minutes, or until lightly browned. Cool the biscuits on the trays, then decorate with the icing (frosting).

To make the icing, beat the egg white in a small bowl with electric beaters until soft peaks form. Gradually add the lemon juice and sifted icing sugar and beat until thick and creamy.

Divide the icing into several bowls and tint with food colourings. Spoon into small paper icing bags and use to decorate the biscuits.

butterfly cupcakes

Not many toddlers can resist helping out when it comes to baking. Let them put the paper cases into the muffin tin, help pour measured ingredients into the mixing bowl and, of course, lick the beaters when it is all done!

125 g (4½ oz) unsalted butter, softened

170 g (6 oz/¾ cup) caster (superfine) sugar

185 g (6½ oz/1½ cups) self-raising flour

125 ml (4 fl oz/½ cup) milk

2 eggs

125 ml (4 fl oz/½ cup) thickened (whipping) cream

1½ tablespoons strawberry jam

icing (confectioners') sugar, to dust

Prep time: 10 minutes
Cooking time: 20 minutes
Makes 18

Preheat the oven to 180°C (350°F/Gas 4). Line 18 holes in two muffin tins with paper cases. Beat the butter, sugar, flour, milk and eggs with electric beaters on low speed. Increase the speed and beat until smooth and pale. Divide the mixture evenly among the cases and bake for 30 minutes, or until cooked and golden. Transfer to a wire rack to cool.

Cut shallow rounds from the centre of each cake using the point of a sharp knife, then cut the rounds in half. Spoon 2 teaspoons cream into each cavity, top with 1 teaspoon jam and position two halves of the cake tops in the jam to resemble butterfly wings. Dust with icing sugar.

Alternatively, do not cut out the centre of the cake and cover each cupcake with buttercream or chocolate buttercream (see below).

buttercream

With electric beaters, beat 125 g (4½ oz) unsalted butter until pale and fluffy. Continue beating and gradually add 1 teaspoon natural vanilla extract and 185 g (6½ oz/1½ cups) sifted icing (confectioners') sugar. Gradually add 2 tablespoons milk, at room temperature. Beat the mixture until smooth.

chocolate buttercream

To make chocolate buttercream, mix 2 tablespoons sifted unsweetened cocoa powder into the above mixture.

teddy birthday cake

A good old-fashioned butter cake makes good sense as a birthday cake for toddlers — particularly when made into a teddy bear.

445 g (15¾ oz) unsalted butter, softened

350 g (12 oz/1½ cups) caster (superfine) sugar

1 tablespoon natural vanilla extract

6 eggs, lightly beaten

550 g (1 lb 4 oz/4⅓ cups) self-raising flour

250 ml (9 fl oz/1 cup) milk

1½ quantities buttercream, from recipe on page 195

30 g (1 oz/¼ cup) unsweetened cocoa powder

DECORATION

five 5 cm (2 inch) jam rollettes (mini jelly rolls)

2 round chocolate biscuits (cookies)

2 milk chocolate drops

1 white marshmallow, halved

liquorice pieces

1 red jellybean

Prep time: 1 hour
Cooking time: 35–40 minutes
Makes 1 cake

Preheat the oven to 180°C (350°F/Gas 4). Grease and line the bases of two 18 cm (7 inch) round cake tins and a 1 litre (35 fl oz/4 cup) basin.

To make the cake, beat the butter and sugar until light and creamy. Add the vanilla extract and eggs one at a time, beating well after each addition. Fold in the sifted flour alternately with the milk until smooth.

Divide the cake mix evenly among the three tins and bake for 35–40 minutes, or until a skewer inserted into the centre comes out clean. Cool for 5 minutes, then turn out onto a wire rack to cool.

Spread the top of one round cake with some buttercream. Sandwich the round cakes together. Cut away the top and bottom edges of the cake sandwich to form a slight ball shape. This will be the fat body. Sit the pudding-shaped cake on top. Secure with skewers. Trim a diagonal slice around the bottom edge of the pudding for a neck.

Cut a diagonal slice off the end of four rollettes and attach them to the body with skewers to form the arms and legs. Cut a slice off the remaining rollette and attach it to the centre of the face with a skewer to form the snout. For ears, make two slits on the top of each side of the head then push a round biscuit (cookie) into each.

Put 4 tablespoons of the buttercream in a bowl. Add the cocoa to the remainder and beat well. With a palette knife, spread the chocolate icing over the body, arms and legs (reserving a tablespoon for piping). Ice the tummy, snout and ears with the white buttercream.

For the eyes, stick a chocolate drop on each marshmallow half with icing. Use liquorice for the lips and nose and a jellybean for the mouth. Ice paw marks on the arms and legs with reserved chocolate icing.

Preparing meals for a child
with a food allergy or
intolerance is not always
easy. This can be especially
so when you want to ensure
your toddler has access to
the widest variety of
healthy foods. The best way
to do this is to prepare the
meals yourself. The recipes
to follow will not only help
you create a good diet for
your child, but will also
allow family and friends to
enjoy meals and celebration
times with your toddler too.

food allergy &
intolerance

problems with food

**FOODS MOST LIKELY
TO CAUSE AN ALLERGIC
REACTION IN CHILDREN:**

- *Eggs*

- *Cow's milk*

- *Peanuts and other nuts*

- *Soy*

- *Wheat*

- *Fish*

**FOOD ADDITIVES MOST
LIKELY TO CAUSE AN
ADVERSE REACTION:**

- *Colours: 102, 107, 110,
122–129, 132, 133, 142, 151,
155, 160B (natural)*

- *Preservatives: 200–203,
210–218, 220–228,
249–252, 280–283,
310–312, 319–321*

- *Flavour enhancers:
620–635, hydrolyzed
vegetable protein (HVP),
textured vegetable
protein (TVP)*

In cases of unexplained problems, a food allergy is often the first to be blamed, but the diagnosis of allergies is a highly scientific exercise and real allergic reactions to food are not as common as many believe. Food allergy is in fact quite rare; most reactions to food are a food intolerance.

A food allergy is an abnormal reaction by the body's defence system to proteins found in food. One of the defining characteristics of food allergy is the almost instantaneous symptoms that can occur when the offending food is eaten. Foods most likely to cause an allergic reaction (see box left) are not usually introduced to babies as first foods for this very reason.

Babies from allergic families are at a higher risk of developing a food allergy than those who are not. For this reason it is recommended that the introduction of these foods into the diet of these babies be delayed by several months or more than the usual introduction times. A dietitian should be consulted for more detailed information about this.

The symptoms of food allergy in young children include swelling (particularly around the mouth), hives, rashes and eczema. Less common is diarrhoea, vomiting, wheezing or asthma. Severe allergies can result in the potentially fatal state of hyperreactivity known as anaphylaxis.

The good news for allergic children is that most will outgrow their food allergy by the time they go to school. The allergies most likely not to disappear are those to peanuts, or other nuts, and fish — these tend to be lifelong.

There may be many other causes of the types of symptoms seen in food allergies, so it is recommended that you seek expert help before changing your child's diet. Treatment of a true food allergy requires complete exclusion of the food or food group from the diet. For young children in particular this needs the specialized help of a dietitian to make sure their diet is adequate for their growth and development.

food intolerance

Food intolerances are reactions to the chemicals found in food — both natural and added. These reactions, unlike a food allergy, are not a response by the immune system but are instead thought to be the result of irritation to nerve endings. Unlike an allergy, the symptoms of food intolerance are rarely associated with the food most recently consumed. Symptoms of food intolerance come about when tolerance thresholds for 'culprit chemicals' are reached. As such they may occur many hours after eating the offending food(s).

Foods likely to cause intolerance in sensitive children are those rich in the natural chemicals salicylate, amine and glutamate. The list of these foods is quite extensive so it is easier to consider those which are least likely to cause a problem (see box right) than those which are problematic. As with the case of an allergy, many of these 'lower chemical' foods are given as first foods, with the higher chemical foods being introduced a little later.

Added chemicals (see box opposite) can also be problematic for some children, occasionally resulting in emotional and behavioural symptoms. Because foods containing added chemicals don't feature highly in the diets of babies or younger toddlers, they are more likely to be an issue in 3 and 4 year-olds.

Food intolerance symptoms are wide ranging and include those symptoms seen in food allergies such as rashes, eczema and hives as well as colic, diarrhoea, nappy rash, vomiting and general irritability. Once again, because these symptoms could have many other causes than food, it is important to have your child seen by an expert before restricting their diet. Treatment of food intolerances is complex and may require complete or only partial elimination of high problem foods from the diet. A dietitian specializing in food allergy and intolerance is best qualified to give you this advice.

lactose intolerance

The natural sugar in all kinds of milk is known as lactose, and is an important source of energy for babies. Lactase is the enzyme in the digestive system that helps to break down the lactose in milk. When not enough of this enzyme is present the digestive system cannot cope and lactose intolerance results.

The most common symptoms of lactose intolerance are bloating, tummy pain and diarrhoea. These symptoms can be caused by other conditions so it is important to seek advice to confirm that this is the problem. In babies and young children, lactose intolerance is not common except as a result of gastroenteritis and other diarrhoea-causing illnesses. This type of lactose intolerance is only temporary, but formula-fed babies should be fed a lactose-free formula for a few weeks. Breast-fed babies should continue to be breast-fed. With toddlers, the removal of high-lactose foods like milk, yoghurt and ice cream is usually recommended. Calcium-enriched soy beverages and processed cheddar can continue to provide much needed calcium until the intolerance resolves itself.

FOODS LEAST LIKELY TO BE IMPLICATED IN FOOD INTOLERANCE:

- *Vegetables — brussels sprouts, cabbage (green and red), celery, chives, choko/chayote, dried peas, beans and lentils, leeks, iceberg lettuce, potato, swede/rutabaga, shallots, parsley*

- *Fruit — pear*

- *Cereals — rice, barley, sago, soy, rye, wheat, buckwheat, cornflour/cornstarch*

- *Fats and oils — butter, margarine (unpreserved, no antioxidant), safflower, sunflower, canola and soy oils*

- *Protein foods — beef, chicken, eggs, fish, lamb, veal*

- *Drinks — cow's milk, soy beverage, lemonade (unpreserved), rice beverage*

buckwheat pancakes

Contrary to its name, buckwheat is not related to wheat at all and so, unlike wheat, is a gluten-free grain. Free of egg, dairy, gluten, nut and soy.

130 g (4¾ oz/1 cup) buckwheat flour

1 egg, or equivalent egg replacer

185 ml (6 fl oz/¾ cup) water

canola oil, for greasing

125 ml (4 fl oz/½ cup) maple syrup

Prep time: 10 minutes
Cooking time: 20 minutes
Makes 16–20 pancakes

Sift the flour into a bowl and make a well in the centre. Add the combined egg or egg replacer and water. Beat with a wooden spoon until well combined and smooth. Pour the batter into a vessel with a pouring lip.

Brush a 20 cm (8 inch) frying pan with oil and heat over medium heat. Pour in just enough batter to thinly cover the bottom of the pan. When the top of the pancake starts to set, turn it over with a spatula and cook for a further 30 seconds. Transfer to a plate. Repeat with the remaining pancake batter, greasing the pan between batches. Serve with a drizzle of maple syrup.

rolled rice porridge

Rice is an important source of energy-giving carbohydrate ideal for small food-sensitive tummies. Free of egg, dairy, gluten, nut and soy.

50 g (1¾ oz/½ cup) rolled rice or rice flakes

golden syrup or maple syrup, to serve

peeled and chopped pear, to serve

pear juice (see page 234), to serve

Prep time: 5 minutes
Cooking time: 20 minutes
Serves 4

Combine the rolled rice or rice flakes and 500 ml (17 fl oz/2 cups) boiling water in a saucepan. Cover with a lid and simmer over medium heat for 20 minutes, or until soft and creamy. Serve topped with golden or maple syrup, chopped pear and pear juice.

HINT: If you'd like a sweeter porridge, try adding a little pear juice in place of the water. You'll need to bring it to the boil before using it.

creamy rice porridge

Free of egg, dairy, gluten, nut and soy.

For a deliciously creamy taste, make the porridge with a non-dairy alternative, such as rice drink. Bring 500 ml (17 fl oz/2 cups) rice drink to the boil in a saucepan, then proceed with the recipe.

potato & leek fritters

If citrus fruits are off the menu, then potatoes become a good alternative source of vitamin C for your toddler. This recipe has more than their daily needs in one serve. Free of egg, dairy, gluten, nut and soy.

1.25 kg (2 lb 12 oz) white-skinned potatoes

1 leek, washed

2 eggs, lightly beaten, or equivalent egg replacer

1 tablespoon rice flour

2 tablespoons canola oil

Prep time: 15 minutes
Cooking time: 20 minutes
Serves 4–6

Peel and grate the potatoes. Pat the potato dry and put in a bowl. Finely chop the white part of the leek and add it to the bowl with the potato. Add the eggs or egg replacer and rice flour. Mix until combined.

Heat the oil in a large non-stick frying pan. Drop tablespoons of the mixture into the pan — you may need to cook the fritters in batches. Fry on each side for a few minutes, or until golden brown. Serve hot or cold either on their own or with baked beans.

HINTS: Use plain brushed potatoes. Red-skinned and new potatoes have moderate levels of natural flavour substances. Peeled potato will discolour if left to stand for too long.

chickpea dip

Legumes such as chickpeas are a 'low chemical' source of vegetable protein plus iron and the B vitamin folic acid. Free of egg, dairy, gluten, nut and soy.

125 g (4½ oz) tinned chickpeas, rinsed and drained (see Hints)

¼ teaspoon citric acid (see Hints)

60 ml (2 fl oz/¼ cup) pear juice (see page 234)

2 garlic cloves, crushed

2 tablespoons canola oil

Prep time: 15 minutes
Cooking time: Nil
Makes 250 g (9 oz/1 cup)

Combine the chickpeas, citric acid, pear juice, garlic, oil and 2 tablespoons water in a food processor. Process until smooth — the mixture should be the consistency of thick mayonnaise.

Scoop into a bowl and serve with crispy wafer biscuits (see the recipe opposite), chilled sticks of soft or blanched vegetables such as celery or carrot, or fresh pieces of pide (Turkish/flat bread).

HINTS: If tinned chickpeas are unavailable, soak 50 g (1¾ oz/¼ cup) dried chickpeas in cold water overnight, then drain. Place in a saucepan with water and bring to the boil. Reduce the heat and simmer for about 2½ hours, or until tender. Drain well and proceed with the recipe.

Citric acid is used in the recipes in this chapter, as it is more likely to be tolerated than lemon juice or vinegar. It can be found at some supermarkets and health food stores.

chickpea & cashew dip

Contains nuts. Free of egg, dairy, gluten and soy.

To add a delicious nutty flavour to the above dip, process 115 g (4 oz/¾ cup) cashew nuts to a smooth paste in a small food processor and add it to the chickpea mixture.

crispy wafer biscuits

These crisp wafers will put your mind at rest if you need to be certain about low-chemical snacks for your toddler. Free of egg, dairy, gluten, nut and soy.

175 g (6 oz/1 cup) rice flour

125 g (4½ oz/1 cup) cornflour (cornstarch)

40 g (1½ oz/½ cup) rice bran

2 tablespoons canola oil, plus extra for greasing

Prep time: 10 minutes

Cooking time: 25 minutes

Makes 40

To make the biscuits (crackers), preheat the oven to 200°C (400°F/Gas 6). Lightly oil two 30 × 25 cm (12 × 10 inch) Swiss roll tins (jelly roll tins).

Combine the dry ingredients in a bowl, make a well in the centre and add 185 ml (6 fl oz/¾ cup) water combined with the oil. Mix until well combined.

Divide the mixture into two portions. Press each portion of dough into a prepared tin and bake for 20–25 minutes. Allow to cool in the tin. Turn out, break into pieces and store in an airtight container for up to 2 days.

HINT: If you'd like more evenly-shaped biscuits, score the dough in the tins with a knife before you bake them, then the biscuits will easily break along the score lines once they're cooked.

vegetable soup

This soup is high in fibre and vitamins. Blend it up for a thick, easy-to-eat meal for small toddlers. Free of egg, dairy, gluten, nut and soy.

200 g (7 oz/1 cup) dried white or red beans

1 tablespoon canola oil

1 leek, halved lengthways, thickly sliced (white part only)

2 garlic cloves, crushed

400 g (14 oz) swede (rutabaga), chopped

3 celery stalks, chopped

1.5 litres (52 fl oz/6 cups) vegetable stock (see allergy-free recipe on page 238)

210 g (7½ oz/1⅔ cups) green beans, trimmed and sliced

gluten-free bread, to serve

Prep time: 15 minutes + overnight soaking

Cooking time: 1 hour 20 minutes

Serves 4–6

Wash the beans and then cover them with water and leave to soak overnight. Drain well.

Heat the oil in a large saucepan over medium heat. Cook the leek, stirring occasionally, for 4–5 minutes, or until soft. Add the garlic, swede and celery and cook for 2–3 minutes.

Add the drained beans and stock to the pan and bring to the boil. Simmer, partially covered, for 50–60 minutes, or until the beans are tender. Add the green beans and cook for a further 5–10 minutes, or until the green beans are tender. Serve with gluten-free bread.

fish patties

A good source of protein for growing toddlers, fish's omega-3 fats are also good brain food. Free of egg, dairy, gluten, nut and soy.

700 g (1 lb 9 oz) white-skinned potatoes, quartered

2 tablespoons canola oil

500 g (1 lb 2 oz) boneless white fish fillets

1 leek, halved lengthways, chopped (white part only)

2 garlic cloves, crushed

30 g (1 oz/¼ cup) chopped spring onions (scallions)

iceberg lettuce leaves, to serve

pear chutney (see page 231), to serve

Prep time: 20 minutes + 1 hour chilling
Cooking time: 25 minutes
Serves 4

Put the potato in a large saucepan. Cover with cold water and bring to the boil. Boil for 15 minutes, or until the potato is tender. Drain well. Mash with a potato masher or a fork.

Meanwhile, heat 2 teaspoons of the oil in a large non-stick frying pan over medium heat. Add the fish fillets and cook for 3–4 minutes on each side, or until cooked. Set aside to cool.

Flake the fish with a fork. Heat another 2 teaspoons of the oil in the same frying pan over medium heat. Cook the leek and garlic, stirring often, for 5–6 minutes, or until the leek softens. Set aside on a plate. Wipe the pan clean with paper towels.

Combine the mashed potato, flaked fish, leek mixture and spring onion in a large bowl and mix thoroughly. Shape into eight patties and put on a plate. Cover and refrigerate for 1 hour.

Heat the remaining oil in the frying pan over medium heat. Cook the patties for 3–4 minutes on each side, or until lightly golden and heated through. Serve with lettuce leaves and pear chutney.

continental chicken sausages

Not only are these sausages low-chemical, but they are also lower in fat and salt than most commercially-made sausages. Free of egg, dairy, gluten, nut and soy.

750 g (1 lb 10 oz) minced (ground) chicken

2 eggs, lightly beaten, or equivalent egg replacer

20 g (¾ oz/1 cup) puffed rice cereal, finely crushed

1 tablespoon finely snipped chives

1 garlic clove, crushed

2 spring onions (scallions), finely chopped

1–1.25 litres (35–44 fl oz/ 4–5 cups) chicken stock (see allergy-free recipe on page 239)

1 tablespoon canola oil

Prep time: 20 minutes + 1 hour chilling
Cooking time: 20 minutes
Serves 4

Combine the chicken, eggs or egg replacer, puffed rice, chives, garlic and spring onions in a large bowl. Using your hands, mix and knead the mixture until completely combined.

Divide the mixture into eight even portions. Using wet hands, shape each portion into a sausage shape. Put on a large plate, cover with plastic wrap and refrigerate for 1 hour.

Put the chicken stock into a large saucepan and bring to the boil. Reduce the heat and bring to a simmer. Add the sausages to the simmering stock. Cover and cook for 10–15 minutes, or until the sausages are cooked through. Remove the sausages from the stock with a slotted spoon and pat dry on paper towels.

Heat the oil in a large frying pan over medium heat and add the sausages. Cook, turning often until browned all over.

HINT: Minced (ground) chicken is available from chicken speciality shops and some supermarkets. It can be made at home by processing boneless, skinless chicken breasts or thighs.

Most commercial sausages contain preservatives. If you know a good butcher, ask to have sausages made up to your own recipe. Avoid contamination by having the sausages made at the start of the day when the machinery is clean.

chicken & carrot sausages

Free of egg, dairy, gluten, nut and soy.

Add 1 small finely grated carrot to the chicken mixture before dividing into portions, then proceed with the recipe above.

glazed drumettes

Small chicken pieces are easy-to-eat protein food for growing children and are great served as a meal or a snack. Free of egg, dairy, gluten, nut and soy.

16 chicken drumettes (see Hint)

80 ml (2½ fl oz/⅓ cup) golden syrup (dark corn syrup)

60 ml (2 fl oz/¼ cup) pear juice (see page 234)

1 tablespoon canola oil

Prep time: 20 minutes + overnight marinating

Cooking time: 25 minutes

Serves 4

Put the drumettes in a shallow non-metallic dish. Combine the remaining ingredients and pour over the drumettes, making sure they are coated all over. Marinate overnight, turning occasionally.

Preheat the oven to 180°C (350°F/Gas 4). Transfer the drumettes and marinade to a baking tin. Bake for 20–25 minutes, turning frequently during cooking and brushing with the pan juices. If the pan juices start to overbrown, add a small amount of water or stock until syrupy. Serve hot or cold.

HINT: Chicken drumettes are available from most supermarkets and chicken shops. They are simply the wing with the tip removed and the flesh scraped back away from the bone and turned inside out.

glazed chicken with garlic & poppy seeds

Free of egg, dairy, gluten, nut and soy.

For added flavour, add 2 finely chopped spring onions (scallions), 2 crushed garlic cloves and 1 tablespoon poppy seeds to the golden syrup marinade. Follow the method as above.

creamy swede purée

Swedes are a good source of potassium, as well as containing vitamin C and the B vitamin folate. Contains dairy. Free of egg, gluten, nut and soy.

600 g (1 lb 5 oz) swedes (rutabaga), thickly sliced

1 teaspoon sugar

2 tablespoons cream (whipping)

ground sea salt

Prep time: 10 minutes
Cooking time: 20 minutes
Serves 4–6

Put the swede and sugar in a saucepan and cover with cold water. Cover with a lid and bring to the boil. Reduce the heat to low and cook, for 10–15 minutes, or until the swede is tender. Drain and set aside for 5 minutes to cool.

Put the swede into a food processor and process until smooth. Stir in the cream and season with salt to taste.

Serve with grilled (broiled) lamb chops or steak.

pea purée with yoghurt

This recipe provides vitamin C and beta-carotene from the peas and calcium and phosphorus from the yoghurt. Contains dairy. Free of egg, gluten, nut and soy.

310 g (11 oz/2 cups) frozen peas

1 large handful flat-leaf (Italian) parsley, chopped

6 spring onions (scallions), chopped

125 ml (4 fl oz/½ cup) pear juice (see page 234)

½ teaspoon citric acid

250 g (9 oz/1 cup) plain yoghurt

Prep time: 10 minutes

Cooking time: 5 minutes

Serves 4

Bring a saucepan of water to the boil, then add the peas, parsley and spring onions. Cook for 2–3 minutes, or until the peas are bright green and tender.

Strain, and reserve 80 ml (2½ fl oz/⅓ cup) of the cooking liquid. Purée the pea mixture reserved cooking liquid, pear juice and citric acid in a food processor or blender. Return to the saucepan and cook over low heat until the sauce is warmed through. Remove the pan from the heat and stir in the yoghurt. Do not reheat once you have added the yoghurt or the purée will curdle.

Serve with lamb cutlets or over baked or boiled potatoes.

vegetable & veal pasta

Rich in energy-giving carbohydrate from the pasta, this recipe also provides the minerals iron, zinc and potassium, as well as vitamin C and beta-carotene. Free of egg, dairy, gluten, nut and soy.

1½ tablespoons canola oil

1 leek, halved, washed and thinly sliced (white part only)

100 g (3½ oz) swede (rutabaga), chopped

100 g (3½ oz) white-skinned potatoes, chopped

2 garlic cloves, crushed

400 g (14 oz) cabbage, core removed and shredded

500 g (1 lb 2 oz) minced (ground) lean veal

2 teaspoons cornflour (cornstarch)

375 ml (13 fl oz/1½ cups) veal stock (see allergy-free recipe on page 239)

375 g (13 oz) rice pasta

Prep time: 20 minutes

Cooking time: 25 minutes

Serves 4

Heat 1 tablespoon of the oil in a large non-stick frying pan over medium heat. Add the leek, swede and potato. Cook, stirring often, for 5–6 minutes, or until the vegetables are almost tender. Add the garlic, cabbage and 2 tablespoons water. Cover and cook for a further 7–8 minutes, or until the cabbage is tender. Remove the vegetables from the pan.

Heat the remaining oil in the pan over high heat. Add the veal and cook, stirring, for 3–4 minutes, or until well browned. Combine the cornflour with a little of the stock in a bowl, then add the remaining stock and a little salt. Add the stock mixture to the veal with the vegetables and stir until boiling. Reduce the heat and simmer for 2–3 minutes, or until the sauce thickens.

Meanwhile, cook the pasta following the packet instructions until *al dente*. Drain and return to the pan.

Divide the pasta among four serving plates. Top with the meat and vegetable mixture and serve immediately.

HINT: If your child can tolerate gluten, both pasta sauces can also be served with wheat spaghetti or other wheat pasta.

rice-crumbed fish with wedges

Rich in protein and energy-rich carbohydrates this is perfect growing food for kids. Free of egg, dairy, gluten, nut and soy.

2 eggs, or equivalent egg replacer

2 tablespoons rice drink

60 g (2¼ oz/½ cup) soy-free, gluten-free plain (all-purpose) flour

70 g (2½ oz/1 cup) rice crumbs

four 125 g (4½ oz) boneless white fish fillets

canola oil spray

iceberg lettuce leaves, to serve

pear chutney (see page 231), to serve

WEDGES

1 kg (2 lb 4 oz) white-skinned potatoes, cut into wedges

canola oil spray

Prep time: 20 minutes

Cooking time: 50 minutes

Serves 4

Preheat the oven to 220°C (425°F/Gas 7). Line two large baking trays with baking paper.

Combine the egg or egg replacer and rice drink in a shallow dish. Put the flour and rice crumbs in two separate shallow dishes. Dip the fish in the flour, then the egg mixture and lastly in the rice crumbs to coat well. Lay the crumbed fish in a single layer on one of the lined trays. Refrigerate until required.

Put the potato wedges in a large bowl. Spray the wedges with oil. Toss to coat. Spread over the other lined tray.

Bake the potato wedges for 30 minutes, turning once. Put the wedges on the lower shelf of the oven. Remove the fish from the refrigerator, then spray both sides of the fish lightly with oil. Add the fish to the top shelf and cook for 20 minutes turning halfway through, or until the fish is cooked and the wedges are crispy.

breadcrumb-coated fish

Contains egg, dairy and gluten. Free of nut and soy.

Commercial breadcrumbs always contain preservatives. You can make your own by putting preservative-free bread slices on baking trays and slowly baking until completely crisp. Process in a food processor and store in an airtight jar. To make breadcrumb-coated fish, combine 1 egg and 1 tablespoon milk in a bowl, put 60 g (2¼ oz/½ cup) plain (all-purpose) flour in a separate bowl and 165 g (5¾ oz/2 cups) home-made breadcrumbs in a third bowl. Dip the fish first in the flour, then the egg wash and lastly in the breadcrumbs. Follow the cooking method in the recipe above.

crunchy chicken bits

Low-chemical food can also be tasty and fun to eat and these chicken bits are a treat as well as being nutritious. Free of egg, dairy, gluten, nut and soy.

canola oil, for greasing

1 kg (2 lb 4 oz) boneless, skinless chicken thighs or breasts, fat removed

40 g (1½ oz/⅓ cup) soy-free, gluten-free plain (all-purpose) flour

2 eggs, or equivalent egg replacer

300 g (10½ oz) plain potato chips (crisps), crushed

Prep time: 20 minutes
Cooking time: 20 minutes
Serves 4–6

Preheat the oven to 180°C (350°F/Gas 4). Lightly grease two baking trays.

Cut the chicken into 3 cm (1¼ inch) pieces. Coat the chicken lightly in the flour, then dip in the the egg or egg replacer combined with 2 tablespoons water. Roll the chicken in the potato chips, pressing down firmly.

Lay out the chicken in a single layer on the prepared trays and bake for 15–20 minutes, or until cooked through and golden brown. Turn once during cooking.

HINT: For extra-crunchy chicken, deep-fry in hot canola oil until cooked and golden brown instead of baking.

crunchy chicken bits with chives

Free of egg, dairy, gluten, nut and soy.

Add 15 g (½ oz/¼ cup) finely snipped chives to the potato chips. Follow the cooking method in the recipe above.

crunchy chicken bits with garlic

Free of egg, dairy, gluten, nut and soy.

Fry 1–2 crushed garlic cloves in a small amount of canola oil until lightly golden. Cool, then add to the potato chips. Follow the cooking method in the recipe above.

chickpea fritters

These fritters are an excellent source of fibre and provide good amounts of protein and iron too. Free of egg, dairy, gluten, nut and soy.

2 tablespoons canola oil

4 spring onions (scallions), sliced

2 garlic cloves, chopped

600 g (1 lb 5 oz) tinned chickpeas, rinsed and drained

1 egg, or equivalent egg replacer

pear chutney (see page 231), to serve

small cos (romaine) lettuce leaves, to serve

crusty gluten-free bread, to serve

Prep time: 20 minutes
Cooking time: 10 minutes
Makes 6

Heat 2 teaspoons of the oil in a large non-stick frying pan over medium heat. Add the spring onions and garlic and cook, stirring, for 1–2 minutes, or until the spring onion softens.

Put the chickpeas and spring onion mixture in a food processor. Process until the mixture starts to hold together. Transfer to a bowl and mix in the egg or egg replacer. Using your hands, shape the mixture into six even fritters.

Heat the remaining oil in a large non-stick frying pan over medium heat. Add the chickpea fritters (cook in two batches if necessary) and cook for 2 minutes on each side, or until golden. Serve with chutney, lettuce and crusty gluten-free bread.

pear & bean salad

This salad is rich in protein, fibre, the minerals iron and zinc as well as vitamins. Free of egg, dairy, gluten, nut and soy.

4 tinned pear halves, drained and chopped

40 g (1½ oz/½ cup) mung bean sprouts

60 g (2¼ oz/½ cup) sliced, cooked green beans

4 spring onions (scallions), chopped

100 g (3½ oz/½ cup) cooked kidney beans

100 g (3½ oz/½ cup) cooked soya beans

1 tablespoon poppy seeds

DRESSING

60 ml (2 fl oz/¼ cup) canola oil

¾ teaspoon citric acid

½ teaspoon sugar

1 garlic clove, crushed

Prep time: 15 minutes

Cooking time: Nil

Serves 4–6

Combine the pear, mung bean sprouts, green beans, spring onions, kidney beans and soya beans in a large bowl. Mix together gently.

To make the dressing, combine the oil, citric acid, sugar, garlic and 60 ml (2 fl oz/¼ cup) water. Pour over the vegetables and stir to mix through. Chill before serving. Sprinkle with the poppy seeds just before serving.

HINT: This salad is best made the day before serving to allow the full combination of flavours. Use any combination of your toddler's favourite beans or use tinned mixed beans.

sausage rolls

Using healthy fats and natural ingredients these sausage rolls will be a nutritious snack any time. Free of egg, dairy, gluten, nut and soy.

canola oil, for greasing

400 g (14 oz) white-skinned potatoes, roughly chopped

1 tablespoon canola oil

125 g (4½ oz/1 cup) soy-free, gluten-free self-raising flour

½ teaspoon gluten-free baking powder

½ teaspoon ground sea salt

1 egg, or equivalent egg replacer

FILLING

300 g (10½ oz) minced (ground) chicken or veal

1 egg, or equivalent egg replacer

40 g (1½ oz/½ cup) gluten-free fresh breadcrumbs

1 spring onion (scallion), finely chopped

½ teaspoon ground sea salt

1 egg, or equivalent egg replacer, for brushing

Prep time: 45 minutes
Cooking time: 25 minutes
Makes 18

Preheat the oven to 200°C (400°F/Gas 6). Lightly grease two baking trays. Boil or steam the potato for 15 minutes, or until tender. Drain and return to the pan and mash until smooth. You will need about 235 g (8½ oz/1 cup) mashed potato for this recipe.

Combine the mashed potato and oil in a large bowl. Add the sifted dry ingredients and enough egg to mix to a smooth dough. Knead on a lightly floured work surface until smooth. Roll the dough out into a 35 cm (14 inch) square, trimming the edges. Cut the dough evenly into three strips.

To make the filling, combine the meat, egg or egg replacer, breadcrumbs, spring onion and salt in a bowl. Add 1 tablespoon water and mix well to combine. Divide the filling into three portions and, using wet hands, form each portion into thin rolls. Lay the filling along the centre of the pastry strips and brush the extra egg along the edges. Wrap the pastry around the filling, placing them seam side down. Repeat with the remaining filling and pastry.

Brush the rolls with the remaining egg, then cut each roll into six pieces. Place the sausage rolls on the prepared trays, prick the tops with a fork and bake for 20–25 minutes, or until cooked through and lightly browned.

HINTS: Sausage rolls can be made a day in advance and kept in the refrigerator. When required, wrap the cooked sausage rolls in foil and reheat at 180°C (350°F/Gas 4) for 5–8 minutes. If your child can tolerate gluten, you can use commercial puff pastry with no added preservatives or antioxidants, instead of potato pastry.

gluten-free pear muffins

With gluten-free flours available in most supermarkets, home-made muffins like these are easy to make. Free of egg, dairy, gluten, nut and soy.

canola oil, for greasing

250 g (9 oz/2 cups) soy-free, gluten-free self-raising flour

2 teaspoons gluten-free baking powder

140 g (5 oz/¾ cup) soft brown sugar

170 ml (5½ fl oz/⅔ cup) rice drink

80 ml (2½ fl oz/⅓ cup) canola oil

2 eggs, or equivalent egg replacer

2 ripe pears (about 450 g/ 1 lb), peeled, cored and mashed

Prep time: 15 minutes

Cooking time: 20 minutes

Makes 12

Preheat the oven to 180°C (350°F/Gas 4). Lightly grease a 12-hole muffin tin with canola oil.

Sift the flour and baking powder into a large bowl and add the sugar. In a separate bowl, combine the rice drink, oil and eggs or egg replacer. Add the rice drink mixture and pears to the flour mixture. Use a large metal spoon to mix until just combined. Spoon the mixture into the muffin tin.

Bake for 18–20 minutes, or until a skewer inserted in the centre comes out clean. Leave for 5 minutes before turning onto a wire rack.

HINT: These muffins need to be eaten the day they are made.

gluten-free banana muffins

Free of egg, dairy, gluten, nut and soy.

Replace the pears with 2 large, ripe bananas, mashed.

gluten-free rhubarb muffins

Freee of egg, dairy, gluten, nut and soy.

Replace the pears with ½ bunch rhubarb, washed and cut into 2 cm (¾ inch) long pieces. Increase the rice drink to 185 ml (6 fl oz/¾ cup).

cupcakes

This recipe will make a gluten- and egg-free celebration so much easier to achieve. Free of egg, dairy, gluten, nut and soy.

125 g (4½ oz) dairy-free margarine

115 g (4 oz/½ cup) caster (superfine) sugar

2 eggs, or equivalent egg replacer

125 g (4½ oz/1 cup) soy-free, gluten-free self-raising flour

90 g (3¼ oz/½ cup) rice flour

3 teaspoons gluten-free baking powder

125 ml (4 fl oz/½ cup) rice drink

icing (confectioners') sugar, for dusting

Prep time: 15 minutes
Cooking time: 20 minutes
Makes 24

Preheat the oven to 180°C (350°F/Gas 4). Line two 12-hole muffin tins with paper cases.

Using an electric mixer, beat the margarine and sugar together well until light and fluffy. Add the eggs or egg replacer, one at a time, beating well after each addition.

Fold in the sifted dry ingredients alternately with the rice drink.

Spoon the mixture evenly into the muffin holes and bake for about 15–20 minutes, or until a skewer comes out clean when inserted into the centre.

Dust the cupcakes with icing sugar.

Hyperactive children can find the natural chemicals in so-called healthy foods just as much of a problem as artificial additives. In sensitive children, adverse effects are dose-related and can build up over a period of time, especially when the chemicals are eaten in many other different foods.

gluten-free pikelets

If dairy is allowed, serve these pikelets with pear yoghurt to make a calcium- and carbohydrate-rich snack. Contains egg. Free of dairy, gluten, nut and soy.

85 g (3 oz/⅔ cup) soy-free, gluten-free plain (all-purpose) flour

½ teaspoon bicarbonate of soda (baking soda)

1 teaspoon cream of tartar

30 g (1 oz/⅓ cup) rice bran

2 eggs, separated

1 tablespoon canola oil

canola oil spray, for greasing

pear jam (see page 235), for serving (optional)

Prep time: 15 minutes

Cooking time: 15 minutes

Makes about 24

To make the pikelets (griddle cakes), sift the flour, bicarbonate of soda and cream of tartar into a bowl. Mix in the rice bran. Make a well in the centre and stir in the combined egg yolks, oil and 250 ml (9 fl oz/1 cup) water. Beat well until smooth.

Beat the egg whites until stiff peaks form, then fold into the batter using a large metal spoon.

Spray a non-stick frying pan lightly with oil and place over medium heat. Place 2 tablespoons of the mixture for each pikelet in the pan, allowing room for spreading. When the mixture starts to set and the bubbles burst, turn over and brown the other side. Repeat the process with the remaining mixture. Place the pikelets on a wire cake rack to cool. Serve with pear jam, if desired.

HINT: Pikelets can be frozen and reheated briefly in a warm oven.

pikelets with pear yoghurt

Contains egg, dairy and gluten. Free of nut and soy.

Replace the gluten-free flour with regular plain (all-purpose) flour. You will need between 185–250 ml (6–9 fl oz/¾–1 cup) water. Serve with pear yoghurt. To make, combine 250 g (9 oz/1 cup) plain yoghurt, ½ peeled and chopped pear and 2 teaspoons soft brown sugar.

carob milkshake

This milkshake is rich in calcium and phosphorus, excellent for strong bones and teeth. Contains dairy. Free of egg, gluten, nut and soy.

1 tablespoon carob powder

1 tablespoon sugar

500 ml (17 fl oz/2 cups) milk, well chilled

40 g (1½ oz/¼ cup) finely chopped carob buttons

Prep time: 5 minutes
Cooking time: Nil
Serves 2

Dissolve the carob powder and sugar in 1 tablespoon hot water. Allow to cool.

Combine the milk and carob mixture by whisking or beating together. Pour into long glasses. Top with finely chopped carob buttons.

HINT: Ask your health food store whether their carob buttons contain dairy and/or soy.

mayonnaise

Young children on restricted diets due to an allergy or intolerance may struggle to gain weight. Condiments like this with lots of healthy fat can help them out. Contains egg. Free of dairy, gluten, nut and soy.

2 egg yolks

¼ teaspoon ground sea salt

250 ml (9 fl oz/1 cup) canola oil

¼ teaspoon citric acid

Prep time: 20 minutes

Cooking time: Nil

Makes 250 g (9 oz/1 cup)

Put the egg yolks and salt in a bowl and whisk together until well combined and thick.

Gradually whisk in the oil, drop by drop until a quarter of the oil has been added. The mixture should be thick at this stage. Very slowly pour in the remaining oil in a thin steady stream, whisking continuously. Beat in the citric acid. Store the mayonnaise in a sterilized glass jar in the refrigerator for up to 3 days.

HINT: Mayonnaise can be made in a blender or food processor. Use the same ingredients as above. Blend the eggs and salt for a few seconds. With the motor running, pour in the oil in a steady thin stream. When all the oil has been added, the mixture should be thick.

pear chutney

Foods with lots of flavour are often the ones food-sensitive kids can't have. This recipe is an exception. Free of egg, dairy, gluten, nut and soy.

820 g (1 lb 13 oz) tinned pear halves in syrup

125 g (4½ oz/⅔ cup) soft brown sugar

1½ teaspoons citric acid

1 teaspoon ground sea salt

Prep time: 10 minutes
Cooking time: 25 minutes
Makes 375 g (13 oz/1½ cups)

Drain and chop the pears, reserving the syrup.

Pour the syrup into a saucepan. Bring to the boil and boil until the mixture is reduced by half.

Add the pears, sugar, citric acid and salt. Reduce the heat. Allow to simmer for about 10–15 minutes, or until the mixture is thick.

Spoon into hot, sterilized jars. Seal, label and date. Once opened, store in the refrigerator and use within 3 weeks.

pear slushy

Here is a safe and sweet treat for toddlers on long hot days. Free of egg, dairy, gluten, nut and soy.

825 g (1 lb 13 oz) tinned pear halves in syrup

1 teaspoon citric acid

Prep time: 15 minutes + freezing time
Cooking time: Nil
Serves 4–6

Put the pears, their syrup and the citric acid into a blender. Blend on high for 2–3 minutes.

Pour into a shallow metal tin and freeze for about 1 hour, or until just frozen around the edges. Scrape the ice back into the mixture with a fork. Repeat every 30 minutes until the mixture consists of even-sized ice crystals. Serve immediately or beat with a fork and refreeze until just before serving. Allow to soften slightly in the refrigerator before using. The mixture should be slushy.

Pile into long cups and serve with a spoon and a straw.

fried flat bread

This recipe helps to fill the need for hard-to-find starchy snacks for toddlers with wheat or gluten intolerance. Free of egg, dairy, gluten, nut and soy.

135 g (4¾ oz/¾ cup) rice flour

135 g (4¾ oz/¾ cup) potato flour (see Hints)

1 teaspoon gluten-free baking powder

1 teaspoon ground sea salt

1 tablespoon canola oil, plus extra, for frying

185–250 ml (6–9 fl oz/ ¾–1 cup) warm water

Prep time: 10 minutes

Cooking time: 25 minutes

Makes 8 rounds

Sift the rice flour, potato flour and baking powder into a large bowl. Add the salt. Make a well in the centre and add the oil. Gradually stir in enough water until a thick batter is formed.

Heat 1 cm (½ inch) oil in a frying pan over medium–high heat. Pour in enough batter to form a round about 10–12 cm (4–5 inches) across. Fry until golden brown, then turn and brown the other side. Drain on paper towels. Repeat with the remaining batter. Add more oil to the pan as needed, ensuring it is heated through before use.

HINTS: Potato flour is often preserved with sulphite, but most of it will disappear during the cooking process. Use this bread as an accompaniment to any meat or lentil dish or top with your toddler's favourite food.

pear juice

This juice is easy to digest and a great source of fibre. It is best if diluted with equal parts of water for toddlers. Free of egg, dairy, gluten, nut and soy.

820 g (1 lb 13 oz) tinned pear halves in syrup

Prep time: 5 minutes
Cooking time: Nil
Serves 4–6

Put the pears and syrup into a blender. Blend on high speed for 2–3 minutes, or until puréed.

Scoop the pear juice into a covered container and store in the refrigerator for up to 4 days.

HINT: Pear juice may be diluted with unflavoured mineral water or cooled, boiled tap water. Pear juice can also be used to naturally sweeten breakfast cereals such as porridge or muesli (granola).

mango juice

This delicious juice is also an excellent source of beta-carotene — a nutrient that converts to vitamin A in the body. Free of egg, dairy, gluten, nut and soy.

550 g (1 lb 4 oz) fresh mango, peeled
55 g (2 oz/¼ cup) sugar
125 ml (4 fl oz/½ cup) water

Prep time: 5 minutes
Cooking time: Nil
Serves 4–6

Blend the mango flesh with the sugar and water in a blender on high speed for 2–3 minutes, or until puréed.

Dilute as desired to serve.

HINT: If fresh mangoes aren't in season, use 680 g (1 lb 8 oz) tinned mangoes in syrup and blend to a purée — you won't need any extra sugar or water. Dilute as desired.

pear jam

When your toddler's food choices are restricted, it is nice to be able to offer a sweet choice to spread on bread. Free of egg, dairy, gluten, nut and soy.

750 g (1 lb 10 oz) ripe, peeled pears, or 1.6 kg (3 lb 8 oz) tinned pears, drained

750 g (1 lb 10 oz/3⅓ cups) sugar

50 g (1¾ oz) jam setting mixture

Prep time: 10 minutes

Cooking time: 10 minutes

Makes about 785 g (1 lb 11 oz/2⅓ cups)

Purée the pears in a blender or food processor. Scoop the purée into a large saucepan and heat over medium heat. Stir in the sugar and jam setting mixture. Reduce the heat to low and stir until the sugar is dissolved. Increase the heat and bring to the boil. Boil for 5 minutes, stirring occasionally, then remove from the heat.

Allow to cool for 10 minutes, then pour into sterilized jars. Seal, label and date. Once opened, store in the refrigerator and use within 4 weeks.

HINT: Use as a spread, filling or topping.

When you have time to spare, the preparation of a few of the basics will stand you in good stead for those occasions when you haven't the time but want healthy and tasty food. Low-salt stocks mean quick-to-make soups, a good white sauce can rescue many a plain meal while our basic tomato sauce can be used for more than just a good pasta sauce.

basics

vegetable stock

Commercial stocks are high in salt and not suitable to include in food you prepare for your toddler or baby. This recipe lets you preserve the natural tastes of vegetables without added salt.

1 tablespoon oil
1 onion, chopped
2 leeks, thickly sliced (white part only)
4 carrots, chopped
2 parsnips, chopped
4 celery stalks, leaves included, chopped
2 bay leaves
1 bouquet garni (see Hint)
4 unpeeled garlic cloves
8 black peppercorns

Prep time: 20 minutes
Cooking time: 1½ hours
Makes: 2.5 litres (87 fl oz/ 10 cups)

Heat the oil in a large, heavy-based saucepan and add the onion, leek, carrot, parsnip and celery. Cover and cook for 5 minutes without colouring. Add 3 litres (105 fl oz/12 cups) water. Bring to the boil. Add the bay leaves, bouquet garni, garlic and peppercorns. Reduce the heat to low and simmer for 1 hour. Skim the froth from the surface of the stock regularly.

Strain the stock. Set aside to cool, then transfer to an airtight container. Store in the refrigerator for up to 2 days or in the freezer for up to 6 months.

HINT: To make your own bouquet garni, tie together with a string or wrap in a piece of cheesecloth (muslin) 4 sprigs parsley or chervil, 1 sprig fresh thyme and 1 bay leaf.

allergy-free vegetable stock

Heat 1 tablespoon canola oil in a large saucepan over medium heat. Add 3 sliced celery stalks, 350 g (12 oz) chopped swede (rutabaga), 1 large leek, halved lengthways and chopped, and 3 crushed garlic cloves. Cook, stirring often, for 5–8 minutes, or until the vegetables turn a light gold. Pour in 4.5 litres (157 fl oz/18 cups) water. Cover with a lid and bring to the boil. Simmer, partially covered, for 1½ hours, skimming the froth from the surface of the stock regularly. Strain the stock. Set aside to cool, then transfer to an airtight container. Store in the refrigerator for up to 2 days or in the freezer for up to 6 months. Makes 2.5 litres (87 fl oz/10 cups).

chicken stock

This recipe makes a flavoursome stock for soups and casseroles without the added extras of many commercial varieties.

2 kg (4 lb 8 oz) chicken bones

2 unpeeled onions, quartered

2 unpeeled carrots, chopped

2 celery stalks, leaves included, chopped

1 bouquet garni

12 black peppercorns

Prep time: 20 minutes

Cooking time: 3 hours 10 minutes

Makes: 2.5 litres (87 fl oz/ 10 cups)

Put the chicken bones, onion, carrot, celery and 3.5 litres (122 fl oz/ 14 cups) water in a large, heavy-based saucepan. Bring slowly to the boil. Skim the surface as required and add the bouquet garni and peppercorns. Reduce the heat to low and simmer gently for 3 hours. Skim the froth from the surface regularly.

Strain the stock. Set aside to cool, then refrigerate until cold. Spoon off any fat that has set on the surface. Transfer to an airtight container. Store in the refrigerator for up to 2 days or in the freezer for up to 6 months.

allergy-free chicken or veal stock

Put 500 g (1 lb 2 oz) chicken or veal bones in a large heavy-based saucepan. Add 1 leek, 1 celery stalk and 1 carrot, all roughly chopped, and 4 parsley stalks (without foliage). Cover with water and bring to the boil, skimming the surface. Reduce the heat and simmer for about 1–1½ hours, uncovered. Strain through a colander, then through a fine sieve. Remove any fat from the surface. Store in the refrigerator for up to 2 days or in the freezer for up to 6 months. Makes about 500 ml (17 fl oz/2 cups).

beef stock

Full of the flavour and goodness of meaty bones, this stock will enrich any recipe you use it in.

2 kg (4 lb 8 oz) beef bones

2 unpeeled carrots, chopped

2 unpeeled onions, quartered

2 tablespoons tomato paste (conentrated purée)

2 celery stalks, leaves included, chopped

I bouquet garni

12 black peppercorns

Prep time: 20 minutes

Cooking time: 4 hours 50 minutes

Makes about 1.75 litres (61 fl oz/7 cups)

Preheat the oven to 210°C (415°F/Gas 6–7). Put the bones in a baking tin and bake for 30 minutes, turning occasionally. Add the carrot and onion and cook for a further 20 minutes. Allow to cool.

Put the bones, onion and carrot in a large, heavy-based saucepan. Drain the excess fat from the baking tin and pour 250 ml (9 fl oz/1 cup) water into the tin. Stir to dissolve any pan juices, then add the liquid to the pan.

Add the tomato paste, celery and 2.5 litres (87 fl oz/10 cups) water. Bring to the boil, skimming the surface as required, and then add the bouquet garni and peppercorns. Reduce the heat to low and simmer gently for 4 hours. Skim the froth from the surface regularly.

Strain through a colander, then through a fine sieve. Remove any fat from the surface. Store in the refrigerator for up to 2 days or in the freezer for up to 6 months.

basic tomato sauce

Keep this sauce on hand stored in small portions in the freezer. It is perfect for a quick pasta meal or use it to top vegetables, rice or poultry dishes.

1.5 kg (3 lb 5 oz) tomatoes
1 tablespoon olive oil
1 onion, finely chopped
2 garlic cloves, crushed
2 tablespoons tomato paste
(concentrated purée)
1 teaspoon dried oregano
1 teaspoon dried basil
1 teaspoon sugar

Prep time: 25 minutes
Cooking time: 25 minutes
Serves 4

Score a cross on the base of each tomato, place in a bowl of boiling water for 10 seconds, then plunge into cold water and peel away the skin from the cross. Finely chop the flesh.

Heat the oil in pan. Add the onion and cook, stirring, over medium heat for 3 minutes, or until soft. Add the garlic and cook for 1 minute. Add the tomato, tomato paste, oregano, basil and sugar. Bring to the boil, then reduce the heat and simmer for 20 minutes, or until the sauce has thickened slightly.

Store in an airtight container in the refrigerator for up to 2 days or in the freezer for up to 6 months.

white sauce

A basic white sauce is a wonderfully adaptable food for young children and a good way to include dairy in the diet of the reluctant milk drinker.

250 ml (9 fl oz/1 cup) milk
1 onion slice
1 bay leaf
6 peppercorns
30 g (1 oz) unsalted butter
1 tablespoon plain (all-purpose) flour

Prep time: 15 minutes
Cooking time: 10 minutes
Serves 2–4

Put the milk, onion, bay leaf and peppercorns in a small saucepan. Bring to the boil, remove from the heat and leave to infuse for 10 minutes. Strain the milk, discarding the flavourings.

Melt the butter in a small pan and stir in the flour. Cook, stirring, for 1 minute until the mixture is golden and bubbling. Remove from the heat and gradually add the milk, stirring until completely smooth. Return to the heat and stir until the mixture boils. Continue cooking for 1 minute, or until thick. Remove from the heat and serve.

cheese sauce

To make a basic cheese sauce, add 60 g (2¼ oz/½ cup) finely grated cheddar cheese to the white sauce when removed from the heat. Stir the cheese through until melted, then serve.

barbecue dipping sauce

Something to dip food into is always a favourite with toddlers. Choose a salt-reduced ketchup and this recipe will be a good accompaniment to finger foods.

2 teaspoons oil

I small onion, finely chopped

I tablespoon malt vinegar

I tablespoon soft brown sugar

80 ml (2½ fl oz/⅓ cup) salt-reduced tomato sauce (ketchup)

I tablespoon worcestershire sauce

Prep time: 15 minutes
Cooking time: 10 minutes
Serves 2–4

Heat the oil in a small saucepan and cook the onion over low heat for 3 minutes, or until soft, stirring occasionally.

Add the remaining ingredients and bring to the boil. Reduce the heat and simmer for 3 minutes, stirring occasionally. Serve warm or at room temperature. Can be kept covered and refrigerated, for up to 1 week.

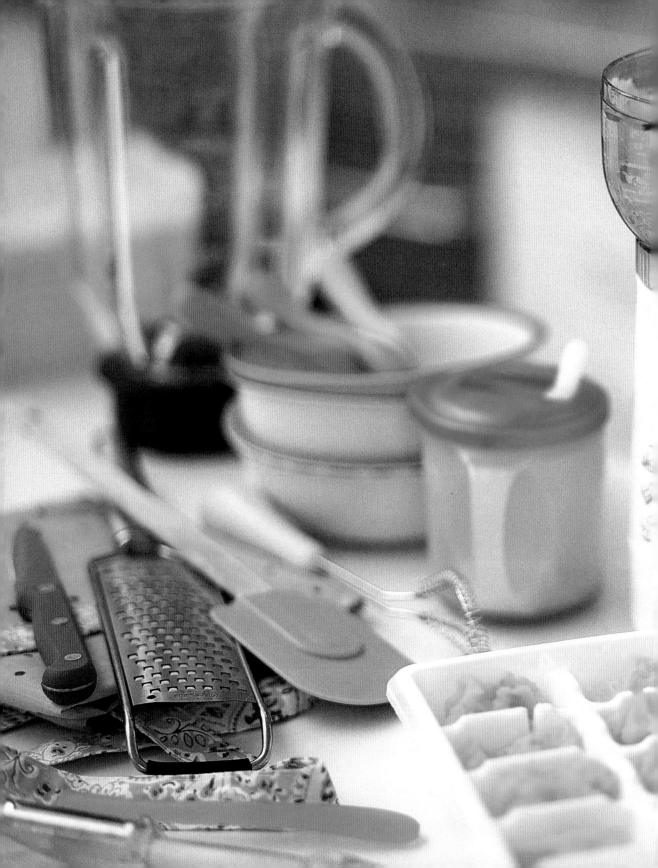

Having the right tools can make feeding your baby much easier. This section includes tips on cooking utensils and feeding equipment. Plus, with all the nutrition information parents are bombarded with, it can be easy to lose sight of the bigger, and much simpler, picture. So we have also provided you with a healthy diet pyramid to cut to the core of what you are trying to achieve when you prepare family meals.

useful information
& index

necessary equipment

KITCHEN EQUIPMENT

You will probably find that you already have most of the things you need to make and store baby food if you already cook frequently:

• *Sieve and/or blender for making purées.*

• *Steamer for cooking vegetables, fish and poultry.*

• *Ice cube containers for freezing and storing food.*

As with most items specifically designed for babies, you can spend a lot of money on eating equipment. However, this is not necessary. Your baby will only need one or two bowls and several flat spoons — you can add a baby fork at a later date. You will also want a few bibs, so you can wash or soak some while your baby is wearing others. The ideal bib covers your baby's shoulders and stomach. Several baby cups with non-spill features will be extremely useful as your baby learns that the drink is supposed to go into his tummy, not on the floor, the highchair, or on your lap. If you have sterilizing equipment for bottles, you can add baby spoons and beaker spouts to the mix. Otherwise, cleaning them carefully and thoroughly in hot soapy water, then rinsing them just as thoroughly should get them clean. Using the dishwasher to clean baby's bowls and utensils is also fine. You may also want to consider a mess mat, which will also need to be cleaned at the end of every meal.

choosing a highchair

A highchair is a major piece of equipment. There are safety and ease-of-use issues with highchairs so look for one that:

• Has a five-point harness to prevent your child from falling or climbing out.

• Is strong but not too heavy for you to lift. Lean on it to check its strength.

• Has no sharp edges and is without removable pieces that could find their way into your child's mouth.

• Fits into your kitchen, family room or around your table. If the legs stick out will you trip over them?

• Has a tray that is well secured when in place, but can be easily removed for cleaning.

• Can be adjusted for height. Also, check if the seat reclines — not all highchairs recline, but this mechanism can be useful when you have a young baby. Any adjustment knobs should be out of a child's reach when they are sitting in the highchair.

• Folds away easily, ideally with one hand. If space is a problem, folding it up quickly and easily being able to lift it will be important.

• Has an adjustable leg rest for your child.

• Is reasonably easy to wipe down.

the healthy diet pyramid for the whole family

EAT LEAST
sugar, fats and oils, salt

EAT IN MODERATION
eggs, dairy products and alternatives, meat, poultry, fish, seafood and nuts

EAT MOST
grains and cereal products, fruits, vegetables, legumes

DEVELOPMENTAL STAGES — A GENERAL GUIDELINE

SENSES	FIRST WEEKS	2 MONTHS	3 MONTHS	4 MONTHS	5 MONTHS	6 MONTHS
REACTIONS	6–8 weeks: first social smiles			Likes to be handled	Enjoys new tastes	May start to cling
HEARING AND SPEECH	Hears from birth. Cries from hunger and discomfort	Gurgling 'oos' and 'ahs'	Brief attention to sounds including voices. Searches for sounds with eyes	Usually disturbed by angry voices. May utter sounds when spoken to or pleased. More consonants		Turns to sounds. Chuckles and babbles
SIGHT	Looks briefly at bright or close objects	Following with eyes	Looking at faces and objects for longer periods of time		Recognizes everyday objects, e.g. a cup. Watches hands	Watches adults across the room
HAND MOVEMENTS			Holds objects which are placed in hands for short time	Reaching out to get objects		Objects put into mouth
BODY MOVEMENTS AND GETTING ABOUT	When placed on stomach will turn head to side. Movements are jerky		Can hold head steady for a period of time. When baby propped in sitting position, head tends to bob forward	Can hold head and chest up when lying on stomach, taking weight on forearms		Lifts head to look at feet. Sits with support. 6–8 months: rolling over

8 MONTHS	9 MONTHS	10 MONTHS	12 MONTHS	15 MONTHS	18 MONTHS	2 YEARS
May cry when a parent goes out of sight. This may last past second birthday	Shy of strangers. Can cling to parents and hide face	Reacts to praise. Understands 'no'		Dependant on adult's presence. Active and curious. Starting to explore. Emotionally 'up and down'	Exploring energetically. Plays alone, but likes to be near adult. Emotionally still dependent on familiar adults	Constantly seeks attention. Clings tightly in affection, fear or fatigue. Tantrums when frustrated
Practising different sounds, e.g. 'googoo' and 'adada'	Smacks lips together and may start to imitate adult noises, e.g. 'brr'		Understands some words and phrases. First words with meaning about this time, e.g. 'dada', 'mama'	Starting to understand and obey simple commands such as 'get your shoes'. Using a few true words	Using both noises and pointing to indicate what they want. Number of words increased	Speech becoming clearer. Puts two or more words together to form simple phrases, e.g. 'go shop'
Sees small beads		Looks for objects dropped out of sight and finds toys hidden under a blanket		Enjoys picture books. Points at named objects		Notices details in picture books. Recognizes familiar adults in photographs once they are pointed out
7–8 months: able to transfer an object from one hand to another		Beginning to use index finger and thumb to pick up small objects		Picks up a lot of small objects using finger and thumb. Can throw things quite forcibly (this is still a game)	Can turn pages of book one at a time	Scribbles lines and rough circles. Feeds self with spoon
	9–10 months: sits alone on floor for 10–15 minutes. Props to side or forwards to balance. Attempts to crawl (some children get around by bottom shuffling or wriggling and may walk later — up to 18 months). 10–18 months: first steps		Pulls self to standing position and lets self down again holding onto furniture	Can climb on furniture	Around this time can usually walk quite well. Runs (with falls). Can climb stairs	Starting to kick and can throw a ball. Very mobile and active

First produced by the Paediatric Health Education Unit, University of Sydney

index

Published by Murdoch Books Pty Limited.

Chief Executive: Juliet Rogers
Publisher: Kay Scarlett

Editorial Director: Diana Hill
Project Manager: Paul McNally
Design Concept and Design: Susanne Geppert
Editor: Ariana Klepac
Food Editor: Rebecca Truda
Nutritional consultant: Karen Kingham
Photographer: Ian Hofstetter
Stylist: Jane Collins
Food preparation: Joanne Kelly
Recipes: Rebecca Truda and members of the Murdoch Books Test Kitchen.
Production: Monika Paratore

National Library of Australia Cataloguing-in-Publication Data: Fallows, Carol. Baby & toddler food: recipes and practical information for feeding babies and toddlers. Includes index. ISBN 1 74045 501 0. 1. Cookery (Baby foods) 2. Toddlers — Nutrition. 3. Baby foods. I. Title. (Series: Food for life) 641.56222.

Printed by Toppan Hong Kong. PRINTED IN CHINA. First published 2005.

Murdoch Books Australia
Pier 8/9, 23 Hickson Road
Millers Point NSW 2000
Phone: + 61 (0) 2 8220 2000 Fax: + 61 (0) 2 8220 2558

Murdoch Books UK Ltd
Erico House, 6th Floor North, 93–99 Upper Richmond Road
Putney, London SW15 2TG
Phone: + 44 (0) 20 8785 5995   Fax +44 (0) 20 8785 5985

IMPORTANT: Those who might be at risk from the effects of salmonella food poisoning (the elderly, pregnant women, young children and those suffering from immune deficiency diseases) should consult their doctor with any concerns about eating raw eggs.

CONVERSION GUIDE: You may find cooking times vary depending on the oven you are using. For fan-forced ovens, as a general rule, set the oven temperature to 20°C (70°F) lower than indicated in the recipe. We have used 20 ml (4 teaspoon) tablespoon measures. If you are using a 15 ml (3 teaspoon) tablespoon, for most recipes the difference will not be noticeable. However, for recipes using baking powder, gelatine, bicarbonate of soda, small amounts of flour and cornflour (cornstarch), add an extra teaspoon for each tablespoon specified.

The Publisher thanks Dinosaur Designs, Mud Australia, Bison Homewares and IKEA for assistance in the photography of this book.